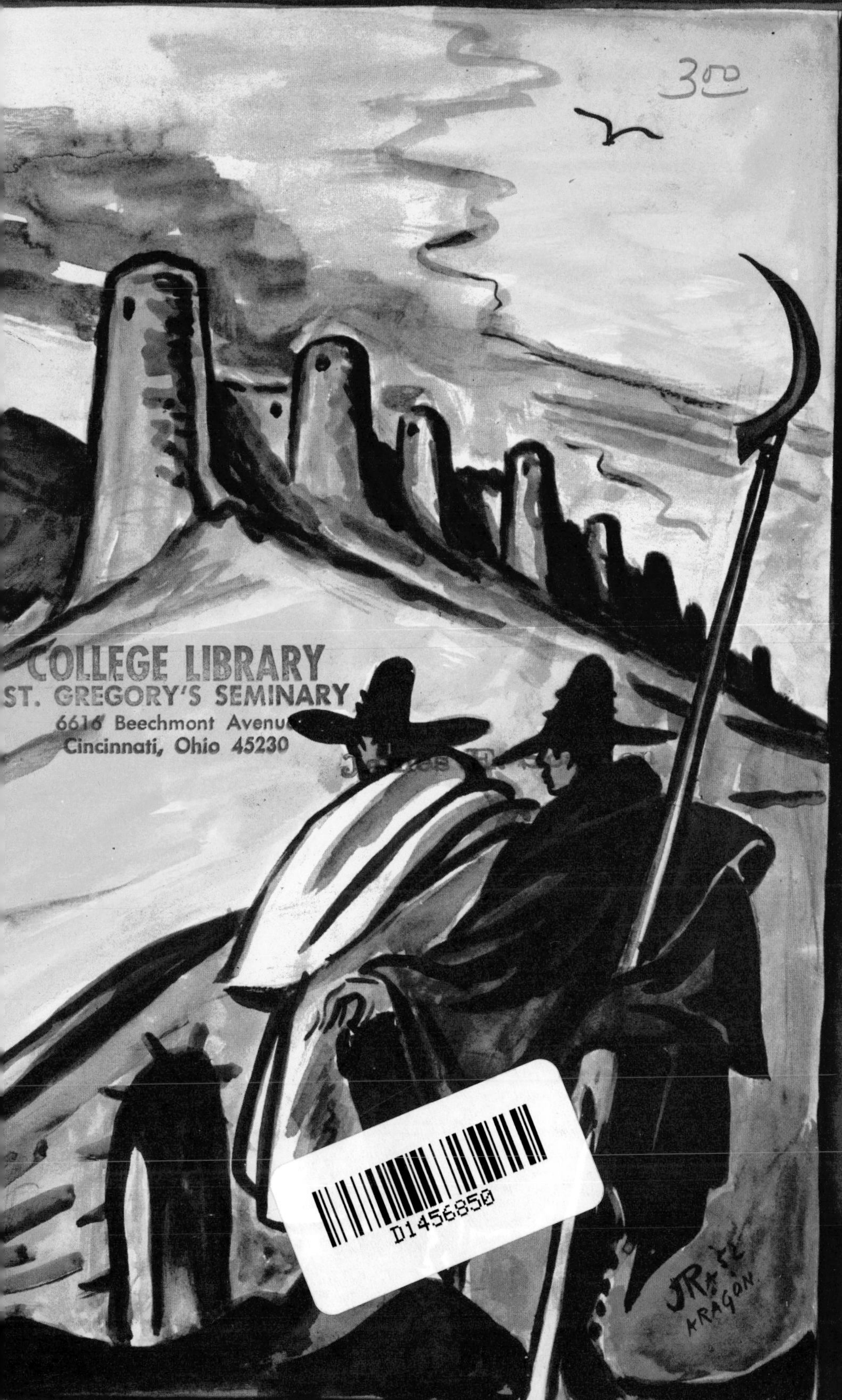
ARAGON

FABULOUS SPAIN

James E. Scanlon

MADONNA
OF THE
CABEZA

James Reynolds

FABULOUS SPAIN

*"Though shalt make castles in Spayne.
And drem of joye, al but in vayne."*

ROMAUNT OF THE ROSE

G. P. Putnam's Sons   New York

MANUFACTURED IN THE UNITED STATES OF AMERICA

VAN REES PRESS • NEW YORK

TO

MARGARET MOWER

Traveler in Spain, whose interest in all
that is Spanish marches with my own.

Acknowledgments

THERE are so many persons I wish to thank for their assistance while I have been occupied with writing this book. The roster of names is a long one. I find I can mention only a few personally. I am particularly and forever grateful to the Spanish people, by and large, whom I met while writing and sketching on the Spanish Peninsula, compiling a portfolio of the Spanish scene. Now this portfolio is bound between boards as *Fabulous Spain*.

I salute the proprietors of the many Paradores Dirección General del Tourismo situated throughout the country. The owners of private houses who offered me warm hospitality along the way, and the interest displayed in regard to my comfort in simple off-the-beaten-track hotels, as well as in the luxurious hostelries, as the Ritz Hotel in Madrid and Hotel Alfonso XIII in Seville, of renowned excellence, of which Spain may be justly proud.

I tender my great thanks to Don Luis Bolín, formerly Director General of the Spanish State Tourist Department in Madrid, now attaché to the Spanish Embassy in Washington. Don Luis was notably helpful, adding to his friendliness and interest in my book the practical imagination of suggestion which has for the past few years so signally distinguished his handling of all facilities for insuring pleasure to the foreign tourist in Spain.

Much valuable help was given me by José M. Coll, Manager of the Spanish Tourist Office in New York. Together José Coll and I clarified some problems which arose. The solving of which was made doubly pleasant by his agreeable and enthusiastic personality.

To my great friend George Copeland, internationally known pianist, who is one of the leading exponents of Spanish music today. I am indebted for his help during discussions about the rhythms of fiery *flamenco*, the dignified *bolero* and the haunting cadences of Moorish inspired *saetas*. All of which contribute immeasurably to the essence of Spain.

Fuentarrabia–September 15.–1952. JAMES REYNOLDS.

Introduction

FOR any writer approaching the adventure of compiling a book about Spain, the singularly individual quality of this storied land must be the first consideration. It seems to me, having traveled in most continents, that no country has so definite a stamp of apartness, so personal an essence. From the moment one arrives on the Spanish Peninsula this fact takes possession of the mind, never to dim as one roams the various provinces. I venture that Spain, of all countries in Europe, has kept intact, immediate to daily use, its customs and racial traits to a degree not found elsewhere today. Perhaps this is so because there seems never to be a moment when there is not a festival of one sort or another in full flare. Religious processions are constantly wending through the streets of towns or along the country roads of pilgrimage. Many of these are sumptuous in trappings. Saints' days fill the calendar and are fittingly observed. Traditional dances spike public interest second only to the corrida, in most parts of Spain. The chief sport, as such, is pelota, a game of ball and wicker-basket-like glove played on a hard court, introduced by the agile Basques. Of course most blazingly advertised and enthusiastically attended is the corrida. Here, His Majesty King Toro, as Madrileños affectionately refer to a fighting bull, is idolized as a national figure, along with his enemy the matador, by everyone in Spain "from the cradle to the grave" as a journalist once remarked to me in Madrid.

The haunting, often fiery music to which the Spanish dance, is ever heard on the wind. The *jota* from haughty, rock-ribbed Aragon is tempestuous, the tempo is wild, the steps as arrogant as the expression on Aragonese faces. In Catalonia the *rájo* is precise, resembling the elegant bolero. Like the stark houses of Catalonian farmers there is something archaic in pattern in the *rájo*, a composed dignity, where the colors are somber. Flamenco in Andalusia is wildness personified. The Moorish cadences which largely compose flamenco music create a rhythm of reckless passion which compels violent footwork of stamping and brings into play the exciting beat of castanets. Let me say that "if music be the food of love," it is also the very heartbeat of the Iberian temperament. Music is heard in Spain everywhere, at all hours. One of the minor mysteries of the land is, "When does a Spaniard sleep?" There is, of course, the three hour halt after midday for siesta. But more than once, when strolling after lunch through some somnolent town, I have paused before the shuttered window of a house to listen. Softly muted song accompanying lightly plucked strings of a guitar, a voice singing in the curiously passionate drone of Moorish rhythm.

A traveler in Spain is always immensely interested in the traditional costumes, so decorative, a part of the provincial scene. In Aragon the rich trappings seen in this proud mountain province attest to a long heritage of royal pageantry. Dark, glowing velvets and brocade, heavily scrolled in gold galloon and embroidery. Gitanas of Granada, and the remarkably handsome women of Seville trail ruffled cottons, coin-spotted in vivid colors or the inevitable Spanish accent of black silk. If I were asked to choose which costumes I favor most, I believe it is the panoply worn by women in the arid plains around Salamanca. Incredibly dramatic, these corded-silk and velvet garments, because of the yards of silver filigree necklaces, barbarically huge in scale, hanging in clattering confusion around the neck and extending to below the waist, sometimes to the knees. Like some pagan deity robed for sacrificial ceremony these women of Salamanca seem to have sprung, ageless, from the earth of their rust-red plains.

In Spain, I am forever conscious of the rightness of the appearance of the inhabitants in their surroundings. Each one seems so much part of the landscape. For variety of texture, the face of Spain is unique. If it were possible to stand on the highest point of the Pyrenees, rising in a great rampart between France and Spain, to look off and away to the farthest reaches of the peninsula where La Coruña breasts the bold Atlantic breakers, the panorama would embrace a vast, wind-swept, color-drenched canvas of sharp contrasts and inconsistencies of terrain. Here great strokes of brilliant, clashing greens, and the golden yellows of fertility. There the stark, muted earth-browns and rose-grays and russets of serrated clay and rock formations, some lying low, gently undulating, others tortured into fantastic cones and hobgoblin shapes. Seemingly limitless arid foothills, devoid of any vegetation, rise suddenly to rich purple and blue distances forming four great mountain ranges. The Cuatro Sierras, as these soaring, jagged-crest mountains are known throughout Spain.

On all sides, the Spanish scene glows with brilliant, luminous color. Native costumes startle the eye, but capture interest immediately. Natural scenery reaches unimagined beauty in Spain, while the evidences of what man has done to complement the landscape, since antiquity, is proverbial. All this awaits you. The Spanish, traditionally a proud, generous people, will welcome you with, "My house is your house," and mean it.

Contents

FABULOUS SPAIN.

Chapter 1

ON ENTERING SPAIN
BY LAND OR SEA

To the traveler entering Spain for the first time, I suggest three routes. Two are by land and one from the sea, by any of the many ports that dot the coast. If the choice is by land there are two mountain passes widely different in aspect, albeit both cross the frontier from France. Both of these mountain roads are good, and by either the individuality of Spain is sensed immediately one passes the frontier customs. The southern route is across the Pyrenees at Port Bou, by the old Roman military road which sweeps in tremendous curves along the sides of mountains, dipping steeply into fern-clad gorges of almost tropical luxuriance, to dart out again and circle little bays so nearly landlocked as to appear inland lakes. The northern route is by way of Hendaye and across a long bridge to Irún. From this point one may choose a wide variety of roads branching out to all the provinces of Spain.

The alternative is to enter Spain by a seaport on the Mediterranean shore, the fabled Costa Brava (the Catalonian coast extending from Port Bou to Barcelona), or at one of the many historic ports of entry all the way down to Cádiz. The coast of the Bay of Biscay in the north is not so well known for historic towns as it is for pleasure resorts. Bilbao is of ancient lineage but commercial pursuits of late years have given the old port a rather brash modernity. The Bay of Biscay shore offers much to the visitor who is not under the tourist compulsion of hurrying from place to place in the "just so I can say I have been there" way of traveling, but who has time for a leisurely visit.

To enter Spain I have used all three routes many times. I can

3

never forget one arrival in Cádiz from a Norwegian liner on an evening just as the sun was setting, drowned in the sea, turning the glassy water to molten gold and crimson. I stood on the quay and drank it in. Cádiz—I had heard so much, read so much, dreamed so often of Cádiz. Now here I was. My first impression of this improbably white town, lying far out in the sea at the end of a four-mile-long causeway, led me, for a while, to believe I had been transported back at least a thousand years in time to some Moorish town ruled by a caliph from a hibiscus-shaded pavilion in the gardens of his rock-hewn casbah. In one way I dreamed true, for walking abroad in Cádiz next morning I found the pavilion secluded among red hibiscus trees. I found as well, in the narrow streets, plenty of evidence in architecture built by Moorish overlords, of their tenure. Eight hundred years of Moorish domination. The longest time in recorded history for a people to feel the weight of a usurper's yoke.

Many persons coming to Spain for the first time wish to enter at Barcelona, undoubtedly one of the finest, most advertised seaports in the world. Barcelona is a fascinating city to wander in. That is, if one keeps to the old, tree-shaded Ramblas, or the San José quarter of noble, geranium-hedged houses. There are long winding parks massed with palm trees and flowers, for flowers seem to drench Barcelona, cooled by fountains and breezes from the mountains which nearly ring the city. The museums are numerous and show a variety of treasures. Certain travelers have maligned Barcelona, calling it a raucous town. I admit a continuous cacaphony of sounds reverberates through the quarters night and day. To say "Spain *never* sleeps, even at siesta" is to use Barcelona as a criterion; but its charm of sheer vitality is compelling. It is the starting point of the best railway and airplane accommodations in the country, next to Madrid. Barcelonese proudly call their city "the nerve center of Spain." Planes and charmingly fitted white steamers ply between Barcelona and Palma de Majorca on alternate days the year round.

Like Málaga, Valencia of the orange-blossom scented air, and Cádiz, a fisherman's paradise, Barcelona is famed the world over for delicious dishes composed of all manner of "fruits of the sea."

The largest seaports in the north of Spain are Gijón and Bilbao; both emphasize their importance as shipping centers. Like the ant and the bee, the inhabitants hurry about their business with little time for or interest in foreign travelers who care only to be entertained. However, the merchants are proud to show their handsome

PLAZA.
TOSSA de MAR.

houses in wide streets. Built of green-gray stone peculiar to the locality, these dignified mansions are elaborately ornamented in carved relief of flowers, fruits, characters from mythology, early Renaissance workmanship, built for the ages. One is forever conscious in Bilbao of proverbial Basque thriftiness.

San Sebastian and Santander are cherished by the Spanish as "pleasure ports." Both extraordinarily attractive towns aptly live up to this sobriquet. Just as Venice is, and has always been, a city of unique character and gay delights to the Italians, so these two seaside resorts on the Bay of Biscay have illusive but very definite character of their own. Both are beautifully situated. Perhaps Santander gains a shade in beauty on its vast circular bay which is an arm of Biscay embracing the mountainous coast. When this bay is unruffled it reflects the improbable Picos de Europa, a mountain formation straight out of Fata Morgana, rising to 8,800 feet, girdled in verdure first, then vaulting terraces of pink quartz blending into black and yellow marble at the topmost crag. This spectacular rock always reminds me of a gigantic striped banner suddenly turned to stone, forever immobile against the sky.

San Sebastian relies on its notably fashionable reputation, coupled with the famed excellence of its hotels, to attract visitors. The Continental Palace has long been one of the most beautifully appointed, completely luxurious hotels in Europe, rivaling the Ritz in Madrid, than which there is none finer. San Sebastian is a city of sharp contrasts. For entertainment to suit all tastes there is the sophisticated opulence of the wide Avenidas de Calvo Sotelo and de España where shops seem to hold all the treasures of the world. For simpler, or perhaps jaded tastes, are the vine and fish-net hung *ventorros* or fishermen's taverns, crouching under the now derelict old fortress of La Mota at the foot of Monte Urgull. *Ventorros* are typical of seaports and serve a hearty bouillabaisse called *cocido*, gilded with saffron. Dancing is crude but compelling in its pagan vitality, a trait for which the northern Spaniard is famous.

During my stay in Spain while writing this book, I talked to any number of American visitors. Some I found were traveling by the splendidly appointed A.T.E.S.A. (which is called simply Atesa) motor coaches, the best run line of its kind I have ever encountered, or by private motor car. A few traveled by the none too punctual or comfortable railway trains. When I asked questions about their Spanish journey and if it pleased them, I was interested to hear all remark on the extraordinarily abrupt and complete changes in landscape. One moment the way leads through a long, winding, mountain-guarded valley, where arcaded white farmhouses bask in the center of sunny fruit orchards, olive groves, and fields of grain. On the instant all this verdant countryside changes to undulating plains and thrusting escarpments of sun-baked earth where a tree would be a rarity. Cutting through this monotony of bone-colored earth loom mountain passes, suddenly thrust up where none apparently had been before. Dark-skinned, haggardly handsome men and women with wildly unkempt children at their skirts emerge cautiously from cave dwellings, cut either by nature or the hand of man (in many cases by the Moors) out of the living rock.

The approach to any town in Spain, no matter in what province or of what importance the place, holds one similarity. The sight of church belfries rising straight and somehow aloof from the huddled mass of tile-roofed houses. Always the church dominating the landscape for miles, just as the church, heart of far-flung papal power, dominates the guardedly religious Spanish mind. I recall a friend in New York once showing me a letter I had written her from Spain. A paragraph was marked:

> Out of the spectacular landscape of Aragon and Asturias rise grim or flagrantly ornate churches. No matter how poverty-stricken a town may appear on the surface, these edifices are sure to be filled with treasures. Frescoes, painted canvas, sculpture, rich altar fabrics, and garniture for observing the ritual of High Mass. A cardinal in Málaga once told me, "In Spain a large portion of all riches in art finally becomes church property in one way or another." As I bade the cardinal good-bye and went on my way I mused on what he had said. I concluded he had been subtly telling me what I had heard many times before. First, last and always, Spain *is* the church, and the church is *Spain*.

Since that day I have traveled widely in Spain and the Balearic Islands. I do not confine my judgment of ecclesiastical dominance to the austere, consummately powerful churches of Aragon and Asturias alone. I find what the cardinal said holds grimly true of every province. Indeed churches in the island citadel Palma de Majorca, a notably devout city, are bewildering in the richness of gilded

7

retablos, somberly glowing religious paintings immense in scale, and jewel-encrusted madonnas.

I was once shouted at by a woman tourist, fidgeting, undecided at a crossroads near Jerez de la Frontera. "Shall I bother with visiting that church?" pointing toward a golden-stone, scrolled façade rising from a grove of dusty, dispirited olive trees. I replied, "In Spain never sell a church short. For you never know your luck. *That* is La Cartuja, one of the most lovely, mellow gestures in Apulian style you will ever see. Don't miss it." She followed my advice and was probably surprised to find that this elaborate Italian Renaissance screen masked a Gothic interior of windy distances.

Starting in antiquity, well before the Christian era, succeeding conquerors down the centuries left their mark of occupancy on customs and architecture in varying degree. Iberians have ever been a race slow to infuse another's point of view into the warp and woof of their daily life. But once there, the pattern remains.

Evidence of early conquerors is scattered far and wide across the Spanish landscape. One comes upon these fragments or semi-ruins in odd places. It is possible in cases like the impressive ruins of the Roman Circus Itálica in Seville or the graceful, crescent-shaped Theater to Diana at Badajoz to let one's mind range backward to evoke what once took place among these marble peristyles and columned porticos fronting tiers of garland-carved seats. Spain offers an inexhaustible wealth of monuments to set one's mind dreaming of the rich pageantry of long gone civilizations.

Today the most signal of all monuments erected in Spain is the Aqueduct of Trajan, one of the four Roman Emperors who was born a Spaniard. Unrivaled anywhere in Christendom, this tremendous engineering feat solved the problem of bringing water from the Sierra de Guadarrama to Segovia in the plain. While I yield not one inch in my long-standing admiration for this double tier of silvery-green stone arches, it has one rival. In a region strewn with ruins is the astonishingly well preserved Triumphal Arch of Bara, near Tarragona, built in the second century B.C. to adorn the Roman Road called Augustus.

Everywhere among these Roman relics we find the advent of the Moor. The Arab, or as it is more generally called, Moorish invasion of Spain was not sudden nor overwhelming. Starting as a series of recurrent "waves," first the Berbers came, guided by constellations in the starry firmament from out the red fastnesses of the High Atlas.

But this Berber tenure was enfeebled by internecine warfare among jealous chieftains and soon collapsed. Then came the Moors, representing many factions, who took their time arranging surprise landings by moonlight or in the early dawn. The whole affair was in a way "a pleasant invasion, merrily planned to delight," as a Spanish historian once told me. The Moors were subtle rather than violent; they brought to Spain incalculable contributions to art, science. learning, and architecture, which later penetrated all Europe.

Rose Macaulay, in her delightful, leisurely *Fabled Shore* says:

> Ghosts from a hundred pasts rise from the same grave, fighting one another still; dig a little deeper, dig below the Moor to the Goth, below the Goth to the Roman, Carthaginian, Greek, Phoenician, and in the end you get down to the Spanish who were here before history began, and will be here after history, defeated and routed at last by this strange land, dissolves in impenetrable mists.

I feel this penetrating insight into Iberian character deeply, for there are tangible evidences of all she says on every hand.

There came the day when the Spaniards realized they were free from Moorish dominance. Then a mighty surge of long pent-up talents flooded the land. Spanish painters and sculptors, who had been working in secret, opened windows and doors of hidden studios and workshops to let in the free Spanish sunshine. The accent in all arts must now be undeniably Spanish. Like fanned flames the word swept across the plains and mountains that Spain must lead the world in art. Craftsmanship in a hundred branches had been taught and fostered by the singularly talented Moors. Of all these the Spaniards made immediate use. The art of decorating and firing tiles, the tanning and gilding of leather, the armorers' tempering of steel blades to prodigious strength and resiliency, had all reached perfection. Toledo, called The City of Steel Apprentices, etched blades and body armor in a fashion termed damascene so skilfully that the art of damascene became world acclaimed. Princely collectors in Europe as well as in far-flung Spanish possessions across the seas adopted everything in "Spanish style." Today, examples of finest craftsmanship are still produced and beautifully displayed for visitors to choose from. Because Moslem law had rigidly forbidden depicting the human figure or animals in art, the question of where Spanish painters had learned so much about drawing anatomy has been widely discussed. Undoubtedly it was the secret teacher in the hidden room. Once the artist was free to paint at will, the subjects chosen were at first largely religious scenes from the Bible.

In the late Renaissance, when the fashion of painting huge allegorical pictures of gods and goddesses of mythology in their eternal dalliance swept through the studios of court painters in Europe, Spanish painters followed in the wake, but their work was very much toned down in character, for the church frowned on such artistic license. In fact, two painters, Herrera and Tomé, came under severe reprimand by the inexorable Inquisition. Herrera died from dungeon imprisonment. For the most part the paintings one sees today in Spain, whether in church, monastery, or palace, are dark, brooding religious subjects, usually the torture of martyrdom, but magnificently glowing in color.

I remember once, after a tour of El Escorial, when I was about twelve years old, my mother asked me what I thought of the riches I had seen *and* why I had glowered so at the broody canvases covering the walls. I answered her. "Acres and acres and acres of canvas, but all so dark I couldn't make out what the pictures were." In her usual crisp manner she replied, "The pictures are dark, surely, but look closely next time, exert your imagination. It will surprise you." Since then I have had many surprises.

After the departure of the Moors, when this great surge of purely Spanish art was gaining volume, it was a field day for architects who went hand in hand with painters, sculptors, craftsmen, all working together to create lasting beauty in dovetailed stone and marble.

Among notable styles is Plateresque, sometimes called Isabelline. Façades are enriched with carved marble and porphyry plaques, caryatid, garlands, and armorial bearings. The Baroque and Rococo styles were given marked individuality, unmistakably Spanish in flavor, by José Churriguerra. In many towns in Spain the recklessly original Churriguerresque style of palaces, churches, and municipal buildings so captures the imagination that one wants to see more of it. Churriguerra, the brilliant son of a fantastically talented family (very like the theatrically inclined Bibiena family of Bologna) is condemned by some critics as meretricious, over-exuberant, or excessively ornate. His style is certainly florid but to me this is saved by his never-failing lyric flow of line and the vitality of his ornament. For example, there is the exquisitely balanced, fairy-tale pavilion called Las Flores por Juana la Paz, in a mimosa glade near Valencia. Fashioned in the form of an octagon, the eight walls are decorated in stucco with a design in high relief of flowering trees entertaining myriad birds in the branches. The freedom of execution of birds and branches imparts to this idyllic retreat a lovely life of its own.

A traveler in Spain is advised to visit castles as part of the treasures of the country. Many of these castles still in good preservation are museums of art. In every province in Spain great or lesser castles affront the sky from mountains or massive rocks on the sea coast. If there is a wanting complement built by man to the natural beauty of Spain, there is little doubt of its identity. In Catalonia, Castile, Aragon, and Asturias, I would say particularly Castile, the almost legendary castles are preeminent. Rock placed sentinels of the plain, Spanish castles have defied the ages and furnished poets, painters, and dramatists with superlative material to exploit their several talents.

Chapter 2

GATEWAY TO FABLE:
The Costa Brava

U NDER a deep indigo sky, so glazed with stars it seemed lacquered in silver, I had crossed the Pyrenees from France into Spain just before midnight. It was now considerably later. At the frontier depot there had been a good deal of scurrying out of army-blanketed cots by the two frontier guards, who smiled sleepily, giving hardly a glance at my passport or luggage. When inquiries as to the kind and amount of my currency were satisfied, I was relieved to be waved on my way by one of the guards, who managed a wide smile and cavernous yawn at the same time. The drive through the mountains of Roussillon had been cold as charity, even though it was the middle of June. The road, while fairly wide and clearly marked, played tricks by dipping down, climbing suddenly heavenward, only to describe snakelike curves, doubling back on itself like a carnival switchback. I remembered this road well, having crossed it once before on a high, hot noon when the air was drugged by the sun beating down on acres of wild thyme which grows like gorse in these parts. The air had been hot and heavy with herb fragrance. Now, in the cold night air, it was the pungence of pine and the salt tang of the sea, off to my left, that overpowered the smell of wild herbs.

Avienus the Roman wrote many tablets about the building of this road. He wrote sarcastically that Roman legions were so eager to forge ahead into Spain, lured by its heralded riches, wide open for their taking, that sappers, or Imperial Engineers, as these military road builders were called in Rome, carved from living rock the military way, keeping only a few leagues ahead of the arrogant

12

legions, who camped sketchily behind but waxed voluble and abusive, impatient to march ahead.

I finally arrived at the *parador* on the outskirts of Port Bou, where I was to stay for what was left of the night, chilled to the bone. Driving had been treacherous because of a heavy slash of rainstorm which had descended quite suddenly just after I left the frontier. Pouring out, unannounced, from a seemingly clear sky, this rather scurvy trick of the elements is often encountered in the wild and unpredictable Catalan Mountains. Suddenly as the storm had raged, it lessened, passing over into the valley of the Sierra Cádi, the first of the numerous *sierras* one sees rising from the plains of Spain. My long ride in an open car across the mountains had left me not only wet but curiously wide awake. Undressing slowly in my room at *Parador Torrella* I stood for a time at the window looking off and away across the Mediterranean, calm-surfaced as a lake under the stars. I wondered just why the sea below should seem so different to me now, than when, after dinner, a few hours before, I had stood on the beach at Port Vendres in the Roussillon, watching the red and umber latteen sails of the fishing fleet set out in wedge-shaped formation for the nightly fishing grounds. It was the same sea. I thought out loud, "Different because this is Spain. The legendary Costa Brava of antiquity. The fabled shore that has known more wars, more pirate raids, more trading in treasures and has been more often described in song, prose and poetry than any other."

I leaned out of the window and looked down the coast, the way I would drive come morning. The sky over Spain was compelling in its brilliance. I traced Orion and the shimmering reaches of the Milky Way. The lights of a fishing boat winked at me and I identified above its mast Castor and Pollux, the mariners' stars, the twin satellites to which Spanish fishermen offer libation, and the best fish of the catch, to ward off storms—a pagan custom which still holds strong along this antique coast.

I turned back to survey my room. A room of simple distinction, not a frill nor an ornament to be seen; low ceiling, whitewashed walls, dark-red painted floor with braided rush mats. A wide, high-bolstered bed. Red and yellow painted chairs standing primly against the walls. Catalonian severity, but comfortable, cool and clean swept, somehow like the silver-sanded beach outside my window. Once in bed I was not long in drifting off to sleep, remembering, however, I planned to get off to an early start in the morning.

13

A cock crowed so loudly, almost in my ear, that I leapt from bed to find a brilliant morning above a rippling sea. The fishing boats were in, drawn up on the shore by teams of sepia-brown oxen. I was sorry to have missed that morning ritual. But I had seen it before and would again, along this coast. On the terrace I took hasty coffee, served me in a yellow pottery bowl. There was smoked fish if I wanted it. Fresh fruit and long, heavily crusted rolls. For a while I traced my route on a big ordinance map of Spain which I had used many times; in fact, it was getting frayed from usage. From the time I drove out from Port Bou until I passed Barcelona I would be driving across the pages of history. All the way to Huelva near the frontier of Portugal, roughly 800 miles away, I would pass through villages, towns and a few cities, built long before the Christian era. Mark Twain said, rather bruskly, of Rome—"An old ruin beside a railway station." One might say of Port Bou—"A jumble of white houses sliding into the sea." Just an amusing name and a jumping-off place between the sea and the elephant-hide crags merging into the gorges of the Alta Ampurdán Mountains.

For many miles along this coast of Catalonia the rock formations are jagged and cleft by innumerable little bays encircling sandy beaches. Some bays are long, spearhead shaped, others may form a crescent or flattened elipse so that as one stands on a height and looks up or down the coast the pattern is a lacy fusing of rocks, sand and water, whose counterpart nowhere else I can remember.

Perhaps the Catalonian embrace of the Costa Brava which remains longest in memory is her fishing villages. Often these are hidden from view. Many are forgotten, even derelict, for wind, weather and succeeding centuries have eaten away the ancient foundations. During the years of the Spanish Civil War many of these villages which had become hideaways for political refugees were blasted from their crags and beaches by gun fire. My first adventure into Catalan solitude was when I walked down a zigzag path along a lonely stretch of coast between Rosas and the grim battlements of Ampuriás. What had particularly attracted my attention, which wanders constantly when driving through a countryside, was a flight of herons, blue, black and white against the sky; the flock seemed to hold a sort of assembly at a pale yellow tower standing sentinel among the wind-tortured pines. I would, uninvited, join this assembly to see what went on. And so I came down to another of the deserted fishing villages which may have been built by the questing Phoenicians, for I

14

SUNRAY COSTUMES WOMEN OF
(BALEARICS) IBIZA:

noticed the long-ago ruins of a barrel-shaped lighthouse, the sort erected by these adventurers from the Greek islands all along this coast. The stillness of death hung over the small village. But a wary, watching stillness. The inhabitants fugitive, the small plaza from which the crumbling church tower rose seemed, in the bright sunlight, waiting only for the return of the native at evening, perhaps singing the good fortune of a bounteous catch. I looked about me, for this was one of many, once thriving, happy fishing villages I had heard about. Glassless windows stared like apprehensive eyes seaward or up into the hills; lizards, always the swift, enameled life of desert silences, scampered in emerald radiance along the white walls. Other than the lizards not a sign of life, for the herons had flown off. Not even the starved cat humping against one's shins without which no "deserted village" anywhere is complete. The golden crescent beach attracted me, so I stripped and went down to bathe. Later, as I was dressing, the silence affected me more strongly than the boom of gongs would have done. For the fabric of all Spanish fishing villages is the clatter of women gossiping at the well. Here the lichened stone wellhead was slimy with stagnant water. No purple-brown nets dried on long poles. No patient menders plunged mussel-shell needles through rents made by fighting crustaceans. Most of all I missed the identifying odor of fish frying in olive oil. Had there been one soul in Tiraola, I could have eaten my fill of fried fish.

Farther along the road I came to Culera, centuries old and more or less deserted now. A few fishing boats start out in moonlight or at sunrise. But all life has migrated to the village of San Miguel de Culera rising in terraces in a lovely, verdant valley behind what was once Culera Port. At San Miguel de Culera molders a gaunt monastery descended from the Middle Ages. In this ruined religious house, once rich and powerful in Catalan church affairs, I walked through roofless chambers. Here were woven resplendent tapestries so fine of stitch, so deftly pictorial, that they were coveted for embellishment of churches, archbishops' palaces and the castles of grandees, even into France and Italy. I learned that as early as the fourteenth century a noble family of Ampurdán, wishing to glorify their name of Oliva (from them a small adjacent town, overwhelmed by high, narrow, shut-faced palaces and graceful but dusty gardens, takes its name), provided the monks with looms and yarn and the much desired silver and gold tinsel threads. A teacher of the mysteries of warp and woof was brought from Flanders, so that for all time Ampurdán might hold renown for the beauty of its woven arras. What most distinguishes these tapestries is a wide border of rocks, pines and thistles interlaced with branches of wild thyme and purple valerian. This border might be heraldery. The absolute Catalonian device.

Driving along the winding coast, with the brilliant or darkling sea always on my left hand, the fishing villages flashed like spangles in and out of the coves, each village bearing a family resemblance. But even more prevalent and arresting are the ruins of Phoenician or Romanesque altars, arches, or plinths, memorials to imperial death or arenas of sport. So far there is no sign of the Moor; his mark will become evident when you approach Cádiz; but in this region, the "destroying Visigoth" who left these pagan and Christian temples in ruin is time.

All travelers along the Catalonian shore remark on the excellence of its sandy beaches, a constant invitation to bathe and drowse on the sand afterward.

Garbet is a pleasant town, the plaza coolly shaded by a mulberry tree promenade. Garbet boasts of its long, curving beach of fine-grained sand. The gold and silver grains are peculiar to this region, mixed with specks of brash red-orange and purple clay washed down from the rock cliff stratas. On the beach I watched an errant breeze riffle this parti-colored sand into stripes. The effect, I thought, was rather like the gaily striped yashmaks worn by the Riff women of Tetuan in Spanish Morocco. Auto-bus companies are wise beyond the usual, halting at Garbet for an hour or more to let hot, dusty tourists have a bathe and cooling drinks served on the beach by youths in red blouses and tasseled black fisherman caps. These caps are for sale, right off the boys' heads. A good trade is apparently done, for I see these caps on the heads of men and women tourists in all parts of Spain.

Leaving Garbet I made a detour, for I decided to have lunch at Llansá, and to wander for a while around the plaza, paved in lapis lazuli and yellow stones, where orange, lemon, and apricot trees grow in tubs. When this ancient town was founded as a recreation resort for high-ranking Roman officers of cavalry, it was called Deciana. Elaborate villas faced a wide quadrangle, famous up and down the coast for the ingenuity of its paving in blue lapis lazuli and gold. Now the quadrangle is the plaza, the center of village life.

The once famous mosaic paving put down in the sixteenth century is a freely translated copy of the original design. An antiquarian whom I encountered in the plaza explained that the design of three horse chariots being raced by Roman officers in gala dress is much altered from the original. When the woefully cracked, chipped, and weather-stained tiles were first unearthed under layers of soil that had for centuries been a garden plot, medallions were found which rivaled in erotic subject the frescos at Pompeii. Only the central design of chariot races was allowed to remain.

"What happened to the fragments of original tiles?" I asked the antiquarian. "Surely they were not thrown on the dust heap, human acquisitiveness being what it is." He smiled, flipped a half finished cigarette to a small boy who had been intently watching us.

"Oh no," he answered. "Collectors are most avidly searching for those fragments of Roman debauchery, as a fine art of course."

I waited, fairly sure of what was to come.

"If you will wait until after siesta, I will show you some I have in my shop."

These fragments were provocative, the pattern in most cases being broken off at the most exciting point of design. I am happy to possess one showing the inevitable nymph in full flight from a centaur, but with a difference. For the centaur wears the armor of a Roman legionary.

High above the plaza at Llansá looms what remains of a once glorious Romanesque church, partially destroyed by anarchists in 1936. The Counts of Llansá, "as far-flung a group of malcontents as you would find in any century," according to Charles VI in his *Chronicles of Catalonia,* built castles on crags of the surrounding hills. For years cousin fought cousin in senseless battles, for what purpose no one knows. Finally, like the feuding McCoys in the Kentucky mountains, the entire clan was decimated. Now the castles rise like monolithic altars shimmering golden in sunlight, black and ominous by night. Half the ghostly hauntings in Spain are traced to these castles of the ferocious Llansá warriors.

I stayed so late at the shop of my friend, the antiquarian, I realized I could never make the tiny village of unbelievable antiquity, called Selva de Dalt, in any kind of time to climb the mountain to the Benedictine Abbey of San Pere de Roda, a towering pile of almost purple rocks that is one of the glories of the Costa Brava.

Just as I was trying to collect my thoughts and decide where to dine and spend the night, one of those sibilant whispers one hears so often in Spain caught my attention. It was a young muleteer who, as a side line, carried on the usual traffic in American cigarettes. I bought a pack I did not need, because I wanted his advice about whether I could get a good bed and good food at Puerto de Llansá a few kilometers down the coast. His smile was reassuring.

"But of course, señor. Beds soft, very fine food, and *lovely* view." He spoke English with a lisp and loud accent on the word lovely. "Where did you learn English?" I asked.

His eyes widened. "I speak *American*, not English," he politely corrected me. "My brother lived in Cuba. Now," he pointed towards the coast road, "he drives an auto truck. He drives like the *hell*."

This was the boy for accenting his conversation if I ever saw one. However, his predictions as to "soft bed" and "fine food, *lovely* view" proved true. For, sitting on a flower-garlanded terrace at a scrap of tavern named Miramar, I ate wonderfully fresh crabs sprinkled with fresh herbs and dressed with lemon and pungent olive oil. A tomato and pepper dish, wedded somehow to chicken livers and saffron rice, was washed down by a light local red wine served chilled. Granted that the food was excellent, the view was better. The kind that loosens the urge to paint what I see to a point not to be denied. So—I sat on the rocks beside the gently lapping sea, painting until I had only moonlight to guide my brush. On a rocky island landlocking the bay rose a reddish-silver castle, crenellated and furiously sprouting battlements. A more warlike pile of feudal masonry I have never seen. Spain is famous for its castles built down the centuries, primarily for defense against every known weapon of destruction. I learned this was Castle Férida. Though besieged numberless times, never had it been reduced. Next morning I asked a boatman to row me out to Férida. The view of Puerto de Llansá and the far-flung coast was one of distant mountain peaks, pine clad cliffs, pink, green, umber, and violet-blue houses rising in pyramid, slightly askew, like children's playing blocks, and the scimitar-shaped beach of golden sand where the fishing boats lay idle, draped with the ubiquitous fish nets without which there would be no life at all along the Costa Brava.

On and on wends the old Roman road, varied in interest. The most impressive natural landmark commanding attention for miles is the Cadaqués Peninsula jutting like Neptune's trident in three-pronged crags of rock into the sea where cross currents churn foam and dash mountains of spray against hidden rocks day and night, no matter how still the Mediterranean may be elsewhere. Here the manner of building villages alters from the usual pattern of huddle and jumble around a church. Like marching soldiers, the houses follow the line of goat paths from the shore to topmost rock. It is difficult even at midday to see these houses with the naked eye, for they have been painted the exact color of the rocks behind. These rocks take rusty hues, dark copper, pale rose, madder-brown, and soft yellow. Only when the sun is setting, when long shadows are cast, can one pick out the individual houses. Even then they seem one with the rock-flank; here is protective coloring at its best, a dodge as old as time. This is said to have been done by the fishermen to outwit Barbary pirates in the days when the Catalonian shore was the happy hunting ground for Corsair plunder. Even today, when night falls, no lights flicker or shine out from windows on Cadaqués Point. No song, no music of concertina or guitar is heard. This is truly "the silent village in the night."

The Port of Cadaqués, apart from the peninsula, has a long, illustrious history. A friendly, beguiling town it is, inviting one to spend a long holiday. I have done so in an earlier year and loved it. In fact, I painted enough pictures in and around the Port to arrange an exhibition in Paris and Rome, later shown in London. One might say with truth that this book stems from that sojourn in Cadaqués Port and the pictures I brought away with me, for it was then my interest in Spain soared.

The notorious French admiral, Count of Foix, lived here after French and Spanish peace negotiations had been concluded in 1285. The count conducted a bit of piracy on his own, up and down the coast. Playing a Robin Hood role, he robbed the rich nobles only to turn his loot over to the poor. Roger de Laurier, a Catalonian admiral, said of Foix, "He is loved on the one hand and loathed on the other. While he is loose, the poor are enriched, and the rich made poor."

My arrival at Port Cadaqués was most salutary. The annual festival of the local saint was in progress. In true Spanish style, flowers were festooned everywhere. In the plaza trellises had been erected. Through the interstices of green laths, roses, overblown and heavy with perfume, had been twined. Beneath a kind of crude plaster proscenium arch tortured into scrolls sat a child-faced Madonna in blue and silver robes. All around this figure were jars of white lilies, already withering to brown in the intense heat. At first I did not notice that the Madonna was enthroned on a bullock cart because of the crowd in front. The wheels of this farm wain, turned for the day into a religious conveyance, were freshly painted in red and green stripes, the spokes interlaced with swags of field flowers. Hovering over the flowers were honey bees whose delicately herb-flavored honey is the pride of the region. I walked around the plaza, sampling the juicy apricots and big purple plums, their skins veined with heavy white streaks that made them look like marble.

An hour passed and still the procession had not started. Children darted in and out of the arcades in holiday clothes, bright as dragon flies. Finally I wended my way back to the wain-enthroned Madonna to find her deserted of devotees; they were now quenching their thirst at the cafés around the square. At one café a painted image of the wine bibber Bacchus covered an entire wall. It was mortally hot and getting hotter. I noticed a wine dispenser was doing well.

In one corner of the square, a group of hugely muscled bullocks dozed, ruminating. I picked up a few hard apples from a basket under an awning and moved toward the bullocks. I have never seen anything more comic than the expression in their liquid, violet-brown eyes. Completely resigned to a hot afternoon of unmitigated boredom, they stood with lowered heads, surmounted by wide leather head bands designed to support yokes of carved olive wood. Great dangles of red and yellow wool hung from the headpieces. I held out an apple in either hand. Each bullock eyed me distrustfully, nibbling delicately before munching.

Suddenly the notes of a cornet wound on the still air and bedlam broke loose. Everyone had, it seemed, an appointed task and rushed to fill it. The bullocks were jerked into motion. Small girls in starched white dresses encircled the wain as virgin maids of honor. Their mothers, in heavily embroidered skirts and gold galloon headdresses worn over black velvet headcloths, lighted long wax tapers and the procession started to move on its ponderous way. As I got into the car (it was far too hot to follow the procession), I noticed that a large portion of the men remained at the café tables stroking their wine flagons, content to leave Madonna of the Wain with female attendants during her sundrenched progress.

I drove later along a road that shimmered in heat waves. Perhaps it would be cooler in the uplands. So I decided on Palamós as a point where I would branch off to inland Gerona. Just as I passed Palamós I caught a glimpse of bright sails against a clear emerald sea through a gap in the rocks, where rampant cacti formed a kind of *chemin de frise*. Broiling heat or no, I must see what went on here for, in the ordinary way, it was far too early for fishing boats to be out. I stopped the car and climbed to a promontory of rock jutting out into the sea. Here was a scene out of fable.

A corridor of dark umbrella pines marched down to the bay, ringed with a silvery gold filigree of sand. Wild flowers in their thousand delicate colors, fragile of petal, seemed about to be crushed under the scarred leaves of sharply spiked cacti. For this was a very carnival of cacti. I counted eight varieties, the leaves of one plant slashing the leaves of another, so that sap ran into designs of purple and dark brown. To me there is something barbaric, like Saracen swords, in the thrusting, gray-green blades of these massive cacti which form a barrier between the road and the sea, along the Costa Brava. It is a rugged shore, surely, as well as a "brave coast."

Through this crosshatching of leaves I saw that the fishing boats were in use to take the children of an orphanage (by their gray pinafores and round black straw hats they are identifiable the world over) for an outing, accompanied by black-habited nuns. In one boat a singing choir was performing, in another food was being taken. What added a fillip to the scene was a dark-haired, devilish youth sitting on a rock, playing on a shepherd-pipes to a group of boys swimming in circles around the boats, bare-bottomed, I judged, by the amount of ducking and shrieks of laughter taking place. The boats sailed slowly, on a calm sea, the orphans fidgeting with curiosity under the stern eyes of the nuns.

Driving along, I thought back on the hours of this day. What a variety of incident! First the rural pageantry of a religious festival at which Bacchus stole the show. And just now a water picnic for hedged-in orphans, where Pan played his pipes and naked brown urchins disported in the sea to its raffish tune. The pagan element in Spain has never died down in country gatherings, no matter how censorious the church in trying to root it out.

As so often happens on terrifically hot days in any land, toward evening masses of dark thunderheads gathered in the western sky to frame the brazen sun. This was to be a day to remember long. I had just reached La Escala, when a big auto-bus crossed a bridge and skidded sharply to avoid running down an ox cart coming suddenly out of a lane. The bus stopped at right angles across the road, forcing me to draw up at the retaining wall to wait until I could pass. I was a shade surprised when the passengers all piled out as if nothing had happened and lined up along the wall to enjoy the spectacular sunset. A last flaming radiance over the land promised a hot tomorrow. The sea spread out below us was colored like Byzantine enamel. For once there was no cackling among the fifteen or more American tourists from the bus. Everyone was silent in wonder.

Gerona seemed illusive, a far longer drive by a devious, twisting road than I had expected it to be. Even the extremely late dining hour of the Spanish would hardly leave me time to reach my hotel, have a wash, and get down to dinner before chairs were being stacked and the chef gone to his favorite wine shop. I need not have given this a thought. It was exactly eleven o'clock when I entered the dining room at the Peninsula Hotel. One would have thought a civic banquet had just started. Waiters scurried around with platters of steaming food. Wine flowed at every table. Each table was full to overflowing, there were even babies in high chairs, for Spaniards like to have their entire families down to the least tot in arms dine together. How the babies keep awake, in smiling good nature, during these late meals, I have never understood. Invariably they do, even close to midnight, devouring heaping plates of saffron rice, *langostinos* mayonnaise, pork chops, black beans and *garbanzos* or chickpeas, all the good, rich local dishes. A table was set for me beside a window looking toward the garden. Above a high wall the belfry of a Romanesque church soared into the night sky, adding lift to the medieval scene. I ordered a *paella*, as I had planned to do since early morning, if I had the good fortune to reach Gerona in time. I have never eaten better. The rice was delicately flavored with saffron, the various shell fish which jostle pork, chicken, sausages, mussels, and lobster in a wonderfully aromatic sauce compounded from the juices of all ingredients, was satisfying to the palate. With the *paella* I drank a full-bodied Marqués de Riscal wine, a claret much favored by travelers, I have found. Even fresh fruit did not tempt me as dessert, for a really fine *paella* is in itself a full meal.

Next morning I set out to wander through the streets of Gerona, an experience like visiting old friends again, for I have often stopped in this old town and come under the spell of a curious kind of Oriental magic which pervades the place, though I cannot tell precisely how or why. Though generally medieval in aspect, in parts it is fiercely Romanesque and Gothic. Perhaps it is the dark, twisting, alley-like streets, some burrowing under arcaded houses, where once

23

lived rich and powerful Catalan noble families. Here are many splendid examples of early Romanesque architecture, but the treasures of Gerona are its situation, and the unbridled magnificence of the Baroque cathedral.

Gerona rises, startling in beauty, high above the River Oñar just where it flows into the raging waters of the Ter, which depends, for its source, on a mountain waterfall, to be seen hanging, like trembling silver, in a high gorge above the town. The façade of the cathedral is eloquent as organ music. A Catalan, Guillermo Boffill, spread himself in genius when he designed the nave, still proudly boasting the widest vault of any cathedral in Christendom, not excepting the immensity of the Cathedral of Seville. Among its art treasures, the cathedral guards a particularly rare piece of needlework, stitched, it is said, by two generations of women, members of six families, purported to be Saxons working in England in the eleventh century.

The work displays a panorama of the creation of the world and has no known counterpart. It is nearly impossible to describe in words the heroic majesty of design. The Creator sits enthroned amid a mélange of beasts, fishes, the winds and planets. Behind the Creator is a vista of the City of Jerusalem. The color is softly luminous, as if the earth were just burgeoning to spring. In the nave of the cathedral a vaulting canopy of embossed silver gleams above acres of red velvet, used to fashion cushions. The antique velvet is the color of ecclesiastical crimson seen only in Spanish or Italian churches. The cushions are piled in stacks forming pillars near the entrance door, for the use of the devout in prayer, and they make superb decoration when not in use.

A story is told that a proud duquesa residing in Gerona had so calloused her knees in youth, being forced by a fanatical duenna to kneel in constant devotion on unyielding stone, that after her marriage she never again entered a church. When she died, sometime during the eighteenth century, she left a considerable sum of money in perpetuity, to supply "velvet knee rests of good quality for all at prayer to cushion their knees."

Everywhere in Gerona one walks up or down, for the town is built on a hillside. Some streets are terraced in a series of shallow-step ramps. Others stretch away into dark caverns, branching off like threads of a spider web under the Roman arches. These contorted byways are tributary to a dramatic set-piece of pure theater, Escalera

24

de Santo Domingo. Rising to improbable height the steps continue straight through a gracefully pillared Baroque doorway to the nave of a church bearing the same name.

In a hurry, I came leaping down the steps three at a time. A tourist, who said he was from Texas, stopped me to ask where to find the museum. "Up those steps," I answered. He gazed upward wistfully, mopping his face with a bandana. Then he sighed, shaking his head. "This is no town for a man with a bad heart."

A brooding castle crowns the highest rock above the streets, for this is the correct finish to any medieval Spanish picture. Gerona is entirely surrounded by high walls. Into them are set enormous plaques featuring heads, in fillet or helmet, of Greek warriors and Roman emperors. The color of the roughly-dressed stone of the walls is peculiar. A repellent, wet-looking gray-green, giving the stones the effect of being still damp and slippery from river water.

Of all sights in this intensely interesting town I feel most drawn to the houses backing onto the river as it flows through the center of Gerona. For the most part, balconies and tall windows are guarded against intrusion by fret-work grills of carved wood (as in La Coruña) or the lower windows by the inevitable iron *rejas*. Terraces hang out over the water. These drip with vines and flowers. The first time I stood on the bridge and looked at this vista of balconied houses, I wondered, "What city, far away from Spain, does this remind me of?" Soon I had it. Srinagar, the last town in India before the bleakness of Karakoram Pass. I had once been poled down the tortuous Jhelum River in a flimsy, canopied river barge, all filigree and jigsaw wooden lace and *no* stability. The River Jhelum rushes in a series of rapids between crazily tottering houses. There, too, were flower-hung terraces. But whereas in Gerona the dignity and vitality of Spanish art manifests itself in the *rejas*, and in strongly built stone houses—in Kashmir one is conscious of the instability of everything except the Himalayas. At night before going to bed I walked out on the bridge in Gerona, beneath a high, white-flooding moon. Again I felt clearly the effect of some eastern city, for moonlight lends enchantment to water-reflected stone work, lightened by delicate iron tracery.

I drove into Torroella de Montgri next day at five o'clock in the afternoon. The town was just returning to life from siesta behind closed jalousies—a longer siesta than usual, for the day had been torridly hot. Usually the Costa Brava is moderately cool in summer with breezes from the sea and mountains, and often too cold at night for comfort. But today had been marked by dead, flat heat, without a breath of air stirring. Once again in the space of a few days I arrived at an auspicious time, for Torroella de Montgri was in the throes of a two-day fiesta, a typical Catalonian *feria*, purely pastoral, without even the mention of a saint to give an excuse for celebration. Actually, it was a semi-annual cattle fair with all the trimmings.

What pleased me most was the chance to see the traditional fiesta costumes of prosperous farmers of the region. Both men and women were, I noticed, in full array. All along the coast, since I had left Port Bou, I had been conscious of women in the plazas of villages or walking along the roads between the long, low white farmhouses, wearing the traditional full, dark cloth skirt, fringed shoulder shawl of red or deep yellow, and crisp white head kerchief, the every day costume of Catalonia. I had even seen a few men standing around taverns smoking long churchwarden pipes of yellowed clay, wearing knee breeches of black or gray velveteen, wide red cummerbunds, and short jackets with silver ball buttons. The hat accompanying this dress is distinctive to Catalonia. Over a black rickrack snood trailing onto the shoulders in the back, is worn a round velvet hat resembling those worn by matadors, lacking the "handles" of flat pompons at either side and the oiled pigtail at nape of neck. For the gala festival, I saw that many women had added resplendent aprons heavily embroidered in silk, sequins, and tiny tassels of tinsel thread. Men milled about the plaza wearing heavily braided jackets slung across their shoulders dolman fashion. Replacing the black snoods, bright silk handkerchiefs were tied around the head under the round black hats.

Dancing began around eleven o'clock. Happily a light breeze had sprung up. Sitting on straight-backed, short-legged chairs, groups of women whispered together. On identical chairs groups of men sat by themselves silent, bolt upright. These groups would, I discovered, supply *palmada*, the rhythmical clapping of hands. This sharp, dry clap-clap-clap accents the dance rhythm when no music is used.

The first dance was a stately treading of steps. It followed the pattern of "stepping off a square" which forms the basis of folk dancing in many countries. Next, two young girls in black dresses and yellow silk head cloths, with clusters of fresh flowers on top, danced a swift, sharply accented pattern. No music was used but the watching men and women, faces immobile as graven images, dealt out a very superior class of *palmada*. When the dance finished, a young man dressed all in black lounged lazily into the space cleared for dancing. He was lean as a whippet and his skin was dark olive. He unslung a guitar from his back and began to play. Here were the haunting, rise-and-fall cadences of Arab melancholy. Although the youth wore the Catalan dress I judged him not of this region, but much farther south. I turned to a pipe smoking individual sitting near me.

"Is that guitarist a Catalan?"

Without taking his eyes off the youth, the man answered. "Pepe was born in San Martí," pointing northward, "that is Catalonia. But he was brought up in Cádiz." He shrugged his velveteen shoulders and spat violently on the stones. "What would you? They of Cádiz are all Moors still."

Collection of Melville Church, III

Chapter 3

ROMAN HILL TOWNS IN
THE SPANISH SUN

AFTER one of my journeys to Spain I was asked to dine with a friend living in Washington who has never been to Europe. Nevertheless, I tell her she has the most "traveled mind" of anyone I know. She has enjoyed a full life of travel vicariously by reading everything pertaining to it. She has hosts of friends who range the world, keeping her on the qui vive by sending her picture cards and detailed letters from some place she has dreamed of one day visiting, or of another she has never heard of. Always avid for stories, she asked me to relate any unusual incidents I had recently experienced in Spain. We sat long over coffee as I told her a tale of having stopped one evening at a little mountain chapel, circular in shape, in the silent fastnesses of Navarre.

In the wall there was a door and, I discovered later, only one tall narrow window, to the west of the altar. Built on a perilous ledge of rock, the chapel seemed poised on a cloud, about to take off for more heavenly pastures. The time was late afternoon when I entered the twilight nave. A last ray of sun slanted through the tall window to pick out and burnish a life-size figure of Christ on the Cross, carved in ivory, which hung above the pine wood altar. So brilliant was this last strong ray of the setting sun that the emaciated figure gleamed somewhat balefully, half obscured by folds of a monk's robe of rusty black velvet. At first glance I thought a swarm of fireflies hovered around the figure on the cross. No—it was the sun flickering on hundreds of tiny garnets suspended on wires from the velvet robe, simulating drops of blood.

When I finished this story there was silence for a time. Then my friend seemed to recall her thoughts from a far place. She said, "To persons like myself you bring a nostalgia for a country they have never seen." Later, as I was leaving, she said an odd thing. Odd because she voiced a thought I had long entertained but had never mentioned. At the door of her house she turned to me, saying, "If I ever *do* go to Spain I want to make a pilgrimage to Sangüesa and the Castle of Xavier. St. Francis Xavier is my patron saint. I have read everything about him I could lay my hands on. Now I hear his birthplace in the mountains of Navarre has been made a shrine."

On my way to Spain this year I remembered the conversation about St. Francis Xavier. I wondered why I had never gone to see the castle when I was in Pamplona or Gerona, for it lies midway between. Perhaps, unknowing, I was waiting to do so this year, the fourth centenary of Saint Francis' lonely death as a mendicant in Sancian at the gates of mysterious China. Now that I had again savored Gerona and come down the mountain to Torroella de Montgri, I was finishing dinner at a most agreeable old inn facing the wide, arcaded plaza. A purely Catalan seaport tavern in every way except the hotel sign, a modern job proclaiming in large electric letters Hotel Nuevo. I sat a while trying to make up my mind whether to stay and browse for a few days in this historically important old town, then continue along the coast to Tossa de Mar and on to Barcelona, or should I listen to a small, insistent voice which had played obligato to my thoughts all day. "You promised yourself the Castle of Xavier. Now get about it." I flipped a coin. Heads—Xavier. Tails—Tossa de Mar. *Heads*. Xavier. I was for it.

Next morning was glorious with brilliant sun tempered by a clean, salty breeze from the sea. I hated to leave Torroella. After breakfast I went down to the strand to look at the arch of azure blue mosaic with a black Moor's head for keystone. This wonderfully well preserved arch was erected by Abdulla El Hadji when he landed here in 1178. This giant of a man—he is said to have been eight feet tall "without his turban"—was one of the few Moorish generals who butchered the Spanish indiscriminately, with such savage ferocity that the populace of fortified towns made no resistance as he raged up and down the coast, but flung wide their gates and fled to the mountains.

By mid-morning I drove past the ruins of the monastery of Ulla. History tells grim stories of the sack and slaughter of the monks of Ulla by the hordes of El Hadji. The riven walls carry no hint of pillage now, hidden under thick vines of flowering grape and passion flower, as though decked out for a festival. Before reaching the mountain road which would land me in the village of Xavier, the landscape is dominated by the flimsy-looking shell of the once impregnable castle of the Counts of Ampuriás. The stone bastions rising sheer from living rock were originally so thick it was possible to house the watch, often as many as twenty men at a time, in guard rooms let into the buttresses. Now the castle is prey only to vagaries of the elements, which have clawed the towers to fragments. I was reminded of a story I had heard concerning the medieval clan of Ampuriás.

It was a large family living remote from neighbors in their stronghold. One member in particular, Count Tobedo, was by nature spiteful, having a mind obsessed with power, a desire to play God. Twice he tried to divert the course of the River Ter. The first try was a failure; floods only destroying the spring crops. The second time he succeeded in drying up the harbor of Torroella. By erecting a series of dams, he diverted the river so that sand clogged the port which had centuries served Gerona and other towns in the hills. So Torroella, lost on a sandbank, witnessed good fortune depart to hitherto nondescript Palafrugell, a few leagues down the coast. I advise visitors to Spain, when driving along Costa Brava, to spend a day or so in Torroella de Montgri; there is much to see to whet the imagination. The town unfolds like a page from Ampurdán history of the great days when the wealth and importance of this magnificent Catalan seaport was synonymous with the grandeur that was Spain.

The way I had chosen, a small back road, to avoid the auto-bus traffic of the main road from Gerona to Xavier, led ever upward into the hills. Coming round a sharp turn I nearly ran down a roadside fruit stall, set up under an awning for roadside barter with passing farmers. It was a casual affair. Catalans are a free-spirited people, uncomplicated in their ideas of how to conduct the daily round. They will pick out a spot beside a road, set up a market, lend aid at childbirth, prepare a sudden fatal casualty for burial, clinch the betrothal of a shy country Daphnis and Chloë, all as effortlessly as telling the beads of the rosary hanging always from the girdle of a country man or woman.

I got out of the car and walked between the mats of woven rushes spread on the grass. These rush mats were for sale as well as the fruit piled on them. Woven of sea grasses and meadow rushes, still green and crunching with sap, they are used in houses and on the floor of arcaded restaurants in the towns. On the mats were pyramids of the local melon, big, golden, and delicious when chilled and served with *jamón serrano*, the pungent smoked ham from chestnut-fed hogs. This combination of melon and ham is an excellent lunch dish served at all roadside taverns in Spain during the summer months. I was persuaded to buy a basket of pears, vermilion peppers, and the luscious silver-dusted blue plums of the region, the kind that are dried in the sun after being brushed with honey, then packed and sent all over the world as prunes.

During the hours of siesta, when extreme lassitude strikes down every man, woman, and child in Spain, like a sudden blight, I ran my car under a twelfth-century arch piercing the half-fallen walls of Sangüesa. As if in the wastes of Sahara desert, I was alone in the dusty plaza. For a while I sat in the car, looking off towards Xavier. The atmosphere was so clear, so luminous, the sky a pale duck-egg blue, the far off walls and single crenellated tower of Castle Xavier, tall and slender as a church spire, seemed within touching distance. In reality the castle is a few kilometers away across a deep valley. All about me reigned quiet, until suddenly I was conscious of a clamor outside the single gate of Sangüesa. A string of auto-busses from Gerona, bound for Xavier, honking loudly, were scattering the footweary pilgrims, so covered with clinging dust as to resemble some white-habited order of monks. It appeared that siesta did not extend to devout pilgrims, nor to bus-borne tourists who had allotted only a few hours of their itinerary to spend at the shrine of Castle Xavier.

Sangüesa is a town of Roman origin with some pretensions to historic interest. It was founded by King Alfonso el Batallador who built two walled towns rising on either bank of the River Aragon, much the same as Buda and Pest were built on either side of the Danube. For centuries bridges connecting most towns built in this manner were of light wood construction, easily burned in case of enemy assault. At Sangüesa there is a most interesting mosaic let into the wall of the gate house, showing three bridges constructed of pine trees with the green tops left intact to wave like pennants on the upright poles. The date of this mosaic is 1278. The Romanesque church of Santa Maria del Real has a splendid entrance door embrasured in a high arch, the architraves carved with figures of saints, hands

31

pointed upward in prayer and all wearing crowns of thorns, a much favored device in medieval Spanish religious sculpture. The interior of the church is unique in having three "lily-shaped" naves, embracing three corresponding presbyteries. The lily form is achieved by slender stem pillars branching out to form petals at the roof.

The greatest treasure here is a magnificent *retablo*. A most ingenious piece of Gothic sculpture depicting Heaven and Hell, the figures carved in scale from infinitesimal to over-life-size. The intricate detail is set off in a wondrous manner by the blaze of hundreds of penitential candles impaled on a forest of spikes in front of the *retablo*.

San Francisco Hospital, at one end of the plaza, resembles the palace of a grandee in richness of Plateresque ornament. There is a curious mixture of periods in architecture in Sangüesa. In one building I saw Romanesque, Visigothic, Spanish Gothic, and late Italian Renaissance, all bidding for recognition.

From the dim recesses of the cathedral I came out into a hot, deserted plaza which resembled a bull ring, being half in sunshine, half in shade. It was just three o'clock. I chose a table at a small café on the shady side, and ordered coffee. It arrived scalding, black as jet, bitter-sweet, and reviving. I noticed the young waiter who served the coffee was still half asleep. He slopped a dollop of coffee in my saucer, grunted in annoyance and said, "It is so early to serve, señor, I am not myself." Invariably I find the Spanish a most polite people, but to a man they resent foreigners interrupting their so necessary siesta.

The drive from Sangüesa is through a severe, blue-gray rocky gorge with a defile of immensely tall pines on either side of the twisting road. I was told later that since earliest times this region has supplied the masts and spars for Spanish ships. One whole mountain was cleared of pine trees to build the luckless armadas of Philip II. I passed the ribbon-thin waterfalls, always lovely in a landscape. Falling like mist from hidden clefts in the towering rock face, these waterfalls become tiny rivers on reaching the valleys to wander as irrigation ditches through farmsteads in the Lecumberri and Careda districts.

Driving along any road in Spain is bound to produce incident out of the usual. I came to a sudden halt to let a funeral procession pass. Perhaps fifty men walking four abreast moved slowly past me in a kind of halting goose step. But I was puzzled that there were only two women, who walked a short way behind the men. The coffin, big and unwieldy as a packing crate, was of new-split pine, decorated in big scrolls of red and black paint. This coffin rested on the backs of four bullocks hitched two abreast. The heads and eyes of these beasts were so covered by black and red wool trappings hung with tassels that a small boy at each bridle had to act as guide. The boys wore bright red woolen capes and broad-brimmed black hats. The male mourners wore long black capes and black knee breeches over red stockings. The faces of the men were almost hidden by huge, floppy red berets. The two women, both fairly young, lent a touch of fantasy to this solemn procession on a wild mountain road. They wore long black skirts embroidered in red and gold, the skirts so full that the back part was turned up to reveal petticoats of red and black striped silk. The overskirt, brought over the head from behind, formed a shawl. Over this was laid a wide band of gold galloon framing the face and hanging down to the knees. This galloon was so rich in heavy tinsel, it bowed the head of the wearer.

The procession passed me in silence, showing no recognition that I was taking in every detail. Later I was told that black and red are the colors, traditional to the mountain people of Xavier, for honoring the dead. I was also told that the two women, so dramatically dressed, who walked behind the men, were the daughters of the deceased. The widow does not show herself in public for a few days, presumably so stricken with grief as to be prostrate. If the funeral is that of a married woman, only women follow the coffin.

The village of Xavier, until recently so quiet that life within its walls was, in effect, one long siesta, is now bedlam. For the summer months, at any rate. From morning to night, bus loads of tourists and motley pilgrims on foot fight it out to gain entrance to the shrine of Saint Francis. I overheard an Englishman, the perfect, "I'll-have-you-know-when-I-was-in-Poona,-sir" type of retired general, growl to his wife, "Outrageous. Obscene I call it. No respect whatever. Why the fella—" pointing the ferrule of his stick at the pushing mass of humanity at the shrine, "deserves better than that." Silently I agreed. Human beings en masse are, each one, bent only on being *first* in all things, no matter what the occasion. In this instance it could be less selfishness than a kind of abandoned ecstasy.

Late in the evening is the time to enter the castle and the shrine. Then the mob has departed, for almost no one stops in Xavier after sundown. There are no facilities for taking care of more than a casual

33

ARCOS
DE LA FRONTERA.
ANDALUSIA.

JR '52

Collection of Hollis Baker, Esq.

diner. The village of Xavier itself might well be hewn from a solid block of rock. The houses seem cheerless cubes of granite. Just outside the crumbled gateway, once the sole entrance to the village, is a tilt yard or tourney court. This was built by an early member of the Azpilcuetas, a noble Navarrish family of which Francisco Xavier was a descendant.

Cold and disused as this long, rectangular courtyard is now, it seems to me there hovers over all the echo of sport and pleasure from the days when in his unrestrained, spendthrift young manhood Francisco Xavier was a notable figure at the joust. Then there would have been gaily decorated booths set on either side against the turreted stone walls. Troubadours would play, pennons fly on pavilions where ladies would set forth their favors of flowers and gauze scarves, as trophies for valor. The lovely light and shade of the famed "courts of love and beauty." All this glitter of life quickened the pulse of Francisco, as his skill with the lance must have quickened the heartbeats of the ladies waving scarves. I like to evoke the scene. Mounted on a destrier, the hugely-flanked horse used in the joust, hauberked in yellow and purple, the colors of his house, plumes from his helm streaming in the wind, this tall, lithe, profligate youth must have seemed a romantic figure indeed to townspeople and noble ladies alike, who had assembled for the day's tourney.

Now, in 1953, the whole world, as if ravished by the saintliness of his regenerated life, commemorates the lonely death of Francisco Xavier on the remote Island of Chang-Shan at the gates of Cathay. The devout flock from every corner of the Christian world to place a candle before the shrine to his memory. Most dramatic of all, to me, is the niche where rests the ancient figure of Christ that used to perspire blood when St. Francis labored under some affliction during his wanderings, seeking to quench his insatiable missionary cravings. The figure has tremendous power to hold one's thoughts as it gazes out under hooded eyes, a curiously archaic figure of eternal suffering.

The Castle of Xavier is perched on a crag, a fortress against the sky, backed by the Leyre Mountains. The walls are forbidding, with no pretensions to beauty or balanced proportions, not the graceful distribution of soaring towers one expects in medieval castles in Spain. The Leyre range of mountains are lovely to watch in changing light and shadow, to gleam in sunlight or under the moon for, like the Dolomites and the Atlas Mountains, strata of rose, yellow, and violet quartz slash the crests. Inside the castle there is one undeniably

35

impressive room with a high groined ceiling. It is bleak, even on a warm sunny day, but stirring in scale, vast and echoing, with dark-patterned tapestries covering the walls. There are three pointed Gothic windows in one wall. From the embrasures spreads a sweeping panorama of mountains and valleys away to the ancient Monastery of Leyre, a tomb-monastery where sleep the Kings of Navarre. It was in this monastery that Francisco Xavier first, in derision, touched the cross.

On the stone seat of one window in this great chamber of Castle Xavier is crushed a tooled-leather cushion, so old and battered the leather is split and worn thin. It is told that the Lady of Xavier, the impossibly pious mother of Francisco, sat here for months at a time refusing any but barest necessities of food, or clothing for warmth against the bitter winds from the mountains. A rosary was always clasped in her hands and a rough crucifix, fashioned for her by a saintly monk from Leyre. In this manner the half-demented woman prayed constantly in an effort to expiate the notoriously carnal sins of her son. When in a hysterical burst of abasement and repugnance against his manner of life he renounced the world and its temptations, his mother is said to have donned the habit of an abbess and founded an order for silent contemplation which is still in existence. She also erected the chapel which occupies one corner of this room.

Accommodations for the night being nil in Xavier, and I doubted if much better in Sangüesa, I decided to drive through the starry night, beautifully cool and aromatic with the odor of pine and wild thyme, to Solsona. I had recently heard about this town at the end of a fertile valley, sheltered by high mountains. Almost no one ever goes there, it is so remote from frequented highways. I arrived past midnight and found the town, for all its remoteness, very wide awake, in the classic Spanish manner. I found a pleasant room at the one inn, the Anna Ribera, that was not a drovers' tavern. In the Spanish tradition of honoring the mother of a celebrated person rather than the celebrity, the Anna Ribera had been named for the mother of Pedro de Ribera, he who designed Puente de Toledo in Madrid, a frantic conglomeration of Churriguerresque architecture much admired by all Spaniards if not by more captious travelers.

Next morning I walked abroad in Solsona to find that life here is starkly Catalan, to the point of being archaic. The Solsonese pride themselves on maintaining the rigid code of conduct for men and women laid down by tradition and culture, to the last dot. The young women, when walking to and from mass, are often escorted by *two* duennas. One walks on either side. The costume for women, young or old, is distinctive, but all-enveloping as that of a Moslem woman in the streets of Fez.

There is a great deal in Solsona to impress a visitor. A great, crouching castle with a long corridor where stone warrior caryatids, immense in scale, carved in full medieval armor, support the painted ceiling. This building of empty, resounding corridors and tiny cell-like rooms, now houses students attending a school of forestry. The church of Maria del Pilar reminds me somewhat of lovely La Lonja in Palma de Majorca. Maria del Pilar lacks the incomparable setting of La Lonja which is reflected in the sapphire blue water of the Balearic tides, but its façade is dramatically set off by a wide paving of black and yellow marble lozenges spread fan-wise in front. A group of young women in the enveloping yellow, pink, and pale green head-shawls, worn over full black dresses, stood in front of the bronze door of the church. It was the first touch of the Moorish influence (of which one sees so much further down the coast) that I had noticed in Catalonia.

I remained in Solsona for another day, for I wanted to drive out into the valley and visit some of the big fruit farms. The fruit market in the plaza in Solsona is a sight to remember. Under awnings of pale blue canvas, stretched as wide as a circus "big top," were piled what seemed like all the fruits of the earth. As always the melons caught my eye. I made a meal of a huge golden melon complemented by *jamón serrano* bought from an enterprising man, who had set up a booth to sell ham and salami right next to a melon stall. All the way along the valley I met wagons drawn by bullocks. The cumbersome vehicles with wheels higher than the men who walked beside them, supported piled crates of fruit on the way to market. Solsona, I learned, is the fruit center of the Catalonia and Navarre provinces.

When I finally left Solsona it was raining. Not the downpour I had driven through crossing the Pyrenees into Spain, but a steady drizzle, a veil of heavy mist making travel along these narrow roads a chancy business. For some reason it seemed to me every living human had taken to walking the roads, nonchalantly preferring to walk in the middle. I blasted the siren until my ears hummed. At a sharp turn loomed a crossroads. I gave up. I had lost my way. The only sign post (and in Spain these fingers of direction are usually dependable) read Vidreras, not Tossa de Mar. If there was one thing

I did *not* want to do, it was to fight misleading roads. Not on a day like this. And then, quite inadvertently, happened one of those things to warm the cockles of the heart. A good Samaritan appeared in a peculiarly Spanish fashion. Out of a lane a man and boy, each muffled in a heavy poncho, preceded a bullock cart. I hastily opened the near window of the car and hailed the man. Would he, I asked, be so kind as to direct me to the right road for Tossa.

He spat in the road, raked myself and the car with sharp black eyes. "What is that?" he asked, pointing to a pyramid of luggage under a tarpaulin on top of the car.

"Luggage," I answered.

He treated me to a most courtly bow from the hips. With the effortless gesture of a grandee removing furred and embroidered robes of state, he tossed his soggy poncho to the wide-eyed boy, shouted some directions to him, and started to come around to get in the car beside me. I saw the man was dressed in the leather leggings and short leather jacket over a dark blue cummerbund which proclaims the well-to-do Catalan farmer. As he settled back in the seat, he spoke.

"I will gladly escort you to Tossa, señor. I have a good reason to do so, beside courtesy." He smiled grimly, staring straight ahead.

A few directions were forthcoming and I was on the right road. The conversation was a monologue, for the man spoke a Catalan dialect, the words fired as rapidly as bullets from a machine gun. But he pointed out farms and told me the names of villages, dimly seen through the mist. I caught a descriptive word here and there. Always he kept me headed towards the sea, which I never could have found on my own. I learned his name was Miguel Aralar. I gathered, too, that there was a man in Tossa de Mar who owed him money. The man was a bandit, a traitor, a liar, and as slippery as an eel for eluding payment of his debt to Señor Aralar. But today this "procurer" was marrying off his daughter. "So," my companion lowered the window and spat monumentally, "yes, the swindler sells his daughter to a rich ancient. I welcome the opportunity of conducting señor to Tossa," he bowed elaborately, glancing at me over his shoulder, "so that I may collect my money, if not from the father of the bride, then from the groom." Again he spat out of the window. "I believe, señor, this old bridegroom, from a proud family, would not like the disgrace which I could bring upon his house. No, not on this of all days."

38

As I swung into Tossa the road followed the serpentine grace of the old Roman walls, in ruins now, but what remained still as lovely in line and texture as any relics of ancient Roman imperialism in Europe. I inquired of Señor Aralar where he would like to be set down.

"Anywhere, señor," he waved vaguely in the direction of the sea. "I will enquire presently where is held the wedding."

His eyes flashed, he doubled his lips under to form a straight, determined line, and drew a forefinger across his gullet, in the age-old gesture encountered everywhere in Latin countries, meaning "or else." Anxious as I was to roam around Tossa de Mar I would love to have been "in at the kill" when creditor met debtor.

Two days in Tossa opened to me a new vista, a fresh conception of how immediate are Greece and Rome as reflected in the lineaments of the people along this Catalonian shore. Tossa de Marians are extraordinarily handsome, in a way that is singularly classical, recalling to mind heads I have admired on antique Greek coins. In the same way I am reminded of the classic mold of feature in the faces of fishermen and the proud women of Portofino on the Italian Liguria. I find the Catalonian and Ligurian types very like. The natives of Tossa are naturally graceful and long limbed. Never have I seen people and their surroundings so complement one another. I do not wonder that for years there was a large colony of artists from all over Europe in Tossa. They lived in little vine-covered houses scattered among the hills that rise from the sea. As in Taormina in Sicily, there would have been no dearth of models to pose for painters.

I was particularly interested in the excavations of Roman villas going forward now, after years of suspended operation, owing to world wars and the grave troubles in Spain. One villa was excavated in 1914. Here one can trace mosaic paths, and the floor of an atrium graceful in a design of triumphal wreaths. There is even a grotto hidden, out of sun and wind, paved with a mosaic of sea nymphs. These villas were complete with hot water supplied by earthen pipes under which fires were kept burning. Three bath chambers were found in one villa. Life must have been both gracious and comfortable all year round. All this was in the first century A.D.

In this villa a portrait was discovered in mosaic, the head of a fierce, strong-jawed Roman. A name is worked into the design. It identifies the builder as "Saliius Vital. Felix Turissa." In a copy of

Avienus' *Ora Maritima,* which I was loaned by Trinity College, Dublin, but which is too unwieldy to carry around, I learned many things about life on this coast. From earliest time it has been a magnet for adventurers, imperial conquerors and pirates, as well as scholars, poets, philosophers, and rich pleasure seekers wishing to live away from the intrigues of cities, in a salubrious climate. Marcus Cadeus, who lived for a time in a villa near Cambrils, wrote a letter on a tablet to send his son Claudius in Rome.

> My villa in Cambrils is more spacious than the one I do not long for in the Alban Hills where you will read this. My droves of black and white bulls delight me and my mules for pleasure driving are as huge and fleet as desert camels.

Perhaps this letter-tablet was never sent. More likely it was intercepted by spies in the pay of jealous factions which split asunder most of the Roman military expeditions. In any case this tablet, with much household gear, even a pair of bronze-mounted chariot wheels bearing the device of a winged griffon, the seal of Marcus Cadeus, were found in sand at Cambrils near Tarragona, where may be seen the ruins of a large Roman country villa and a small museum.

The natives of Tossa enjoy an almost pastoral life. Tourists come and go, but pleasures and crafts remain simple. I watched old women in the black, indigo, and white of Catalonian dress sitting in front of their small houses, bare of ornament, sparsely furnished, scrupulously clean. Owing to phosphorus in the whitewash, the outside walls glow like mother-of-pearl in the sun, and take sharp, purple shadows. All day long the women sit on hard, high-backed chairs fashioning trinkets from sea shells. Boxes, sticks for mounting fans, little altars in which to stand a figure of the Virgin, pocket books, and tassels to wear at the belt. Most engaging are the seahorses contrived from plaited cane leaves. I would rather buy these than most of the souvenirs I consistently dodge in my travels.

The plaza of Tossa is typical of port towns, for every day is wash day, if judged by the amount of bright garments whipping in the breeze. Every house on the plaza has a flower-filled window box in each window. The effect is of high carnival all the time. There are other inns, and one or two private villas whose owners take guests *en pension.*

Avienus wrote that blackberries "of ambrosial sweetness" grew on Roman farms and in the gardens of villas all along Costa Brava. Blackberry canes bend in the sea wind today, as they did in Avienus the Roman's day. On my last morning in Tossa I had a big bowl of the rich, dark berries with fresh oranges squeezed over to bring out the flavor. My host at the inn told me the berries came from his own garden near Lloret, worked by his six sons. "I have one more son but he is in Barcelona doing his military service." He shrugged, rolling his eyes heavenward. "I train them all to become gardeners to work at the big villas where the *big* pesetas are."

At S'Agaro, quite near, Hotel S'Agaro has been opened. It is luxurious, but not overly expensive, for the comfort and excellent food you get, and the location in a large garden is very fine. Casa Blanca is a charming inn, set high on a small plateau overlooking the many-towered citadel and the emerald-bronze water of the little fishing port of Codolar. Ventorro Marina, a good hotel-restaurant type of place, in the usually breezy plaza, is rapidly becoming well-known for good food.

I stopped only a short time in Lloret, a pleasant town with palm-shaded streets and a particularly lurid history of Greek depredations and Roman (they called it Loryma) sacking. This sacking, it appears, was systematically carried out because the Spanish inhabitants stoutly refused to pay outrageous taxes imposed by succeeding Roman governors. Later the Moors leveled the town for the same reason. Lloret has an ancient name for sullen resistance to foreign influence in any form. Today the town seems flourishing, the people quiet and dignified, as is the case with most of the Catalans. One senses everywhere along the way an innate reserve that nothing can jar.

Lloret has but lately become a point of vantage for motor-coach tours to stop for passengers to lunch and have a bathe. The food in the quayside *ventorros*, as picturesque as any along this coast, is notably good. A platter of cold fish salad, made doubly enticing by a side dish of big yellow tomatoes of the region sliced and dressed with oil and lemon juice, is a satisfying luncheon after a long, hot morning ride.

After Lloret the Costa Brava starts to draw in its antique horns with one last cluster of little villages lying sheltered, many completely hidden, by rocky escarpments, accessible only by narrow roads or steep foot-paths. Canet, Blanes, and Malgrat are lovely, romantic towns. So ancient are the houses, they totter on their foundations, but there is great activity in the port. There is an ornate red and yellow church at San Francisco, a scrap of village named in

41

memory of the saint. Ghost-ridden La Pola is a carnival of cacti with its one, desolate villa, hideous beyond nightmare, started as a *pavillon d'amour*, but never completed, by a profligate member of the Martorell family, whose habit of beginning outlandish ventures in architecture only to leave them uncompleted, is flamboyantly manifest in the unfinished Sagrada Familia church in Barcelona.

Piñas del Mar seems to sleep under the wand of enchantment, quiet, unhurried, almost drugged by the smell of hot sun on the pine trees. La Forcenera has a small shipyard for building the high prow boats for fishing fleets, the identical model used by the early Phoenician traders, long before the Christian era. Leta, on a high promontory, once had a large villa occupied each summer by a princess of the royal house of Habsburg. The villa was destroyed in 1936 by anarchists. Now remain only wild and lovely gardens cascading down the water stairs. I walked among these gardens and thought the hand of man had never touched them, only Demeter, in ebullient mood, had twined the garlands of roses and willed the dragon lilies to drift in waves of red and gold along the chipped balustrades.

It has been said the only way to see the villages of Costa Brava is to sail along the coast and view each one from the vantage point of water. I have before now done just that and agree it is a sight to cherish. But not many persons can do it that way. Only rarely does an excursion steamer skirt the coast between Barcelona and Puerto de la Selva, in the shadow of thrusting Cap Creus, where an important depot for military training is situated. Even these steamers, always crowded to the gunwales, ply too far out at sea for one to get a really good view of the villages. I prefer to drive along the coast road I have described, long and dusty as it is, for then one can leap out to investigate when the glimpse of a red sail, or the belfry of a Baroque church catches the eye. Then one feels the pulse of a village that has beckoned. *Only* then does one savor the real flavor of timeless Costa Brava.

Chapter 4

BARCELONA AND MONTSERRAT

A<small>T</small> Mataró it is wise to leave the coast for an inland road through Sabadell and Rubí, a road by which one enters Barcelona majestically from the mountains, as the Roman legions must have done. High above a nearly insurmountable ring of serrated silver rock rears sentinels Tibidabo and Montjuich, called "the twin towers." Barcelonese are vastly proud of their mountain "girdle" and point it out to the visitor at every turn, as if one could escape seeing it. The first sight of Barcelona when coming down the mountain road is characteristically Roman. For the Romans, at command of Emperor Trajan, rebuilt the sprawling seaport in the Spanish Marches when they started an exhaustive campaign to Romanize all Spain. Near the Tibidabo Gate three marble columns, Corinthian capped, said to have been part of the portico of the Temple of Hercules, rise in golden splendor, for the marble was once plated with gold leaf, traces of which remain to catch the sun's rays. Once past this reminder of the antique world, isolated in time, the city rapidly becomes active as an ant hill, in purely modern pursuits.

More than any other thing in Barcelona I am attracted by Las Ramblas, a thoroughfare of Arabian Nights delight, comparable to no place else that I have ever been. The broad walk, shaded by a double row of plane trees, stretches on and on through the Old Town. On every side is glitter, the people possessed by a kind of healthy confusion, an insatiable appetite for investigating shops and bazaars, with brief halts for a glass of *manzanilla* or hot, strong coffee. People sit all day and far into the night at small tables no larger than a tea tray, for many of the Rambla cafés are in full fig until dawn.

44

Every imaginable sort of business is transacted. The evening of my arrival I was seated at one of these tables enjoying a glass of *manzanilla*. My friends rightly accuse me of ordering successive glasses of this dry, chilled sherry simply to get the accompanying little plates of shrimp, olives, anchovies, bits of roast pork in tomato sauce, and *patatas fritas* or potato chips dusted with saffron. All this "free lunch," incidentally, is offered with an ulterior motive. The more salty appetizers one eats, the greater thirst for more *manzanilla*.

Having a long evening before me in which to enjoy the sights of Las Ramblas, I was suddenly conscious of a hysterical voice next me. Sitting at the usual infinitesimal iron table were four young men. A raffish crew if I ever saw one. The youngest of the group was dressed in somber black, almost blatant against the light colored summer suits of the other three. But this gesticulating individual sported a red silk necktie drawn through a gold ring set with a diamond. He was bareheaded, nervously running long, nicotine-stained fingers through a mass of black curls. In agitation he was positively shrieking at his goggle-eyed listeners. This brouhaha, I gathered, concerned some woman who had done the fellow wrong. Suddenly the youth leaped up from the table, slopping wine over the knees of his friends. He struck his brow with the flat of his hand with force fit to break his neck, and shouted, "If I do not kill her tonight, I will become weak, as always, and forgive her again. *No*—I must kill her tonight." He gulped what remained of his drink, and rushed away down the Rambla. I carefully noted the effect of his threat on the faces of the youths sitting silent, hunched over the wine-slopped table. Not one of them seemed unduly alarmed. One bought a newspaper from a cigarette-cadging urchin. He immediately turned to the page announcing a future corrida. Another picked his teeth. The third followed with speculative eyes the voluptuous behind of a woman walking with a man old enough to be her grandfather. I ruminated, remember this is Barcelona. Life here is full-bodied. *Everything* goes. No one gives a damn. Viva Barcelona!

Many visitors rail against the noise, the continual "upheaval of the stately life," as Chopin, who loved Andalusia but loathed Barcelona, wrote to George Sand, warning her not to set foot in it. But the more I see of it the better I like Barcelona; it is a tantalizing town. Often when walking through the teeming streets I will come, suddenly, upon a space of stillness, some tucked away court or plaza faced with shuttered old houses, as if I had happened on a country

45

retreat. Then I am reminded of an old Chinese proverb. "Noise is not in the market place, nor quiet in the hills, but in the ever changing hearts of men."

That intrepid traveler of the seventeenth century, Lady Mary Wortley Montague, wrote of her Spanish travels:

> Barcelonese are a volatile people, their activity around the clock has no compare. To noise they are impervious. Anyone of them, I vow, could sleep on the clapper of a tolling bell.

I will add to this statement that there is never a dull moment in Barcelona. No building in the city typifies this ebullience of spirt in so startling a manner as Templo Expiatorio de la Sagrada Familia.

The Legend connected with the building of the church of Familia Sagrada in Barcelona amounts almost to the farcical. At first the idea was talked of by a man, an arrivist contractor named Lardo, who elicited funds to build a "modern" church in the eighteen-nineties. But the citizens of Barcelona, while pretending interest were luke-warm in dipping into their pockets. Finally three architects were enlisted—Gaudi, Martorell, and Font. Martorell seemed to be the most go-ahead of the three. He went about telling the new rich that if "they" (whoever) would put in a substantial sum to get on with the building which Gaudi had designed, that person would be said to have literally *donated* the edifice. Different men were approached in secrecy, each one believing that he, and he alone, was the bounti-ful benefactor. So money began to pile up. Gaudi did his part: de-signed the church exterior. Martorell is said by some (opinions and guide books *differ here*) to have designed the astounding, bewilder-ing phantasmagoria of writhing architectural detail called "the crypt." In any case the church was worked on by fits and starts for fifty years. Indeed, it is far from completed to this day. In style it is the last blast of L'Art Nouveau in Europe and a definite forerunner to the Paris Exposition Buildings of 1900. The exposé of who had or had NOT contributed to building La Familia Sagrada caused cleav-age in family relations, until many persons were called in mockery "La Sagrada." Martorell who let it be known that *he* was the man who had put in the largest sum of money was most ridiculed. He had used in decoration his recent family coat-of-arms, a flower opening its petals, as a motif. This can be seen both inside and out on the orna-ment of the church. This man bore two sons, both of whom being pampered in youth became notorious libertines and profligates. There were many stories, perhaps apocryphal though many are sworn to be true, told of their peccadillos. While not actual twins, they were of so near an age, they went down in Barcelonese history as *"Las Sagradas."*

The edifice has been variously described. The late Sir Edwin Lutyens called it "Ridiculous—out of all reason—mumbo-jumbo." Sacheverell Sitwell, in his wholly admirable *Spain* says:

> The church of la Sagrada Familia is not less peculiar than the most extreme works of Dali and Picasso, more particularly when it is realized that it was begun as long ago as 1881, the year in which the latter painter was born.

In any language it is a fantastical erection in stone and might just as well be the cloud palace of Little Nemo, the bewitching child of an American cartoonist's dream, instead of a weird gesture in architecture, so controversial that it provokes the most bitterly contested disputes, and even wilder adjectives, from all who see it. I must in this statement except the Barcelonese, who think it the "supreme masterpiece of modern building," the exact words used to me by a Spanish admirer of Gaudi.

An annotation on the margin of a description of this church is an incident in which I took part in this manner. I was visiting the gardens of a country house near Aranjuez. The châtelaine of Los Fontanas was showing me a garden where hundreds of varieties of trees had been planted to form a maze, an ever widening circle with a grass path between. Somehow the conversation turned to the Sagrada Familia church, and the notorious Martorell twins.

I asked, "Just what were they celebrated for, except the odd combination of extravagance, piety, and philanthropy?"

She stopped in her tracks, put a forefinger to her lips, seemed a shade puzzled, then said, "Oh yes. The Martorell raised magnolia trees." She pointed her fan to a magnificently shaped, wide-spreading tree, the blossoms massed in full bloom. "There. That tree was given me as a child, for a San Jeronimo Fiesta present by Manolo Martorell, a grandson of the church builder."

I must have shown the surprise I felt at this remark, for the tree she had pointed out must be at least one hundred years old, if the size of the ones in the cloister of the cathedral in Barcelona, two centuries old, are a criterion.

Seeing my surprise, she blushed. "How ridiculous I must seem. I

47

do get muddled sometimes trying to remember about all these trees. It was *this* one Manolo gave me. Here." She indicated a considerably smaller specimen in early bud. We laughed, but I pursued the subject. "Do you mean the Martorell family conducted a nursery garden?"

"Oh no," she answered. "They grew them for pleasure on their estate, just to give away as presents. Look on the four spires of the church sometime. If, in all the welter of ornament you can find the rosettes, you will see they are carved magnolias. It is the Martorell device."

One morning I "made promenade," as they say in Barcelona, along the Ramblas which extends from Plaza de Cataluña to Puerta de la Paz and on to the Old Port. In various sectors of the city Las Ramblas bear different names—Canaletas, Estudios, San José Capuchinos, and Santa Mónica. Sauntering along my eye was attracted to the beautiful doorway of Virreina Palace. The building is a Spanish simplification, in this case not *elaboration*, of Louis Quinze Rococo. The frame of the high doorway, surmounted by a window, is exquisitely carved in trophies of ribbon-bound musical instruments. Figures of woodland nymphs cast garlands of ferns and flowers across the window pediment. The tracery of the iron balcony above the door repeats this fern design. This pastoral motif imparts an air of a house in a park, or at the end of a country lane, rather than a town palace in the very heart of Barcelona. However arresting is the façade of this house, the haunting story of The Lady of the Violets (Manuela Lariosy Ribériz) captures my imagination even more.

The lady lived during the height of Francisco Goya's fame. He painted her full length in silvery gauze carrying a tray of violets, and in miniature on ivory—a rare medium for Goya—to please her husband. What is most extraordinary about Doña Manuela is not the fact that she was considered the most ravishingly beautiful woman in Barcelona, but that she was deaf, dumb, and blind. Her one passion was violets, especially the dark purple, heavily-perfumed Parma violet. Her legion admirers filled her salon with tribute to her beauty in the one way she could enjoy. She could feel the cool texture of the petals, she could smell the perfume, and when the petals were crystallized in sugar she could taste them. The fresh violets were probably bought at what may easily be the most extravagantly stocked flower market in the world today. The market occupies an entire city block on the Ramblas not far from Virreina Palace. It is said that when

The Lady of the Violets died in her fiftieth year her funeral surpassed any seen in Barcelona before or since. Six white horses to draw the hearse were caparisoned in violet velvet covered with trellis of silver cords and tassels. Panache of violet plumes nodded from silver bridles. The funeral cortège was formed of a *guard d'honneur* of young men wearing violet velvet capes, some carrying silver staves topped by bouquets of violets. Others held aloft in the misty atmosphere lighted silver candelabra which, unfortunately, guttered in the wind. Barcelona has never forgotten The Lady of the Violets nor her funeral.

The Liceo Theatre on the Rambla de Capuchinos has a flamboyantly Rococo façade and the interior is what all theatres should be, vividly theatrical and sumptuous. Red and gold promenades, with doors to the boxes discreetly curtained against intrusion at the wrong moment. The boxes are elaborately festooned in red brocade. To my mind, the abode of drama should be primarily dramatic in itself.

Perhaps my favorite quarter in Barcelona is Barrio Gotico surrounded by the original Roman wall of the city with Plaza de San Jaime as the center. Here, out of the moil and broil of the daily round is a collection of buildings largely medieval in style. The focal point of all is the cathedral, sometimes called Cathedral of the Golden Fleece, for the stalls are dedicated to knights of that coveted order. The somber palace of the Kings of Aragon stands apart in a kind of arrogant isolation, characteristic of the Aragonese, who, according to the fifteenth-century poet, Juan de Mena, were born "silent of tongue, thunderous in the dance, but the soul stifled in wrappings of gold samite and black velvet." The façade of this once royal house is plain faced with only an elaborately-carved doorway to lend distinction to the whole.

Plaza del Rey is composed of tall houses mostly painted gray or pale yellow, but here as everywhere in Spain the housewives cannot resist window boxes of bright pink or red geraniums. A famous, beautiful building, beloved of traveling architects, is Casa de Convalecencia. I cannot remember when Baroque style has been better served than here. The walls are pale rose color, pierced by long lines of perfectly proportioned windows, which form a kind of frieze. Nothing more simple can be imagined than this double line of windows with no ornamentation other than pedimented tops. Yet this is a building that impinges on the imagination by its very simplicity. I have heard countless people in Barcelona remark that La Casa, as it is popularly referred to, is their favorite. When asked if I do not agree, I reply, "La Casa is architecture at it best, fluid and emotional. I can give no higher praise than that."

Of museums there is great array. And of curiosly intriguing sort. Museo Marítimo in Puerta de la Paz is epic for everything to do with nautical tradition. Particularly, Catalan maritime life down the centuries is here wonderfully well displayed. The most spellbinding collection of ship models probably in existence sends boys of all ages into spasms of delight. In fact, boys and their fathers can hardly be pried loose from this museum. I heard an American boy, perhaps fifteen years old, say to his mother, who was urging him to leave because they must catch a plane for Majorca, "But I could live here *always*. Why don't you and father just go to Palma and pick me up on the way back?"

Barcelona boasts of the finest, most comprehensive collection of primitive paintings in the world. The oldest Catalan paintings are morbid, amazingly modern in many respects. Attenuated bodies, long, sallow faces. The pictures display a kind of fanatical indecision of just what it is all about. It has become almost a pilgrimage while in Barcelona to visit Museo de Bellas Artes de Cataluña, housed in Palacio Nacional de Montjuich. One sees work by artists little known outside of Spain. Jaime Serra, Ribalta, the Basque painters Botte and Coll, as well as Murillo, Tintoretto, El Greco, Zurbarán, Valezquez, and Ribera. Ribera is represented by ten meticulous drawings in sanguine of the exciting fifteenth-century Cathedral of Zamora, more like a caïd's pleasure pavilion than a stern Spanish religious house. Large paintings by the ill-starred Herrera, who ran afoul of the Inquisition and died from the effects of torture and imprisonment, have a malignant fascination curious to define. The masterly draughtsmanship is dark, and smouldering is the color. However, I was told by a custodian, these Herreras are a star attraction at the museum.

On all sides while traveling in Spain I had been hearing someone somewhere call out to another, such questions as, "Have you been up to Montserrat?" If the answer was "No," the scathing retort came, "Don't be a fool, man. You'll never see anything like it as long as you live."

Although I have been "up the mountain to smell the fog" as the Barcelonese say, for the monastery is invariably smothered in the clouds, I decided to refresh my memory at the feet of the black Virgin and Child of Montserrat. It was a dark morning when I left Barcelona, but sun burst forth as I climbed the steep road to Monistrol. The monastery itself has no beauty, was probably never impressive, and after falling into decay in the nineteenth centry it has been wretchedly restored in the past few years.

The Basilica gains stature from the galaxy of figures carved as if in procession above the Gothic doorway. The Twelve Apostles march magnificently accoutered, some in a kind of fancy dress, some in full armor; all are mitered and bearing croziers in almost papal splendor. The interior of the Basilica is so dark and windy one feels repelled by damp shadows and choked by the heavy odor of ancient incense which saturates the place. In a side chapel stands Our Lady of Montserrat, alone and peaceful. She is said to have miraculous powers for aiding barren women in their desire for children, so Our Lady does not lack attention. Like other very old and greatly venerated images, the Virgin and her Child have black hands and faces. This is not the color of the wood, which is neither black nor primitively painted. Through the centuries the smoke from innumerable candles has stained and blackened not only the hands and faces of the Virgin and Child but the garments of satin and brocade. No one dares to touch so sacred an image which, year after year, gathers an over-all patina of smoke and grime. An obsessed young monk who acted as my guide said to me, when I suggested the devotees of the Virgin might welcome a cleaning of her garments, "No—Oh, no, the very color of the ages has taken on an adoration of its own." So I had no more to say on that score.

In what is called the Old Shrine at Montserrat can be seen the exceedingly decorative frescos of Juan Llimona, a Catalan painter who became a monk after he finished the richly colored panels. From the time of receiving the tonsure he became a famous painter of illuminated missals. His work is found in many Spanish museums. To my mind, a far greater cause for marvel than anything the monastery has to offer is the rock formations of San Jerónimo rising behind the Basilica. La Momia and her "daughter" La Momieta with El Massif de San Salvador overtopping the lot. At one side of San Salvador is arranged by nature, in demented mood, a set of six grotesque rocks called Las Santas Magdalenes. The whole group forms a conversation piece out of a hashish eater's dream, and could not possibly be more entertaining. The British sculptor of abstractions Henry Moore, with his featureless-faced women, could not even at his best, approach

51

these elephantine hulks which bear a slight resemblance to a Victorian lady entertaining the girls of the sewing guild at tea. Behind all this monolithic charade towers a cluster of pink cones like a monstrous pipe organ.

Someone once said to me, "Why does Barcelona have so many good hotels when nobody ever goes to bed? Why not just doze in the Ramblas and save money?"

The Ritz is the best hotel, located centrally, and the rooms are beautiful. Majestic and Principe and the Gran Via are all pleasant places to stay. If one wants quiet there is La Florida on Via Tibidabo a little way out of town, situated in the midst of a garden with lotus flowers floating in a lagoon. I like this hostelry, using the word in the grand, expansive Edwardian sense. There is a custom here which is unique nowadays, even in Spain. When a lady arrives, a majordomo in gold-laced livery presents her with a massive bouquet of roses, lilies, and perhaps violets. When the lady departs she receives a box of *marrons glacés* and a smaller bouquet than on her arrival, one more easily handled on her journey.

In Barcelona the choice of restaurants is large. Rigat, like La Florida, is reminiscent of the great days of Alfonso XIII (almost everyone in Spain privately sighs for the return of the monarchy, that life which was so like *la Belle Epoque* in Paris and Vienna). The food here is epic and the surroundings dashing. I recommend heartily Solá for all manner of fish dishes. Ladies like the swank of Parellada. Big lunch parties are in order all year round; the custom of presenting each lady with a fresh bouquet of flowers on leaving is a mark of the elegance of this house. Near the Old Port there are many famous small restaurants where the speciality is *paella*, with an accent on *langostinos*, lobsters and crabs served in various ways. Les Set Portes has individual atmosphere; everything is pure white, floor, walls, even the uniforms of the waiters. If a hurrying waiter chances to spill a bit of sauce on his jacket or wrap-around apron, he must go immediately and put on a fresh one. Two chefs attend to the cooking, which is done in full view, on the toes, very much in the tempo and with the gestures of a ballet.

A feature which attracts customers to Les Set Portes is the dancing of the *sardana*, performed nightly around ten o'clock in front of the *taberna* by young boys and girls, in a kind of frantic romp.

I am very taken with a small *taberna*, so close to the waterfront that fresh fish are kept in a floating "cage" and hauled out on order. It is

MOORISH FORT-LIGHTHOUSE
TORREMOLINOS · NEAR MÁLAGA.

called La Concha. Besides the marvelous food are two attractions, Pablo Catolica, a guitarist from the gitana (Triana) quarter of Seville, and Loto the patrón, who is a gigantic clown. He sings constantly during the evening, in a piercing falsetto voice, even when extolling his menu. He told me once that in his boyhood he had been the leading boy soprano in Barcelona, adding that he had sung in the choir of the Royal Chapel of Santa Agueda. What his bulk, even as a child, must have looked like in cassock and cotta in a choir stall must have been a sight. He assured me "I am now a magnificent cook." His *zarzuela*, composed of many varieties of shellfish cooked in a pungent sauce, is a Spanish version of bouillabaise. With this dish Loto, if he likes you, bears proudly to the table a steaming platter of saffron rice studded with anchovies and black olives. I have steered many a traveler to La Concha to eat this dish. One night I told Loto a story of how saffron came to be used, to impart a tinge of gold and an illusive flavor to food. Chef Miguel at Hotel Miramar in Málaga had told the story to me.

To begin with, many Spaniards claim that Olympian Venus was of their race, and that she rose from the sea near the Pillars of Hercules between Spain and Africa, and was raped from Spain by an infatuated Jove. Tiring of her, Jove gave this stupendous beauty as wife to Vulcan the Armorer, most ill-favored of the gods. When Venus wished to soothe her surly, uncouth spouse, eternally begrimed from his forge, she would prepare for him a soup of game birds and lace the broth with herbs and saffron. "Since then," Miguel said, "it has been believed, indeed proved, that saffron is not only the most delicate and subtle of flavors, an ingredient which smooths to satin texture any food with which it is seasoned, but a notable aphrodisiac as well."

The decorations at La Concha are as bizarre as the host. In the corners of the room stand wooden columns on which someone has pasted decalcomanias of a variety of subjects. From the columns rise tall vases of yellow pottery painted with huge roses in brilliant color. The vases are filled with sheaves of cattails, dried grasses, pheasant, and peacock feathers. Loto will tell you, with a prima-donna wave of the hand, "I gathered them all myself." On the yellow walls of La Concha hangs a motley collection of pictures in all conceivable mediums and as many subjects, presents from painters who have eaten Loto's grand food and passed by. I am represented in this galaxy by a sketch in oil. A fragment of Tarragona. The castle on its crag, blood-red against massed black clouds. All the sound and fury of ancient days, in color; the red stone work that is so the essence of Tarragona.

One evening I sailed for Majorca. Flying there is much quicker—under an hour from Barcelona to Palma—but I have a deep feeling that one should approach one of the loveliest harbors in the world by ship. It is an over-night trip, in complete comfort, and if the sunrise favors, the first sight of golden La Lonja and the pinnacled cathedral rising above a forest of masts and sails is a rather breathless one. My arrival at Palma was auspicious. A number of gleaming white yachts, both steam and under sail, dragged anchor in the roadstead. Like an imperious protector defying man or the elements, the Conqueror's Church, built by Jaime I of Aragon, rises above the maritime activity of the harbor. This young Aragonese warrior drove the Moors forever from his homeland and then turned in high exultation, split a rock with his sword, and decreed that a cathedral should rise on the spot whereon he stood watching the last Moorish felucca dash toward Africa and safety. No monument to victory was ever better placed, nor more spirited in design. Each buttress of the church ends in a finial, sharp and pointed as a warrior's lance against the sky. Seen from out in the bay the whole lace-like structure appears to rise from a forest of palm trees.

The nave is famous for its width and is said to be higher than the cathedral in Seville. I have wandered for hours in the Conqueror's Church. For me there is a special kind of magic in the high, slender columns of the nave, unlike any I have ever seen elsewhere. Massed together in a martial array, they are so delicate in form as to resemble straight sheaths of rose-gray velvet.

In 1420 Guillermo Sagrera built La Lonja as a gold exchange. A wholly beautiful building of soaring proportions in the grand scale. In the vast hall the roof is supported by spiral columns in Venetian style so much admired in Spain during the early Renaissance. The walls of the rooms once used as an exchange are covered in cut crimson velvet. Behind La Lonja bulks a ferocious old watchdog in smooth-dressed golden stone. A notable landmark, the Castle of Bellver. The massive circular towers are unusual in design, being rather squat with two-story crenellations. The courtyard is circular too—so large in circumference it was used as a jousting yard. If the cathedral dominates the harbor level of Palma with a lovely air of sanctity, old Bellver seems to roar a challenge of defiance from the heights. Over the sea-reflected town of Palma hovers, for me, an air of enchant-ment. I once had a vivid dream that the fairy Morgan le Fay had touched the sea with her wand and lo, Majorca had appeared to ride the waves. The enchantress was so astonished at her prowess to produce so delectable an island retreat that forthwith she took up residence. Whenever I am on Majorca I feel that I dreamed true, and bow to every lady I meet lest she be Morgan le Fay.

To most people, the Balearics mean Majorca, but Minorca and Ibiza are also well worth a visit, if only for a day, by sailboat from Majorca. Minorca is splashed with vivid color in house fronts and the sails of fishing boats. Mahon at the head of the landlocked Bay of Mahon is a village of great charm. It reminds me somehow of Cobh, near Cork on the south coast of Ireland. Certainly an Irish air rides the tall gray houses with terracotta chimney pots, and the great castellated house built by Irish General Mahon. Ibiza is small, actually a great promontory sprouting three jagged peaks. San Juan Bautista, one of its towns, slumbers in the shadow of a centuries-old convent of the Cistercian order, with an arcaded ambulatory surrounding a vegetable garden divided into square plots by borders of cinnamon pinks and pansies of every imaginable color. A sweet green cordial called Eubarca, with a lingering taste of verbena, is brewed here. It is widely used in Spain to crystallize fruits, which are a delicacy much favored by the Spanish. No dinner party is complete without a tray of whole crystallized apricots, lemon and orange slices, plums, cherries, and so on, being passed with a thimble-sized glass of Eubarca before coffee. In the big shops of Madrid, Barcelona, and Seville are always to be seen huge baskets and boxes, decorated usually with spirited scenes from the corrida, in which these whole crystallized fruits glow like jewels.

The small verdant island of Formentera appears to cling like the tail of a kite to Ibiza. For fifty years Formentera has had a small community of painters; even a few sculptors now have built small houses near Cap Paládo. Most of the residents, some of whom remain all year round, are British, as in Madeira and the Grand Canaries. A few Americans and Frenchmen are to be seen, either painting industriously or sun bathing on the beaches. These householders do not welcome chance sightseers. If you want to be received here you must rent or buy a house and settle down, to work or loiter in the sun.

One Englishman, the oldest inhabitant in the colony, told me, "We don't like strays here." No one could possibly call this man a stray. He came here sixty years ago for a fortnight holiday. Since that time he has been *once* to the mainland, to Barcelona to row with his bankers, who he thought were cheating him on his quarterly allowance from his family, a firm of distillers. I was allowed for a few moments in the drawing room of this man's house. Formentera or not, this room was "forever England." It was like the Charge of the Light Brigade in cluttered mementos of Victorian and Edwardian military victories.

Personally I like Minorca better than Ibiza. The houses are spacious and furnished in skillfully painted furniture, all handmade by the man of the house before he brings his bride to her new home. The "bespoke" woman visits the house while the work of decorating—and each Minorcan is his own decorator—is in progress. No doubt there are many differences of opinion. I was asked to lunch one day in a house at Fornells overlooking Ponto Bay. The room was painted white, with a heavily beamed ceiling of smoke-blackened beams. The floor was red tile. Tables, chairs, and a spaciously planned wardrobe, taking up most of one wall, were all painted pale yellow with a pattern of sea serpents in red, green, and black. I asked if there was any particular significance for the sea-monster motif. The man replied briefly, "I saw one once in Ponto Bay." His wife flicked her bright striped apron in annoyance. "He *thinks* he did." She cast her eyes over the furniture. "I'll never see the last of it."

The young men of Ibiza wear, on all days when they are not fishing or painting furniture, a most entertaining costume. A hand-woven white linen shirt with full sleeves and white linen knee breeches with red leather leggings. A wide red sash is wound tightly around the waist, to resemble, as much as nature allows, the slim waist of a favorite matador. A sleeveless jacket of dark colored leather sports wide revers. The entire jacket is embroidered in bright silk and tiny mirrors. A red wool Phrygian cap is worn rakishly. To say a young dandy of Ibiza "flashes" in the sun is strictly true. This is an eye-compelling get up, and full well the youths know it.

When walking through the streets of Palma one is conscious of the Catalan ancestry of Majorcans. Rapid-fire conversations catch the ear, short, sharp sentences, like those one has but lately been hearing up and down the Costa Brava. But in appearance natives of Majorca differ widely from their mainland forebears. Everywhere here are blondes with blue or gray eyes and many women have red or light brown hair. The Majorcan blonde has dusky skin, much like

Lord Byron's "dusky-blonde Venetians." The reason, according to historians, stems from days when the Moorish caliphs would pay exorbitant sums for beautiful, golden-haired Venetian women to regale them on the harem divan. Often Barbary pirates, plundering the mainland, made sudden forays far into the interior to abduct some fair-haired beauty to tempt a Moorish caliph. In Málaga and in Seville one sees supremely beautiful golden-fair women today, in the tradition of Eugénie de Montijo, Empress of France, who was born near Málaga. Moorish influence is felt in countless ways when one goes into the interior on Majorca. Formentor, Valldemosa, Sóller, Pollensa, Miramar were long occupied by the Moors. The highest mountain on the island, Puig Mayor, distorted into a lolling shape, like a drunken Bacchus molded in red rock, was once crowned by a Moorish casbah. Now little remains of the fortress save a long, undulating wall with a high, jagged-saw watch tower leaning as crazily as the mountain crest. This is a wonderful place to picnic by day, in the shadow of the tower. It can get mortally hot on this rock; I suggest it is better to picnic at evening. Watch the sun drown in the sea and turn the crag of rock, reminiscent of the Dolomites, to molten bronze. Watch the moon rise to turn it all back into silver. For a picnic supper, my advice is to have a man on the quay in Palma boil a few lobsters and crabs for you. Then take a basket of fresh vegetables and salad lettuces, a flask of olive oil, a few lemons, a loaf or two of dark-crusted fresh bread, and an assortment of fruit. Add to this a flagon of wine, Marqués de Riscal, if you can get it, or any good *tinto* (red wine), of which the shops stock an assortment, and then proceed, with whatever friends are available, up the slopes of "Old Puig." Eat all you can hold. Drink deep. Sleep a while between sunset and moonrise. Then just sit and realize how wonderful life can be. You will tell your grandchildren about this picnic on Majorca, covertly wishing you could repeat it.

I like to ride horseback along the roads leading from Palma to Valldemosa or Pollensa and Sóller. Long furrows of tilled fields stretch on every side. Artichokes, celery, asparagus, onions, eggplant and, of course, peppers and garlic destined for markets on the mainland are the mainstay of the big farms. At many of these farms one may buy lunch, served on a table under the trees. One day I rode out towards Sóller. I stopped at a farm called Los Moros. Over the stone gateway was carved the decapitated heads, without turbans, of three Moorish miscreants, eyes popping, lips stretched in agony, so lifelike the stone mouths seemed to shriek in defiance. I pulled in my horse and paused to read what was written underneath. But it was in Arabic. Just then the owner of the farm appeared. We gave greeting *"Por Dios."* He told me that when Jaime I of Aragon drove the Moors from the island, three wretched, starved slaves hid in a cave on this farm. The owner had routed the slaves out, fed them a Gargantuan meal, and then, his ancient hatred for all Arabs returning to mind, he cut off their heads, after depriving each of his turban, thus ruining the Moors' chances of being received by Allah into Paradise. The three severed heads were hung, like so many apples, above the old stone gateway to rot. No one knows when the three stone heads had been carved.

"So," I asked, "this farm has been in your family since the eleventh century?"

The man smiled and stroked the neck of my horse. "Yes, señor, and long before that. We are the Torre Hermosa family. We lived here before the Moors ever set foot on Majorca."

A boy was called to water and stable my horse, then I was treated to a lunch of cold sliced veal, and a big platter of wild asparagus served with lemon and "the best olive oil in Spain," my host advised me. Pink and yellow peaches, ripe with juice and redolent with the irresistible perfume of the fruit completed a refreshing meal. Usually too active to sleep at midday, this was one time when I welcomed siesta in a cool, shadowy room, where I dozed on a painted bed as big as the Ark.

As it turned out this was to be a day of country favors, for Torre Hermosa had told me to be sure and see the farm of his brother Donédo a few miles along the road. "It is all windmills and strangled olive trees," he said. "The Moors tried to destroy the olive groves before they fled. But," he shrugged, "it takes more than the slash of a scimiter to destroy the hardiest tree on earth. Though the trees were hacked and bleeding the fruit was harvested and the seed renewed."

I rode perhaps two miles through olive groves bordering either side of the road. The olive trees in Majorca are said to be the oldest in Europe still to bear fruit. The tangled, paper-thin trunks are as warped and split-in-twain as a skein of silver threads, and, it would seem, as tenuous. Olive trees in North Africa, Italy, and Spain have always fascinated me beyond understanding. How these grotesque shapes, seeming to have no roots, to skip crazily over the ground, can yield a crop of olives century after century is beyond reason, but they do. Some of the groves still producing around Sóller are known to be two thousand years old.

At the farm of Donédo the windmills are typical of the hundreds that loom against the sky, rising from the flat plain around Sóller to Puig Mayor. All are tall, whitewashed stone towers, much like a light-house in construction. On one side close to the conical top are fitted immense wings made of cedar poles. These are covered by a netting woven from thongs of bull hide. Over these wings are stretched tarpaulins of heavy linen. I watched these tarpaulins being woven in the dooryards of the white stone cottages. The linen is dyed in big exposed vats, yellow, plum-brown, or bright blue. On a day when strong wind sweeps across the plain, and there is much grinding of wheat, maize and rice, all this revolving color presents a brave show. Sóller houses have thatch roofs and always there is a stork balanced on one leg in his ridge-pole nest. Bad luck is supposed to attend the house where no stork nests.

For an hour or so I sketched the windmills. I was ready to mount my horse, which had been cropping so much grass that I was afraid I might have to dose him against colic when I got back to Pollensa, when Señor Donédo arrived on the scene, accompanied by one of his sons. The young man carried a flagon of wine and three gourd cups. This cool wine proved to be a refresher at the right moment. A light, white wine of the region called Father Junipero Serra. A bland wine, gentle as its namesake, a young monk from Majorca who first distilled wine, blending it to his taste, from his father's vineyards near Valldemosa. After a time the monk went to California where he founded missions. Always he made a point of imparting to the lay brothers the secret of how to make his favorite wine. It could be that some of the white wines distilled in California today derive from this recipe.

It was nearly dark when I rode back through the olive groves towards Pollensa where I planned to stop the night. A rasping wind had sprung up which twisted and tortured the slender olive trees. As twilight darkened, even my horse became skittish. A kind of Witches' Sabbath seemed to be taking place in the groves. With branches waving, the trees reminded me of the legend of those storied whirling dervishes of Sidi Boursa, appearing on the African roads, improbably ancient and attenuated to affright travelers bound for Mecca. As the pilgrim laid about with his staff, the dervishes would

60

disappear in dust, only to appear again in front or in back to harass the man. At least one old tree, whirling dervish, or wraith, crashed down in the gale, frightening my horse so that we galloped into Pollensa at the double.

The day before I was to leave the Balearics, I was invited to a celebration at one of the big farms famous for a famous breed of beef steer. Torre del Drach (The Tower of the Dragon) it is called. All farms on the island are named Torre something or other. Torre de los Cinco Zaguanes (Tower of the Five Patios) is another farm famous for beef cattle. I had been asked to come in mid-morning, if I wished to sketch and take photographs, for the banquet to terminate a local religious fiesta would get under way soon after evening mass. Each farm is a small village, completely selfcontained. This is a holdover from the days when all farms were fortified behind walls, as were fortress castles. At Torre del Drach there is everything from blacksmith shop to an infirmary providing efficient first aid. I heard of one proprietor who employs three hundred men on his estancía and who has a registered nurse always in attendance in case of emergency. Before the festivities began I was taken through the main house. Here were gilded leather screens from Córdoba, and sets of the coveted Majorca red and gold painted chairs, upholstered in red, yellow, or almond-green velvet. The many branched repoussé silver chandeliers, which are a speciality of island craftsmen, blazed with wax candles. The floors were strewn with rugs woven by hand from loosely-carded sheep wool, dyed brilliant colors, the pattern invariably of ships and flowers ingeniously distributed. These rugs, many of them very large, are another product of the island.

The feast to Santa Maria de la Paz was laid on long trestle tables under an arbor of grapes. A whole steer was roasting, not in an outside pit, but in a cavernous fireplace in a separate bakehouse where ordinarily hundreds of loaves of bread are baked daily to supply all the farm workers. During the roasting I was taken to pay a visit to the bakehouse. What a grand, mouth-watering sight it was! A man wearing a leather apron swathed about his hips prodded the beef with a long pike like those used by a picador. The huge carcass revolved slowly on an iron spit with a crank at either end. Two boys turned the cranks to keep the spit constantly in motion. The embers in the pit glowed and sputtered as the rich juices from the beef ran over the lip of big brass bowls set on low iron tripods to catch the juice. When the bowls were brought to table later I found that an

61

added flavor was juniper berries tossed into the bowls along with salt, pepper, and garlic. As I turned to leave the bakehouse one of the two boys poured red wine over the roasting carcass. The rich steam that rose hoisted my already full-bodied appetite a few more notches. I hurried back to my place at table. When great slabs of beef, platters of vegetables, salads, and fruit were placed on the board, I was convinced that Pomona, Goddess of Plenty, keeps an affectionate eye on Majorca and its great farms which so bountifully produce her fruits of the earth.

On the way back to Palma I stopped for a little while at Miramar, a beautiful country estate with gracefully arcaded patios in the true Majorcan tradition. During the feast at Torre del Drach, I had been told an amusing story which had to do with an erstwhile owner of Miramar. An Austrian Archduke, Ludwig Salvador, had once fascinated the countryside by his luxuriant red handlebar mustachios. Such hirsute splendor drove every young male to try and raise something comparable on his upper lip. But the result was largely failure. Whatever did appear in the way of mustachios was not red. One resourceful young man ordered a hairdresser in Palma to make him a false one, even more impressive in color and flow of line than Ludwig Salvador's. The result set a fashion which became so widespread among the young dandies of Palma, so vulgar, and incidentally, made the hairdresser so rich, that the infuriated archduke shaved off his mustachios in a fit of pique.

In Palma I stayed at Hotel Mediterraneo, where lobster, either hot or cold, is supreme; indeed this is so of all shell fish one gets anywhere on the island. In Cape Formentor, I stayed over night at Formentor Hotel, so beautifully situated under a red rock promontory. The bathing beach and sailing facilities at Formentor are the best. In Palma, both the Victoria and Alcina hotels are well considered. If anyone craves thick steaks, or beef in any form in summer, they will find it excellent in quality and cooked in any desired way at the hotels and restaurants bordering the Rambla in Palma. At the moment Majorca, which has always had staunch admirers, is enjoying great popularity, full well deserved.

Chapter 5

THE GOLDEN MOUNTAIN
OF TARRAGONA

THE finger of good fortune touched me on the shoulder, surely, the morning I was booked to fly by a commercial plane from Palma to Barcelona. From there I planned to continue on my way down the coast to Tarragona. During the fiesta at Torre del Drach I had met an agreeable young yachtsman from Portugal, one of the Quina family who win most of the yacht races in Mediterranean waters. Now, he and two cousins of the same name asked me to join them in a fast sloop for Villanueva y Geltrú where he was to enter his yacht in a regatta. We put out in a slight mist, necessitating reefed sails, then lay on deck discussing Villanueva where we hoped to land next morning. We spoke of how crowded it was for regatta, of the famous wine of the region which does not suit all tastes, having a distinct flavor of resin, and the beauty of the Villanueva women. "But," the youngest Quina cousin remarked, "they are no fun—cold as icicles."

A Quina in the galley acted as chef and produced for supper chunks of lobster fried in egg batter, a Portugese speciality of an excellence which reminded me of the way the Chinese prepare shrimp. Considering the sloop was named Lotus, I thought this Chinese-out-of-Portugal delicacy eminently fitting. So—it was solemnly entered in the log as Langosta Lotus. Soon I turned in. The sleeping accommodations on board the Lotus were narrow but comfortable. I lay thinking how happy I was to be able for once to arrive at Tarragona, one of my favorite towns on earth, unhurried. Always before it had been by train or the weather was against me. Now I could leave Villanueva fairly early, lunch perhaps at Calafell or

64

Portos, driving slowly on to reach Tarragona about sunset. I wanted to drive at walking pace and view to my heart's content "the golden wonder of Tarraco," as the Roman Martius wrote home in a series of paeans of praise.

I had wired from Palma to have my car meet me. I set out in a cool, bright morning and was so eager to reach Tarragona that I did not stop at Calafell for more than a glass of beer in the pleasant but undistinguished little plaza.

From afar off I saw the Arch of Bara. It was like seeing a much loved friend after too long a separation. I hurried forward with, theoretically, my hand stretched out in greeting. But the hand, as so often it does, held a paint brush. The day had come on very hot since I left Villanueva and passed Torredembarra with its al-fresco fish markets high smelling as all such markets are the world over. My nostrils tingling, I was grateful for fresh salty air and the swathe of fairly cool shade cast by the arch. Once settled, I just sat for awhile in silent wonder that this Roman arch is always so much more tremendous in stature than one has remembered. I have said elsewhere it is my favorite monument by a Roman architect left in Spain. I was once asked, after holding forth on the beauty of the Arch of Bara, just why it moved me to such a pitch. I replied, "Because in the night watches its image thunders across my imagination like a comet. Next day I can write or paint like a streak."

Spanning the Via Maximus, sometimes called Augustus, the arch is much simpler in design than most of its kind. No single ornament intrudes to confuse the rise of four Corinthian columns on either side of the arch. As arms reaching upward, these support the massive carved cornice. This soaring mass of champagne-colored stone, athwart a road crossing the lonely plain of Consturti, gains in importance by its placing. It dominates the plain, solitary under the blue immensity of the sky, translucent as sunlight filtered through water. Sitting under the great arch I felt as if I were in a cool cave, with heat shimmering all around me.

I drove across the Campo de Tarragona towards "the golden mountain." Perhaps no storied city anywhere is so gloriously presented, so grandly situated to view, as Tarragona. It has the stature of an acropolis and blends every conceivable shade of gold. In the shadows the rose patina of polished bronze lingers long after the gilding sun has set. If Toledo, as one approaches from the arid plain, seems the illusive cólor of myrrh, then in Tarragona we have a golden casket to hold this perfumed resin from out the East.

The origin of Tarragona is lost in the mist of prehistoric times; the most compelling relic is its Walls. The oldest part is built in gigantic scale. The masonry has been called "Cyclopean" because of its similarity to the remains of walls and foundations of palaces found in Mycenae and Tyre and the Carthaginian catacombs under the palace of Dido. Because the oldest part of the Roman construction is built of smaller stones (about one kilometer is preserved in good condition) the part so often termed "Cyclopean masonry" is thought to have been built by early Iberians. This method of construction can date as early as the twentieth to the fourteenth centuries B.C. Two tall round towers, Paborde, or Archbishop, and Tower Magin, rise on the walls. These may have been used as lighthouses, for a rocky headland juts far out into the sea at Port Las, where ships once entered to serve this imperious city on the heights. For some unaccountable reason these towers infuriate the elements, and attract lightning. Both have been struck many times. Except for showing black streaks and gaping fissures in the masonry, the towers seem impervious to Olympian Jove and his thunderbolts.

I am always deeply moved by the first sight of Tarragona glowing on the rocks above the Catalonian Marches, close to the provinces of Aragon and Valencia. In early Iberian chronicles, which I saw in the library of the Nobles College at Salamanca, historians eulogized the city. Many speak of its being "Romanized" too systematically. I always feel Tarragona fiercely Iberian in atmosphere. For despite evidence of successive Phoenician, Greek, Roman, Goth, and Moorish sojourn, it retains a strongly individual air that is none of these. It is Iberians who walk the streets of Tarragona today.

The historian Fray Bartolomeo de Las Casas wrote, "She (Tarragona) endured periodical sack and pillage when walls were reduced and towers laid down." But, like the legendary Phoenix, the Tarragonese always revitalized their city from the rubble and ashes of destruction, using many of the "Romanizing" stones from the walls to build the existing houses. The cathedral is said to have been the foundation of a Roman governor's palace. The Presbytery housing the imposing tomb of Archbishop Juan de Aragon is built of stones from the ruins of a barracks erected by the Emperor Hadrian for his Roman Legions. Hadrian often came to Tarragona, then called Tarraco. Indulging in his favorite whim for theatricals he caused a

66

theater to be built high on the walls overlooking the sea. One wonders, was this before or after he built a theater at his ill-starred villa at Anacapri, from the balcony of which his much loved Antinoüs, it is sometimes said, leaped into the sea after he had been ridiculed for appearing on the stage as Apollo?

An Aragonese writer Pablo Comeña says that when he saw Tarragona after the expulsion of the Moors it was "a heap of golden dust, inclosed in ruined walls with little signs of life about." However true this may be, the place must have been a paradise for builders with all the stone blocks from the Clot del Medol, the Roman quarries, ready to hand. Today this immense, circular Clot del Medol is one of the sights of the coast. A natural park of flowers, trees, a lagoon, the rock walls radiant with hanging vines.

Not only did ancient Tarraco abound in well-cut stone for rebuilding walls and houses, but after each succeeding destroyer, a wealth of Greek and Roman capitals, cornices, fragments of statues, either complete or minus limbs, were salvaged. This antique beauty in marble or porphyry sculpture, as much admired by Romans as it was later by Venetian architects building palaces on the Grand Canal, may be seen today set into walls and arches or standing in gardens. Tarragona is richly ornamented. I saw handsome statues of Roman athletes carved from beige marble standing, half-hidden by ilex trees, beside the Paseo, a broad avenue which sweeps in a great curve under the still monumental walls. Today Tarragona is lived in by Catalans who appreciate its enthralling historical past, as well as the beauty of panorama, miles of mountains, seascape, and rocky headlands as far as the eye can range. The city is kept in wonderful condition, for all its exposed ruins. I was amazed at the lack of dust, for it was hot and dry when I was there. Seen through binoculars from my grotto, as I sat, under the Arch of Bara, the hill seemed to float and recede in gold dust, as if one would never quite reach it.

Latin civilization entered Spain through the gates of Tarragona. In a short time the hill town became so renowned for learning, for high-style social gatherings, theaters, and the largest sport arena in any Roman colony, that Julius Caesar sent one of his favorite courtiers, a patrician of the Julian house, accompanied by a retinue of three thousand companions and soldiery, with a baggage train of costly gifts for distribution among the populace. The envoy of Caesar bore a golden tablet wrapped in silk of Imperial purple. On the tablet was inscribed *Colonia Julia Victrix Triumphalis Tarraco,* thereby honoring the city with his name. The Roman historian Pomponius Mela built a villa near the sea and wrote lyrically of Tarraco as *urbs opulentissima*.

The ruins of Augustus' palace, called Pilate's Castle, show that the foundations covered an area making it the largest building in Spain, larger even than any known building in Rome. Enclosed within the walls of the palace was an amphitheater. Of this only a few steps and part of a wall remain. In the same case is the Theater of Augustus and the Circus. Both were built on a slope facing the sea. Under the Circus may be seen a few of the stalls for the hundreds of horses used by chariot racers and by the cavalry. Not long ago the bronze hubs of a chariot were found here as well as mountings for a harness. These hubs bore the device of a scorpion, the emblem of Emperor Trajan.

One of the monuments in a fine state of preservation is an aqueduct. It was thought to have been built by Augustus, to convey water to the magnificent baths, in the building of which every succeeding emperor during Roman domination had a hand.

The Catalan-Romanesque Cathedral is reached by one of the most gracious flight of steps known to architecture. They seem to have been conjured from golden stone and to be poised on air. Yet there they rise, through the centuries assisting uncountable pairs of feet to ascend to the lovely door of the church which rests on foundations formed by part of the Roman walls. When seen from the rear the great circumference of the cathedral reminds me of the immensely circular Castle of Bellver in Palma de Majorca.

The interior of the cathedral has the sublime austerity of a stone sarcophagus. The kind of deliberately unadorned alabaster or obsidian coffins affected by Roman emperors, who, sensing the rising resentment of the populace against their outrageous profligacy, attemped to delude them into believing they were men of simple tastes. There is a hollow grandeur in the nave that the flickering candles do nothing to dispel.

But like so many Gothic interiors with thirteenth and fourteenth century carving, a stone cutter was allowed to do as he pleased so long as he put on a good show with a sprinkling of wit to add zest to the design. A kind of Christmas pantomime atmosphere pervades the cloisters which were erected and embellished in the thirteenth century by the Tailors' Guild of Cloth Cutters. The mood is gala. Here are cats and dogs in a free-for-all fight. Birds are busily engaged

68

MOKO

CUIDAD REAL.
JR✕'52

in pulling worms from the earth. Ants as big as conies are building an ant metropolis. Gargoyles are feeding their hideous young from flaming spoons. A dunce stands on his head with a dunce cap on his feet. Rats, dressed as noble personages, are chasing a flagrantly obscene Adam and Eve from a garden where trees are composed of writhing snakes. This is a galaxy of make-believe in stone, disreputable as it is entertaining, and wholly unique in ecclesiastical decoration.

I was greatly drawn to Pallol Square, a cul-de-sac behind a screen of crenellated walls, probably of Catalan construction, built around a Roman arch. Seen through the arch, Pallol might well be the stage setting for the market place in *Kismet*. The houses are of tawny to rust-pink stucco, scarred and stained by mildew to a quality of green-veined marble, imparting an effect of richness of texture splendid to the eye as any *sgraffito*-etched palace in Florence.

Long flights of iron-railed steps wander up the fronts of the houses to the roofs and most of the windows are large, but screened in the Moorish style by jalousies of delicately carved cedar. Like so many of the small, shut-away plazas in Spanish cities, Pallol seems to have a life completely its own. Groups of women in both bright and dark-red skirts and black shawls, carrying yellow pottery jars on head or hip, gossip or scold children in the immemorial way of women at fountains. Some of the women wore a headdress I had not seen before. Tied over the hair, almost covering the eyebrows, a bright colored scarf was wound turban fashion to tie in a loose knot at the nape of the neck trailing long fringed ends nearly to the heels. On top of this, worn at a decided dip forward, were round black felt hats, the narrow brim bound in red, very similar to the headgear worn by women of the Canary Islands. I asked one of the women at the well if she, by any chance, was from *Las Islas Afortunadas*, the Fortunate Islands, as the Spanish call this gem of their possessions. She smiled. "No. I am not, but my mother and many of them," she included most of the other women, "are Tenerifese. We are all tapestry weavers." I remembered then that generations of women in Tenerife have been skilled with wool and shuttle, their designs drawn from nature and the sea.

In the Corridor of Tapestries in Casa de las Conchas in Salamanca hangs a tremendously powerful arras woven in the seventeenth century in Tenerife. Against a gray-green sky clear as crystal, rises the misty snowcap of Pico de Teide, the "magic mountain" of the Canaries. What gives this arras vitality, and style far out of the ordi-

70

nary, is an immense and ancient Dragon Tree. A few of these trees grow on the Canaries, with leaves like metal scales and the sap is red as blood.

That evening, I strolled in the gardens of the Tarragona cathedral cloisters. The belfry is more like a lighthouse on some rocky coast than the usual church tower forever with us in the Spanish landscape. Creamy white at the base, a wide band of pink circles the upper half. I stood with pencil poised over my sketch book. "Where?" Then I remembered. Barnegat Light transported from the New Jersey coast to a cloistered garden in Tarragona. I have a special fondness for lighthouses. I will go miles out of my way to see one. Next to the black and white striped Cedar Point Light in California, I like Barnegat best.

A young monk was standing in the doorway of the belfry earnestly regarding his wrist watch, against the moment he would have to man the ropes to ring the bells for evening mass. I admired the watch, a very handsome Swiss timepiece. He said, "My brother, who is a mechanic in Philadelphia, New York (his geography was slightly awry) sent it to me. I would not be allowed to wear it," he grinned like a schoolboy, "only that I must be prompt with the bells." I pointed to the belfry and told him I knew its nearly identical twin in America. When I mentioned that Cedar Point Light was in California he repeated the word "California" two or three times. "That is where all the Spanish Missions are," he nodded sagely. "If I am devout and do not let my mind wander in bad paths, I hope some day to be sent out to California."

Much later in the evening I was sitting at a café called Ferreras Aqueduct, in the small plaza facing La Purisima, the only Baroque church in Tarragona, hurrying to sketch in the writhing convolutions of its façade before the light failed entirely.

I noticed a small boy dithering on the curb in front of me, peering anxiously into the faces of the people occupying the ten or twelve tables on the pavement. Finally I heard a loud hiss. It seemed to come from a dark corner at the side of the café. I could not make out the shape, but a ray from the street lamp picked out the whiteness of a finger pointed at me. Then the boy darted from the curb, snatched off his cap and bowed low. "For you, señor," he said, handing me a piece of paper. Unfolding it I read, "Be sure and go to see Castle Tamarit. It is a lighthouse. You will like the villages of Prades and

Montblanch, where I come from. Go with God and the Blessed Virgin." The note was signed "Fray Jesús."

Over my glass of *manzanilla* I decided to reward the thoughtfulness of this pleasant young monk by changing my plans for tomorrow and doing just as he bade me. I wrote him a note of thanks in return, thereby starting a correspondence which I shall endeavour to keep alive, for I want to know if he ever arrives at the missions of California.

At six o'clock the next morning I started out, for if I covered all the points suggested by Fray Jesús I would have a long day. First I drove to Castle Tamarit, a few miles out of Tarragona on the coast. Commanding a lonely site, the high, rough-laid stone walls rise steeply from the ruins of a Roman retaining wall built for the dual purpose of defense and of repelling the sea. This wall must once have been impressive. Now it is riven by storms and in between the buttresses, itinerant fishermen have built huts thatched with reeds. The effect is of a gray mother hen sheltering a brood of chicks under her feathered wings. Save for the fluttering of washing hung on fish nets, the place has a long-deserted air. A lovely beach of white sand stretches on either side. What gives the castle individuality is the arcaded loggias high up under the lichened tile roofs. Because the buildings of Tamarit vary in height, the loggias are on different levels, connected by steps. This is a deviation from the usual style of Spanish castles. From the center of this mass rises a slender watch tower. This is the lighthouse. I learned from a man weeding a straggling vegetable garden, under a wall out of the wind, that the tower was much older than the castle. From the stones of a Phoenician drum-shaped lighthouse, in which bonfires had served as beacons, the tower had been built by the Romans. The castle was Spanish, of much later date, probably late Gothic, incorporating the tower within its walls.

I had a bathe off the rocks under the tower and a spot of "raw" lunch from the vegetable garden, augmented by bread and cheese and a bottle of surprisingly good wine, a *Riojo* from Ribarroya in the hills, supplied me by Vicente, the caretaker, along with information. Like his father and grandfather before him he had climbed the winding steps in the tower nightly to light the beacon. For eighteen centuries light from the Tower of Tamarit has warned mariners of treacherous hidden shoals.

Along a rocky road full of pot holes I drove to the Castle of Escornalbou not far away from Tamarit. I had been told of this place, once haunt of the Knights Templars, by a friend in Madrid who knows I am interested in ghostly happenings. Even the approach to this castle is ghostly. One drives through a darkling woods where I am sure, an ax has never felled a tree. There, against a pine-clad mountain lies, according to guide books, "the peerless castle of Escornalbou." I will not subscribe unconditionally to the "peerless," not while still stand Castle Olite in Navarre, Ponferrada near León, Real de Manzanares, or that erection in stone out of the realms of pure fable, Coca, in the environs of Segovia. But Escornalbou does have a brooding grandeur all its own. I walked around the high walls regarding the place from all angles.

"Safe and well furnished with castles," Alphonso the Wise said of Spain. In construction and front the Spanish castle is unlike any other, giving an impression of great austerity and unconquerable might. There are two distinct types of castles to be seen in Spain: one was designed for purely military purposes, of which Real de Manzanares and Bellver in Palma de Majorca are good examples; the other, built as a fortress to protect the residence of a noble family, is exemplified in Escornalbou. Placed on a rock one does not see, because the base is hidden in olive and hazelnut trees, the castle is built from stone quarried close by. This stone runs a remarkable range of color from all tones of purple and brown to red and ochre yellow. Four tremendous towers flank the outer wall or bailey. These circular towers sprout crenelations, which seen from below the walls, appear oddly at variance with the air of mighty strength of all the masonry. So lace-like as to remind one of the stone tracery of Gothic windows in the Monastery of Santa Creus in Tarragona, among the finest known to exist. When one walks out on the platform of the tower the sense of delicacy is instantly dispelled. The stone tracing is twelve feet high, a forest of stone and iron spikes from which cauldrons of hot oil and lead were poured on the heads of attackers. I walked around the platform of two of the towers, forever convinced that whoever built this barricade knew all the tricks of combining defensive power with beauty.

In the great hall of Escornalbou is a superb collection of medieval armor and all manner of battle harness and accoutrement. As the boy in the Marine Museum in Barcelona told his mother he could "live there" among the ship models, just so could I live, in a state of high excitement, in the Hall of Armor, in the rooms and corridors of the castle haunted by the ghosts of first, the braggart Alzára family—so violent they drank the blood of bulls—later, the recluse order of Knights Templar.

To reach Prades and Montblanch I had to drive inland a few kilometers through most agreeable farm land. Here were big, substantial looking red stone or whitewashed houses, set foursquare to the elements in the midst of grain fields. Men and women wearing enormous straw hats were working in the wheat. A huge, black-bearded man, rather startling, for one sees few beards in Spain, stood over the workers telling them a story in a voice so sonorous I am sure it carried to the distant mountains. The man seemed a Biblical figure with flowing beard, wide brimmed straw hat, and flowing cloak of white linen. This custom of a local bard narrating legends or village gossip to field workers has come down from the Moors. It keeps the workers entertained and speeds up the day's work as they gather and bind the wheat sheaves in rhythm.

As so often happens, I arrived in Prades in the middle of siesta. I was amazed to find a few shops open and people in the streets. The reason for this activity was soon apparent. The wool embroidery market, held one day a week, was in full swing. On this day farmers come into Prades to buy the tiara-like headpieces one sees across the brows of bullocks. The bands are usually of leather, sometimes of heavy felt. All are elaborately embroidered by the diligent small boy apprentices one sees sitting Arab-fashion in the shops. Half the young boys in Spain are apprenticed to some sort of craft, which keeps skillful craftsmanship alive in an age gone berserk on machine-made gadgetry. I can never resist buying these embroideries. Especially the big bunches of tassels to hang at either side of the bullock's head for festivals or gala events. These run the gamut of the spectrum and are embellished with tiny mirrors, sequins, and silk pompons. No self respecting bullock will appear in public without this adornment.

Prades itself is a medieval town with blank-walled houses save for the beautiful Gothic doorways of polished oak studded in iron, much the same in appearance as Montblanch where I later stopped for coffee. What most impressed me in Montblanch were the cobblestones used to pave the streets. As big, and about as comfortable to walk on, as a field of cannon balls. There was a most charming inn with tables set out under a large pomegranate tree, which was the first sign to tell me that I was not far from the Province of Valencia where I would see whole groves of pomegranates.

In time for eleven o'clock dinner I arrived back in Tarragona. I went to my room at Hotel Europa for a hot bath. Tarragona is not enriched with hotels, however rich in treasures from antiquity. I had tried one meal at the Europa but not again. There are many excellent *tabernas* with comfortable accommodations.

I chose Taberna de los Sastres (the tailors' inn) where, I knew from past pleasures, I could get fresh mushrooms cooked in red wine, served with chicken roasted on a spit. Jaime II of Aragon conferred royal patronage on the tailors of Tarragona for their performance with scissors, thread and needle after one of them, a man called Pablo Cordaz, had on short notice fashioned for him from finest wool a warm, hooded cape with inset sleeves. So pleased was the king that he ordered more of these cloaks, the *capa de honras*, which was to become in the middle ages the most popular garment in Spain.

Spiked by royal patent the Tailors' Guild waxed rich. To exalt their importance they built a chapel, Capilla de los Sastres, spending a vast sum, for that time, on a rarely beautiful stone reredos, as luminous as burnished silver. An unusual feature of this reredos is that some of the members of the guild wanted the stone carving gilded, others, with better taste, decried this. A compromise was reached. Half of the reredos on one aisle is lightly touched with gilt. The other half is virgin stone. There are some lovely, delicately carved panels in the chapel by Master Aloy, who worked in the fourteenth century as both tailor and sculptor.

Someone will probably ask, "What about the museums in Tarragona?" There is the archeological museum, where the greatest treasure is a statute of Bacchus as a slender youth playing with a panther. This is extraordinarily beautiful in the Praxitelean style. A rare exhibit is a Roman doll in ivory, with jointed arms and legs and a kittenish expression on the crudely painted face. In Museo Diocesano, a long, unfortunately dark room, houses a notable collection of medieval tapestries. I had to use a flashlight to see the detail and overall effect of most of them. One pair shows the figures of Judith and Holofernes and attendant soldiery, woven in close stitch like French petit point, while the mountain background of a tent-city is coarse, its stitches loose and shaggy like a Kashan carpet. This Biblical scene casts a strange spell, more Oriental in mood than medieval French, which the catalogue tells you it is. The color of this tapestry is sumptuous, its general scheme is green, black, and tawny, with Judith in a scarlet robe girdled in gold over darker crimson. On her pale gold hair is a helmet with waving panache of scarlet plumes. Holofernes receives her in full body armor of gold, a lion skin swathing his loins. Behind him a blackamoor carries his helmet of gold in the image of a lion's head crowned with black plumes. This panel was given to a Tarragonese noble family in the fifteenth century by Don Jesús Maria de Guzman, a member of the powerful Guzman family, second to the Albas in lineage in Spain.

As far as museums are concerned, if there was ever a city that in itself was one vast museum, lavishly displaying its treasures, surely it is Tarragona. Wander wherever you will, all the arts are represented in some measure from antiquity, through Roman, Moorish, and Renaissance to Baroque and Rococo.

Leaving Tarragona on the road for Castellon de la Plana the scene changes rapidly. I started at night, and as I passed through small villages I was to hear the last of Catalan songs, the Antillean *habanera* sung by fishermen and sailors all along the Costa Brava, with variations in each region. Actually *habanera* is the fisherman's song inherited from sailors who sailed the Spanish Main and brought the cadenzas back from Cuba. Along the Costa Brava proper, before one reaches Barcelona, the *habanera* is controlled in rhythm. The *cuento* which I heard outside Castellon is spacious, its notes are throbbing with seduction and deception and fiery love.

I had come down from the mountains, to drive along a road bordered by tilled fields, orchards, and groves of hazelnut trees, all turned to greenish silver under the moon. I did not want to sleep under a roof tonight, so I drove into a grassy lane, got out my sleeping bag for comfort on the ground, not for warmth, as the soft night air was delicious. I found I had a neighbor. A small donkey was in the field, hobbled against wandering. I offered him some wine from my bottle which he refused, and, after a one-sided conversation, I slept until dawn.

The drive through early morning mist in search of some likely looking place to get a bowl of coffee was abruptly brought to a halt when I approached a wood of cork trees. In Spain where there are cork-bearing trees one will find charcoal burners. Like Romany gypsies, or tinkers walking the roads of Ireland, Spanish charcoal burners are a race apart. They are people of the bush and the forest, haters of towns and none too fond of people in general. If it were not that selling *carbon* was their only means of existence they would probably not stir out of their green glades. But they know a Spanish housewife cannot prepare the daily *cocido,* which must simmer on a slow, hot fire for five or six hours, without her bundles of charcoal sticks.

This morning I saw ahead of me a member of this woodland gentry sitting on the rump of a donkey, leading three more of the dun-gray beasts. In pannier fashion, bundles of charcoal were tied with rags with a red flag on top to attract attention of customers. This wily fellow had maneuvered his pack train across the road, so I had no alternative but to stop. He was tall and cadaverous, and like all his breed his hands and face had acquired a patina of black grime from years of bending over smoking fires. He regarded me from little red eyes, put one hand under a kind of dingy *serape* and drew forth a string on which were threaded little figures of bears, wild boars, deer, and other creatures of the woods. He held it out and I took it. This, I thought, is like the necklace of some barbaric god of fertility such as I had seen at Knossos on the Island of Crete. Carved in hazel wood, during long vigils over charcoal fires, the silvery brown figures were enchanting. I bought all he had, and drove on towards a distant village just seen through the trees for my long delayed bowl of coffee.

Chapter 6

VALENCIA GUARDS THE HORN
OF PLENTY

FROM a rise of ground above Tortosa I saw the mightiest river in Spain. As if some giant had cut a wide breach between the Catalonian Marches and the Valencian Plain, then laid down his sword, blade up, the Ebro reflected the sky. What a glorious sight it is! Even Amposta seems to run up a hillside on its bank for fear of the churning waters where the river empties into the sea forming the Ebro Delta, violently fought over for twenty centuries. The houses pile one upon another, even the castle on a crest of rock seems puny in contrast to the Ebro. It is a navigable but treacherous river. Boatmen will tell you "Old Ebro is a Cid of a river. Long, wide, and terrible in anger." The reference to Le Cid, the hoary old conquistador, is often used in Spain to denote unpredictable temper and force.

History tells that Amposta, guarded by the castle built by Count Ramond Berenger III was impossible for an enemy to reduce though variously and in great numbers they tried. It would seem that Count Ramond lived in a fever of warfare equaled only by his tireless and extravagant way of building castles up and down the Catalonian coast to defend towns which did not belong to him but which he hoped to annex. When I was looking up the history of Spanish fortress castles in archives in Madrid, I came upon at least twenty which still rear battlements in more or less ruinous state from Ampurías to Sagunto, labeled "built (in whatever year) by Count Ramond Berenger III."

Tortosa is a town with panache, like a proud beauty dressed in her best, and if she has no place to go, then her interest is centered

78

in the huge Baroque cathedral. This façade is a riot of ornament, very much like the front of San Moisè in Venice, in the shadow of which gondoliers love to gather for their lunch and, while sharing bottles of wine, sing lachrymose ballads.

· I find the cathedral in Tortosa singularly handsome, for the perhaps excessive ornamentation is so cleverly integrated in flow of line that the effect is no more disturbing than a richly patterned lace altar cloth. The interior is fourteenth-century Gothic of pure Catalan style. The massive flying buttresses lining the outside walls are repeated inside the nave, allowing for a series of chapels of noble families. The only other example of this rare feature that I can recall is to be found in the Cathedral of Beauvais.

Approaching the village of Vinaroz I first inhaled the odor from orange groves that interlace the fields of Valencia. The intense blue tile domes of the churches, the typical royal blue *azulejos*, glazed and fired in ovens in practically every dooryard, rise above the orange groves, for one is as typical of this region as the other.

In the Baroque church of Vinaroz, which seems to fling its massively scrolled façade into the heavens, is a chapel so tiny as to escape notice unless you have been told to look for it. In a glass case no larger than a jewel box is a smaller crystal box mounted in filigree gold. In this reposes a glove of yellowed kid, stuffed with floss to give a lifelike appearance. The fingers hold a posy of flowers, colorless, nearly dust. A ruffle of tarnished silver lace encircles the flowers. This is the tomb, if you can call it such, of a young girl of prominent family in Vinaroz, who disappeared from the face of the earth on her wedding day. This happened sometime during the early part of the nineteenth century. The distracted mother kept vigil in the church for years praying for her daughter's return. At last, having no body to bury, an elaborate funeral was held. The glove and withered bridal bouquet were "interred" in the glass box.

Through a fragrant landscape the road winds towards Peñiscola. The wide farms, called *huertas*, with golden wheat fields become more numerous. Fertility stalks the land. Groves of pines are still with us and will be until Algeciras is passed. But there is a difference. No longer pine-clad mountains or hillsides, but broad savannas where blue-purple myrtle grows beneath the pines.

"Peñiscola is not true." This thought always leaps to my mind when I see it from afar. I feel very much the same about the improbable titan in stone, Penón de Ifach at Calpe, further along the

79

coast. But where the Penón de Ifach rises from the sea shaped like the prow of a Roman trireme, Peñiscola floats on the sea like the entire ship.

The pyramidal town lies midway in the curve of a white walled jetty. As I saw it from the road, I felt as I so often have in Spain that the curtain had just gone up on the transformation scene of an extravaganza. It is so quiet now, a kind of desuetude has settled on the place, but its history rings like a gong, with tales of plunder and siege. When Jaime Conquistador strove to oust the Moors who thought they were firmly entrenched, the wells of fresh water gave out and thousands of Moors died from drinking salt water. The small remainder, rather than capitulate to infidels, garrotted each other until only one man was left to leap into the sea. The Conquistador rebuilt the citadel which gleams like a mosque in alabaster, but is falling to ruin from neglect. The Knights of St. John next held Peñiscola and built a church and a castle. The heyday of this gem of the ocean was certainly pure theater, a kind of Restoration comedy with scandalous overtones.

In 1415 anti-pope Benedict XIII was mysteriously presented with Peñiscola, "by Avignon," it is said; but everyone connected with papal Avignon denied vigorously having anything to do with the gift. Papa Luna (many acid tongues said Benedict should be called Papa Loco, that he was crazy as Mad Juana ever was) decided to retire to Peñiscola. He arrived in a gilded barge with cardinal purple sails, attended by a court of cardinals—"the most corrupt sinners outside of Hell," read a papal Bull sent to Avignon at the time. This scarlet-clad crew lived a life of sumptuous idleness, indulging in intrigue among themselves while bleeding Papa Luna, slowly failing into second childhood, of his considerable worldly goods.

There is little to be seen inside Peñiscola. As you drive away, turn again and see the town rise like the tiers of an amphitheater, reflected by the bluest of Mediterranean water.

For a while I drove through a locality where the ovens for firing tiles dotted the landscape like huge beehives. It is a brave scene, for the white cones are splashed with green, yellow, and blue glaze. Even the highway was as gay as a circus parade. Winegrowers were bringing grapes down from the vineyards on the hillsides. Donkeys stumbled, heavily loaded with rope panniers of grapes, piled in saddle-bags called *alforjas*.

In Castellon de la Plana there is little of interest, save perhaps the

Baroque houses of the rich orange dealers or men who have for centuries had a corner on the tile trade. There is an older town of Castellon on top of a mountain, curiously double-humped, rising from orange groves outside the town. Here are the ruins of a once splendid Moorish castle of a caliph. This overlord maintained a harem numbering hundreds of wives and concubines. After the extermination of the Moors from the province, it was discovered that the caliph had personally decapitated his entire household. He buried the heads of his victims in a tile-lined tank where once the ladies of the harem bathed, and the bodies in the dungeons beneath the castle. To this day country people when picking grapes in the hills, give this crumbling old rookery a wide berth.

Sagunto is a town after my own heart. It is ancient and awesome; withdrawn from the world, it broods like some barbaric god, lonely and serene, or like a vast mural painting sharp in drawing against the sky. The old castle and surrounding walls far flung on the blunted hilltop are powerfully imagined. When Sagunto was one of the richest of the Roman military centers along the coast, the pride of imperial governors, many of whom had villas here, it must have been singularly impressive in scale. Though much of the walls and fortress is ruined, scarred by centuries of wars, it still retains its grandeur. The Roman walls ascend the hill in almost serpentine undulations, like a tired old dragon scaly with age.

When the town was called Murviedro by the Romans, there were gypsies in caves in the surrounding hills, more industrious than most of their tribe, for they molded pottery beads. Strings of these beads may be seen in the museum in Sagunto today. To tie the old with the new, I saw an old woman sitting underneath cypress trees near the Baroque arch, where the road leads to the Port. Her lap was full of clay beads glazed in vivid color. The old ones from "the caves" sit silent, staring through time, stringing beads to sell along the roads.

Cypresses appear now, to stand sentinel before the Moorish houses in the plain. As I drove out of Sagunto, I passed a bronze shield embedded in the spike-topped wall, and near it the gate leading to the Roman dungeons. This shield marks the spot where Hannibal, wounded while besieging the city, lay bleeding to death, to be saved by a Nubian servant who transfused the blood of a stallion into his master's veins.

I turned inland here to see the little village of Pedralba Arzobispo, famous through the centuries for its silk of particularly sheer texture.

81

The village was given royal patronage by Alfonso VI, in the eleventh century, creating the silk weavers "purveyors in perpetuity" for all silk used in the veils of saints and madonnas throughout Spain. This was a pretty formidable order to fill, considering there must have been more images of saints and Virgins in Spain in those days than there are today. The *alcalde* of the village made a journey to the court of Alfonso at Valladolid to ask that the silk from his village be woven only for Madonnas; let the saints be coiffed by someone else. This request was granted. Today, the silk whimple of which the Pedralbese are most proud is swathed around the head of *Virgen de Las Angustias* (the Virgin of the anguished) by Juan de Juni, in the Cathedral at Valladolid. This silk is reserved today exclusively for her, it is of a muted silvery green, the color found in the velvety shells of green almonds. An exquisite shade, and considered by the silk purveyors to be the most beautiful color and texture ever produced by them.

The mulberry trees are planted in circular rows and when I was in Pedralba the leaves were being picked by groups of young girls in red bodices and white turban head cloths. The leaves are picked singly, leaving a tuft of leaves at the end of each branch, dropped into baskets of lacy straw, so large each one is held by four girls. Great care is taken to guard against matting and crushing the leaves, else the silkworms will not feed. At an inn I saw workers from the silk factory having "elevenses" in the form of a light white wine drunk from *porrones*, glass bottles with a long thin spout. A drinker starts the wine spurting close to his mouth, then lengthens the jet until it is eighteen or twenty inches from his lips. Great dexterity in this mode of drinking often ends in contests and prizes awarded to him who can drink from the longest jet, without spilling a drop on his chest.

The entrance to Valencia is wreathed with oranges. Groves by the wayside, and orange sellers everywhere. The Valencia orange is not, by a long shot, the best in the world. The fragrant rind is delicious crystallized, but the orange pulp itself is bitter, far best used in marmalade.

Valencia has been called "the most coveted city in Spain" from Roman times, when Pompey sacked it in wrath because the townspeople failed to give him sufficient revenue, right down the line of conquerors, including "old rapacious," El Cid. An assault on the city was always contemplated but never put to the test by "young rapa-

cious," Cesare Borgia, Duke of Valentinois whose family came from Játiva, a small hill town close by. Gustave Flaubert said of Cesare:

> The first Borgia sprang full-horned like a bull from the cork forests of Játiva. Slowly the horns turned to sword blades, then to poinards with a drop of poison on the tip. The Borgia bull in the Vatican (a play on papal edicts) is outmatched in craftiness by the Minator of Valentinois.

Cesare always hoped that by some stroke of the famous Borgia luck his banner, emblazoned with a black bull wearing a jeweled gorget, would fly from the archbishop's palace where as a boy he had spent months at a time with his uncles. After Cesare died, there was found in his palace in Rome a model of Valencia as it was during his lifetime. He had commissioned a sculptor to spend years on this model cut in alabaster with a panorama of the surrounding country, complete with Gandía on the Sérpis and Játiva. It is said that this toy, the product of wishful thinking on the part of Cesare, was destroyed or lost when all his valuables were looted by his servants.

Once the walls of Valencia rose as proudly, if not so massive, as those of Tarragona. The beauty of eight entrance gates, emblazoned by the armorial bearings of noble Valencians (the Borgia built one gate) was renowned. Then came the deluge. The Moors attacked, breached the walls in many places, but rebuilt to leave art and beauty behind them. El Cid, marauding up and down the coast, bent on convincing posterity that he was the greatest military strategist in Christendom, destroyed four of the gates with "elephant" battering rams. These deadly machines of war had been invented by the Cid in the form of heavy poles with iron heads, mounted on the backs of twenty or more teams of bullocks. It is told that after this onslaught of destruction, even so callous a man as the Cid suffered qualms of conscience. He partly repaired the walls and built a magnificent castle, rivaling his fortress in Valladolid, placing an arrogant equestrian statue of himself above the gateway. I wonder where this statue of the conquistador, mounted on his charger, is today? No one ever hears of it.

In mid-nineteenth century a wave of demolition of historic walls and monuments in Spanish cities was started. It rolled across the peninsula like a tidal wave. This was found later to be a political move by shysters who masked it under the banner of "give work to the poor and provide them with decent dwellings." Down came walls and ancient buildings. In Valencia the worst desecration was the Albufat Tower with its interior walled in armor shields, left in barracks by the fleeing Moors, and the Puerta del Cid crowned by his now lost statue. The world must be grateful to the father of the noted painter Sorolla y Bastida for pleading with the Queen, Maria Christina, mother of Alfonso XIII, to use her influence to stop this wholesale wrecking which would soon leave Spain a desert of antique art. The Queen responded wholeheartedly and it was halted just in time.

To me, of greatest interest in Valencia are its eighteenth-century houses facing palm-studded plazas, the beauty of the Valencians, dark, flashing, their features decisively cut in classic mould, the fantastically beautiful sequined lace shawls, and the iridescent pigeons. The latter make the sunset hour glorious by flying in flocks of purple, green, peacock-blue, and gold round and round the bell tower of Santa Perellonet, the whirring of their wings so loud the strident bells are hushed. These Spanish pigeons are far more rich in plumage than their San Marco Venetian cousins, eternally gorged by tourists and drab in color. No one appears to feed the pigeons in Valencia, for they are a wild breed from the mountains and are as big as hawks. All day long they are hidden to return at sunset radiating light from ten thousand gleaming wings. There is a saying in Spain, to denote the beauty of a woman's eyes and smile, "as flashing as the wings of a pigeon of Perellonet."

Valencians are notably hospitable. Like Virginians they dote on entertaining a stranger. And food is ranked high as entertainment here. Foremost is rice prepared in "twenty-one ways," they say. All kinds of fish dishes appear too, and the baby chicken broiled on a spit over charcoal embers and served with green-almond salad is epic. Every night the women of Valencia dress up. Silk brocade flaunting great peonies, roses, grape leaves, and Baroque scrolls welds the designs into the realm of fabulous. Flowered brocade woven in Valencia has been famous since the middle ages. A piece of five or six meters is so heavy that if pinched into a pyramid it will stand alone. A man with whom I was discussing this brocade said, "In the Vatican alone there are probably many acres of our brocade, in copes and vestments."

The combs worn by women of Valencia are different entirely from those worn in Seville, Madrid, or the north of Spain. Here they are of gold, beaten thin and embossed in a flower design. No mantilla is worn, but a graceful, and even sumptuous sequin-embroidered shawl of heavy lace is draped across the shoulders. Often a full silk apron, sequin-embroidered too, is worn over the brocade skirts. With gold combs, plastrons of intricate pearl and semi-precious stones, rose or green satin slippers, and apron ties of patterned satin ribbon, the women of Valencia, strolling in Plaza Puerta del Palau at bell-ringing time, strike me as being every bit as glittering as the pigeons. In fact, the young men drinking the bitter cognac called *aguardiente*, white and powerful, will tell you the pigeons and the jeweled and gilded ladies are the star attractions of the city.

The silk exchange La Lonja is to me the most lovely building in Valencia. It has grace of proportion, the gay air of the people, the color of sunshine. Inside are framed sample lengths of brocade woven to send as gifts to Elizabeth I of England, the Bourbons, Habsburgs, and the Medici. And a magnificent display of color, texture, and ingenuity of design it is.

Probably no house of Rococo feeling has been pictured so many times in books and magazines and, for the most part, brilliantly described, as Palacio del Marqués de Dos Aguas, facing the small plaza Dos Aguas. The façade as a whole composition I find exhilarating. Stand off and get the entire effect with its twin pavilions at either corner of the mass. Then come closer, examine the proscenium of figures, imagined from out the middle mist of fancy, placed to enclose the entrance door and outline the niche above, where stand a Virgin and Child. Heroic male figures, caryatids of a sort, yet too undulant to uphold anything, typify the swirl of water, for these are *"dos aguas,"* the two rivers, from whence the palace takes its name. The fusing of waters is the theme employed by Hipólito Rovira who studied in Rome and came to Valencia around 1723. This man must have dreamed nightly of Zaragoza Sea, Lyonesse, The Islands of the Blessed, and East of the Sun, West of the Moon. There is a concern with imagination and dreams, a grace of flowing line, in this embossed and tinted stucco decoration which covers the entire façade of the house, as lyrical as the color of a field pied with spring flowers, so tender, so illusive as to seem only the memory of some flowered vale once seen, long ago.

My last night in Valencia I went to a small theater to see Pedro de Córdoba dance flamenco in the grand style. He is the leading male dancer in Spain today and flamenco is his forte. Córdoba's popularity

86

with the public is on a par with that of the reigning matador, say Aparicio and Litri, who fight bulls as a team, Dominguín or the rapidly rising Manolo Vázquez and Juan Posada.

The great secular celebration of the year, usually held in July though the date is flexible, is the *Falla*. I have witnessed it twice. It depicts the reign of Señor and Señora Gargantua, with daughters Sarcasm and Libel on either arm. All ages dote on this fiesta. The *Feria* in Seville may be just as gay with music and dancing but not so original nor bawdy in carnival mood. Through the streets are paraded gigantic figures of painted cardboard and papier mâché. These are dressed in outlandish costumes, the odder the better. From second-story windows whole families put on a kind of Punch and Judy show (the window acting as proscenium), humorous to the hilt, and often caricaturing some local bigwig. Grotesque masks with tinsel headdresses attached are sold in the streets, while firecrackers and cap bombs explode in the air and under foot. This civic charade ends with a parade of the giant buffoons carried on poles, the streets lighted by colored fire. The night ends at dawn in clamor, explosion and extreme fatigue.

To me the *Falla* meant Pedro de Córdoba. I had seen him the previous year in Madrid and remembered him as lean, lithe, with the narrow, sallow face of an El Greco grandee. Now, during *Falla* celebration he appeared in Valencia. He nearly always dresses in black with a relief of white, but this time he danced an interlude of *Triana* with two gitanas, a man playing a gypsy panpipe and two women singing *saetas*. This motif is an ancient dance which always opens the *Fiesta de Triana* in Seville, a *marcha torera*, slow at first, but ending on a high, wild strain of music with fast, intricate foot work on the part of the dancer. For this dance de Córdoba wore a vermilion velvet jacket and *Triana* sombrero. Then came the flamenco. I realized as I watched that, perhaps unknown to the Spanish, this dance of seduction, the male playing hard to get, women (gitanas in this case) sweeping yards of ruffled trains around him, enticing, is *L'Après-midi d'un Faun in Valencia*.

All life centers around the Mercado, one of the largest plazas in Spain, with its acres of stone paving that in the past was used for knightly tourneys and as a place of execution. On one day, to the sound of trumpets, jousts took place, with all the rich panoply. On the next, shrieks and stench of heretics being burned, or drawn and quartered rent the air. The Inquisition at its height of insensate

87

cruelty laid a heavy hand on Valencia, mistaking the essentially gay nature of the people for looseness and impiety.

The Alameda is gay and aristocratic, a long, tree-shaded walk extremely fashionable at all times, but most delightful at eight o'clock in the evening when the brilliantly-dressed nursemaids from rich households are taking their charges for a ride before bedtime in red and yellow carts drawn by donkeys, so hidden under embroidered harness and the inevitable tassels, that all one can see is big ears above and trotting hooves below.

Valencia has little to offer the visitor in the way of good hotels. Metropole is fairly comfortable, but small and usually full of South Americans who consider Valencia a "resort" in the manner Italians do Venice. Surprisingly, the best pension and restaurant is called Hans Christian Andersen. Seeking relief from a chronic nasal disorder Andersen stayed in Valencia for a year in 1864. He rented a tall ornate Rococo house in a quiet street with a tiled patio and a view of the sea. But he constantly complained of the excessive heat. *"Mucho calor—mucho, mucho calor,"* was his habitual greeting as he walked abroad. Today, a large sign informs you that the yellow stucco house in a street of dusty, decayed elegance is Pension Hans Christian Andersen. In the leafy patio where excellent food is served at small tables, one is handed an outsize menu. In flowing script across the top is written, "Mucho Calor."

For a while after leaving Valencia for the south, the suburbs seem to go one forever. Suddenly this dullness ends when the road runs under a Moorish arch emblazoned with the Borgia bull. The countryside becomes marshy and soon the lagoon of Albufera lies unrippled, flat as a silver salver, under the pale sky. This fresh-water lake, separated from the sea by a narrow neck of land, is a fishermen's and hunters' joy. Fish are plentiful, and in spring and autumn duck shooting becomes not only a pastime, but an occupation for the men living in little *barracas*, whitewashed mud huts thatched with reeds, which seem to hide in tall plume grass at one end of the lagoon. These men work fast during the short duck season to fill the pot and to sell the birds to markets in Valencia and fashionable Alcira where there are a number of big villas and two good hotels.

A curious sight among the marshes of Albufera is the boats, narrow as Mohawk canoes, with yellow, delta-shaped sails, that ply the canals cut like spokes of a wheel to connect the many small hamlets with the lagoon. Thousands of herons nest on the lagoon or in the marshes, and there is the continual whirl of aquatic bird life.

The road to Denia leads through vineyards, where drying racks for grapes cover the meadows way up into the hills. The raisins of Denia are world famous. It is a lovely pale ivory town under tall, waving palms. Oliva, nearby, is ancient and mildewed in appearance because of the houses built from marsh mud, so porous it sucks in all moisture. The town is purple with racks of grapeskins used for dyes. In some places honey is diluted and sprayed on the grapes. This honeyed raisin, full of juice, is in great demand all over Spain and sometimes one is served a small plate of them at restaurants along the coast. One is supposed to sweeten the coffee with a honeyed raisin, then lift it out with a spoon to eat. I remarked on this custom one night in Valencia. My host lifted an eyebrow. "If a Martini cocktail in New York can have an olive, or a Manhattan a cherry, why not our coffee a few honeyed raisins?"

"*Bon.*" I ate my raisins and drank the coffee in silence.

A Moorish castle, largely ruinous, dominates the village of Denia (the Roman Dianium) where there is said once to have been a temple to Diana on a pillar-like rock standing out of the sea. Scholars, Professor Rhys Carpenter to name one, dispute this theory, some say the temple was at Calpe atop the Penón de Ifach. As there are no signs of ruins there it is doubtful if anyone will ever know for sure, though indefatigable digging for this temple and foundations of Roman villas still goes on. As I passed Calpe the huge jut of Penón de Ifach was ablaze with sunlight at the top, but cast a deep purple shadow over the bay at its foot. More than ever the fabulous rock formation looked like the prow of a Roman galley. If I could paint a gigantic eye on both sides to ward off evil spirits and monsters of the deep, long white-rimmed eyes with staring black pupils, such as the galleys and triremes once had, I am sure the old gods would come to the Penón, unanchor the rock and set sail to some unknown sea.

The road to Alicante has the Moorish air. Pale blue and white houses like those seen on the sea road between Tangier and Casablanca crowd so closely together the appearance is of one long-drawn-out village. More and more I am persuaded that the Moor is still in Spain in spirit if not in person. I drove into Benidorm, huddled on its palm-fringed beach, at sundown. Bells in the tower of a church faced with blue and yellow tiles rang out the call to evening prayer. A fleet of fishing boats was just putting out. Wide-beamed, dark-brown hulls rode low, stern down, with prows high and pointed as a Phoenician spear. The design of these boats has not altered since antique times. Each prow was painted with the familiar eye to ward off evil spirits. The triangular sails were either solid color or fashioned from patchwork in green, rose-red, and silvery blue. I looked for, and found, just as I had done in the Aegean Sea, a votive offering on each mast. A pair of crudely carved heads wearing Phyrgian caps of red wool, cut and sewn by the fisherman's wife. A lighted lantern swung above the heads. Thus lighted, Castor and Pollux, twin patrons of fishermen the world over, gazed searchingly ahead, or perhaps winked at the stars in the firmament bearing their name. All this has held from pagan days when more then twenty centuries ago Greeks from Phocaea sailed along this coast.

I watched for a while this departure of men who nightly drag a livelihood from the chancy sea, then walked along the scimitar curve of beach so primly fringed with palms. The sun seemed long a-dying but its last rays cast glorious color on the water. Great swathes of cobalt blue where restless currents churned, mauve and rich green among the rocks which, in this last light, gleamed like enamel. And then, just as I turned back to the village, a group of boys, naked save for loin cloths and wide brimmed straw hats, drove bullocks, yoked together in teams, into the shallows to be rubbed down with fistfuls of seaweed. Had I somewhere in Greece beheld this same scene? I had, but then it was painted on the blood-red walls of an excavated Minoan palace.

After Benidorm the country changes suddenly to a dry, dusty, mauve-and-cinnamon aridity. Here the sepia rocks are piled crazily along the sea road as if some giant, interrupted at play, had abandoned a long wall he was building.

As the environs of Valencia are orange laden, the country around Alicante is one vast vineyard. Alicante grapes are famous for an oddly different kind of wine, for perfectly symmetrical bunches of table grapes, and for plump, juicy raisins. The bunches of grapes marked to sell as fruit are tied up in gauze bags. I saw swarms of angry bees and frustrated birds hovering over these unattainable grapes. An amusing effect in the vineyards is the scarecrows. Not a lone figure in tattered garments, but sometimes as many as a dozen figures made of straw, dressed in gay, colored costumes, are grouped together. In order to ward off the flocks of birds eternally bent on ravaging the grapes, all sorts of devices are used. Some of the scarecrows have branches of trees stuck into the hatbands, from which dangle rattles. A breeze will cause the rattles to whirr and a high wind sets up a din to be heard for miles. If the birds become too obstreperous crowds of small children are hired to dash along the rows of vines beating the air with long sticks.

The harbor of Alicante which is fringed with the most luxuriant palm trees I had yet seen, is predominantly Moorish. It even seems an Oriental port. All sorts of ships are either warping at the long, curved mall or raising anchor to sail away. The Alameda is wide and bordered with cafés. From morning to morning, straight through the night, these cafés remain open to serve townspeople and tourists the Alicante wine. Like a casbah in some Moorish town, the old Castle of Santa Barbara crouches on a hill overlooking the harbor. Across the bay is another castle, San Fernando, of later date. For centuries the two fortresses have frowned at one another across water. The evening I arrived at Alicante a local fiesta was in progress. Roman candles, skyrockets, and colored flares were being set off from the parapets of the two castles. The sharp red and green light on the old town and the ships in harbor was a luminous spectacle.

The food in Alicante is renowned, to match its much-touted wine. I lunched at one of the numerous restaurants on the sea front and ate for the first time an excellent dish called *bacalao a la vizcaína*, fresh codfish in a cream sauce with tomatoes and a cheese topping, all browned under a quick flame.

After lunch, when the narrow streets of Alicante were deserted for siesta, I drove out to the Cabo de las Huertas region. No one traveling this part of Spain should miss El Cabo, as it is called. White farm houses, tropical vegetation, red, black, and curiously spotted cattle feeding knee-deep in green grass reminded me that charcoal grilled steaks, veal cutlets, and tender calves' liver are unsurpassed in this province.

I visited the famed Hermosa vineyards of Alicante grapes, tasted three or four different wines and sampled the raisins, big, purple-black and, oddly, tasting of raspberries. I drove to San Javier at sunset and sat for a time awestruck with wonder at the sight of an old, battle-scarred castle (Los Alcazáres) bristling with towers and craggy battlements, which crouched like some wounded heraldic beast on a high escarpment overhanging the almost circular bay of Mar Menor. Again it was the sun setting in splendor that bathed the castle in crimson, gold, and slashes of yellow until it seemed to dissolve into molten gold. Always in Spain it is the sun which points up these castles, half in ruins, and deserted by man, lending for a brief time a glory they once knew.

Murcia lies inland in the mountains of the Province of Murcia, remote, hugging to its heavily-jeweled and gold-lace breast all the old customs of Spain. It was once called the Kingdom of Murcia and in effect it still is. I always feel transported to the days of Philip II in this proud city all gray and silvery pink, embraced by barren, serrated mountains. Once this capital was walled, but the Moors pulled down the walls to make way for an elaborate system of irrigation ditches to reclaim the city and environs from the arid waste of desert dryness that was causing a mysterious plague which was rapidly decimating the inhabitants.

Murcia is in some ways a festival of Baroque architecture. Corinthian columned porticos abound, and the cathedral is Churriguerra personified. Winged angels swathed in belling draperies, playing on flutes and trumpets, seem insubstantially poised on scrolled cornices all around the plaza. The Palacio Episcopal is magnificently flamboyant in scrolls and carved swags of fruit over the high windows. The great audience chamber here has a painted ceiling in extreme bravura in the manner of Tiepolo. The curtains and walls are of heavy cardinal-red silk, lit gloriously by the sunlight filtering through the small panes of glass. On fiesta days the women wear the traditional red and black velvet costumes with gold lace and heavy jeweled bodices.

Mojácar in Murcia province rises from an arid plain. The houses are square and flat-roofed in Moorish style, gaily painted. The piled up effect is that of building blocks entirely walled by the cactus with its huge paddle-like leaves. I first saw Mojácar early in the morning when a heat mist made the town appear to be floating in space borne on green lily pads.

Cartagena is the most modernized of all the cities of the south coast. It is a city rich from adjacent silver mines, just as it was when Sir Francis Drake sacked it in the sixteenth century. I found it noisy, but with a different kind of stridence from Barcelona. The sound of machinery is rampant. Industry reigns supreme. The shrieking of sirens and blowing of steamship whistles finally drove me out.

I drove to Lorca, Moorish in name and architecture, so that I could stop at a beautiful old inn, curiously called Comercia, probably because the cattle market used to be held in front of its iron-studded doors. I found the inn, built in the seventeenth century, delightful.

The room I had was paneled in wood and painted a pale icy green. A most refreshing room to stay in for the weather was very hot.

One of the things to visit in Lorca is the Potters' Market. Here on a flattened hilltop dwell two hundred or more families whose ancestors were Moriscos, the converted Moors who after expulsion of the caliphs stayed in Spain. All who live in this plaza are potters. The gamut of household utensils is run in molded clay. I was fascinated watching the big lumps of red or brown clay turn into long necked jars, under the bony, deft fingers of the potters. Vases as gracefully shaped as the calyx of a lily, or huge round platters took sudden shape. Little boys tie the platters on the backs of donkeys, fill them with almonds and the apricots which grow in profusion around Lorca, and hawk their wares through the streets. The loveliest building, I think, is the Colegiata of San Patricio. The image of St. Patrick which stands in a niche under aloe trees at the head of a long flight of steps was carved in Ireland and brought here in the eighteenth century by a monk called Brother Patrick. This monk is said to have been massive in build, with a riot of red curls around his tonsure. His voice boomed like heavy surf on rocks. Unwittingly, he frightened women and children out of their senses. Nevertheless, he became a powerful man in the church and is buried in the cathedral in Salamanca. Little boys with turbans wound round their heads in Berber style, lead reluctant donkeys up the steps to the niche early in the morning to be blessed by St. Patrick before setting out on the round of fruit selling.

When I left Lorca, I was headed for Andalusia of lovely memory and beckoning delights. The road out of Lorca is Spain, Moorish Spain, at its most desolate. Burnt red hills undulating like the swell on a Red Sea seem limitless. Soon I traced on hillsides, the vineyards of Baza. This is a hill town definitely Moorish, but with the undeniable stamp of Andalusia. Big woven baskets and pottery jars for olive oil were stacked in the plaza. Wineskins, fatter with wine than they ever were when covering the carcass of a goat, hung dripping on the walls. A dark Moorish-looking woman in a ruffled gingham skirt with a black shawl pulled across the lower part of her face like a yashmak hurried past me.

The street climbed to the old Moorish castle where I had been told I would see some fine carved cedar ceiling, for a rich Morisco had once lived in the castle and brought all his treasures from Granada. The oddly metallic effect of intricately-carved cedar has the patina

93

of oiled bronze. In one of the rooms the carving was touched with green, red, and violet, as one sees in the Palais Bou Jaloud in Fez. Particularly arresting were the great cedar doors carved in huge bosses and flame motifs. There was not a stick of furniture in the rooms; all was dry as dust.

Finally I went out into the deserted garden. There I got a surprise. Seven or eight boys and girls ranging in age from six to ten years were playing some sort of a hop-scotch game in the hot sun. All were stark naked as the day they were born and I realized that, except for the fact they were intensely animated, they might have been carved from the cedar of the castle ceilings. Just as I started to leave the garden and the leaping nymphs and fauns a woman all in black, with a shawl almost concealing her dark face, came out of a door in a small pavilion. She paid no attention to me, but walked over to a well, drew up an earthen jar of water and proceeded to sprinkle it over the hot, brown children.

I almost failed to get the car down the narrow tortuous street leading to the plaza. Finally I made it by scraping half the paint off the sides and took the road to Alcudia in the Sierra de Baza where I planned to spend the night and get a start in early morning for the cave dwelling of Guadix and hence on to Granada of the myriad roses.

Chapter 7

THE ROSE-RED PLAINS OF ANDALUSIA AND GRANADA

IT gives one a curious feeling of utter isolation to drive through
an arid sea of low, dry, undulating hills, where no sign of man
or his habitat can be seen, where almost no vegetation breaks the
monotony. Loneliness encroaches, with only the rasping wind scyth-
ing the intermittent ridges of *esparto* grass, and above that, the nerve-
wracking call of cicadas which you cannot see. Ever since leaving
Valencia I had been conscious of the ubiquitous cicada, and a fine
noise to currycomb the nerves these waxy-scaled insects make. There
are many different kinds of cicada in Spain, especially in the south.
The most infernal species comes out, I remembered, in romantic
gardens where one walks, swept away in dreaming, through tangled
rose arbors, or beside lily-strewn lagoons lying quiet in shadow.
Suddenly this contemplation of beauty is shattered by a strident,
metallic sound, something between a file scraping and the twanging
of steel wires. The rise and fall of this whirr serves the male cicada
as a sexual call. He keeps it up indefinitely. I admit a nostalgic garden
is the place to call to a desired mate, but I have often wished the lady
would respond sooner. So—as I drove along the blistering road to
Guadix I had as escort a cacophony of sound worse than all the harbor whistles in Cartagena at their shrillest. On I drove, hoping for at
least the sight of a gray hare, the savage jackrabbits who are said to
infest these tufa-rock hills.

Finally, on the horizon loomed a dim smudge of misty violet, the
Sierra Nevada Range, to excite my dreariness with thoughts of Granada. Suddenly, an individual, tall, lank, dressed in blue canvas jacket
and knee breeches peculiar to the inhabitants of the Guadix el Viejo

plain appeared beside the road. I slowed to a halt. The man regarded me silently. I noticed he carried a rifle of obsolete German make, a heavily-mounted field piece. At his side hung a bulging bag wet with blood, with long ears protruding from the flap. I remembered then that I had heard gun shots a while back. It turned out the man did not want a lift. He was waiting for his brother who would meet him somewhere along this stretch of road. Meanwhile he had shot a few hares. Would I like to have one? I declined, saying I had no way of cooking it. I inquired if there was any village or hamlet, even a wayside *taberna*, where I could get a bottle of wine or a gourd of water, for my throat was plastered with walls of red tufa dust. He answered that there was a small hamlet, the one where he and his brother kept the wine ship. He motioned to a hill, higher than the rest.

"Serón, only a few houses," he said, "just as you come into the Sierra Baza gorge. But why wait? Have some wine now." With the courtly gesture one becomes so used to in Spain, he took a bottle of wine from his pouch, uncorked it, flicked a dollop into the dust to moisten the bottle, and handed it to me. It was as sour and raw as well-mothered vinegar, but wet. I drank thirstily. Recorking the bottle I heard the clop-clop-clop of hooves. Over the ridge rode a single horseman. By the lift of the hunter's head I surmised this was the awaited brother. And thereby hangs a tale, an incident of the road, which of the many chance encounters I have had in one country and another, could have happened only in Spain. It bares to the bone the principal obsession of the Spanish mind.

However startling in appearance the skeletal rider was, his long skinny legs nearly touching the ground, his mount was even more marvelous. A barrel-ribbed, spavined pinto pony, the kind known to horsemen as crow-bait, was smeared with lather and red dust, and in the last stages of exhaustion. The brothers hailed each other in a give-and-take of explosive words. This over, the new arrival smiled broadly at me. In a deep, hollow voice, oddly at variance with his rather child like smile and excited eyes, he said, "One little moment, señor, while I show you my treasure." Whereupon he proceeded to unfold a dusty *serape* from across the pommel of his saddle. I had thought by the shape that the *serape* wrapped a rifle, but no. What I saw was a dingy sword, such as are used by matadors in corrida, when delivering the final, lethal *suerte*.

"Regard," the man said, first to me, then to his brother. He rubbed his finger lovingly along the blade. "This is the blood of El Bolero Moro, the last bull killed by Miguel Gorríto. You know Gorríto, señor?"

I shook my head.

The man regarded me narrowly, disbelieving such ignorance. He continued. "Gorríto was so contemptuous of wild bulls, even the most savage, he fought them on stilts." He sighed and hugged the sword to his thin chest in a kind of delirium of possession. His brother shrugged and leveled at me his small black eyes.

"You perceive this is Manolo's heart. Do you not? In his own mind it was *he* who killed the bull called Black Dancer with that sword. He wanted to make his life the corrida. But," his hand measured in the air, "he is too tall and his chest is weak. No strength. So—what will you? He spends all his money on relics such as this sword."

Dreamily, Manolo spoke. "I will hang it on the wall of the wine shop where it will attract many customers to drink," he narrowed his eyes at the brother—"our detestable wine. No?"

This story of El Gorríto the matador, a monument to bravado, who fought bulls on stilts, was to have an unexpected aftermath a few days later at Antequera on the road between Granada and Málaga. One of those occurrences that seem too well planned by the Fates to be merely coincidence. I will tell of it later on.

I bade good-day to the tall brothers from hidden Serón, which, I learned later, was a small community of cave dwellers. As I drew closer to Guadix the mood of the country lightened considerably. The welcome green fringes of cork-tree branches and avenues of mulberry trees leading to small thatched farmhouses caused my spirits to rise. For this had been a long, hot pull and the resinous wine by the roadside had not quenched my thirst one whit. Crossing a high-arched bridge over a dry river bed, dry since Roman days by the look of it, I began to wonder if I would see water again when I spied a clump of fig and pear trees heavy with fruit close to the road. Two little boys standing in the shade held out trays of woven rushes piled with bronze pears and big, blue-streaked purple figs. Never had any fruit looked so refreshing. I stopped and bought the lot. The pears were cool and juicy and the figs at the proper ripeness. I made a feast. The boys watched me with the intense absorption a foreigner always induces in Spain. When I sprinkled pesetas in their hands there was a flash of white teeth in both brown Andalusian faces, and a scramble back to the trees hoping I would want more pears.

A long road lined with small villas with blue or green tile roofs, all tight shut against the heat, led through the environs of Guadix. A tomb-like quiet prevailed. Not a soul stirred though it was approaching sunset. A little wind had sprung up and the red dust swirled and eddied ahead of me. I turned a corner and there lay a cool avenue of broad old mulberry trees, magnificent in spread of leaf. These swept up to a long flight of steps leading to the cathedral. I stopped for a while under the luxurious shade of the mulberry trees and wondered how this cool oasis could thrive in so drought-tortured a place. It hardly ever rains in Andalusia. The sun shines as much in winter as in summer. Even when it does rain moisture never sinks into the baked earth to any depth. It seems to me a miracle of nature that in this region such luxuriant gardens flourish.

Close to the walls on which the cathedral stands is a garden of delight. Neglected now, but still riotous with geraniums, roses by thousands, lilies, carpets of myrtle, tall cypresses rising in exclamatory black points above pomegranate and jasmine and the lacquered ilex tree. Hidden in the tangle of vines is the ruins of a Roman villa built by Emperor Theodosius, who was Spanish by birth. Once this was a pavilion in a perfume garden. All flowers planted here were cut to distil the perfumes in the essence of which Theodosius lived and had his being. Only the merest fragments of mosaic floors remain and a long wall of what was once a tank for bathing. Now, in the cracks, skeined by thorny vines, run the largest and brightest green lizards I have ever seen. It is said that Theodosius hated Rome and loved to compound his spices and perfumes in Spain. Indolence, which amounted at times to torpor akin to that of a hibernating animal, was attributed to his obesity, by indulgent friends, or, more likely, sycophants. From young manhood Theodosius was so huge he had to be carried about on a litter or supported by slaves. At the luxurious villa he had built near Blanes, at the end of Costa Brava, when he wished to bathe in the sea, slaves had first to empty great jars of perfume into the water to deaden the salty tang of the sea at the spot where he would be carried on a gold litter, curtained in azure silk. This litter was so cunningly fashioned that it could become either a coach on land, by the attachment of wheels, or a raft in the water on which the sybarite emperor floated over waves of rose perfume. Perfumes were so great a passion that he lived in a perpetually scented mist. When culprits were brought before Theodosius for judgment, they had first

99

to be sprayed with perfume, no matter whether the man was of high or low degree.

Today traces of the emperor and his passion are still to be found in the Attar de Rose Theodosius sold in perfume shops; and in milestones placed by him on the road from Blanes back into the hills toward Guadix and his now obliterated villa. On these plinths is carved, in low relief, a full-blown rose, very like the one used as private device by another ruler of Empire, certainly different in spirit, Elizabeth Tudor.

Guadix presents a curious, high bosomed appearance, planted on a terraced hillside in a desolate, burned-out region. I walked around the wide *paseo* in the dying light of evning, my favorite time for wandering through Spanish towns. Slowly I climbed up the long flight of steps to the cathedral. From this vantage point I got a tremendous sweep of the *vega* and the façade of the church, so blazing in sunset color the convolutions of yellow stone seemed to crackle. I looked up at the Madona de las Vegas, staring straight ahead from her shell-domed niche above the pillared doorway. A lovely, lonely figure with an inherently sad expression. I thought of *The Trojan Woman*. Of old Queen Hecuba on the walls of Troy, gazing mute in grief, out across the burned-bare wastes of her tormented country.

For this is true of the hard red vega of Guadix; it is ever tormented by heat. It has been known not to rain a drop in two years in this part of Andalusia.

I stayed the night in a small, infinitely clean inn. My room was all white with peasant furniture of plain hazelwood scrubbed white with sand. From the window I had a view of the plaza where copper pans and immense pot-bellied earthen jars for storing olive oil were piled so high as to give the effect of protective barricades. I was told this piling up went on until the plaza was impassable to donkeys or pedestrians. Then everybody made a holiday and loaded the products of the town on lorries. Whoever had ordered them was probably surprised at this sudden, overwhelming delivery. Then the whole procedure of piling started over again.

Next morning the air was made cooler by a latent wind from snow-capped peaks of the Sierra Nevada. I remarked on this relief to the *patrón* of the inn.

"It is well," he said while filling my bowl with coffee. "We nearly perish with the heat. But just as we are about to send for the priest, *Olé, Olé,* the good God, He sends us a cool wind from the mountains, even if not a drop of rain as our prayers have asked for, and we decide to live a little longer." From out of the shadows of the patio came the voice of his wife, "His next gift *might* be rain, so I shall continue to pray for it."

Into almost every conversation with the Spaniard, no matter of what import, is introduced some allusion to the idiosyncracies of the Almighty in answering prayers.

The caves of Barrio de Santiago, hollowed out of the twisted and pinnacled hills behind Guadix, are marvels of nature in themselves long before man got to work on them. There are many cave communities scattered about this farflung *vega*, variously similar to this one. A few miles away is Benalúa, far more wild and primitive. The gypsies of Benalúa congregate in the open to do all their cooking. A coarse bread is baked in natural stone ovens and the inevitable stew brewed by Romany tribes the world over is cooked cooperatively in a huge iron cauldron bearing the insignia of a regiment of Irish Fusiliers. If questioned about this the gypsies turn evasive. But on inquiring in the town of Guadix later I was told this cauldron had been salvaged, if not boldly filched, from a regiment of Wellington's army when it was preparing to leave the military station of Guejár-Granada after the Peninsular Campaign.

I have been in Barrio de Santiago when the paths, twisting among the caves, were eerily silent, as if the shut caves with cobalt-blue doors and crazily-askew chimneys were deserted relics of Moorish days. But on this morning activity, even clamour, reigned. The gypsies were snatching from off the lines newly-washed or -dyed finery, preparing to go off to neighboring Benalúa to attend a wedding. It was, as I watched, like a spirited ballet. Donkeys were being loaded with big earthen jugs of wine gaily stoppered with plumes of straw. Wicker-protected jars of olive oil were strapped on the backs of small girls in pigtails astream with bright ribbons, a compensation, I supposed, for being classed along with the donkeys as beasts of burden. The men were more lightly laden with rolls of gaudily striped rugs from Alhama de Granada, high in the mountains, a village of weavers. These rugs are used as bedding, or as cloaks against a sharp wind, or to form wind-break tents for gypsy women during childbirth. There is a superstition of dread, extending as far as the tinkers in Connemara and the *bhuls* of India that no child must be born to a Romany woman except under the sky, preferably the sky in full complement of stars.

THE
SILVER
MADONNA
MALAGA

Collection of Mrs. C. Suydam Cutting

In the confusion of departure I walked along the cave-bordered "street" unnoticed. Suddenly I was hailed by a man in the doorway of a cave and offered a hasty glass of *blanco*, a thin, white, slightly effervescent wine, very like cider. By a branch of dry and withered grapevine hanging over the door I took this cave to be the wine shop. A crudely lettered sign hanging by one nail read *El Zorro*, the gaunt gray fox which stalks these barren hills with a price on his flattened head. Peering into the dark interior I saw the walls covered with gray fox skins. I can never resist a potential fur rug. I love to step out of bed on a cold morning into the warmth and softness of the fur of wild animals. I bought two beautifully-marked skins, dark gray on the backbone, a black stripe at the shoulders, shading to pale gray under the belly. Finally the wedding cavalcade started down the hill, and I went down to Guadix, followed by a few goats and pariah dogs. Here I found my car the center of interest. A group of small burned-brown boys in breech clouts and immense straw hats milled around the car, reminding me of the lone shepherds I had but lately seen on the hills above antique Sagunto. I drove slowly away from this blanched outpost of Moorish hideaway, thinking of its history. For it was in Granada and the surrounding tufa caves that the Arabs made a last stand. Droves of slaves fleeing their masters holed up in the caves that are now Benalúa, Guadix and Purullena. Some died of thirst, but many more infiltrated into Spanish life to establish the strongly Moorish cast of feature, the proud carriage of the head. "Hold thy head as if a mosque was thy turban," bids the Koran. I had just seen this pride in the boys who laughingly drew signs in dust on the body of my car.

I have seen many of these cave dweller settlements scattered about Spain. For example, at Guadix near Granada and at Purullena in Andalusia. Always I am reminded of pueblo villages in the American Southwest. In many of these caves the cleft entrance is high and wide as a cathedral door. I have explored any number of caves in various provinces, to discover long, winding corridors with steps cut down, down, ever down into dark subterranean chambers, cool, but perilously damp and slippery from dripping springs.

The immemorial caves in Spain caught the imagination of an Italian traveler in 1720. Carlo Moretti of Milan wrote in his journal:

> Spain appears to be formed from a series of gigantic steps. Some lead upward to plateau pastures. Others wend, dark and

slippery, into the maws of forgotten caves. Some of these steps I find lead to Heaven. More often they lead to Hell.

I was shown this journal, preserved in a private collection in Seville. So delicate was the milky-brown of faded ink it resembled Islamic calligraphy in design of graceful curlicues. Moretti proved to be a most observant and lucid chronicler. His account of the rigors of coach travel in Spain during the first quarter of the eighteenth century is a story of rugged adventure laced with treacherous quagmires, tempests, and high banditry. He tells of ascending to plateaus to "range after range of mountains, drifting like the tides of ocean into the clouds." These are his "steps leading to heaven." During his journey Moretti was surprised by bandits in the Sierra de Gredos, imprisoned and held for ransom, far down in a dank cave. This duress, of what length he does not say, was unquestionably his steps "leading down to Hell."

I drove on to Purullena on the road to Granada. Here the cave dweller is his own architect. A tufa mud frontal, according to the builder's taste, is modeled in a big square frame surrounding the cave entrance, often projecting a foot or more to be roofed in red or blue tiles. The caves, I find, become delightfully cool in the hot summer days and warm and dry when it rains, or when the harsh winds of winter blow for days at a time across the plains. A few caves have electric light. There are even two wireless sets in Purullena, a few bathrooms of a sort, and many shower baths. The village boasts a mayor, a judge, an able young electrician, and a senile poet. A huge community cistern, often low in water but always replenished after the Virgin of Purullena de la Cruz has been loaded with votive offerings, supplies water from a hidden spring.

I liked the immense oval stable hewn from the bowels of the highest hill, where at night nearly one hundred donkeys are made comfortable on thickly scattered straw. In Purullena a pig may have his own little cave. But the riby, mangy curs found in all Spanish towns roam the place in packs to scatter roosters and hens, so red with tufa dust they all seem gory.

When Purullena is seen from the lower road the effect is of a weird, scarred canyon of cliffs, and pyramids of twisted rock, dotted with squares of whitewash or strong blue where chimneys shaped like bee hives sprout from solid rock. The very strangeness of this sight beckons the traveler to examine this Troglodyte empire at close range. The inhabitants are largely farmers. They cultivate the surrounding plain by intricately cut irrigation ditches. Beet root is the staple. I ate a beet-root soup, rather like a Russian borscht, spiced with peppers and mixed with sour cream. Hot or cold, I find it extremely good. And the generous portions served in the huge, saucer-shaped bowls make you blink.

Leaving this tufa land, the way to Granada is steadily upgrade. First by gradual spurts, the road going berserk in hairpin turns, often strewn with boulder-size rocks lying in one's path. But the views, caught momentarily between jagged peaks, richly compensate for this slight annoyance. The rising sierras ever in the background glow at the base and shimmer at the top, sharply etched against a sky dramatic in itself with piled thunder heads catching black and purple shadows underneath. But this is Andalusia, so there is faint hope these magnificent cloud monsters will split open to drop rain.

It was late evening when I approached Granada. A crescent moon hung luminously over the improbably remote peaks of Los Nevadas. Granada, like Toledo, Ronda, Tarragona, Gerona, Aragon, and old battle-ground Sagunto, gains in stature, presents a poised, serene beauty by its setting. Placed high, carefully set, as a jewel might be, to center interest, the first glimpse of the "Hill of Pleasures and Fountains," so named by Mohammed Ibnal Ahmar, is unforgettable.

From gently undulating hills, crested in rose gardens and cypress, rise two of the world's most famed palaces. Alhambra and the exquisite Generalife. For walls so strongly built the whole cluster of towers and pillared pavilion seems ethereal, as if about to soar lightly into space. All the color seems to stem from the Alhambra, which means Red Castle, a perfect example of Maghrebine (west of Islam) style. All reds are here, from deep garnet to rose, to red-orange and faintest pink. But time has muted the reds to a silvery cast in which no one tone thrusts forward. Rose light and mauve shadow abound. The crenellated towers seem luminous as pearls against the mountains.

Below the Alhambra gardens lies the wide arm of the Darro and the gray city of Granada. The Albaicin and gypsy caves of Sacromonte lie in a curve of the river edged by gardens. Granada is rich in Moorish gardens. The typical *caminos*, long shaded garden walks, were laid out by Mohammed Ibn Al Ahmar and finished by effeminate Yusef I. This sybarite was garroted by a demented Nubian slave whom he had tortured, in an aisle of the *caminos*, while Yusef was gathering mimosa to line the walls of his pavilion for a fiesta. In a private collection in La Coruña I saw a series of Moorish tiles, so delicately painted as to resemble early Persian miniatures, retelling in brush strokes this whole episode.

Before entering the gates to climb the rose-studded cypress paths which lead to the Alhambra and on to the gardens of the Generalife, stop for a while below the walls and look upwards. No scene embracing hanging gardens that I know of anywhere has the singular allure of this one. First, are high-piled walls hung with rose vines. Then, rising from the jet of cypresses and pomegranate, the red and orange towers. Behind this, to hold the eyes in focus, the snow-ridged shoulders of Sierra Nevada, plumed in clouds. From these peaks swift-running slaves used to bring snow, packed in straw, to cool the rose-flavored sherbets of the sultans.

More and more as one penetrates deeper into Spain, and begins to savor the richness of its beauty, the fact becomes apparent that the color of its ancient towns and cities, coupled with the golden quality of light, distinguishes them from any others in Europe. In many countries a city when seen from a distance, presents nothing of particular interest, and too often, once inside the town, one must hunt out the beauties of architecture of which one has read or heard. It is the light and splendor of color that even in Spain places Granada apart. There is one arrogantly *red* building, Hotel Alhambra Palace, fronting a steep chasm overlooking the *vega*, the mountains, the Alhambra, Generalife, and the lower town. The hotel is stark, Moorish red. High, rounded towers and spiked walls give the effect from the forecourt, of the casbah of a Berber caïd in the fastnesses of High Atlas. The rooms are big and comfortably furnished, and visitors are enchanted by the wonderful view from their rooms. At night, when they take coffee on the terrace hanging sheer over the gorge, the moon striking fire from Sierra Nevada snows is a sight to remember.

Moorish sultans and caliphs believed the fabric of life must be serenity of mind, never stinting bodily pleasures, the whole lived in the midst of beautiful surroundings. The sultans of Granada, from Rahman I, down the line to King Boabadil, expelled at last in 1492 by Ferdinand and Isabella, strove to attain perfection in pavilions and fountained courts, belvederes and miradors and towers against the sky. How nearly perfection in decoration was attained, one sees today. For example, the Court of the Myrtles and the Hall of the Ambassadors, with green and alabaster tracery delicate as the rivulets of water in the fountains. The Belvedere Temple of Daraxa with its ceiling of "stirred-around" fretwork, like swirls of clotted cream. The most original court is perhaps the Hall of Abencerrajes, its tulip-shaped cupola lit by windows cut to ape the scales of a pineapple. This filigree lets in threads of light to pick out arabesques of violet and rose-pink enamel. The effect is dazzling. By more than any other thing in the courts and colonnades, I am attracted by the fountains and runnels of singing water. So many of the fountains were placed to be seen as finials to a flowery vista or a sun-flecked pool where, from a silken-spread divan, the sensuous lilt of running water could be faintly heard.

The arches of colonnades at Generalife were called "miradors of love," from which could be seen the terraced gardens in moonlight. The scent from jasmine, violets, and roses, strengthened by dew, must have been heady, provocative of strange desires.

Even a man as occupied with Spartan living and the stratagems of war as the Duke of Wellington, was moved to unaccustomed tender-ness by the spell cast by the Alhambra and the Generalife. He once had quarters in the latter palace. From his apartment a stairway led down to a walled rose garden. Wellington wrote to his mother, Lady Mornington, in Dublin, in a lyrical style far different from his curt messages to his wife and officers:

> I rest in Granada of Ten Thousand Roses. For you I inclose in this roll *one* of the ten thousand roses I see from my balcony, which I cut at sunrise. A rose by any other name is Granada
>
> ARTHUR.

Generals of his day used a japanned tin tube in which to send both military dispatches and personal letters, hence his mention of a "roll."

Wellington was offered the Alhambra as a gift. After some delib-eration he rejected the offer, saying the palace was too impractical to live in. He asked instead for a few rose bushes to transfer to Ireland. The answer to this request was a deluge of "Rosas de Granada." In appreciation of this generosity, Wellington sent a gift of hundreds of nightingales. Today if you walk among the jasmine and ilex groves of the *caminos* nightingales still sing at twilight. Listen carefully and if it is spring mating time you will hear two or three amorous males fighting a duel of song in a concert of desire.

After Wellington left Spain, terrible calamity fell upon the Al-hambra and Generalife. It became partly an asylum for maniacs and a haunt for thieves, beggars, and vagabonds. Cooking fires were lit in the lovely courts. The tiles and mosaics were broken and blackened. Horses and bullocks were stabled in the Court of the Lions and the walls of pavilions were defaced with indecencies as far up as arms could reach. The gardens were plundered, in short such havoc reigned it was thought the palaces never could be repaired for public view. But within the past hundred years, by a miracle of restoration, the buildings have been restored to their ancient beauty and once more stand forth in all the perfection of their delicate detail.

Every visitor to Spain is interested to hear about the castles, convents, and country houses that have been turned into *paradores*. These are hotels run under the auspices of the Spanish Tourist Department. One of the most agreeable *paradores*, from every standpoint, is the rehabilitated Convent of San Francisco close to the Alhambra gardens in Granada. Here, under arcaded terraces awash with huge pink, yellow, and red roses, one may lunch or dine in shade and quiet. The excellent food is enhanced by a wondrous view. In the walled garden one may wander and pick peaches, figs, and apricots for dessert.

While Granada is triumphantly Moorish, the cathedral is a grandiose gesture of Renaissance magnificence, as befits the tomb-church of Ferdinand and Isabella. The naves soar into infinity and a cold gloom rides the place. But it is unquestionably grand. The *reja* in front of the recumbent effigies of the royal pair is sumptuous in black bronze with intricately carved figures of heretics enduring the tortures of the Inquisition. This work of Bartolomé de Jaén, despite its gruesome subject, with the figures of courtiers watching all manner of torture, forming a frieze across the top of the screen, is so beautifully wrought, the design so richly flowing, that the entire screen does not accent horror any more than the many manifestations of the Crucifixion. From any standpoint this *reja* of Ferdinand and Isabella of Castile and the Infanta Juana is considered by the most critical beholder to be a masterpiece of wrought metal. The remains of the king, queen, and infanta are interred in a dark crypt under the tombs reached by a treacherous staircase. In a vault, off by itself, lies the Infanta Juana, the pitiful religious fanatic whom the people called Juana la Loca; as lonely in death as during her life, imprisoned, and for half a century tormented by hallucinations that it was she, not Christ, who hung nailed upon the Cross.

The church, Cartuja of the Assumption, has a robust gaiety, a carnival of ornamentation. The high naves are fluted and scrolled to the last inch. Chapels, confession boxes, and cabinets for reliquaries are a mélange of ivory and ebony inlay, colored marbles, tortoise-shell doors topped by gilded candelabra holding forests of candles. An immense urn of brilliant flowers is painted in each of the lunettes over the sacristy. I have seldom seen a church where the air of spectacular frenzy was so sustained.

If Cartuja of the Assumption was frenzy, when I arrived at Sacromonte it was bedlam. It was "men's day" with a vengeance. Hundreds of men were squatting on their hunkers watching a series of cock fights, and the wine flagons passed from hand to hand rapidly. True to form, the sun was dying in a rage of Spanish red and gold. The nondescript clothes of the men took on a patina of gold, lending the scene the unreal quality of an old, frayed tapestry.

Usually the brilliant hackle feathers are the beauty of fighting cocks, but the breed of cockerel raised in Spain for fighting is a most curious fowl. Long and rangy of leg, with big sharp spurs, the body is small and the neck scrawny, and devoid of feathers. Oddly nervous, the cocks seemed to be afflicted with St. Vitus Dance, hopping up and down, pecking savagely at their breasts and wings. I was told the birds are fed ground hot peppers in their cornmeal just before a bout. Ragged of plumage, dirty and drab in color, these miserable looking cocks, depending for weapons on natural spurs and needle-point sharpened beaks, fight to the death like fiends possessed. As I watched, a sallow individual blared forth on a cornet. Instantly all the rings were cleared of fighting birds which were crammed into wicker cages. Then two men, each bearing a much finer specimen of fighting cock, appeared from either side of the square attended by a group of admirers very like the entourage of a popular matador in Seville. This was to be the prize event of the day. As a ring was being staked out, the women from the caves of Sacromonte approached in weaving columns like a parade. Arm in arm, by twos, threes, or in groups, the gitanas circled the square. The men, for the moment, were intent on the fight. Shouting encouragement or invective, the bout was staged. In a short time blood and sodden feathers lay all around, but the victor, a lethal-eyed bird, was held aloft and acclaimed. By now it was nearly dark. The whole mob retired to the caves and the floors were cleared for *zambra*. Beds, chairs, and tables were hoisted by rope and tackle to hang from the roofs of the caves. Big shaded oil lamps shed light in a pool in the center of the floor. Dancing started. Dark-faced men in tight black suits and flat-brimmed black hats worn dipped forward over the eyebrows sat with guitars at the ready. Gitanas in the full, ruffled skirts of pink, red yellow, and green, dotted with black coin spots, adjusted short black neck shawls and took castanets from old women who had once been dancers. A few twangs, a clack-clack-clack, and the evening was away.

I saw flamenco and *seguidilla Manchega* danced till the furniture hanging from the ceiling rattled in unison with the *palmada* of clapping bystanders and stamp of dancers' heels. A halt was called after about an hour, and I was shown some of the caves, considered the last word in luxury. Some gitanas, like Lolita Medina and La Carmenita (Pilár Carmen) are renowned dancers, who live in caves of four and five rooms, where pictures, mostly of themselves, cover the pink or blue walls, brocade portières divide the rooms, crystal chandeliers hang from the ceiling, and a modernly equipped bathroom is shown with tremendous pride.

I like the less luxurious caves, the ones that have not changed in way of life or in manner of decoration in the four hundred years gitanas have lived on Sacromonte. One cave in particular, where two old sisters, La Lolita and La Faraona, live together. It is a small one, the walls rough-hewn and plastered with posters of matadors of fifty years ago, vying with all sorts of relics, images and chromos of La Macarena, a Virgin especially loved by gypsies. The walls and tables are covered with copper and pottery cooking utensils, made in the old Moslem bazaar in Granada. Strings of peppers, garlic, hams, sausages hang in pungent array. On a rack hang brilliant, slightly bedraggled shawls, worn long ago by the sisters when they danced *seguidilla* and flamenco. La Lolita, wizened and gray, once danced *sequiriya gitana* (vaguely related to *seguidilla*) and *cachucha* for King Alfonso XIII when he visited Sacromonte. From a tortoise-shell box La Lolita took a gold comb, much like those worn by the women of Valencia. King Alfonso had given it to her for her spirited dancing of the difficult *cachucha*. But of all the treasures in the cave La Faraona's bed, of red painted wood, so high with mattresses she must have had to climb in by ladder, was her pride. Tied to each of the four bedposts was a bunch of cerise, magenta, pink, and yellow paper flowers she had once worn atop her raven hair.

I took the road to Málaga by way of Loja, a dusty village in appearance more African than Tetuan. Archidona appeared as I drove out of a long stretching cork forest. It proved a gleaming pink town, where I saw for the first time banana trees march round the plaza instead of palm.

I came away with the memory of an excellent wine. A *tinto*, Marqués de Murrieta, a tart, full-bodied vintage that I have asked for elsewhere many times since. A dessert was placed before me which I liked exceedingly, bananas cooked in orange juice, chilled, and sprinkled with slivered blanched almonds.

I had just sighted the sapphire-blue tile domes of churches in Antequera, gleaming against a paler sky like so many inverted tulips, when I had a flat tire. Luck was halfway with me, for only a few hundred yards down the road I saw a bunch of grape vines hanging from a yardarm, which in Spain denotes the ever-welcome wine shop. I parked the car on the side of the road before the shop. Soon I had made a deal with two young loungers to put on my spare tire, for which I would give each a bottle of wine, plus whatever pesetas they should ask. Inside the shop I took a glass of wine myself. On the wall over a long bench I noticed a strange sort of picture. A kind of still life or shadow box arrangement enclosed in a cheap gold frame. Glass, thick with fly specks, covered a large square of black velvet. Spread fan-wise on this was a yellow satin cape, embroidered in red and pink carnations, heavily accented with spangles. Light from a small candle in a glass cup, such as are placed under the image of the Virgin, flickered fitfully, striking sparks of light from the spangles. A name was traced in gold on the velvet. I squinted to read out loud. "Miguel Lopez Gorríto."

A voice called from behind a long table where the *patrón* had been polishing glasses. "El Gorríto, that brave one he fought—"

I turned quickly around. "I know—on stilts—the wildest bulls. I heard all about his fearlessness a few days ago in the middle of hell."

The man looked surprised, so I told him about meeting the brothers from Serón in the Vega de Guadix, hot as inferno. Then I asked him how it happened that so many of the personal belongings of El Gorríto, all having to do with his prowess in corrida, were scattered hither and yon around the countryside. The man said that after the matador had retired from corrida he fell desperately ill. His savings dwindled away on expensive operations. His mother was destitute. So friends of Gorríto gathered together his considerable wardrobe from palmy days, his swords, and presents from admirers not yet gone for pawn, and made a caravan around the country selling each article for what they could get.

III

"I would not take gold for that cape, señor. El Gorríto always wore it on his entrance into the ring on Easter Sunday corrida."

The *patrón* poured me a glass of wine just as the two young fellows came in announcing my spare tire was ready for the road. Wine was poured for each of them. Four glasses were raised to the cape. Again I had encountered—was it the ghost of El Gorríto? This being Spain and myself traveling its length and breadth I would doubtless meet him again.

Antequera on the road to Málaga is a lazy town. The atmosphere is Moorish and Baroque with none of it noteworthy. There is, I am told, a good *parador* in a garden, but the town is mostly a stop over for lunch by persons driving between Málaga and Granada. I did see one fine palace, the walls pastiche, blanched pale violet, set in a tangle of crimson oleanders. The Rococo iron-work balconies were handsome. A nearly obliterated ruin of a Roman circus was excavated a few years ago near the town. It was then discovered Antequera had once been a large Roman military center when Marcus Aurelius was bearing down on Málaga (called Malaca then) to sack the opulent city of her silver mines.

As I drove towards the mountains over which I must pass to reach Málaga, I saw old, flat-roofed houses, Moorish in style, standing in banana groves, the ragged leaves like Fringed Banners under the tall elegance of shivery hazelnut trees. High walls covered with yellow, black, and green Moorish tiles divided these gardens from the road. A cheerful point was the green luster pineapple finials atop the gate posts. These caught the light in a thousand facets and attracted flocks of starlings, as moths are bemused by candle flames. Along the road, ever since I had left Antequera, I had noticed roughly carved, lichened milestones, bronze-scaled with age. These bore deeply incised Roman numerals and the name Marcus Aurelius.

Up and up the road climbed, through elephant-hide rock defiles until suddenly I drove out onto a plateau. The first stirring panorama of Málaga lay far below, shaped like a harp—a silver harp, for silver has for centuries been the shield and buckler of this coveted city, first mined by the Phoenicians, who, through laziness let her slip through their loosely-held net. Then under Marcus Aurelius, Malaca was made to disgorge her treasures. Like Cádiz it was the Moors who turned Malaca from her iron and silver mines to become a great seaport and a city of earthly pleasures. I came down from the mountains at Vélez-Málaga, and drove through vineyards of Muscatel and Málaga grapes toward the walls of the town.

Chapter 8

"AND SO WE CAME TO RONDA, ON ITS STUPENDOUS GORGE...."

THE road from Vélez to Málaga is like driving between furrows in a vineyard. On either side are terraces of Muscatel and Málaga grapes, the fronds so curling and far reaching they seem to clutch at passersby. Inland range low hills, streaked with the vivid purple of saffron blossoms. Nowhere, save the Vale of Kashmir, is saffron grown in such quantity as in Andalusia. Few persons who use saffron know what this precious spice is, or where it is grown. In flower the saffron plant looks much like a crocus. It thrives on plateaus or terraces where the sun is caught in full radiance. Saffron powder is the sun in color and, to taste, probably as near the flavor of sunlight as mortals will ever know. Along the road from Vélez to Torremolinos, when saffron is in bloom, large areas of pale mauve and dark purple, for the blossoms vary in tone, add a strikingly beautiful effect to an already beautiful landscape. The flowers are dried in the sun and the pollen extracted by hand. This pollen constitutes the powder that is sprinkled in food to impart a golden color and a subtle flavor. The "imperial flavor," a Spanish chef once said to me, as he added a pinch of saffron to a cream of celery soup, thereby turning it to liquid gold. When mixed with water, saffron forms a rich yellow dye. Málaga saffron is famous for strength of color and bouquet. It is used in Spain not only as a spice but as pigment for watercolor paint and, in Andalusia, to dye the hand-woven linen shirts and capes worn by men on market days.

The all-year-round equable climate of Málaga is legendary. Avienus, that first famous tourist in Spain to write of his travels, said, "Malaca has a glory all its own. It is haunted by the sun." I asked a

Málagueño about the much-touted climate. "Do you ever have dull days?" He answered, "December is cold and gray, it can even be very wet. Do not plan to spend Christmas in Málaga."

An Englishman who has resided in Málaga for twenty years, raised a glass of old Muscatel wine of notable vintage, and answered my question in this manner. "Taste this wine slowly. Let it lie on your tongue, then slip warm and soft down your throat." He did just this, and nodded his head. "You will know then what the climate of Málaga is like."

Whatever the weather in the long run may be, her devotees are amazingly staunch.

I find the city has a worldly elegance akin to Seville. Málagueños have an air of refinement, an easy balance, a sway to the eddies of life, which is exceedingly attractive. Their señoritas are bewitchingly beautiful. Time, *as* time, means nothing to the Málagueños. No one ever makes an appointment for a definite hour. "I'll meet you between siesta and promenade" (from four to seven o'clock).

Everywhere one is served Málaga wines or sherry. The famed Muscatel wine is too sweet for my taste, but the pale dry sherry drunk from tall, slender glasses like the "specimen" vase for a single perfect rose, I find a wonderful spur to appetite. And appetite is important in Málaga. Food, particularly fish in any form, is carefully selected here and prepared with the infinite care seldom found outside of Paris. Fruit from the sea is infinitely various, but my prime favorite is *boqueron*, the regional specialty. *Boqueron* is fresh anchovy, which is netted in the rich fisheries from Estepona to Nerja. When *boqueron* is served, either by vendors with portable charcoal cooking braziers on the sands of La Playa de Carmen or at Hotel Miramar, it comes fried in fan-shaped bunches, five fish to the fan, with a slice of lemon and a small dish of crisp, hot almonds dusted with saffron.

Málaga is a rewarding city in which to wander. I have great affection for the cathedral fronting on Plaza del Obispo. I *should* keep away from this plaza with the rousing Baroque air. Shops for antiquities line the square, the windows piled with loot or treasure. What *is* treasure, and the longing to acquire? To me treasure is, after one has dreamed one's fill, yet *more*.

Having an inflated acquisitive instinct I walk up and down del Obispo murmuring, "No, no—no more," under my breath. The allure of these windows is insidious. My purse is flattened in no time.

But it is lovely loot. I have bought moonstones so luminous the chain of stones glows in the night. Spanish brocade of green and yellow, heavy with tinsel threads, and old red velvet, the color so rich and deep the folds seem to have swallowed the fire of rubies.

The cathedral has an endearing nickname, diminutive for so huge a pile. La Manquita, or "little one armed woman."

If one asks a boy in the street where the cathedral is he will hold one arm flat to his side, the other straight up in the air and ask you, "La Virgen de la Victoria, or La Manquita?" knowing perfectly well all the while which church you mean.

The story of the cathedral is rife with superstition and fatal accidents to its builders. On the sight of a Moorish mosque, the walls of the cathedral began to rise in 1528 from unfinished plans by Enrique de Egás and Diego de Siloë. Both architects were killed in mysterious accidents within a fortnight of one another. All work was suspended because frightened workmen said it was the spirit of the mosque which had been torn down, haunting the scaffolds. Not until the eighteenth century was construction renewed. This was entrusted to Jose de Bada who altered the Renaissance design to exuberant Baroque. No one seems to know why, but of the twin belfries planned by de Egás and de Siloë, to add dignity and symmetrical balance to the towering yellow stone mass, only one was ever built. It was this architectural deformity that caused the nickname.

Inside, the cathedral seems too ponderous in ornament. The naves are encrusted with pink, white, and gold embellishments, a blaze of relics. Forests of candles flicker on the usual dark paintings of maternal sorrow and saints in anguish. It is the three great carved outer doors, opening from flights of steps, that I find as important in design as any in Spain. Immense in scale, these doors are important in ecclesiastical art, for there are no others quite like them. And each one bears an appropriate and resounding name. El Sol's (Sun's), Las Cadenas' (Chains') and Perdón's (Pardon's). Everything about the cathedral has a high, imposing air, even the worshipers. For morning mass, stand in front of the Palace Obispo, seat of the Archbishop of Málaga rising at one side of the sweep of steps leading from the plaza to the door called Perdón's, and watch the arrival of highly-varnished broughams, with teams of beautiful bays, liveried coachman and footman on the box, the black curtains tightly drawn against glare of sun or peering eyes. A line of these equipages will drive up, out will step elderly women, or young girls attended by duennas. All are in black, some wearing a comb and mantilla. This pageantry of devotion in black elegance, against the high yellow steps, is the definition of Spain as it has been for centuries. The Spanish see no reason for changing.

The church called Santiago's (St. James') was founded by Ferdinand and Isabella, first as a monastic order, housed in a long stone building. Later this was enriched to church status, and we see here the fine Castilian hand of Isabella la Catolica. Santiago's is somber, ponderous, as grim as the pallid face of her daughter Mad Juana, gazing out from painted canvas in the sacristy. It is said in Spain that Isabella always rejected the fact that her daughter was insane, whether from religious mania or from deeper cause. The queen practically cannonized the infanta, so that her image, in one form or another, stares out of dark naves in countless churches in Spain. Santiago's has a magnificently graceful Mudéjar belfry where hang bells said to have the deepest tone in Spain. It is indeed so low and deep, as to be sepulchral, and a horribly depressing sound to be awakened by.

A sixteenth-century palace of the Condes de Buenavista has elaborate architraves bordering the windows featuring pine tassels and cones. Wooden shutters, floridly painted in scenes of the hunt in the mountain regions of Spain have long interested me to the point where I have promised myself to paint shutters in the same manner for my house in Ireland.

The Moors really spread themselves when they "rebuilt" Málaga, which was their boast. According to historians Málaga was rivaled only by Granada as their favorite city in Spain. In conception the citadel, or Alcazába, above the port is unrivaled for beauty of line and proportion of the slender flanking towers. The long, undulating walls of the Alcazába are built of a stone more porous and gray in tone than the red and ochre of Alhambra. A sort of rose blush, which turns to deep violet in the shadows of twilight and under the moon to a silvery tone of pink, like Orient pearl. Because of the porous nature of the stone, time has pitted the walls and towers until Alcazába is hung with vines and rock plants, valerian, cactus and spicy pinks. The seeds were planted, I was told, by "winds, and birds from Africa."

No matter where one walks along the wide alamedas or in narrow, huddled alleys of the old quarter, where leaning houses were built by the Phoenicians, the eye is always coaxed upward to the castellated Alcazába.

In antique times the crescent port of Málaga vied with Tyre and Carthage as a magnet for merchant ships. Avienus wrote, "So clouded with sails is the roadstead of Malaca that some ships must anchor in the open sea."

When Carthaginian and Roman ships put into this port their captains were driven demented trying to keep their sailors in hand. It became the fashion for sailors to desert ship, to live in idleness in this salubrious city.

Today Málaga is still a magnet, and ships wine, raisins, cane sugar, honey, cotton, and dates, to most countries in the world. The famous *bodegas*, establishments where grapes are pressed, and where every step in preparing wine for market may be seen, are worth devoting an entire day to visit. The method of showing the various stages of making Málaga and Muscatel wine is a leisurely process and should on no account be hurried. I was conducted through Bodega Hermosa by a most charming woman, a director of the firm, who regaled me with stories of how certain visitors react to the wine sampling. I saw every phase of wine making and sampled seven or eight choice vintages, without mishap, because I ate olives and almonds in between sampling. Walking through the long aisles of casks, dark mahogany in color, aromatic with long cradling of the rich liquid, a halt was suddenly made.

"Here," said my guide, "is our special pride. A musky liqueur type, our oldest recipe."

A man was summoned who pipes the wine by long metal tubes from the casks. A different glass is used for each vintage. But when I was taken to a large reception room for the last sampling—the greatest of all Hermosa wines, a Málaga grape brandy, Hermoso Oro—the glass was drained, then cut by a diamond with my device J.R.* and placed on a long shelf in an even longer corridor, among thousands of other marked glasses.

I was intrigued by swarms of honey bees droning around the open vats, particularly those where sweet Muscatel grapes had been but lately pressed. In a constant state of mild intoxication some of the bees fall to the ground to be trodden on, while others fly away through the ventilator slits in the roof, to line their wax combs with redolent syrup. This wine-flavored honey is rare to come by, consequently much sought after.

Next to distilling wine, Málagueños are most concerned with celebrating *Semana Santa* (Holy Week). What most distinguishes the procession through the streets in Málaga from those in Seville, Granada, and possibly Valladolid, are the *pasos*, or floats, always carried in twos, one for Mater Dolorosa, one for a representation of the Passion. *Penitentes* in costume, often barefoot, represent the various *cofradias* of the city. The *penitentes* of the *Sepulcro* pass silently in cypress black. *Santo Domingo de la Soledad*, in azure blue capes with sashes of crimson. *Misterios Dolorosao* are wrapped in mantles of black over tunics of purple and silver, but all wear the penitential *capilla*, a tall pointed hat with a circular cape covering the face like a hood, falling to below the chest. On the front of this is emblazoned the insignia of whatever fraternity. Slits are cut for the eyes in the manner of the conical masked headdresses of the Misericordias of Rome.

The sound of organ music heard through the open doors of the churches proclaims the procession is about to start, and a hush falls on the people packed tightly on either side of the "penitential way." Eyes are watchful, in awe, for the figures forming groups on the *pasos* are almost frighteningly lifelike, and no detail of gore or suffering is spared. Mater Dolorosa is tragically beautiful, her features modeled in the last despair of anguish. Mantles of gold- and silver-embroidered velvet spread out fan-wise, trailing to the ground. In the light of torches and myriad candles the sumptuous fabrics seem brilliant as lunar scarves trailing from Aurora Borealis. Violet and pink tissue veils crowned with a tiara of jeweled spikes or stars sway perilously, as the Mother of Sorrows is carried, none too steadily, on the shoulders of strongly built porters from the dockyards. Sometimes twenty bearers are needed to support a *paso* on its long journey through the streets.

As the night wanes, the silent throngs become articulate. Prayers and chants murmur, rising to cries of ecstasy, as the *pasos* are heaped with flowers tossed at the foot of the cross. Mater Dolorosa becomes almost hidden in heaps of roses, carnations (the most Spanish of all flowers), sheaves of lilies tied with gauze and ribbons, and knots of jasmine. The air becomes almost stifling with warring smells. The acrid and musty effluvia of humanity, spice, incense, the burnt-wax odor of guttering candles and, inevitable at any gathering in Spain, appetizing *patatas fritas,* thin shells of potato frying in olive oil.

Hotel Miramar is a most agreeable place to stay in Málaga. Not so

Moorish in style as most of the buildings, it has rather the air of a big neo-classic house in Madrid. Situated on a point of land surrounded by palms and flowery gardens, from the terraces one has a sweeping panorama of the sea and harbor. The rooms are airy and those facing the sea have a balcony, so desirable a place to have one's breakfast on a sunny morning. A whole book of infinite variety could be written about the pleasures of balconies in Spain.

Food is notably good at Miramar. I ate *gazpacho* here, of an excellence. This soup, served iced, is, if one may call it so, a liquid salad, because of the wide variety of shredded raw vegetables, with an accompaniment of croutons, served on a big tray, to spoon into the tart soup. This soup base is a bit like a clear *madrilene* with a dash of lemon juice. For lunch on a hot day I know of nothing so refreshing. There is an excellent *parador*, Hostal Nacional, featuring its arcaded terrace restaurant more than guest rooms, which are small and few in number. Situated on a hill behind Málaga, it is a wonderful place to have late dinner and watch the lighted city and harbor activity with the string of lighthouses trailing beacons up and down the coast. In the daytime the view is equally splendid, but completely different. Now the coast is seen for miles, as far as Salobreña with its "little Gibraltar" rock, covered in pines. Follow along with this bird's-eye view and look down into the arena of the bull ring, dramatically situated at the end of a palm-fringed alameda close to the sea. On down the coast to Point Cala del Moral with its crumbling Moorish village long deserted, but still haunted by a sultan on an Arab stallion, who of nights rides down the hill to frighten motorists on the road to Torremolinos.

On the same ridge as the hostel is a landmark well known to mariners since the days of Carthaginian coasters. The Gibralfara, a Phoenician-Moorish fort, built on foundations of an earlier Iberian fortress castle. One of its towers was a hollow "drum" lighthouse. Slaves were forced to cut wood in the nearby forests to keep the fire stoked. Even during the day it was not let die out. Fresh fuel was added at the hour when Helios drove his horses of the sun down the sky to send them plunging in clouds of steam into the darkness of Ocean. For centuries this furnace of flame and sparks raged into the sky at night to warn sailors they were nearing the Pillars of Hercules, guarding Outer Ocean, which was to superstitious sailors only The Great Mist where the world ceased in Limbo.

Today Gibralfara, a once forbidding hulk, has been tamed to

shelter gardeners growing produce for market. Around the base of Moorish walls twist pumpkin vines. I saw golden cucumbers and melons near a little pool shaded by fig and mulberry trees, where children were singing their lungs out having a birthday party of juicy melons. I asked if they had no cake. One little girl, who I thought looked a bit green around the gills, pointed up to the *parador*.

"Yes, a big cake. It is up there, for later," and then she rubbed her middle. "It will have to be a lot later. I've eaten too much melon."

The seacoast suburbs of Málaga are highly thought of all over Spain. People come from as far away as Oviedo, in the gaunt Asturias, to build small villas at Marbella, Torremolinos, or El Limonar which are always surrounded by large gardens. One reason for the popularity of this region, besides the delicately-balanced climate, is the long string of sandy bathing beaches. Near Málaga is the enchanting La Playa de Banos del Carmen, where, after a bathe, I eat my weight in freshly grilled or fried *langostinos, boquerones* and crabs-mayonnaise (a sauce now international, which was invented in Spain). Torre del Mar has a most charming house, Pension La Roca, to dine or to stay for a holiday, provided you can get in, for it is extremely popular. It is an old manor house with a galleried hall like a medieval castle, but much more comfortably furnished in chintzes and gay colors. One eats at tables on the rocky headland jutting out into the sea. Torremolinos is lovely and pine scented with a number of agreeable hotels. The one I like best is Santa Clara. The house has the air of a happily lived-in Spanish country house. A regiment of dolls of all nations sit stiffly on the staircase appraising the arriving guests. It reminds me of a notable collection of dowagers at a court ball.

Of all the villages near Málaga, I like staying at Nerja. It is a simple village, given over to fishing and crushing olives for oil. The two odors mingle pleasantly, leavened by the salt tang of the sea. I have stayed here before for a week, painting from morning to night. So I drove out from Málaga to stay for a night, just to renew my acquaintance with the almost mythological white oxen who act as nursemaids to get the unwieldly fishing boats out of the narrow harbor into open water. Outside my room was a wide balcony. I was standing there waiting for the nightly pageant of oxen, fishermen, boats, and the devious sea, when I was told the story of a local Romeo and Juliet drama which had happened on this very balcony a few months before.

The beautiful granddaughter of the *patrón* of the *taberna*—I was assured she was "like a madonna" by everyone from whom I heard different versions of the affair—had come to live with him. She and the village ne'er-do-well promptly fell in love. Sudden young love, that consumes and pays no mind to anything else. The grandfather raged. Twice the boy was caught climbing to the balcony. Further meeting was forbidden the two young lovers. One night they took a boat and rowed into the path of the moon. The boat was found drifting near Melomár, but the boy and girl were never seen again. I was asked by a raffish-looking individual, smelling very high of garlic and wine, if I would paint for him a picture of the tragedy as he described it. I got out of that one by drawing a bleary-eyed portrait of himself.

After I had disposed of my sitter and he was showing his portrait to cronies, I watched the teams of oxen hitched to the fishing boats by ropes. The oxen are so white, so hugely built, yet wonderfully gentle, wearing red embroidered headdress with élan and no fuss. It is a tricky business to maneuver the bulky fishing boats across the sandbar and into open water. After the oxen have performed their job, they are allowed to swim by themselves. I could tell they were enjoying this swim, holding their decorated heads proudly out of the water.

In the pine forest of Fuengirola, where the dark branches sweep into the sea, I spent a night at Hotel Alhamar. This is an experience not to be lightly missed, for in one way it is like staying in a great Spanish house that is a museum of treasures of the Renaissance. Not a cold, roped-off museum but a wonderfully comfortable series of rooms, where are grouped pieces of furniture, gilded leather screens from Córdoba and so on. If for no other reason one should visit Alhamar to see the tremendous fireplace breast of carved and gilded wood extending from floor to ceiling in one of the rooms now used as a lounge. In rare beauty of carving and patina this piece compares with some of the notable *rejas* and *retablos* in Spanish cathedrals.

Many sportsmen come here from Madrid and Seville, even from London and New York. I saw the name of a friend of mine from Virginia in the guest book. I had not even known he was in Europe. The shooting all around Fuengirola is excellent. Rough shooting in the sand grass close to the sea where wild duck and snipe abound. Woodcock, quail, and partridge are found in satisfying numbers nearer Torremolinos and back in the brush of primitive Monda and Torro. In the reedy marshes around Estepona a species of big-bodied wild swans fly over from Africa to nest. These heavily-plumaged birds (the beige feathers are used by women of Estepona to make little shoulder capes to sell to tourists) make remarkably good eating when roasted on a spit over a slow fire, and served with mushrooms.

In Estepona ancient shipbuilding yards have flourished there ever since the enterprising Phoenicians set up "ways" of pitch-hardened pine on which to lay the keel and ribs for their questing ships. Pine "ways" still creak, hammers ring on hand-made cleats and rigging is twisted on winches in the old manner, as fishing ships take form under the skilful hands of men who have inherited the art of ship-fashioning down the centuries. Nor do these craftsmen vary the design of the hulls or alter the triangular shape of the sails, still called "Phoenician cut."

I should have liked to stay longer at Taberna de la Mar in Estepona to eat a dish of *calamares*, a curious fish found in crevasses of the rocks when the tide is out. When freshly fried in olive oil these fish resemble French-fried onions. But I had had this fish in Málaga and I was eager to get on to Ronda to arrive at my favorite hour of sunset.

I left the coast road to drive into the mountains at Casares where Moorish houses are painted so many variations of strong blue the town seems a kind of orchestration of the color with each shade striving for first place.

In Dublin I once picked up a small, tattered book on a stall in front of a musty old second-hand shop in Ashton Quay. Bound in leather, the book had once been brilliant red. That was probably what first caught my notice. Flipping over the pages, my eye was caught by the opening words of a chapter. "And so we came to Ronda, on its stupendous gorge." That was all I needed. I bought the book and read a sort of honeymoon travel journal, the kind of stilted phrasing and rhapsody so popular in the early nineteenth century, but full of interesting detail of an older time. A young Englishman had taken his bride to Spain some time after Waterloo. I gathered he had been in Wellington's famous personal guard although he never said in what regiment. The young officer and his bride had intended only a brief visit in Ronda. It turned out that they stayed the rest of their lives. In fact, they were ancestors of the man who first started the Hotel Victoria. Fronting the gorge, it is a landmark in the country-side for many miles.

A strange, barbaric "never-never land," however long I plan to stay at Ronda it is hard for me to resist making it much longer. Entirely surrounded by sierras, Ronda bulks against the sky as a figure-head massively carved from living rock. It seems the mighty keystone for an arch over the amphitheatre of the Tajo, a chasm that divides the town in two. After I had left the blue houses of Casares the road became more lonely. At first I passed one or two villages on rocky crags, hardly discernible for the houses are built of slag from the rock face. Then solitude enveloped me for a while until I passed a church that looked as if somebody in desperate mood had swiped a whitewash brush across the portal and then run off. Goats bounded in front of the car, coming from nowhere and leaping apparently into infinity. Finally began the ascent in earnest, through desolate gullies. I ran out from Plutonian shadows past a cluster of half-derelict houses marked on my map as Pedro Alcantara. This ruin was given over to goats and dark-visaged goatherds curious, but poised for flight, wild as the hawks circling overhead. Wildness upon wildness piled, in this always ascending, tortuously winding road over the mountains. Villages and people are left far behind. Now and again a dust-covered man, a road patrol, flew past me on a motor-cycle.

Gaining the top of the watershed, I seemed lost in the immensity of panoramas on every side. Indescribably grand is the sight of three great mountain ranges glazed in umber, brown, rose, and the metallic colors of oil slick on green harbor water. Spread above is the limitless sky and soaring eagles. For these rocks are the empire, and the battle-ground, of the largest and fiercest eagles this side of the Himalayas.

Coming out of a high walled defile, at last there was the sight of Ronda, seated among the clouds on its gorge with an air of the un-attainable. Down from the mountains the road leads through the *vega* to the foot of the Tajo or Ronda gorge. Now the Roman fragments appear. I passed half ruined arches of two Roman aque-ducts, a lesser triumphal arch, a few pillars lying in dust, and rank grasses, which once had marked a victorious way. Many gateways and parts of Roman walls stood stark in the *vega* or in the midst of plowed fields. These were once the entrance to fortified farmhouses, with walls intact and gates working properly as late as 1700.

The actual arrival at Ronda, after climbing the last steep road through the impressive Arco Romano, does not let one down. From the old Arab bazaar quarter to what Rondese call the new quarter, one crosses the high, single-arch bridge over the Tajo. At the end of the bridge is Plaza Puente Nuevo. Cafés around the plaza were

FIESTA COSTUMES. MOTHER AND DAUGHTER
Puebla de GUZMAN (HUELVA·ANDALUSIA)

just filling up as I arrived. Waiters were carrying pitchers of the highly regarded *sangria*, an iced punch made from a light Marqués de Riscal red wine spiced and enriched by sliced peaches, oranges, and big strawberries from the lower farms, with a dash of cognac added for "fire."

The café habitués were, I noticed, looking eagerly toward the bridge. How well I knew why. The usual entertainment put on, gratis, by the starlings was about ready to begin. I had sat spellbound by this show before, and fully expected to again. No one knows for a fact in what era it all started. Around five o'clock every afternoon, except in rain or gales of wind, not too rare at this altitude, hundreds of starlings appear from nests down among the rocks to dart through paper or cardboard hoops made by small boys or "boys" of all ages. The hoops are about ten inches in diameter, scarcely more than the breadth of the starling's outspread wings. These hoops are skimmed into the air above the bridge (the birds scorn to perform except at the Puente Nuevo entrance to the bridge). At dragon-fly-speed, twittering in hysterical excitement, a starling darts through the hoops. A bird almost never misses the hole; sometimes two or three birds may try for the same hoop, to fight it out in mid-air. Many a paper hoop falls to earth torn to pieces. I skimmed some hoops offered to me by a little boy whose eyes were popping with the exertion of trying to be three or four places at once. Action in the air is too swift to tell how many bull's eyes I scored by proxy. The starlings keep up this performance at high speed for perhaps half an hour, then, as suddenly as the flock arrived, they are off again to rest and preen their feathers on the roof tops. There will be no repeat performance until next day at the same hour. I expect there is a sort of gymnasts' guild to which the starlings belong, forbidding them to perform more than once a day. The whole affair is taken very seriously and the boys and men argue over the weight of heavy paper or cardboard for skimming as intently as crack tennis players discussing the weight of a racquet.

The Moors made a last stronghold of Ronda as they tried to do in Granada. Because of its position they managed to hold out longer in Ronda, which they had retained for eight hundred years. The extremely handsome houses one sees today, facing on narrow streets in the Arab quarter with the rear of the house terraced in gardens and glass-walled patios looking out over the sierras, are either incorporated into the Moorish walls or actually become a part of the old houses built by rich Arab merchants and caïds. Many *hidalgo* families from Seville and Granada have palaces here. Unfortunately economic crises have forced the owners to keep their houses shut for most of the year. But Ronda is an elegant, highly cultured town and the autumn season is noted for musical concerts and literary gatherings and lectures which attract many visitors. I have been in Ronda when it was perishing cold and windy after sunset, the crystal-clear cold of the high mountains, the indigo firmament advertising the constellations. But the summers and autumns are largely still air, sunny but never hot.

A short way from the Puente Nuevo is a small cleared space, semi-circular in shape, to follow the Baroque curve of the eighteenth century Plaza de Toros. In all Spain, I believe this whitewashed stone bull ring has the greatest charm. A perfectly simple, mediumly scaled roundhouse pierced here and there with iron barred windows fitted with coral pink shutters, and solid black bulls'-hide doors. All this serves to point up the magnificent entrance gate, a pendant jewel of yellow marble columns, Rococo scrolled iron balcony surmounted by a garlanded cornice of richly indented molding, and a pediment displaying a flaming marble urn. So splendid, so arrogant in style is this entrance it might grace any Baroque palace in the land. I painted a group of youths in front of this iron-studded door, wearing old torero costumes from the museum. Black netted snoods, red stocking-caps, purple and yellow breeches, and short fringed jackets heavily braided in black silk. The costly gold bullion used on Torero suits today was introduced for the wedding celebrations for Maria Christina of Austria.

The bull ring, the smallest in Spain, is seldom used now for corrida, because important matadors, whose very names on the billboard would insure a record crowd, get claustrophobia when fighting bulls in this restricted space. If they even entertain the idea of coming to Ronda, the price they ask is so prohibitive the mayor shakes his head "No." In fact many Rondese shake their heads likewise and say wistfully, "We must go to Málaga or Seville to see El Toro receive the *suerte*. If our ring were only not so small!" Now, in summer, it is often used for outdoor film shows.

Walking down the hill from the Arab bazaar toward Arco Romano, one sees a strange time-worn structure of great character, the early Renaissance palace of Marqués de Salvatierra. Built in a long wavering line at the triangular junction of two roads, the walls are three stories on the upper incline, six stories on the lower. The high, narrow façade is a glorious piece of theater scenery. Atop a bronze-studded door, leading into a patio walled and floored with ancient Moorish tiles, stand life-size figures of Adam and Eve carved in jasper. Such frank detail is displayed in the carving of the anatomy there is no doubt as to the gender of the figures. There are streets of fine Baroque houses with bold embellishment, as contrast to narrow lanes of two-story white Moorish houses, the front almost entirely swallowed by black or red *rejas*, bordered by hanging vines and plants of fuchsia and geranium.

A curiously unstable old house built precariously on a hilly street cobbled in cannon-ball stones is shown as the place where Cervantes wrote a greater part of *Don Quixote*. From the window of a low-ceilinged room under the tiles spreads a view straight out of the first days of Creation. Chasms, mountains, sky, and then more distances to far sierras. The day I looked out of this window the sky was raging for storm, like the most tortured El Greco canvases.

The church of Santa Maria Mayor is elaborate, scrolled and floriated in Baroque style, with groups of "engaged" or collected pillars of jasper. The sacristy is hung with fifteen or more pictures of the Virgin, all dark and emotional in mood. An odd thing is that each one was painted by a different artist in a different period, yet in each presentation the Virgin has the same face and expression, to the last tear.

There is a convent called Las Floras, where the chapel opens out of a patio to display a Virgin in carved silver, clothed in sky-blue velvet. The face and figure are childlike, but a curiously pagan air surrounds the niche. The tips of silver toes touch a silver crescent moon carved with a grotesque gargoyle satyr-like face. A compelling silence reigns, all is bathed in luminous sub-aqueous light.

One of the major sights in Ronda is the Roman-Moorish baths. Within the past few years a remarkable discovery was made by a man who was out with his dogs for a morning walk. While ranging fields in the *vega* not far from Arco Romano, his foot slipped into what he supposed to be a badger hole. But hearing the crunch of glass he looked more closely. Red, blue, and green glass splinters clung to his muddy boots. He had stepped into a window over a ventilation duct in one of the many rooms of what proved to be subterranean Roman baths. At his own expense, the man started excavations. It was found that with pools, long intersecting corridors, and rooms once used for steam baths or rubbing down, the whole foundation covered two acres of ground. Water was supplied from mountain springs brought across the *vega* by aqueducts. There had even been a system for heating water by fires under brick furnaces. The government became interested and took over the excavating job. Millions of pesetas were allotted. Some of the most experienced archeologists obtainable were soon put to work. It was a stupendous task. Now, open to public view, a once vast, luxurious bathing establishment, built first by the Romans, later much elaborated by the Moors, is there for all to visit for a small fee. Marble and stone statues, fluted columns, cornices, and pediments, all the panoply used by the Romans to enrich whatever they built, along with necessities for baths, such as jars for oil and perfumes, old leather buckets, and perforated bronze pipes for spraying unguents adorn the rooms. Moorish glass, tiles, and mosaic were found in good state of preservation. The entrance is down a long ramp, with stables on either side for chariot horses belonging to Roman clients, and later, presumably for Spanish-Arab barbs, the fiery mounts of sultan and caïd. There is even a domitory for bath attendants, with bull's hide hammocks hung from iron rings. It is estimated that three hundred men could have been housed in this great underground room. One wanders at will, then takes refreshment at a small rustic pavilion near the gate. There is a woman, the wife of the caretaker, who walks among the tables, and most old she is. Dressed in voluminous black skirt and gold-laced red bodice, she has a mission, and a story to tell.

While you drink *manzanilla* or coffee, perhaps a cool *sangria* if it is hot, she will pick for you a bouquet of jasmine, from gnarled old bushes of great size. A nosegay tied with red ribbon for the ladies, a boutonnière for the men. Bent almost double with age, Señora Ballta is still smiling. When she presents you with the jasmine she becomes the local historian, relating in a loud cracked voice that the bushes were planted by a Roman emperor. A trifle mixed, some days she says it was Trajan, another day Hadrian, or again Marcus Aurelius. No matter. The señora's ancient charm is winning and the jasmine lovely.

When the Romans held Ronda it was a "pleasure dome" of pavilions in the sky as well as a military center. The long, uphill gradient, winding from the *vega* to the walled town, was known as the "prostitutes' quarter." On one side of the road is a wall. In the thickness of masonry one can still see small, cell-like rooms, each with a tiny slit window. Along one side of the room is a couch of stone. On the other side of "this gay libidinous way" as Via Aphrodite in Alexandria was called by Mark Antony, rises the sheer rock walls of the gorge, with the inevitable caves hollowed out. From preserved documents it is learned this quarter was once the seething heart of Ronda in Roman, probably even more so in Moorish, times.

Prostitutes lived in the caves but carried on their profession in the "room with a view" across the way. The Moors offered all manner of attractions along this road, even opened a bazaar at the foot of the hill and one at the top. The latter called Plaza del Moro, is still in use, but the bedizened whores, representing odd types of women from outlying lands, their faces masks of carmine and antimony, have long since departed. The caves and little cubicles for pandering love at a price are now used by rutting sheep and goats. Here one feels the antique world is still with us but, alas, shorn of its enticing daily round.

As all of us know, savagery has not gone from the world anywhere. In Spain it is manifest in curious ways. It may be indulged in as sport, for revenge, or for survival of the fittest. The evening before I left Ronda I was standing in my window at Hotel Victoria, looking down across the gorge, so close that had I leaped from the window the Tajo would have swallowed me. Far off, the Sierra de Algódonales had caught my eye, graven ramparts of purple and silver fading into black in the dying light. Across my thoughts flashed what Akbar the Mogul emperor called his hashish-eaters' fortress in the Hindu Kush. "The haunt of eagles, the dread of man." Suddenly, against the last pale primrose of the sky I saw first one eagle, not majestically wheeling as so often they do over the gorge, but darting in savage strokes at another eagle below him. I got my race glasses into focus and witnessed an epic battle between two white-hackled male eagles, that fairly ripped the sky apart. Both birds were titans in wing spread, neither gave quarter, this was a fight to the death, with wing quills rigid as sabers, neck hackles sprung straight out; it was a stupendous sight. In rage the eagles let out almost human screams, as one would rise, expand his talons and poise for the stoop. Bloody feathers torn from wings and breasts fluttered earthward. It was darkening rapidly, but in the last rays I saw that the largest eagle was nearly spent. In a mighty swoop he rose, paused and stooped like the Black Avenger, then grasping his opponent by the neck in taloned death grip, shook the life out of his heart. With a last scream of triumph the victor dropped the dead eagle into the dark gorge. For a second he hung motionless against the sky, then rose in sweeps to soar in bloody splendor back to his eyrie.

Collection of John Lindquist, Esq.

Chapter 9

THE PILLARS OF HERCULES
AND CÁDIZ

F rom Ronda to San Roque the road winds always down hill,
erratic as a carnival switchback. For a while the only life one
sees is road menders who clear away boulders fallen from
the crags. These men are so covered by rock dust one can hardly see
them when rounding a curve. Then comes silence and an unpeopled
world. The silence of these unfrequented Spanish mountain roads
always amazes me. A silence, ominous and profound, like a corporeal
presence, so that when gunshot sounds, far off among the crags
(there are chamois about, consequently hunters), one feels that the
silence is as shocked by echoing reverberations among the fastnesses,
as one's self.

For twenty kilometers I had not seen a human being nor a house,
not even a goatherd's hut. I was just pulling out of a gorge into a
space with a view of Gibraltar rising from the sea, far away in the
heat mist, when I met an old, earth-colored woman leading a burro.
The backs of both woman and burro were piled high with bundles of brush and twigs. Where these drudges go is a mystery
of the road. Deep down I went, into a gorge black as pitch, the road
slimy from dripping springs. Then it curved out into civilization.
Below me blazed the blue and ochre town of San Roque.

I sat for a while at a *ventorro* with fishnets hung over the front
from roof to the quay, casting a latticed shade. I drank *sangre de
toros*, a strong red wine, too strong for midday, but there was nothing else to be had. Always it is the bull which is eulogized in Spain.
Even his blood is drunk, literally by the old mountaineers, or figura-
tively, in the wine of that name, by the less venturesome.

132

San Roque is prideful, holds itself aloof because of sheltering in the church of Santa Maria de la Coronada, an image of the Virgin, rushed from mother church in Gibraltar in the dead of night just before the British took The Rock from Spain. The Virgin is not generally on view, or so a verger told me, but I noticed his hand wavered half outstretched, so, for a few pesetas, I was shown the image. She lives most of the time in a plain olive-wood cabinet, very like a confessional box. She is rarely beautiful. Delicate, aristocratic features of pale ivory, untouched by color. To me, her greatest feature is repose. Twice a year she is paraded through the streets and down to the beach to bless the fishermen, the latest catch, and the nets. What gives this Virgin special point is that when she was being brought through a raging storm from Gibraltar to San Roque, in some manner never known, both arms were lost. Now, she is tremendously revered. For a time other arms of wood were attached to her shoulders, but legend has it that these always fell to the floor. After a time no attempt was made to restore them. A voluminous cape of midnight-blue velvet, heavily encrusted with silver embroidery, conceals the lack of arms. She wears a tiara of jeweled stars with a halo in the form of the full moon, emblem of fishermen, the omen of a good run of fish, and she is hung with votive chains and rings.

At a crossroads close to Algeciras is Los Barrios, a most engaging little hill town. Only a clutch of brown and umber houses in Moorish style, struggling to keep upright on either side of a street which is narrow and steep as a ramp. What gives the village character is the bull ring crowning the hill. As one drives toward Los Barrios, this round, white building looks like one of the squat Moorish castles so often seen high above these coast towns. A curious placing of a wide door, a circular window above it, and two oblong windows at the sides, give the effect of a face eternally arrested in surprise. This bull ring is a very thriving concern. A once famous matador, El Bruno, long since retired from corrida, now runs a school for boys who wish to learn the exciting and dangerous profession of bull fighting (and find me a boy in Spain who does not). I watched fifteen or twenty serious-faced youngsters learning from the fat, genial El Bruno the subtle difference between handling the magenta silk cape held in both hands to "dominate" the bull, and the red serge *muleta* held in one hand to conceal the sword from the bull while taking a stance to deliver the final sword thrust.

For miles the seascape is dominated by Gibraltar on one's left, so compelling it fills the eye, for it is ever changing in color. The Moors said of it, "Jebel Tariq raises the sun out of the sea at morning, bathing its flanks in gold, and drowns the sun in the same sea at night bathed in a red glare."

To walk along the quay of the "old port" of Algeciras, or to sit on the terrace of Hotel Reina Cristina is like seeing Gibraltar from the dress circle of a theatre. The Bay of Algeciras nearly encircles both the town and The Rock, the popular way in these parts of referring to Gibraltar.

The port of Algeciras is noisy, smells vilely of fish and rank harbor mud, and has little else to offer. On the other hand Hotel Reina Cristina is far enough away from the port so that this reek is not apparent. Situated in the midst of luxuriant gardens, where every rose in the roster grows in profusion, it is a horticulturist's dream. In fact a rose lover from California told me he comes to Reina Cristina every year in May and June, just to sit and sip *Amontillado Primero* sherry among the roses. "Then," he added, "when I am ready to return to Santa Barbara and my own garden, I send a few cases of the sherry ahead of me." He sighed. "When I was young I thought life was champagne, a satin slipper to drink from, and the lady to waltz. Now I find *Amontillado* and roses and sunlight suffice."

If there is a full moon, a most curious atmospheric phenomenon takes place. Dark old Jebel Tariq of the Moors seems to be so close to the gardens of the hotel that you could put out a hand and touch it, or step onto the terraced plaza half way up the side.

The way to Cádiz is over the stones of Roman history. In the second century B.C., Julius Caesar set up tablets in this region, all the way from roughly what is now La Linea, the British Customs Depot, to Tarifa. Inscribed on the tablets was *Colonia Libertinorum*. Tarifa was the headquarters of the Roman fleet under Crassus before his fall from favor. The mole at Tarifa defines antiquity alive today, almost as much as Cádiz. This ancient breakwater, with a fishing village at the end, was once shaped like the three prongs of Neptune's trident. In the harbor depths this foundation, built of Cyclopean stones, can still be traced. Statues of boys playing on pipes and cymbals and what appear to be castanets—for the present Spanish castanet was used by temple dancers in Attic Greece—have been found submerged among the crevasses of the Roman stonework. These figures of young dancers and musicians are believed to have formed finials, or a kind of frieze, for a pavilion facing the roadstead. Perhaps an admiral took his ease under marble cornices, canopied in silk and topped with these marble youths, while reviewing his fleet.

Tarifa has often been called the most Moorish town left in Spain. When seen from the Gulf of Cádiz, Tarifa, with the stark whiteness of its square, flat-topped houses and white crenelated walls, all overlooked by a casbah fortress, has no longer a counterpart even in Morocco. Surely the finest remaining example of Moorish fortress castle is here. Abd-ar-Rahman I, founder of the Omayyad Dynasty at Córdoba, built the castle with walls so high, unpierced by apertures of any kind, that the lofty mass blazes in incredible whiteness to shed a glare over the whole town. Black rejas cover all the windows in the houses. This strong accent on black is most noticeable in the costumes of the women of Tarifa. Standing in the doors of houses or walking in the treeless streets they appear like exclamation points, black habited as nuns, stark black against the white walls. Long black shawls conceal half the face, permitting only one eye to show. All are dressed identically, the shawls folded all alike. The women of Vejer, of Zahara in the mountains, also affect this concealment. In a gayer mood, the extravagantly dressed *tapadas*, those veiled women of Spanish ancestry in Peru, wear dresses of coral pink, magenta, yellow, and emerald green, under long black veils imported from Tarifa, again concealing all features save one eye.

I could not resist driving up the almost impassable road to Vejer de la Frontera after I had seen it in the clouds glowing like pearl, from the Laguna de la Janda, a small lake where from one side rise the twin peaks of Sierra de Retín. The road winds from the lagoon around the mountain so that the town behind its nearly circular walls presents a series of enchanting pictures as you climb to the one entrance gate. The houses rise sheer, as part of the walls, but towering above all an ancient castle raises its proud silhouette flaunting age-eaten turrets, where eagles nest. One Moorish house on the battlements has a roof of Mecca green-glazed tiles, like the hundred mosques in Fez. Sun flashing on this roof can be seen by sailors far out at sea. The castle, once one gets close enough to pick out detail, shows Roman, Gothic, and Moorish detail, the buildings all piled helter-skelter together, like the turreted castles all askew in old tapestries.

Once I had arrived in the arcaded plaza, where the walls, thick with centuries of whitewash, have a patina smooth as Parian marble,

I looked around for a place to stop the night. It was, I saw, to be a night of stars, and a nearly full moon would rise about nine o'clock. There is no inn at Vejer, but the patron of a *venta* under the arcades told me he had a room, "small but clean, with a goose feather bed." Later in the night when the mountain cold descended like heavy dew, I was glad of the goose feathers.

I wandered for hours that night in Vejer de la Frontera under the moon. What I most remember is silvery light, luminosity of walls, silence, and a fleet of silver ships. The ships were in an old palace, now partly used in the day time as a school for girls learning to make lace mantillas. The façade of the palace stands out among Gothic and Moorish houses in an arrogant Renaissance style. Once inside the patio, where the only flowers were madonna lilies in two great octagonal tubs of Moorish tiles, six immense doors of red córdoban leather, tooled in gold, give a hint of unguessed treasures lying in wait behind. And so it proved. I was shown through the rooms by a caretaker steeped in lore of Vejer and its resounding history from days when Avienus says it was called Herma, when Tariq beat Roderick the Goth to his knees and when Jaime I, before he set sail to drive the Moors from Majorca, came to admire from the castle battlements the view of Cádiz lying far away in the sea.

One room has gold leather walls and cornices of red velvet. Another, silver paint spattered over red, giving the walls the effect of a clouded ruby. On the second floor a room stretches clear across the front of the house, embrasuring six tall windows. To this room I lost my heart. The walls are covered in dark green brocaded velvet. The ceiling is painted to ape the sea, with figures of the four winds blowing from bulging cheeks stupendous gales, or gentle breezes. Monsters from the deep, fancifully conceived, writhe and disport among green and peacock waves. But the glory of the room is the fleet of silver ships hanging from the ceiling. This fleet was once replica in miniature of the entire Armada of Philip II. Just as it appeared in Cádiz harbor, in readiness to sail against Philip's "thorn of womanhood," Royal Elizabeth, the brazen Tudor. Some of the original one hundred and thirty odd ships have disappeared, but the effect is still remarkable. There remain sixty ships hammered from thin silver, perfect in every detail from silver wire rigging to pearlcolored silk square sails. Each ship hangs from delicate silver chains. In the center gleams the *San Martin*, flagship of the Duke of Medina Sidonia, admiral of the Armada. Grouped about this high-pooped galleon are hung at different levels, *Real Capitana*, *San Cristobal*, *San Francisco*, *Florencia*, and the *Santa Ana* and *Ragazona*, the largest ships of the fleet. These silver ships resemble castles of the sea. Only a few pieces of furniture, of dark wood or Renaissance gilt, stand on a floor of ebony, inlaid in ivory with stars and signs of the Zodiac. At a long writing table is a throne chair gilded and carved in motifs of sea shells and waves. The chair is covered in claret velvet, fringed and tasseled. Old, worn to shreds, the bloom of beauty seen only in silk velvet still triumphs. This house once belonged to a member of the de Cisneros family who had set his heart on accompanying Medina Sidonia in his flagship to attack the English fleet under Sir Francis Drake. Due to a grave illness, young de Cisneros was forced to give up the idea. Facing a life of invalidism, confined to his palace in Vejer, he asked his friend the admiral for a model of his flagship. Before Medina Sidonia left Spain on his ill-starred voyage he commanded his personal silversmith to construct from scale drawings this fleet of silver ships.

Except for the caretaker, I was alone in this nostalgic room. The lace makers had all left. I asked him if I might open one of the windows, for there was scarcely a hint of wind. The man nodded his head. I opened a window through which a long ray of moonlight slanted across the dark velvet walls, picked out golden glints in the furniture, and turned a few of the ships to molten silver. But best of all, an errant breeze stole in, lightly belling the silk sails, so that the fleet seemed to dip and gently roll as on a phantom sea.

The way to Cádiz lies through San Fernando, a long drawn out village of low white houses, the *rejas* over windows nearly as large as the houses, painted dark or brilliant colors. San Fernando is a town rich from the salt industry and has been called in guide books *Ciudad de los Rejas*. As one looks along the street as far as the eye can range, it is not houses one is conscious of but a long corridor of *rejas*. A big, high belfried church looms behind a garden of wind-tortured palms. To right and left, spread the salt flats of las Salinas. Now the wind howls, the marsh grasses bend almost double in the gale, and flocks of white ibis, wings streaked in black, build nests on stilts like aborigine huts and are so used to motor cars speeding back and forth along the narrow isthmus road, that they cross in front of the cars on stiff red legs, unconcerned as market women.

The causeway through salt flats seems never to end. Pyramids of salt like white canvas circus tents catch the sun in myriad facets, flashing like crystals, fit to blind one's eyes. Supremely cool and virgin white the town lies at the end of the long straight jetty, yet memory of its importance in the pagan world, of its luxury and vices, stirs the mind to sensuous flares of imagination. Possibly the most haunting thought of all is its fabled antiquity. Who founded Cádiz, and when, is forever questioned.

The earliest Roman writers call Gadir or Gades (the inhabitants are still called Gaditanos) "an ancient city;" Pliny said "a fragment of the lost Atlantis," and so on. To Emperor Hadrian, born not far away in Itálica, it was a "pleasure port"—Juvenal and Martial called it *Gades Jocosae*. To me it is still Cádiz the Joyous. Across the inlet lies the Isla Léon, once known as Erytheia, the haunt of the herdsman Geryon, who fought Hercules to save his sacred cattle. The Phoenicians built a wall around the island and a Temple to Hercules in the center. In the surrounding waters are still found fragments of statues and utensils used for votive oil and burning myrrh. These are of embossed bronze which craftsmen who came from Phocaea in Asia Minor, wrought in exceeding beauty. Among the many legends concerning the birth of Cádiz, one claims that Hercules lies buried beneath the stones which mark the temple site. On any day of the year small brown Gaditano boys with gray Berber eyes sit on the seawall in wait. Each one will entreat you to let him row you across to "see the bones of Hercules," as he puts it, adding importantly that he alone knows where they are. I have never done it, albeit I have been to the island, only a litter of huts and age-pitted stones. But I will bet a long-handled silver spoon (the symbol of Cádiz sold as lapel pins in any shop) that the boy would produce a pile of blanched bones to prove his boast. Possibly bones from a carcass of Geryon's sacrificial bullocks.

Beyond myth or question Cádiz was once adorned with temples and sacrificial altars to Melkarth (the Phoenician Hercules), Pallas Athena, full panoplied as she sprang from the aching head of Jove, Mars, and Priapus, rampageous deity of the Saturnalia who was linked with maritime Aphrodite. The two were held in unrivaled popularity by Phoenician sailors who crowded the port at all times. There is a fragment of sacrificial altar to Aphrodite to be seen on the quay where these most superstitious of all mariners used to offer a libation of freshly produced semen, publicly ejaculated as a bid for the Goddess' protection before daring to set out upon a voyage "into the unknown mists."

138

Cádiz was once the most cosmopolitan city along the coast from Cadaqués to the Tartessian Gulf (Gulf of Cádiz). The sumptuous style of living practiced by rich merchants, scholars, military governors, traveling emperors and their court, as well as charlatans and courtesans of both sexes, produced luxurious and diverting vices to attract adventurers in such numbers that Pliny said, "Gades will one day sink into her own encircling waters from weight of the population."

To savor Cádiz fully, I like to start walking through the narrow shadowed streets of the La Viña quarter. Black, white, blue, and yellow tiles form window casings, and rust-brown jalousies hang like tableau curtains from bamboo poles slung across the streets from roof to roof. This effect of striping along the cobbles, with broad bands of sunlight and shade, is wholly Moorish. Now and again one sees a tiny plaza set back, a mere gap in the close-packed rows of houses. This space is filled with market stalls where every commodity needed in the daily round is sold by bargaining at full lung power. Women in La Viña wear total black much like the women of Tarifa. The difference lies in covering the head with an over skirt, upswung to form a shawl, giving a curiously divided-in-two silhouette. From the waist down to the heels is a narrow skirt. From the waist up the skirt forms a full blouse, tightly wrapped around head and throat. The women of Tarifa are black-wrapped, silent, morose. Those of La Viña black-bloused, riotous in laughter, cackling and yelling their heads off. Unique in so many ways, La Viña was the last Moslem quarter in Spain to be abolished. In 1826 the mosques were closed and the *muezzins*, "The Voice of Allah," departed from Cádiz for Tetuan and Riff country in Morocco.

From the balcony of my hotel, the Atlantico, I looked out on a scene of wide, palm-fringed alamedas, rocks, harbor life, and the encircling sea. Every time the tide changed a miraculous occurrence kept me always on the alert, to stand in wonder. When the sea was at high, I looked across the hotel gardens to a few jagged rocks sticking but a few feet out of the water. When the tide was half out I saw the barnacled walls and broken columns of a ruined Roman city. When the tide ran out entirely, I saw below the Roman town the arcades and catacombs of a Phoenician port, on which the Roman town had been built. Below these age-defying stones, gleaming bronze-green and purple with subterranean life, who knows what buried city lies? Day after day I watched this rolling back of time

139

take place. I could well believe the boast that Cádiz is the most ancient city in Europe. Strabo wrote that Iberians (Spanish) had built a port here two hundred years before 1100 B.C. I had only to walk a half-circle mile from my hotel to again watch the restless tide reveal under the Castle of St. Catherine (Santa Catalina) a fort and the old Phoenician (Fenicio in Spanish) markets, with stone-pillared stalls and oval tanks for keeping fish. How wise were these marketeers to know that to keep fish fresh in captivity they must continuously swim. Square corners annoy fish, who in ramming their heads against corners become torpid. So the tanks were built with oval walls.

In some respects Cádiz resembles an immense, pear-shaped fort. The high walls that surround part of the city are of earliest Moorish construction; the remainder, including the actual citadel and gates displaying grandiose armorial bearings in stone, were built by Alfonso X. I suggest a bird's eye view to see Cádiz at its best. From a high point, to get the *La Tacita de Plata* (Little Silver Cup) version, so dear to all Gaditaños, go up in the Tavira Tower. From here you see a panorama of vitality in architecture and green, sea-blue and shattering white radiancy. It is the incredible whiteness of Cádiz that has always impressed visitors. The Italian writer, Edmund d'Amicis, finds Cádiz, "The whitest town in the world. Write a thousand times the word *white* with a *white* crayon on blue paper and add a marginal note, *Impressions of Cádiz*." From Tavira Tower one gets the impression that Cádiz has been bathed in whitewash from head to foot.

The city is encircled and crosshatched with old gnarled magnolia trees of great age. Avenues of oleanders and dark enameled ilex bushes cast dappled shade. Pointing to heaven are the towers and belfries of the castles of San Lorenzo, Santa Catalina, and any number of churches. A great many of the important houses in, for instance, Plaza de España, and a few public buildings are in Neo-classic style. This style is beautifully represented in Cádiz. The cathedral with its famous carillon raises twin belfries exuberantly Baroque. At evening mass these chimes are arresting in purity of tone, played by a master of ecclesiastical music.

The cathedral houses many treasurers in sculpture by Juan Martinez Montañes, so richly flowing in line I am always reminded of the modeling of tempestuous draperies on the figures of The Italian Renaissance sculptor Bernini. Some thirty pieces of sculpture were sent to the cathedral in Cádiz from the ruined Carthusian Monastery at Jerez de la Frontera, but many figures were lost or stolen en route. The Capuchin Church is stern, austere in the plainness of its walls inside and out. There seems always to be something implacable in the cold stone of Capuchin houses, like the hooded habit the monks wear. In the church of Santa Catalina is "The Mystical Marriage of St. Catherine" by Murillo (painted for the Capuchin Friars), delicate in line with a curious misty mood, appropriate to the subject, but completely unlike any picture by this painter I have ever before seen. It is unfinished, for Murillo fell to his death from a scaffold while painting it.

Cádiz comes to life in its street scenes. Gaditaños love to parade, the women wearing impressive corsages; as in Málaga and Seville, flowers in Cádiz are rampant, the gardens overflow into the streets and flower sellers do a rousing trade. When I am in Cádiz I like each night to try for dinner one of the old seafront *ventorros*. Of these there is a wide choice. Favorites are mentioned pridefully by Gaditaños whenever a visitor asks "Where shall I eat?" The answer is sure to be in this wise. "Puerta de la Tierra for atmosphere, Las Palmas and Ventorro del Chato for good food, and El Telescopio for a combination of both." Puerta de la Tierra is very spacious inside, as well as the garden under red and pink oleanders. The waiters, like the Horse Guards in London, are chosen for their height and good looks. The service is as smooth as their best olive oil. Ventorro del Chato is over two centuries old, vine hung, redolent of rare vintage wines on draught—a rare innovation—the food superbly prepared, and served in huge blue and yellow pottery dishes. An added attraction for cat lovers is a kind of corps de ballet of tortoise-shell cats which live the life of Riley on fish scraps fed by admirers who cannot possibly eat all of the huge portions served them.

Of all the old *ventorros* I am partial to El Telescopio. At high noon I sit under the arbors, watch the strollers and eat my fill of *gazpacho*. For late dinner I return to eat a luscious *paella* or perhaps *bacallao*, codfish en casserole, with celery, mushrooms, tomatoes, and olive oil, nowhere in Spain so well cooked or served, on a trolley under a glass dome, with such élan. After dinner, while the hot black coffee is "on the drip," trace the starry firmament, identify the Pleiades, Venus, Orion, through a huge telescope, which stands on the waterfront terrace like a propitiatory altar. The custodian of the telescope is a well-known but mysterious character in the *alamedas.* His long, sallow face has the aristocratic look of a Greco hidalgo. He wears a brown velvet jacket, the pockets bulging with red, green, yellow, blue, and white rosettes. His beret is worn as a Basque wears it, pulled tight down to the eyebrows. As far as anyone knows, Pedro lives on "a fee for my services, señor?" asked with a low bow, small tips for the pinning on of a badge with which he rewards the tipper. Around midnight at El Telescopio the scene is a gay one. Groups of people sitting at the red and white checkered tables sporting big, bright rosettes and smug expressions because of their recently-acquired planetary knowledge.

The Provincial Museum in Cádiz has a small but extremely fine collection of pictures. In this museum are six of the finest Zurbaráns in Spain. His occupation with the use of white pigment, his absorption in perfecting white upon white, thereby creating a sense of radiant color by shimmering highlight and smouldering shadow, using only brown, black, and white, is masterly. (Never better displayed than in his incomparable St. Francis in the Prado.) Here his St. Bruno is a *tour de force* of radiant whites so skilfully painted in the cowled habit and the white hands holding white-bound books. Never is Zurbarán's white flat or chalky.

I went through the museum with an architect who had just finished doing over a Moorish house for a doctor. We had been discussing the Zurbarán canvases and the spectacular use of luminous pigment. I asked the architect, "Considering this is Cádiz, is your Moorish house white?"

He looked surprised and then laughed, "What else would it be? Isn't Cádiz the whitest town in the world?"

I nodded. "Yes. Walls, patios, staircases, pillars, floors and—"

He interrupted me. "And birds' nests with eggs and fledgling birds in them. The whitewash brush and bucket is ever ready. Why, will you believe that a servant is not hired in Cádiz if he doesn't know how to whitewash?"

"I'd never doubt it," I answered. "But there is always the cerulean sea to give weight to the scene. In other towns the sea is accidental. In Cádiz it is *essential.*"

So many small towns, more or less similar to one another, lie in the curve of coast until one reaches Huelva and high-walled Ayamonte breasting the frontier of Portugal, that I need give space to only a few that stand out. Sometimes a town will live forever in my memory because something occurs that dramatizes for me a characteristic that seems peculiarly of the people. Such a town is Medina Sidonia, with its white arcaded streets, where that power of detachment in the Spanish mind, that trait of projecting one's thoughts into far places and other times was brought instantly into focus.

It was, perhaps, half past two o'clock, the middle moment of siesta time. From behind some of the ornamental iron *rejas* which protect the lower windows in Spanish houses, came snores and grunts of deep sleep. Farther along the street was a house where a curtain had been carelessly drawn behind the *rejas*. From within the shadowy room came the sound of a guitar, accented by the tap, tap, tap of heels and clack of castanets. A breeze conveniently blew the curtain apart so that I could see into the room. There were five or six small girls, none more than eight or ten years old. Each had a fringed shawl crossed over her thin shoulders and castanets in her raised hands. Here, I realized, was a dancing lesson in progress. What lent a most eerie quality to the scene was the woman who sat on a brass bed in the middle of the room. She was a gitana, dark complexioned as a Moor. Her eyes were half closed, a cigarette drooped listlessly from heavily rouged lips. The song she sang was hardly audible, a lament from out of the desert, and nothing at all to do with the dance she was supposed to be teaching her eager pupils. Her mind was far away, lost in remembered ecstasies, and the children danced on oblivious. "There," I thought as I walked on under the arches, "is *Spain* writ large."

Sanlúcar de Barrameda holds a bold position on the coast at the mouth of bronze-green, lazy old Guadalquivir, the river that, as the Spanish say, "only opens an eye as he flows through Seville, to wink at the girls." The lower town is boisterous, occupied with fishing and tinning the catch so fast there is a feeling of perpetual motion in town and inhabitants alike. Watch always for the contrasts in Spain. Directly above this dynamic "new town" is Sanlúcar de la Montaña, a drowsing cluster of houses where the Romans once built villas and a fortress.

The Moors pulled this down and erected a frowning castle of dramatic proportions cresting the hill. The castle is now partly given over to housing restive young soldiers, doing their compulsory training stint, but they spend every possible free moment in lively Sanlúcar de Barrameda. The castle fortress is so huge and sprawling that I walked through empty, echoing halls, rooms with painted frescos and carved cedar ceilings where once in unbridled splendor lived Guzmán el Bueno, created Duke of Medina Sidonia by Alfonso the Wise, for his brilliant generalship during the wars that so continuously plagued Alfonso's reign.

Close by the river mouth is a small spa called La Barrameda (Sanlúcar de Barrameda on the map). An arcaded farmhouse with a square tower room, half hidden in aloes and the tall plumed canes of marsh grass, was a retreat for Goya. He used to bury himself in the breezy reaches of this rather lonely spa to paint in summer. It was at Sanlúcar that he induced the Duchess of Alba to "take the air in long walks with your little dogs" which he cordially hated, complaining the "little beasts either ignore me or bite my heels." The duchess stayed in a small rustic villa; after her death, and when the house was being dismantled, were found dozens of parasols of lace covered silk, spangled tissues, satin, even taffetas painted in fanciful designs by Goya himself. Every possible conceit in handles from lapis lazuli to pink pearl and filigree. The Prado has Goya's sketch books with page after page of spirited sketches made at his Sanlúcar retreat, showing the duchess dancing, haughty in wide beribboned hat, or weaving garlands in a meadow. Many sketches show her in sultry or melting mood, lightly clothed.

The small but historically important port of Puerto de Santa Maria is dominated by a church with vast, silent nave, scaled to such heights it reminds me somewhat of the cathedral in Seville. The Castle of St. Mark, where Columbus stayed while deciding whether or not to set sail from Santa Maria, is old and tottering now. Juan de la Cosa lived there in a tower room under the patronage of the wise Duke of Medinaceli who bade him draw a map of the newly-discovered continent of America and its relation to the rest of the world.

Chiclana is a "pleasure port" given over to tree bordered *alamedas* and very fancy villas with a gay night life where a card game resembling faro but bearing the same name as the town is played from sunset to sunrise. Ubrique, although much smaller, tries to rival proud, aloof Córdoba, with the beauty of its tooled leather. Many of the ornamental headdresses worn so capriciously by ponderous bullocks in most parts of Spain are made in Ubrique.

Huelva is a rich and green town with the haughty Medina Sidonia air, selfconsciously calling attention to its size and commercial importance, because of the Rio Tinto mines. Standing on an advantageous delta where the Odiel and Tinto Rivers join, its wealth was so loudly extolled by the Phoenicians that the Romans, under Emperor Trajan, wrested it from them in the same sudden storming stratagem used by Marcus Aurelius to acquire the silver mines of Málaga. Through the centuries Huelva has grown fatly rich on silver ore extracted from the Rio Tinto mines, on its fisheries (a very superior tunny run far out in the Gulf of Cádiz), and on tanned bulls' hides for harness leather, an industry as old as Roman times when light racing chariots and cavalry saddles were made.

Trajan, who was born in Itálica near Seville, built an aqueduct at Huelva. This aerial waterway was unique both for transporting water and as a magnificent piece of stone ornament in the landscape. Under the arches the emperor dedicated altars to Jupiter, Aphrodite, Mercury, and other deities much favored by him. So lofty was his self-adulation that he caused a heroic figure of himself, sculptured in different attitudes and variously accoutered, to alternate with the representation of each Olympian deity.

After Roman tenure had ended, the Moors built castellated walls and a citadel for defense, but largely concentrated on mining and refining silver. The damascened blades from Huelva of Moorish workmanship are seen in supreme beauty in museums and shops for antiquities from Seville to Tetuan. When the haughty de Guzmans, Dukes of Medina Sidonia, rose to the unrestricted power hitherto reserved for a sultan or king, succeeding dukes tyrannized the coast from the village of Medina Sidonia (environs of Cádiz) to Huelva. Besides erecting monuments, the engineers in ducal employ uncovered stone-laid military roads put down by the Romans, and built triple-arched bridges over the marshy inlets. Possibly the most stirring example of Medina Sidonia domination to be seen today is the great square castle bristling with four deeply-pronged towers, rising against the sky like unfurled banners to temporal power, unique for flaunting majesty, even in richly endowed Spain. Huelva, a spacious town, clean swept, with a cool and fragrant climate, backed by green pine forests, is definitely worth a visit.

The lower reaches of this coast are in a region unspoiled by tourist traffic. After leaving Cádiz, the hotels are not of first- or even second-class ranking. But soon there will be *paradores* opened near Huelva and Ayamonte.

La Rabida is a Mecca for American tourists in Spain. Columbus, after a night spent on his knees in prayer at the monastery of La Rabida, set sail from the nearby port of Palos. The *Niña*, the *Pinta*, the *Santa Maria* were destined to lose their way in storms until Columbus chose to follow a flock of strange-looking birds winging landward, to mark a new page in history. At La Rabida is a beautifully situated Hosteria de la Rabida near the Franciscan Monastery. At this restaurant is served a soup of ancient lineage. *Sopa de Diego Colombo* is lentil soup, into which is stirred the yolks of eggs, then it is sprinkled with croutons. When seeking audience with the Duke of Medinaceli Christopher Columbus and his young son Diego came to the door of the Monastery, road-weary and nearly starving, a young monk Fray Juan Perez offered them food, shelter, and to the father, sustaining spiritual comfort and courage. But it was young Diego who ate ravenously of the simple fare, all that the friars had to offer. A lentil soup, laced with eggs and chunks of bread.

Addicted to mountains and the inspiring panoramas offered as one drives over them, I started to Jerez de la Frontera by an unfrequented road. I thought, this road would lead over the silvery rocks along the banks of Rio Tinto. But I lost my way and after many turnings and false directions given me by goatherds, or polite but noncommittal farmers, I found myself on the most eccentric road in all of Spain. At first I was heartened by a bosky stretch of country lane bordering the River Tinto, and running through a straggling white town, La Palma Bollullos. After this I had been told I would come to Almonte, then cross the marshes. For a while I bumped along, suddenly I rubbed my eyes. Either this was mirage or I had been transmigrated to Cambodia. For the church and houses bordering a long treeless street aped Cambodian temple architecture to the point of rippling roof lines and façades faced with tiles—yellow, green, and black *azuléjos*. The church has the most entertaining cornice, up-tipped at the corners, supporting a parade of faience saints carrying parasols and wearing long chains of ceramic beads, which loop them one to the other like a celestial chain gang.

After this charade of Almonte, I struck a marvel of nature, Las Marismas, "the great marshes." It had been cool all along the coast from Cádiz to Huelva, but here, veils of humid heat rose in capering waves. The yellow-green stretches of coarse grass seemed as limitless as the Hungarian *puszta*. The surface of the track—only by honorary title could it be called a road—varied from aquatic to rock-pile to mattress-soft marsh roots. Great herds of cream-colored cattle stood, too heat-stunned even to chew their cuds, immobile as marble statues lining a triumphal way. Flocks of nesting sea fowl, "from

PROMENADE

LADIES OF ARCOS de la FRONTERA.

Africa," as one is always told in this part of Spain, rose in the air yawking with anger at being disturbed. The most curious sight of all was one I saw many times again in the arid stretches of *vega* in other parts of Spain. Great flocks of huddled, motionless dun-brown sheep. From a distance I first thought the dark patches, isolated like islands in the marsh, were low rock formations which I should probably have to cross. But no. Two or three hundred sheep packed closely into one mass to cast a block of shade for the lambs to lie in, lest they perish in the unremitting sun. This sight reminded me of a gigantic football squad. Instead of bleats, I listened for "Eight—six —six—nine—four—twelve" signals.

At Lebrija once more I arrived within the borders of sanity and peculiarly happy fantasy in dress. Here were familiar white houses with black *rejas* bordering a vista of window gardens with flame-red carnations and the climbing passion flower. Just as it is impossible to enter a Spanish town and not see something personal, indicative of that town and no other, the women of Lebrija wear brilliantly-colored sombreros tilted forward over long white shawls, deeply fringed, and black skirts with ruffled trains carelessly sweeping the dust. They walk with the swing, the nonchalance of Anna Karenina in a pink sombrero.

In every sense Jerez de la Frontera has a lovely approach. Often in Andalusia one will see the name of this town written simply Xeres (which is its old name) without the de la Frontera which is attached like the tail of a kite to the name of so many towns in this province. The word "Frontera" signifies that the town once formed part of the eastern border of Moorish domination and in most cases a fortress still dominates the reaches.

The town is beautifully set, as might be a shallow bowl of vintage wine in a circle of banked greenery. The green hills are the world famed *Montanitas de Xeres*, "little mountains of Xeres," which the English pronounce "sherris" and hence their name for the wine. Low lying, undulating, the hills are covered with vineyards, twenty-five of which belong to the family of Domecq of Macharnudo Castle. The entire population of Jerez live by, or for, the grape. There are many *bodegas*. Marqués del Mérito *bodega* is like a great country house in a garden famous for its fountains, and that of Gonzales Byass, is of British origin. But possibly the most noted, certainly the largest, is Bodega Pedro Domecq. To pass beneath the great entrance gate of cartouched stone is to enter another world, a sweet-scented world, a realm where if one could stay and sample, day after day, the pale gold, or rose-bronze sherry, all worldly cares would drift away.

In the year 1730 Pedro Domecq arrived in Jerez de la Frontera from France to sample the famed vines. As so often happens (Jerez is full of families with Continental ancestry) he decided to stay. He bought a castle and devoted his life to perfecting a particularly dry and fragrant brand of sherry, transferring the color and sunlight of the grape to the palate with a little something added. To be conducted through the cellars (guides here are linguists who explain every facet of Domecq vintages to foreign visitors) is to wander in the caves and galleries of a fabulous medieval castle. Immense distances roofed by tiles with great windowless walls—"the temple of the grape," Théophile Gautier called this. On either side, piled in tiers of three, are the "aging" casks, all of which are made from American oak. Bodega Pedro Domecq maintains a fleet of ships for the express purpose of bringing the seasoned oak planks from America. One after another the huge dark casks are pointed out, the contents described, then a man is summoned and the particular vintage piped into a glass. Names of the different brands lie as pleasantly on the tongue as the wine itself. First, one is told that to the conditions of soil and climate which produce the inimitable qualities of true sherry must be added the *flor*, a delicate yellow or pink flower of this region, its flavor most apparent in *Amontillado*. To Spaniards the most highly regarded short story ever written is Edgar Allan Poe's "The Cask of Amontillado." Picture postcards of Poe, in white stock and black cravat, are sold in most shops in Andalusia with pamphlets of the story.

Extra Amontillado is the palest gold and the driest sherry in the world. I sampled *La Ina Libarita*, a wine for connoisseurs. *Solera Fundador*, a very special wine to honor the two-hundredth anniversary of the founder, has a tang, reverberating on the palate the way the "rip" sound of the word strikes the ear. *Fundador* rips the silence. *Guitar*, a sherry of light and delicate bouquet, is a favorite with Spanish parents who bring up their children on it, so they will appreciate good wine. The favorite sherry of "ladies and English vicars for two hundred years" is *Nelson Brown*, nicknamed "Horatio" at the *Bodega*.

An alcove with black-and-white striped pillars at the end of a long gallery, houses the Domecq museum. Dark casks set high on trestles are marked with gold armorial bearings or replicas of signatures. The Duke of Wellington, Lord Nelson, Maria Christina of Spain, a galaxy of arms and quarterings of most of the Spanish Bourbons and Habsburgs. Light flickers on a lightly traced signature of John Ruskin. The handwriting of Lord Byron seems cramped, while the name of Fyodor Chaliapin is "deceitful caligraphy," tiny as miniature for a man of such huge frame and sweeping voice. Poe is here too— the name looks precise, cold. But the name Alexander Fleming, inventor of penicillin, is bold, with dash. It is told by the guides with great relish that as Fleming wrote out his name to be copied and emblazoned on a cask of his favorite brand, he remarked, "Your sherry is far more pleasant to take than my penicillin."

In another *bodega*, smaller, but much older than Domecq, the museum is more precious, with vintages of the almost effeminate delicacy of the Moors. In glass vitrines standing on gilt tables is a collection of fantastically fashioned Moorish goblets and Saracen carafes and filters, tall and slender like scent vials in the souks (bazaars) of Marrakesh. These are filled with dark, cloudy wines like syrup, so old that a taste upon the tongue, a moment of savoring and all the gold of Muscadine is yours. Like lambent fire is the lizard-green wine of Beziers, which was once transported in porcelain jars on the backs of slaves to the Omayyad sultans in Córdoba and Seville. One old brandy smells of musket flint and tastes like cordite spiked with the flames of Hell. I tasted a liquid pot-pourri of rose and violet petals, orange peel and jasmine buds, steeped in *Oloroso* brandy five hundred years ago for a Venetian doge of the Foscari, who must have had a prodigious sweet tooth. Above the bottle hung his scarlet seal, flaunting a gold-winged Lion of Saint Mark's. This decoction of gardens and sunlight was musky to the tongue. I thought of Turkish Delight from Constantinople, or the Hindu conserves of exotic fruit one is served for breakfast in the water pavilions of Udaipur.

Jerez de la Frontera tolerates no bleak, shuttered palaces such as I had seen in Ronda. The town's life and prosperity is based on its wines. All kinds of buildings are put to business use. Big oak casks from the different *bodegas* are stored in cellars and empty rooms of old palaces. People of Jerez will point with pride to the beautiful portal or embrasured window entablature of a baroque palace in the palm-shaded *alameda*, saying, "That is our lovely palace of the Doros," adding wistfully, "no longer do we dance there. It serves a purpose now, not originally intended." But it is often because the family has died out, or the younger members prefer to live in Madrid. And there are many such. Some palaces, however, are still lived in by the original families, for there is great wealth in Jerez, which has long been noted for its fashionable pursuits.

I walked along the streets remembering stories I had heard about this or that palace, of some erratic, or too notorious member of the family. Great stories could be written of comedies or stark drama that has taken place in these high-ceilinged rooms. I have collected a number of these fragments of incident to write one day myself. Palace de Pedro Aladro, Palace de Requelme. The Ponce de León with its patio fountain inset with rose quartz. Los Morlas, the white and gold Rococo ballroom now filled with casks of aging *Amontillado,* and the exquisite Plateresque bijou of a house los Davila. Two old houses in the main street were made into a hotel, Los Cisnes (the swans) where one dines in a charming flowered-trellised patio.

In the utterly quiet, simple Convent of St. Francis is the tomb of Blanche of Bourbon, the queen of Peter of Castile. She lies in effigy on a catafalque of remarkable richness, of pomp and circumstance, almost articulate, seeming about to disturb with sound the hush of piety which always hovers about these ancient Spanish cloisters. Blanche was a woman ever to the fore. It was to enrich her wardrobe, legend says, that rare chinchilla was first introduced into Spain. A conquistador named Ruy Mondoro sailed home from La Paz in Bolivia, dodging Drake and the English buccaneers, to present this new fur to the Spanish queen. It was not long before Spaniards and Indians all over the new lands were hunting chinchilla fur for the rapacious court in Castile, where, to own even a few skins to edge a collar or gloves, became the rage. This pearl-gray fur, soft as down, was so prized that by gun and powder fuse, by poisoned arrow, steel trap and ferret, chinchilla were driven from their refuge among Andean rocks. In museums in Madrid, in Aragon, Navarre, wherever vestments and old court costumes are displayed (the Escorial has a tremendously representative collection of costumes of the courts of Philip I and II), I have seen robes, capes, and traveling clothes variously trimmed with this costly fur.

To go from the sumptuously bejeweled presence of Blanche of Bourbon in effigy, to the decaying grace in golden stone of La Cartuja a little way out of the town is to step into a world apart. Here in the dying evening light I saw, in effect, architecture like music, but the last strains of music; stone so delicately carved that it has all the elements of music, and so fragile that experts have deemed it unwise to try to restore or preserve the church.

When Ribera carved the fluted columns in spiral lines and mounted one garlanded cornice above another in 1570 he worked with a great sense of theatre. All this enriched façade is only a harborage for St. Bruno, St. Catherine, and many other saints rising in shell-domed niches to a zenith pediment where on a cloud rests God the Father.

To give lift to the pediment, to add the last heavenward sweep, Ribera placed an amazing collection of urns, flaming and pinnacled, urns of all sizes, grouped like spires of a cathedral. Gold these are, in stone, gold they caught the sun as I walked away through the thistles and the barley stooks which lean against the trembling walls of La Cartuja.

I thought long upon the vicissitudes of this glorious church, which is really only an alcove of long echoing halls of the derelict Carthusian Monastery, three times sacked and mutilated, the priceless Zurbaráns sent for safety to Cádiz. Used for a time by farmers for a stud, it is now a granary in the midst of fields of grain. Perhaps Demeter, who watches so carefully over neglected beauty in buildings such as this, when gracing her fields, will preserve La Cartuja much longer than is thought possible. The delicate strength of the golden stone, however frail I thought, has weathered many centuries. There is about the carved façade an imperishable quality, subtly suggested, as there is about the Parthenon.

Chapter 10

FIESTA IN SEVILLE

THE road to Seville winds through a veritable sea of olive trees. Near Bornos there is an *almazara* or ancient olive oil press owned by Señor Gonzales, which I never fail to visit when I am anywhere in the region. The road to the house passes through a gully ridged with olive trees over one hundred years old and still bearing lustily. I once asked Gonzales about how many trees he had for yield. He scratched his chin. "I have not got 32,000,000 trees like they have in Jaén Province, but my grandfather planted 10,000 trees and most of them are still bearing."

Over half of the world's supply of olive oil comes from Spain and, I learned, one fourth of Spanish olive oil comes from Martos district of Jaén.

My arrival at Los Cabras, the Gonzales place, was heralded by yelping of hound puppies, quickly squelched. I was pressed to eat immediately. It was only ten o'clock in the morning, so I said a glass of wine would do. We drank a *tinto* from the hills, a pale pink, very light sherry. Then we walked up onto the ridge nearest the house. For miles, I could see nothing but the gray-green of olive leaves, shivering as if in a breeze, though the air was still. There was great activity abroad. The method of gathering olives varies in different provinces. In the Jaén and Córdoba groves the gentle touch, "milking the trees" by hand, is favored. But here in Bornos and Lebrija, *bravo* or rugged beating of the trees with long sticks by women and boys is considered the proper way. At the sudden sound of a kind of reveille played on a bugle by a fat, red-faced youth, we went down to the press. The grinding stones are eighteen feet in

154

diameter and nearly three feet thick. I asked Señor Gonzales where these monster stones had been quarried, then cut circular for grinding olives. He told me that his grandfather had come to Bornos from Jaén as a boy to work on a farm. One day while investigating the gully, bare of trees of any description then, he had found the two gigantic stones half buried in mud. That was the beginning of this *almazara*. Perhaps the Moors ground their olives with these stones. I have seen Moorish oil presses bigger than this in the hills around Córdoba and Seville.

Baskets the size of hogsheads used in breweries for malt, stood in a row on a ramp, filled to the brim with bronze-black olives. The effect was like that of the stage extravaganza *Chu Chin Chow* in the scene with tons of black diamonds in jars. The entire olive, including the pit, is ground to a black paste. Men shovel this paste onto mats of coarse marsh grass, piling mat on mat in layers until a stack is ready to go again under the stones. This pressing goes on until the oil has oozed out and the mats are covered with black gum. Vats lined with tiles collect the oil to be sent through troughs. Water is now drained off and boys skim off impurities. The olive oil thus primitively extracted must go to one of the big refineries (probably Cádiz or Seville) to be purified for export. I like to taste the oil just as it comes from the press. Before I left Los Cabras I accepted the invitation "to eat" which had been my greeting. Now, I was hungry. A sort of sandwich called *comida* which means "a meal" is eaten by all the workers for their lunch. To my mind it could not be better. The top is cut off of a small loaf of bread, which in this case was fresh and still hot from the oven. The inside is scooped out. Freshly-pressed olive oil is mixed with the crumbs to which are added tomatoes, anchovies, and a clove of garlic. When kneaded together this is put back into the hollowed loaf, tamped down with a wooden masher, until it forms a core. This is formidable in the hand. If you are *brave*, eat it just like that. If effete, have it sliced. I ate a *comida*, as was, on the spot, and was handed another for the road. This I ate later, washed down with a bottle of Valdepeñas, as I stood in the grassy *vega* gazing up at Zahara brooding on its rocks, gaunt and scaly with years.

A few miles from Bornos is Zahara and Arcos de la Frontera. There is something sublimely unreal about the whole picture of Zahara and Arcos that pleases every fiber of my imagination. Each can look across a wide valley to the other. Each village is perched on a high rocky crag. But there the likeness ends. Zahara is a magnificent, dying old warrior queen. She has withdrawn from battles of the world, and stacked her spears, her head held proudly high. The serried rocks are black, rust-red and gray, the haunt of owls. There is a desolate kind of charred patina to the ancient houses struggling up to the castle with its three truncated towers. Even when I climbed the broken steps to the windy plaza the town bore a medieval, beleaguered look. The women were all wrapped closely in black shawls, their wind-burned faces hid.

Now, Arcos is proud and high set, enjoying to the full a panorama of sweeping mountains, grim Zahara and the far off lovely vineyards of Jerez. Tall eighteenth-century houses bordering the square are supremely elegant. The culture of the old noble families who have for centuries lived quietly behind their scrolled façades is proverbial in Spain. The cathedral, its belfry a beacon for miles, is immensely rich in tinsel brocade vestments, crystal and gold altar garniture, all the treasures of churchly pomp. The women wear black velvet gowns; over these are draped in full-circle black lace shawls. Multitudinous petticoats with pink, heliotrope or yellow ruffles bedewed with sequins flick as they walk. Their faces are dead white with rice powder, their eyes dark lashed, shadowed with kohl or mascara, in the old eighteenth-century elegance of *maquillage*.

Arcos has one long descending street from the cathedral to the Roman gate leading to the *vega*. The cobbled street, lined by white houses with black *rejas* presents an alabaster calm. There is not one flower in sight. Arcos has for me the air of a great Spanish drama about to commence. Everyone seems to be holding his breath. But the proscenium curtains have never parted on the first scene. In Seville or Madrid when I have mentioned Arcos de la Frontera in a gathering of some sort, invariably women unfurl or clack shut fans, men shrug shoulders. "Arcos?" they say. "Yes, Arcos is beautiful. But there are no hearts in Arcos. Simply white faces and figures of elegance in the clouds."

There is a fairly straight road to Seville by way of Utrera and Dos Hermanas through uneventful countryside, albeit distant views of rich brown and purple mountains, as seems always to be the case in Spain, a kind of "visual reward" no matter how monotonous the immediate surroundings may be. Yet if the burned-bronze or ivory-gray reaches of *vega* are monotonous, it is as grandly evocative a monotony as one will see under the canopy. Always on the horizon stands forth some storied city, a dreaming village or castle carved in living rock, to keep the eyes alight in anticipation.

I chose to enter Seville by way of mountain-bound Marchena, in order to pass the wayside shrine to La Macarena where gypsies from Triana quarter in Seville come to hold wedding ceremonies. My way was a Roman military road across the end of two minor sierras, Algodonales and La Puebla de Cazalla. This road offers wide panoramas of endless variety, if the atmosphere is clear. As it turned out the day was cool and crystal clear, the sky that pale primrose yellow, so faint as to be the color of eggshell, with massy white clouds at the horizon which cast purple shadows on the earth. The curious pagoda-like peaks of the Sierra Yeguas, far off to my right near Osuna, caused Li Hung Chang great concern when he visited Spain. "My pagoda mountains," he called them. In fact he sent a Chinese painter to Spain the next year to paint panels of the Yeguas range. Li Hung Chang wished to have a record, but he spurned photographs as spawn of the "devil's machine." So the painter, Li Hu, painted a series of panels in black, sepia, and white on gray silk. Before returning to China he presented Queen Mother Maria Christina with a set of the exquisitely painted panels. Now made into screens, these may be seen at the Escorial.

As a relief from implacable rock, however fanciful or Oriental in shape, it is the broad farmlands lying in the valleys and the El Greco sweep of cloud-shadowed *vegas* on the horizon that attract the eyes here. Checkerboard fields in a range of barley-pink, wheat-yellow, bordered by swathes of tilled earth, red as copper-veins in the sierras and all the greens of cork, olive, and mulberry leaves, fuse into a lovely pattern. Long farmhouses flash whitely in groves of acacia and hazel trees. I saw storks flying low and again eagles circled in the sky, but not the great-winged warrior breed that had staged such an unforgettable battle in the night sky over Ronda.

I came down from the last mountain pass through an all but deserted copper-mine village, the huts dyed blood red from whitewash that had been mixed in buckets once used to transport copper ore. A few laborers, thin as rakes, picaresque faces grinning, shouted "Salud, salud, puedo fumar?" ("Hello, hello, may I smoke?") I knew this way of asking for a cigarette. I tossed them a package, carried just for such demands. One fellow grinned and shouted "Feliz viaj, señor."

With his good wishes for my journey I coasted down into verdant fields to be stopped in the highway filled with bellowing bullocks being driven to a cattle fair farther along. As I waited for this formidable road block to amble past, urged by shouts from an army of small boys with pronged sticks, I took note of the inevitable head-dresses of the cattle. A veritable millinery display, this one, to enhance the beasts' appearance to a prospective buyer. Red, green, and yellow leather bandeaux and wool boblets to discourage the flies. A great deal of the farm profits must be expended yearly on bullock trappings. But no matter how poorly dressed the farmer, his bullocks are always suitably turned out as custom and his pride demands. Once the bullock herd came to a turn in the road and the dust settled, I saw that I was in front of the gates of an *estancia*. Twenty or more buildings, including a pillared chapel, surmounted by a gilt saint, were clustered around the manor house, much in the way a medieval village used to be built under the shadow of a castle. I have, on two or three occasions, stayed in country houses near Seville, usually *ganaderías* where bulls are bred. This place I could tell had no bull pens nor wide grassy savannas for bulls to roam. These houses vary, in size and appearance of course, but mainly the old *estancias* are built on the same general plan.

"Estancia Calderón," read a sign. I recognized the place the moment I could see the gate through clouds of dust. The sign alone is unique anywhere. Carved in wood are four large animals painted to ape life so cleverly that the ram, heifer, bull, and hog seem to be the real article hoisted in the air. Estancia Calderón raises cattle, sheep, and hogs for the markets in Seville. Locally the place is called "*Tenera, carnero, cordero, cerdo.*" In the rapid-fire speech of Andalusia it sounds like one word, "vealmuttonlambpork." I drove into the big cobbled courtyard and was fortunate to find myself welcomed by Señor Calderón in this manner: "Oh yes. The Irish horse man." Not horseman, I noticed.

The house is built around an inner court. A double-tiered colonnade marches around four sides with a big arch to drive a carriage through in front and walls in back. On one side are living rooms, bedrooms for the family on another, service rooms on a third, and apartments for guests on the fourth. In the courtyard, a large octagonal fountain centers a lead figure of a very stout, well-fed appearing Virgin de los Vegas. Inside, the house is furnished in Spanish Renaissance. Some pieces are dark wood, richly carved, others are painted in flowers and fruits. The private chapel in the house (the one outside is for the workers) is all Rococo floriations of white and gold. The principal reception room is seldom aired and lighted save for ponderous family conclaves, when ramifications of the Calderón y Martorell families assemble to settle betrothals, marriage settlements, and christenings, a very distinct part of Spanish provincial life. This room has the stern-fronted Spanish air of being smothered in materials that feel rich in the hand, stiff velvets, damask, and acrid smelling gold-metal galloon. Once I bought some old silver galloon in a shop in Seville. Hefting it, I realized the silver thread was so heavy that with a meter or two folded into a clout one could bash in a man's skull or pole an ox.

After a Gargantuan lunch consisting mostly of four kinds of roast or broiled meats, washed down with Marqués de Riscal, rather groggy I went on my way. The landscape around Marchena takes on a completely unreal look, the look I often see in pictures by Mexican painters, adept in the primitive style of painting lurid Baroque ruins and piled blue mountains. This country side where red cattle stand knee-deep in bronze-green grass is not flat *vega*. The terrain rolls restlessly as I have seen a groundswell in the treacherous Bay of Biscay. But there is no treachery here, only a limitless sense of peace and plenty, with far off, in a luminous mist, the Giralda Tower to mark Seville of a thousand delights. Ahead of me I saw that the ground, swept bare of grass, rose suddenly to form a knoll. On the crest of this natural dais a bridge spanned a wide river bed with only a trickle of water winding snakily among dry stones. And it was the sight of the bridge that stopped me like a blast of cannon fire. Once it must have been architectural "sound and fury" in the peaceful *vega*. There is fanfare still, but muted, a Churrigurresque dream in sculptured golden stone. Almost wholly ruinous, the entrance ramp climbing the first arch is still brazen with twin truncated plinths in rusticated stone. How vibrant in the sun must once have been this carnival of heraldic beasts, angels blowing trumpets, trophies of war, and the scrolled cartouche of some hidalgo family. When bright and new, heroic figures must have fought for prominence in the confusion of design. Now all this panoply lies shattered in vine-grown heaps, a paradise for my wary friends the lizards. In the hot sun this graveyard of Rococo architecture seems as if some Temple of Mars had suddenly been struck by a bolt from the hand of jealous Jove. I gazed around to marvel. It is a remarkable sight from any angle, and I wanted to find a spot from which to sketch.

Wandering among plumed helmets, ringleted angels, the mouth-piece of a trumpet still grasped in a severed hand, a sandled foot, a winged Hermes hat, I halted to sit on the back of a fallen warrior, tracing the richly curving design of the cuirass, carved with lions' heads and paws. Sketching these roughly broken fragments I wondered, why has no one ever removed them to enrich a private garden or a museum? But then, all over the world I find forgotten grandeur, in houses as well as ornament, left to the elements, to lichen and mold, and to me.

A few miles further along the road loomed another, far simpler bridge across a bone-dry river bed, but now the mood was stillness. Lonely and serene was the figure of La Macarena. Sometime recently she had officiated at a gypsy wedding. Her breast was still looped with necklaces of brightly-dyed shells, paper flowers, strings of copper charms and bells, and tiny glass cups on wires, a few still filled with oil and a thread of wick. Passersby would halt to light these "stars of La Macarena" to bring good fortune along their way. At the annual Romería del Rocío when the most lovely of all pilgrimages is made in great white-hooded caravans, proceeding from Seville through the countryside, gitanas place one of these "stars of La Macarena" alight among the carnations and mimosas posed on top of her head. A woman of the Triana quarter once told me the reason for this.

"It is for us the same as a trip to the confessional for those señoritas." She flicked a thin brown hand towards two young girls in black shawls. "We light La Macarena's star and put it on our head. Then we go our way. Dance, sing the saeta, what you like. If the flame does not go out, and all the oil is burned, we are of no sin. But," her black eyes with muddied whites rolled in the sockets, and the corners of her thin, snake-lipped mouth drew down, "if the flame goes out before the oil is burned away, then we must do a penance. A long penance, before we can sing to our Mother again."

I stood looking at La Macarena thinking what a tremendous hold she had over the gypsy mind. Then I looked down at the foot of the pedestal on which the figure stood. The ground was littered with gaudy trash, the usual aftermath of a pagan ceremonial since time began. Trampled paper flowers, empty wine flagons wound in red and yellow ribbons, a burst tambourine, a few broken fans. Swarms of bees and flies hovered over baskets of rotting fruit that had been placed at the feet of the Virgin as her share of the feast. I paid my respects to La Macarena by placing an orange in her outstretched hand, thinking how much the carved face reminded me of The Lady of Elche, excavated at Elche in Murcia Province and now dreaming the years away in the Prado. La Marcarena's was the same flat-boned face, cheek bones set high to narrow the far-seeing Asiatic eyes. Even La Macarena's headdress, swirls of wheat studded with paper flowers, was, in effect, like the tambourines at either side of the Carthaginian head of—a sacred prostitute? Or was The Lady of Elche a temple virgin? No one has ever found the answer, though there are many conflicting theories. I believe her to have been a dancer (sacred prostitute) in the inner temple of Aphrodite, known as Tanit in Carthage. Quickly I sketched in this wayfarer's Madonna, then turned to leave her to the importunate bees. I noticed a lone man sitting patiently on the rump of a dozing burro. He paid me no attention, removed his sombrero and sat in silent reverie, gazing up into the face of the Madonna. Far down the road I turned to look back. There he sat, a small, rather shriveled black figure in the rustling landscape. A cruel sun blazed on his bare head. He sat watching La Macarena, one figure as graven in quiet as the other.

Possibly no city anywhere enjoys the peculiarly romantic reputation of Seville. Famous capitals in Europe such as Paris, Rome, Madrid, London, and the old Vienna, have devotees who will not give an inch in comparison. Each of these cities has a special time to see it at its best. Constantly, one hears someone say "I am off to Seville for Easter," which means *Semana Santa* (Holy Week). To me Seville is in season at any time. I can arrive there, stay at Hotel Alfonso XIII, one of my five favorite hostelries on earth, and be content to just wander about the city day and night. Many times I have done this, and always find new and memorable delights.

I heartily subscribe to the idea that if one's first visit to Spain can coincide with *Semana Santa* in Seville or for the Feria, a few weeks later, his stars are in the right orbit. *Semana Santa* is the people's celebration. The panoplied, unapproachable hierarchy of the Church, notably powerful in Spain, stays rigidly in seclusion during this entire week. *Cofradias* (fraternities) arrange everything, from who shall bear the richly conceived *pasos* tableaux of scenes from the passion, to what resplendent robes Our Lady shall wear. The procession always follows the same set line of streets. As is the custom all over Spain, in Málaga, Valladolid, Zaragoza, and so on, *hidalgo* and peasant alike walk "The Way" hooded and barefoot, carrying

161

forests of lighted tapers, without which no devout Spanish Catholic can move. The blare of trumpets and deep roll of drums as each *paso* approaches, the glare of light, church doors standing wide, every altar candle flickering in clouds of incense, stir the senses. The wail of *saetas* when the human voice becomes an emotional instrument to express the grief of Holy Mother and Christ on the Cross surpasses any cries of anguish one can imagine. All this visual beauty and strain on the emotions is strong fare. It takes even the Spaniards a few weeks to recover from *Semana Santa*. But it is a tremendously moving experience.

The *Feria* creates an entirely different mood. Seville comes exultantly to life with distinctive Andalusian brand of gaiety, which never lags day or night. Once upon a time *Feria* was a huge cattle fair drawing crowds of thousands from miles around. Gitanas came from Barrio Triana, the gypsy quarter of Seville, to dance *flamenco*, the *jota*, *seguidilla*, and sing the haunting, piercingly shrill *saetas* to express their emotions, religious or otherwise. This boldly planned, highly entertaining cattle fair, first held on the Tablada, or tableland environs caught at the heart of Sevillaños, who by nature dote upon companionship, music, dancing, and good food and wine. As the years passed the *Feria* grew in importance until, today, it is known the world over. While *Semana Santa* is for the populace at large, the *Feria* takes an aristocratic turn. The *hidalgo* no longer hides his face or walks barefoot in penitence. He dons a gray, plum-brown, or black suit, the breeches cut to perfection, high in the waist, and as tight as his own hide. A short jacket braided in black or dark color soutache and the low-crowned, stiff-brimmed córdoban hat worn at the admired tip-forward angle, completes a singularly smart mode of dress in Majo style, infinitely becoming to the lithe, dark good looks which seems the heritage of most Sevillaños. The streets are crowded with pedestrians and lacquered open carriages. Spike teams of three black or white horses, or the milk white mules bred in this region, are adorned with red tasseled harness, clanking with silver. The women who fill the seats to overflowing are as so many brilliant, hugely petaled flowers, their wide flounced cotton skirts spread out over the mud guards to trail half way to the pavement.

Many of the younger women ride side saddle in tailored habits cut, except for the classic wrap-around skirts, exactly like the braided suits worn by their cavaliers. As contrast to this tailored elegance, girls from the country, or perhaps gitanas, wear wide ruffled cotton skirts of vivid color, coin-spotted in black, short fringed shawls crossed over the breasts, their black hair piled high with combs and rose geraniums. I saw two young ladies in pure white, closely wrapped in lace mantillas, drive past; their mother, or perhaps a duenna, all in black, was sitting close beside them. The women were all blazing with diamonds. Women wear splendid jewels at *Feria*. In fact, except at the opera in Rome in the great days of the monarchy, I have never seen more magnificent jewelry, better displayed than in company with lace mantillas, long gloves, a skillfully wielded fan, all this dazzling in the sunshine.

The girls dressed in wide-skirted crinolines who ride pillion behind a brother or perhaps fiancé, fill the eye. They seem poised as centaurs. They scorn even to touch the slim waist of their partners in front. The animal grace of riding in perfect balance, arms akimbo, embroidered shawls slung over one shoulder and allowed to trail down one flank of the horse, is true *Feria* style. The men are forbidden to turn to look at or touch their partners. But pride in the grace of the girls behind them, shines in their amused eyes.

The street where *casetas* are placed in rows is the heart of the *Feria*. These small houses are set up year after year so close together one neighbor can touch the hand of another to pass a glass of *manzanilla*. Gay at any hour, it is at night when, lighted by candelabra, oil lamps, or silk lanterns, the filigree, jigsaw pavilions seem like boxes in a Rococo theatre. A certain style is observed in decoration. Curtains may be of lace, heliotrope, rose, almond green, or primrose silk or net. Spindly gilt chairs are stiffly placed with perhaps a few tufted satin armchairs for elderly relatives. This mode sets the tone of Victorian rightness for a *caseta*.

There is a story which kept Seville in gales of laughter for a year. A rich, spoiled, extremely fashionable young duquesa went to Paris. While there she met a chic decorator. She engaged him to do her a "modern" *caseta* for the forthcoming *Feria*. The *boite* arrived and her footman set it up in the street the morning of opening day. It was a black and white cube room devoid of filigree or any of the fanciful *Feria* touches. A zebra skin rug lay on the floor. Plastic glass chairs and tables stood around, and a radio cabinet in plastic. This oddity had a short life in Spain. Not a nine-day wonder. A nine-*minute* wonder, for a crowd of onlookers declared this contraption was no *caseta* and promptly tore the thing to pieces.

Triana gypsies have their own *casetas* in a street by themselves.

CARMEN
OF SEVILLE.

Olé Olé

PALMADAS
ANDALUSIA

The little houses are smaller, few of them have filigree verandahs, but make up for this in garish fronts frosted in tinsel and powdered mica, like old-fashioned Christmas cards. Urns, lent by Triana potters who make highly glazed faience jars, are filled with the favorite Triana decoration—magenta, cerise, and pink paper flowers mixed with real roses and carnations. In front of the *casetas* a great deal of cooking is done, for gypsies eat all the time. The classic stews and broiled *langostas*, the big lobsters from Cádiz. Triana bread, of dark barley flour and ground hazel nuts, is baked in the embers. Every little way there is an open air Triana restaurant where fish and pork fries in oil. Old women peddle fresh, crisp *patatas fritas*, calling out their wares so weirdly that I always think they are announcing the arrival of Nurse *F'tatatita* to claim the recalcitrant Egyptian "Kitten" Cleopatra. *Feria* or not, a gypsy pitch is still the wide Romany world. The dark, withered faces of the older women, scrawny, leather-skinned, peer out under shawls. The younger women with savage, eagle-sharp faces, their lank black hair drawn into strange knots and twists, kick long cotton dresses sweeping the ground as they snap their fingers loaded with cheap rings. Just by squatting over a cooking pot, or sliding from behind a tree, palm outstretched to tell your fortune, these wanderers create a world entirely their own.

During *Feria* I watched twenty Sevillaños dance the *seguidilla* in the light of a great bonfire, their shadows thrown, magnified to giants, on the white wall of a bull pen. The flow of line of resilient bodies, a sudden accent in the lift of a chin to notes ripped from a guitar. The sharp twitch of one hip, an answering twitch with the other. A backward shrug of shoulders, the delicious crescent curve of a lean back flowing like water into lifted arms, to point it with the stamping of feet. All this play of muscle and curve of line is as natural to them as drawing breath. No people in all Spain can dance flamenco and *seguidilla* as they do in Seville. I talked with a man, once a great flamenco dancer, who has made a long study of the ancient background of these dances, primarily the skill with which Sevillaños use castanets, a skill, he says, that comes down in their blood from earlier than Roman times. The Phoenicians brought temple dancers to Cádiz. Later the Romans danced to castanets in the theater at Itálica. Hadrian had a troupe of Spanish boy dancers who were adept with cymbals and castanets. In antique days Andalusian men moved as nomads, feeding their great herds of bulls in the swampy plains around Cádiz and Sanlúcar and the marshes now called Las

Marismas. They slept out under the stars. The women camp followers danced the men drowsy, taking the dance pattern from the leap and scut of animals, the sudden flight of birds, but more than anything from the dart, the writhe, the sudden slither of snakes, which in olden times, infested the southern marshes. As the centuries waned, these nomad herdsmen and their women wandered to what is now Seville. Even their dress is Gaditanian in feeling. Skirts fitting close to the hips, then flaring out at the knees, like those of the temple dancers in Tyre and Carthage. I was shown old tiles depicting dancers that had been copied from wall paintings in Crete, and sacred prostitutes in temples in the Groves of Sidon, which might just as well have been portraits of gitanas in Seville today.

Whenever one mentions the play of castanets in Seville the talk turns to La Malina. She has a *caseta* during *Feria* which is always so crowded with her admirers that the walls burst at the seams. La Malina is of the old *cuedro*, the great dancers who are a legend while still alive. Old now, and immensely fat, La Malina can still dance rings around most of the young dancers of today. In Spain you will hear that no one has ever touched her fire, her subtlety, or her thunder with castanets. I saw her dance a few years ago in a *caseta* of a woman from Madrid, before a few guests. The great style of La Malina was her intricate footwork, the language of her heavily-ringed hands, as she held them small and pointed as the head of a cobra. She was spellbinding to watch.

To walk or drive in an open carriage through the parks of Seville is an event during *Feria*. The crowds from all parts of the province stroll through the leafy alleys which border the drive. The women wear a variety of lovely dresses, different each day, creating a magical effect. Days before the fair starts, the *Feria* carts piled high with dust-covered luggage can be seen moving through the city to whatever lodgings the country people stay in. I saw a group of five or six young girls walking in Parque de Maria Luisa. Each girl was a startling beauty, camellia skin, black hair and eyes, the panther grace and proud carriage of the head on a slender throat of the pure Andalusian. They wore full, ruffled dresses with tight bodices and long sleeves. On the head, instead of mantillas, net and chenille ball fringe (*madroños*) covering the back of the head only, to fall to the waist behind. Long earrings of jewels, or fresh jasmine buds (which are sold by street vendors) touched the shoulders, and each girl carried a long handled stick with a panache of fresh flowers, as in the time of the Duchess of Alba.

There are three parks in Seville, Paseo El Cid, the Parque de Maria Luisa, and Paseo de las Delicias, bordering the Guadalquivir. The latter is a wooded stretch of drives where every vista of jasmine, roses, hibiscus, and camellia, sprinkled by fountains, is as exquisite as its name. Across the Guadalquivir lies Barrio Triana. Go there at midnight during *Feria* when gitanas dance *flamenco*, the wild acrobatic *talladas* and the most difficult of all gypsy dances, the sensuous *cachucha*. The men dance in tight black suits, their slim figures pliant as a Toledo blade. Women stamp in a tornado of red and yellow ruffles, a single flower wobbling on top of the head above mascaraed eyes. All is gleam and glitter, from flashing teeth to tiny red slippers. Guitarists in the shadow strum strangely-accented rhythm, scraggy boys set off fireworks, house fronts glow, lighting the window watchers, the din vying with crescendos of shrill saetas. In even the most blasé spectator I wager the blood will race.

One will see great crowds moving across Plaza El Cid toward a flat, hard-baked plot of ground called the Tablada. Follow this crowd, who will toss salted and sugared almonds at you as they would confetti. A trick is to catch the almond in the mouth in mid air. Brightly decorated corrals are set up in a circle. This is to pen bulls for tomorrow's corrida. From *ganadarías* scattered all over the plains surrounding Seville come the fiercest fighting bulls. Like everything else in the city during this week, the corrals are decorated to the last corbel on the peaked entrance gates. Banners stream in the wind. The name of *"Ganadería de Don Urquijo," "Ganadería del Duque de Pinohermoso"* as I swiftly sketched in some of the restless bulls, I noted the name painted over each pen. *Brillante, Granadillo, Pelon,* and *Flordenardo.* Visitors, their eyes and imagination caught by the stunningly vital posters of matadors and bulls in wild contact, displayed from every wall and shop window, are always trying to buy these vivid placards. A go-ahead young man had set up a stand in the Tablada where posters, paper-frilled banderillas, and other souvenirs of the corrida could be had without the chore of hunting them out. The fellow was, I noticed, doing a rushing business. I added to my collection of posters. These I keep in a huge portfolio designed for this purpose. One time when I was in hospital in New York, I insisted, in violation of all hospital rules, on having ten or more of these nostalgic banners pinned up on the walls of my room. By the time I left the hospital, not only my own nurses and doctor, but many more on the staff had come to see my show and could converse on the styles of Pepe Dominguine versus Antonio Ordonez.

I seem always to be strolling in Seville. Something is always happening to engage my attention. At seven o'clock every fine evening occurs a parade that warms the heart. For want of another name I call it "the children's hour." The first time I saw this event it was heralded by a clop-clop-clop of hooves on asphalt pavement. I turned to see a single hackney approaching at a smart clip. There was a flash of yellow wheels and passing me an open wagonette with a man on the box in braided Majo jacket of fiery red, and a black córdoban hat. Happily laughing and wriggling on the side seats were five or six children and two small babies each in the arms of its nurse. As this turnout sped past me down the lane of Parque de Maria Luisa, the children waved and called out gaily to no one in particular. I waved back. Carriage after carriage, mostly traps or wagonettes, passed me. Later I learned this custom of sending children with their nurses for a whirl around the parks, originated in the eighteenth century when the Duquesa de Albuquerque felt her brood of ten, doubtless energetic children, too many to cope with on a leisurely evening drive in her landau. The duquesa ordered two or three carriages fashioned with side seats. From that time out, when she took the evening air through flowery drives, her children, according to age, followed her in their own carriages. What interests me are the strict rules, observed by everyone today, that were laid down, presumably, by the duquesa. Only one cob is harnessed to the wagonette. A team would conflict with the style of the mother's equipage. One man does duty as coachman and groom. Nurses must wear black with voluminous white aprons and frilled caps with long starched streamers to dance in the breeze.

Aside from all the aimless strolling, music, dancing, wine, beautiful women, and dashing young men, there is much to see in Seville during *Feria*, or at any time. The Barrio Santa Cruz is a labyrinth of shaded *calles* where the walls of old houses are hung so thickly with baskets of growing flowers the stonework is concealed. In this quarter there are many beautiful old palaces, mellowed by the years, for it has the aristocratic *hidalgo* air. Many a grandee of Spain will tell you, "I was born in the Santa Cruz quarter in Seville." An antiquarian, his eyes far away in dreams, once told me: "More than half of the greatest treasure of Moorish and Renaissance art and furniture in Spain are in shuttered rooms in the Barrio Santa Cruz." From my window in the Alfonso XIII, I looked across a garden to the Real Fábrica de Tobaco, a square pink and yellow Baroque building two stories high, built around a patio as big as a football field. For some reason a moat surrounds the factory, a wide, deep ditch now given over to rank weeds and few strangled flowers. Obelisks set at intervals on the pink-frosting cornice lend a festive air of candles on a birthday cake, in scale with the famous *Gigantones*, the grotesque puppets which in most Spanish towns entertain the crowds to the point of hysteria when carried in processions.

This factory is in a garden, walled by iron spikes set into a yellow and black tile dado, and one is told it is where Carmen worked. One man added, "—and scratched out all the other girls' eyes." I hope some day to hear the opera *Carmen* sung by a diva dressed as a gitana of Triana quarter. Lucienne Breval in Paris, for example, did so, and was painted in costume by Zuloaga.

In Spain, I saw potential Carmens at every turn, wherever there are gypsies. I wondered what any one of them would say to the batch of Carmens who appear in various opera houses. They would doubtless spit in the dust more ferociously than they ever spat before.

The splendors of the Alcazar in Seville are well known to the world by photographs. The Gate of the Lions, with the arresting curve of "Allah's turban" arch, and vaulting height of wall at the side (hung thickly with climbing jasmine and passion-flower vines when I was there) leading into the spacious Court of the Miradors, delicately arched and colonnaded, gives the Alcazar its distinctive character.

One day I followed the great swags of linked chain, swag by swag, that encompass the four long façades of Biblioteca Colombina. Then I *knew* it was the largest archives in Christendom to harbor documents devoted to a single historical achievement—Columbus' discovery of America. The red and yellow Renaissance building is elevated from sidewalk level on a dais of stone. This lends great prominence to a building of no appreciable height in the heart of Seville. On the cornice rise stone plinths, like those used in ancient times to mark a harbor entrance, usually reserved in architectural ornament for the abodes of admirals. For example, one sees these symbols on Plazzo Papadopoli, reflected in the Grand Canal in Venice.

For archives ablaze with riches, give me the velvet canopied palanquines in the cathedral where robes for the Madonna used during *Semana Santa* are displayed. Not even in the gardens of Carthaginian Salammbo, or Queen Sophonisba, "who walked on a carpet of peacock's tails radiating the sun," were there ever such embroidered velvet trains spread under light. The depth of color—purples, claret reds, and larch green—is sumptuous as a background for the spun-gold threads. The Virgen del Gran Dolor has a casket of ruby-and-emerald-hafted daggers to be plunged into her heart for the procession, and the tears raining down her cheeks are real pearls. Christopher Columbus is buried in an elaborate sarcophagus under a tasseled canopy supported by four bronze grandees in court array.

The Giralda Tower close to the Gothic cathedral seems a Moorish arm forever pointing toward the cloud realm of Allah. "Giralda is one of the three sons of the Moor Jebir," or Yakout-el-Mansour, a Berber will tell you in the coffee houses of Marrakesh. Holding up one hand he continues, "The Hassan in Rabat. El Kuttubbiya," pointing to the gardens of the mosque, "in the shadow of which all muezzins wish to be buried."

The cathedral in Seville is a deeply-moving experience. Coming in out of the sun, into such unimagined size and soaring spaces, leaves one almost too stunned to comment. On every side is the most glorious ecclesiastical art. I met an American woman who told me she had "done" the churches of Europe and felt she never wanted to do another. Then she came into this cathedral. "It is far more filled with the beauty of Spain that I have read and heard about than any museum, even the Prado. I have been in Seville ten days and spent most of every day just walking and looking. I'm not half through yet."

I like to hear how different persons feel. An Irish Mother Superior of a convent in the wilds of Connemara once said to me after a rapturous trip to Seville, "The naves embrace the firmament and bring all heaven within reach." To say it is the second largest cathedral in the world is not enough.

In all this vastness of the power and glory and formality of Spanish Catholicism, an engaging earthy touch is a series of outside chapels. In the thickness of the mighty walls, set at intervals, is a series of tiny chapels facing on the street, each one an altar and glass covered reliquary for anyone passing by to stop, as at a wayside shrine. I have seen before these shrines touching pictures of devotion by the poor.

The Capilla Mayor, a forest of iron grills and *rejas*, is of tremendous scale yet delicacy of design. The altar lace alone would fill a museum. Altar cloths are folded many times to be opened and used as curtains during *Semana Santa*. One cloth alone is from the realm of fable. It is said two hundred nuns in Segovia worked for many years, a lifetime for some, on this cloth. In appliqué cord lace are panels showing The Stations of the Cross, The Crucifixion, and The Resurrection. All figures are life size. When completely unfolded the cloth measures twenty square yards. In religious processions it is sometimes carried on poles by fifty men as a banner against the sky.

Seville has a wealth of old palaces. Most of them are lived in so quietly that only the families and closest friends ever get beyond the armorial gates. The Spanish family and its ramifications is a very closed corporation. Sevillaños entertain to greater extent than most Spaniards, for the nature of the Andalusian is expansive. Everywhere one finds the greatest courtesy and good will. But the family circle is inviolate.

Casa de Pilatos is most representative of the *Mudéjar* style. Plain walls use four stories. A magnificently sculptured set piece surrounds the entrance door. The Dukes of Medinaceli have for centuries collected the furnishings with consummate taste. Although this family have many other houses, it is said the finest pieces of Spanish Renaissance in their collection are in Casa de Pilatos.

The palace one hears most about is Las Dueñas. In a small, crescent-shaped plaza rears a huge gateway flanked by peak-roofed gate lodges. Above the gate it appears that all the armorial bearings, trophies and banners in Christendom have burst into splendor in blue and yellow glazed tile. This is the entrance to an old Moorish palace, unquestionably the finest of its kind left in Spain. Las Dueñas is extremely old, mellowed to the red gold color of vintage wine. Set in gardens, on the edge of town, one can walk out into open fields, strewn with meadow flowers. The walls are pierced with jalousied windows, and balconies cling to all the walls like the old houses of grand viziers and caïds in the palm-shaded environs of Marrakesh. The Duke of Alba comes here for one week only, during *Semana Santa*. The gardens are open to view every day, and a custodian with the ascetic look of an El Greco saint and a musical way of telling legends of the house, will show you around the lower rooms. The carved cedar ceilings, some oiled only with attar of roses centuries ago which gives them a dark patina, others touched with red and green enamel, are superb, carved in honeycomb and stalactite design.

There is a unique museum in Seville which attracts many visitors. I notice many tourists go there around five o'clock in the afternoon hoping to catch a glimpse of some famous matador showing friends how toreros dressed in the time of Goya, who eulogized the bull-fighter. Here are displayed on figures all stages of the classical torero dress. Of special interest is the change from, say 1800, to the present day, in the dress of *matadores de toros*. The suits worn when Goya lived are much more pastel in coloring; the faintest of peach pinks, robin's-egg blue and breath of violet. Matadors wore their black hair long, confined in silk or velvet ribbon nets, and no hat. There is raiment of today stronger in color, the traditional pink silk stockings embroidered in roses and sequins, the ten yard long silk sashes. A few on show are spattered with blood of a gored matador or some particularly brave bull. I saw one young man, a *novillero*, demonstrating to a companion how he dances into his girdle. A servant or a friend (a great honor, this) holds one end, then the matador pirouettes and spins until the wide silk sash grips his waist as hard as armor. As for armor, the weight of all the gold and silver bullion and sequin embroidery on jackets and down the outside of the knee breeches is as much protective armor against the bull's horns as to display rich texture in the sun. The small black bicorn, uncompromising in line, is worn straight on the brow; a marvelous foil to all the vivid finery.

Hotel Alfonso XIII is one of the great hotels of Europe, with the Spanish version of Edwardian atmosphere. I suggest you walk through the gardens where aviaries of singing birds in tile pavilion cages live always within the spatter of fountains. The dining room at Alfonso XIII is world famous. Santo Domingo mahogany, red brocade, and gold. High ceilinged, with a row of tall windows giving onto a dining terrace, there is no more splendid room in Europe. The hotels in Seville are notably good. Hotel Christina is perhaps the gayest. In the grill one can eat, drink, and watch flamenco. The Inglaterra has a fine cuisine. The Madrid, in the charming Mendez Nuñez quarter, has the aristocratic Andalusian air. The old Colon is full of magic. The majordomo wears Barber of Seville livery, the housemaids are more like English nannies, middle-aged, plump, smiling; they wear red and white striped uniforms and mob caps straight out of nursery rhymes. Added to this *opera bouffe* atmosphere, the food at Colon is exceptional.

One of the most entertaining experiences I had in Spain was the night I drove out to the ruins of the Roman city of Itálica. A bright moonlight night in a carriage as unwieldly as the Ark, drawn by a team of white mules in red harness hung with brassy-toned bells. The turnout was positively philharmonic as we clashed along. I felt conspicuous, but no one we met seemed to take the slightest notice.

Once I had become accustomed to the brassy tinkle of the bells on the harness of Castor and Pollux, as I had christened the pair of white mules who drew my red and black landau, I became so attached to the whole turnout that I engaged Vulcan, who handled the reins, to call for me next day so that I, like an idolized matador, might arrive at Plaza de Toros with a flourish. I must explain all this roster of names from mythology. The mules wore pointed Phrygian caps of red cloth like those of the firmament twins, perched precariously between long ears. And no animal on four legs has such expressive ears as a mule. As for my driver, if Vulcan is supposed to have been the least favored of the gods, with abnormally long reach and armorer's strong hands, heavy torso, short bowed legs, and simian countenance, then, reincarnated, he sat upon the box of my carriage. Vulcan wore a picador's hat with a black chenille hood behind in the old bull-fighter tradition. Walking around at Itálica, I noticed he limped badly, which he explained by saying he at one time had been a picador, "—until I ran my *pic* through my own leg," he grunted.

The ruins of the Roman amphitheater are more imposing by moonlight than I remembered them by day. An immense semicircle with columns and pediments better preserved than many in Spain. It was so bright I could make out the lascivious expressions on the masks carved above doors supposed to have been private boxes. The dressing rooms under the stage were all equipped with tanks in which the actors could bathe. The star system seems to have been in existence then as now. Scipio Africanus built this vast theater and arena for games, to entertain his veterans from the Carthaginian wars. It seems curious that in Itálica four Roman emperors were born; Trajan, Theodosius, Hadrian, and Marcus Aurelius, yet for all the monuments built by them in other parts of their native land, in Itálica the prominent remains of the Roman era are not of their doing, but of a soldier of fortune who loved the men who fought under him in his African campaign so greatly that he devoted the rest of his life and

173

hard-earned private fortune to keep the veterans in patrician luxury.

We drew up at my hotel at about three o'clock in the morning. I turned to say goodnight. Castor, Pollux, and Vulcan all smiled or nodded, "*Buenas noces.*" A more infectiously gay group, when all's all, I never expect to see.

Before I begin to describe one of the great sights of Seville, (the day of a great corrida, in almost any town in Spain) I want to explain for the reader who does not know the history of *tauromachy* (the art of fighting the bull) just why this dangerous sport has such a hold over the Spanish mind. It is not a cult or just a popular fad, but a great national *force*. I once visited the rancho of a retired matador, who in his heyday had been the most popular idol of the bull ring. He was entertaining a group of friends at dinner. The main topic of conversation was bulls with, toward the end of the meal, a little politics. To end the topic of too heated political import my host turned to me and said, "If there *is* a Messiah in Spain, it is El Toro."

He who goes to Spain to see and to savor all that is Spanish, should make a point of attending a bullfight, and it is necessary to understand its peculiarly vital meaning if Spain is to be comprehended. The aesthetic part of the spectacle, the parade of toreros across the sunlit ring, the color, the arrogance of lithe matadors, every one a potential dancer, is an essential part of the corrida, but not the principal one. The bull is the *axis* of this contest between strength and agility plus split-second timing, whereon all the spectators' interest is focused. The fighting bull from Spain is veritably a savage beast. He is bred to absolute freedom on wide grassy plains. He hates barriers as he hates men. His brain is a tangle of sudden rages in which he spends his tremendous strength. When a fighter enters the ring to confront the bull he fully appreciates the bravery of this horned thunderbolt. Yet he must set his mind to dominate and master the animal for the kill. Here enters the consummate grace and dexterity of the fighter. The flash of personal style on which the reputation of a matador rests is now brought into play. The pitting of man against beast in deadly combat for sport is as old as man or beast. If one wishes to understand the fine points of bull fighting, the nearly incredible popularity of the sport in Spain, watch carefully the hair-trigger emotions of the crowd. It is the *bull* who gets first consideration. I have often seen a crowd burst out in fury as one man against a matador who had not dealt fairly with a brave bull. There are many stories of bulls who have shown such courage in the ring that they were accorded that rare shout from thousands of throats, "Don't kill—don't kill!" and sent back to grassy pastures never to fight again.

Next day was Sunday, dedicated to bullfights in Spain, so that every working man may attend. Vulcan called for me at five o'clock. He was festive in red braided *Majo* jacket and had a yellow silk bandana under his round brown hat. Branches of bright green lemon leaves had been hung as tassels to the Phrygian caps of the mules, to ward off flies during the time they should stand and wait. I felt a drab figure indeed in a dark suit, but we set off with cracking of whip and a dissonance of bells, in fine style.

As Vulcan drove with great skill and much acid badinage through the streets, the bells on the harness were drowned out by countless other bells on the harnesses of horses, mules, even teams of little burros. To arrive at Plaza de Toros on the evening of a "supreme extravagant corrida," according to the legend on the posters, cannot be compared to any other sensation I know. Two of the most popular matadors in Spain are to dispatch three bulls apiece. The bravery and ferocity of the bulls, from a famous *ganadería*, are treated to as many glowing adjectives as are the matadors. On every hand is shouting and surging color. The exciting arrival of toreros in wagonettes, fully turned out in gold galloon and satin. Women, many beautiful and flashing, in high combs and mantillas and all the jewels they possess, arrive in victorias.

At six o'clock to the minute a fanfare is blown on trumpets. The gates of the barrier are flung open, the parade comes in. The opening gambit has great flare. Two *alguaciles*, in medieval black velvet, crimped ruffs, and plumed hats, ride beautiful, long-maned Arab mares. Today the featured matadors are Juan Posada, with the face of a poet, dressed in yellow satin, and Manolo Vazquez, wearing green, walking like a panther, causing moans of delight from the assembled women. There is possibly no other costume for sport to show off the male figure with such grace as the gold-and-sequin-embroidered jacket, the tightly wrapped silk sash, and knee breeches of a torero. For the entrance parade the extraordinarily beautiful *capa de paseo*, sometimes embroidered in jeweled saints, is worn slung over one shoulder, wrapped tightly about the hips and held with one hand. *Banderilleros* stride in, often tall men, whose agility "on the toes," arms upflung to drive the goads into the bull's shoulders, is proverbial. Picadors are older men, hard-bitten like my driver Vulcan, riding nags well protected, in these days of upholstering the

175

nags, in wadded quilts. Another trumpet blast and a black or sepia
bull stands in the open gate. Head lowered, undecided, little red eyes
blinking in the sudden light. From now on it is flashes of speed, flicks
of red, alternating long pauses, while man and bull eye each other,
calculating just how near is death. A horn one inch too close and it
means for Posada or Vazquez being borne out in the arms of fellow
toreros to a narrow bed in a candle-lit chapel under the arcades, to
wait for recovery, or death. For the bull there awaits a perfectly
placed sword point just behind the skull, a quick downward thrust,
gouts of choking blood, and an ignominious exit across the sand,
dragged by a mule team, whipped to a gallop by red shirted *monos*.

The style of several prominent matadors varies. Some depend on
quiet subtlety of handling the capes in masterly *verónicas* or double
verónicas, flipped in an arc sudden and swift as bird flight, to surprise

and dominate the bull. Others display contempt, or arrant bragga-
docio such as a matador kneeling with his back to the bull or, like El
Gorríto, fighting the beast on stilts.

In the history of tauromachy, stories of the tricks to which matadors will resort to catch the interest and spike the imagination of the
audience are legion. As a slim youth, Litri first appeared in the bull
ring, and the audience greeted the grave faced *novillero* with no
enthusiasm. "The student," he was nicknamed. In surprisingly short
time, the boy flashed like a meteor across the Spanish sky. After a few

corridas Litri was mentioned with the immortals such as the incomparable Manolete, courageous Juan Belmonte, survivor of many gorings, who became the greatest teacher of bullfighting in Spain today, and Marcial Lalanda, whose mariposa or zigzag swirl with the cape was like a swarm of crimson butterflies.

Of a sudden, at the age of twenty-two, Litri has announced his immediate retirement from the bull ring. In an interview with representatives of the press in Madrid, Litri gave his reasons as a not-to-be-denied wish to devote his time to studying the classic literature of Spain which his absorption with the technique of cape and sword had so far prevented. After the first thunderclap of this announcement had reverberated to the farthest sierras, the youth of the country raised their disconsolate heads and are now loud in speculation as to which matador or precocious *novillero* will be the reigning idol of the bull ring. The humming of conjecture in the cafés and *ramblas* will for a time sound like the swarming of all the bees in creation. For, as Pindar said of youthful athletes "Bright are the laurels and high held the young heads to encircle."

Chapter 11

CATHEDRALS AND OLIVE GROVES
IN JAÉN

THE day I left Seville it rained in torrents until I was well past Fuenta Palmera, an old hill town of clustered houses, looking in the misty light like a Spanish Mont-Saint-Michel when the tide is in, standing up stark from the flooded plain. A few miles before I reached Córdoba the sun came out, not in accustomed Spanish splendor, but so I could faintly see this Moorish bastion city as if built from pale jade. Almost it seemed to float in La Campiña, the wide plain between the Guadalquivir and the Gothic pointed peaks of Sierra Morena. Today these usually brilliant purple-blue mountains, frosted with the silver of jagged crests, were but lightly sketched in mist, with spears of black rain jabbing the plain. By the time I had reached the Roman bridge over which I must pass to reach the Omayyad Gate the mist rose again. Pale sun filtered through rain, lending the proper Oriental illusion to the most Oriental of all towns in Spain. After I had gone to my hotel, the Simón, I walked through the Gran Capitan, a wide promenade regarded by Córdobans as fine and important to their open air life as the Rambla de las Flores is to Barcelonese.

The pride of Córdoba is the Mezquita, or mosque, sometimes called "the most Moorish building in the world in or out of Morocco." This may be true, but inside the effect is a forest of confusion, where long corridors of lotus-petal arches and columns, alternating in stripes of red and white, form a tortuous maze through which one gropes one's way to reach the Court of Oranges, with its range of yellows, drifts of perfume, and music of fountains.

The Street of the Miradors is to my mind the loveliest part of

Córdoba. Some of the old palaces are so ancient that parts of the walls were built by members of the emir's court in the tenth century. I divert my mind with evoking a picture of the Omayyad emir, Abd-ar-Rahman, in his two-story palanquin, reclining on cushions behind tinsel gauze curtains on the top tier, while his favorite concubines, masked and turbaned—as Pierre Loti said, "the women of the Omayyad wrap their heads in the rainbow"—lolling on the lower platform, awaiting a summons upstairs.

When Abd-ar-Rahman fled Damascus after the massacre in which his entire family was slain, he landed at Cádiz. There, for a time, he stayed. Then, listening to a soothsayer who told him his destiny lay in Córdoba, he founded the Omayyad Emirate of Córdoba in the tenth century. Soon after Abd-ar-Rahman had become the most powerful Moor in Spain, the soothsayer added to his prophecy the rather frightening warning that the emir would be assassinated if he entered the door of his palace, or the door of any other house, from ground level. To insure a long life, the emir never again walked in the streets, but was carried in a double-decked litter said to have been "half as big as a mosque," borne on the backs of Arab stallions. He decreed that all upper windows in houses be as large as doors. Instead of entering a house from the street he used the upper miradors, thus the high arched windows give the street its name. The precaution of using upper windows for entering seems to have worked, for there is no record of Abd-ar-Rahman meeting a violent death. Córdoba was a city of nearly half a million population when the Moors were driven out of Spain. The memory of the learning, the luxury, the craftsmanship fostered here by the Omayyad emirs caused all Spain, as well as the courts of Europe to wonder if such splendor of the mind and the arts would ever be known again. The world had long marveled at the glorious silks, tinsel gauzes called *dibij* and *tiraj*, the damascene silver caskets, jewelry, and screens for the miradors. Leather, under the tanners of Córdoba, became soft as velvet, or burnished as a ripe chestnut shell. Now, only in the museum can one see the famed gauzes in which perfumed beauties of the harem were wrapped by eunuchs to be carried to the emir's couch.

In glass cases are meters of silk tinted like the plumage of exotic birds, so sheer it can be drawn through the hoop of an earring. I saw a purple damask named *Ispahani* with an underlay of crimson silk, glowing with changeable bloom to rival the purple dyes of Tyre.

179

While all this silk and tinsel beauty is as unattainable today as the langorous ladies who once wore it, the shops of Córdoba are filled with all manner of articles of leather which one can buy. In one shop, where old loot was enticingly displayed, I saw a screen of dull polished leather, the green of larch forests when a few rays of sun pierce the dense glades to give life to the green. Etched on the leather panels were ships and waves and seahorses in silver gilt. A perfect example of seventeenth-century Córdoban art.

Notwithstanding the Mezquita is considered a wonder of the world, completely alone in the field of architecture for individuality of design, ask any man in Córdoba what is their greatest treasure and he will tell you "The shrine at the grave of Manolete." In 1947 the unquestioned idol of Spain, the tall, shy, dignified *matador* Manolete was to fight Miura bulls at Linares. Of all fierce *toros*, the Miura breed are the "black death." Manolete was killed that day by a "dead bull," by reflex action of the horns as he bent over to remove his sword after delivering a brilliant *suerte*. He is buried under cypresses in Córdoba, and his grave has become a shrine.

In so many towns and cities in the world I have a special spot I like to go alone. A pilgrimage, sometimes for a reason I scarcely know myself. In Córdoba I go at late evening, just as the lanterns are lit, to the ancient monastery church of El Christo de Los Faroles. This shrine is outside the town in an ilex grove. All here is completely medieval Spain, nothing to do with the Moors. The old white walls, and rose-gray lichened tiles of the long, undulating roof, might have been brushed in under a thunderous sky by El Greco. I saw El Christo at night when a moon was struggling behind clouds casting a chiaroscuro of light and shade on the walls and low, square belfry. In the courtyard rises a Gothic cross in mightiness of simplicity. It might have been hewn from stone by the verger in a long brown cloak who came out of the cloisters to light the row of iron lanterns surrounding the cross. On tall iron spikes, quavery and rusted with age, the lanterns are not very bright, they glow fitfully like will-o'-the-wisps. Yes, this is what I came here for. It is an El Greco canvas come to immediate life.

Linares is a big, rambunctious mining town. The bull ring is one of the largest in Spain and the townspeople work hard, but are so enthusiastic for good corrida they will cheerfully go without bread, chick-peas, oil, and garlic, then pool the money thus saved to attract the best talent in matadors. Its situation is spectacular in the wild region of Sierra Morena, Bailen, Andujar and Ubeda. All about here range pine forests, thundering waterfalls, wild gorges where the sun never penetrates, and ragged peaks thrusting into the clouds. This is nature's prolific game preserve, like the Val de Aosta in Italy. Wild boars and stags are hunted the year around. Great brown bears, wolves, and lynxes are the scourge of hamlets on the lower slopes. Hunters from all over the world come to stay in *paradores* in Ubeda and Andujar (where a splendid *hospederia* is open the year around) to stalk the illusive, almost legendary mountain goat with the great scythe horns, *Capra hispanica*.

On the road from Linares to Andujar I passed a group of hunters. The road was so narrow I had to drive at a crawl to pass them, for all were heavily laden from, I judged, many days of sport in the mountains. Three foresters who had guided the shooting party were as striking to behold as mountaineers always are. A father and his two sons, I should say. The father was a giant in cape-like jacket of mountain-goat skin lined with brown bear fur. The band of his wide-brimmed felt hat was stuck full of bears' paws and boars' tusks, eagles' wing feathers and wolves' tails. This was real panache. His sons wore the wrap-around leather leggings I had so often seen in Catalonia, cross-gartered in strips of bears' fur. Each wore a leather cape, fur-lined, slung across one shoulder dragging the ground arrogantly, and his hat was a pale imitation of the father's. Three as proudly stalwart denizens of the chase as I have ever seen.

Andujar is a curious hill town of great character. Nearly all the houses have fronts covered in a diapering of huge iron rosettes. Stars, lions' heads, bears' masks, and so on, in the manner of the plaster shells on the façade of Casa de las Conchas in Salamanca. This iron ornamentation gives to the houses a rusted stripe effect, which is as decorative as it is original. In this region sudden, tempestuous rain storms are frequent, so the iron stripes become rivulets of red; the same effect is seen on the rust-stained houses of Zamora, where ornamental eaves are cast in iron. I asked about these iron bosses in Andujar and was given an illuminating answer. The town had once been a Roman fort, with houses either forming part of the old wall, or later built into it. In the sixteenth century, in order to shore up some ricketty masonry, iron bolts were set into the stonework to strengthen it. With the well-proven Spanish sense of decoration combining utility, the bolts were given ornamental heads. Once the effect was seen, everyone in town followed suit, whether their walls were sagging or not.

If it were not for frequenting *hosterias, ventorros, tabernas,* by whatever names these wayside inns are called in various provinces, to take a glass of wine during my journeyings, I would not see half the entertaining things I do. In Spain these inns are the pulse of village life, and the haunt of traveling gossips who give all manner of information for the lift of a glass, gratis. I was about to quit Andujar for Ubeda when I saw two men, whom I instantly recognized by their clothes to be from Barrio Triana in Seville. The men came out of the dark wine shop which is part of the *hosteria,* mounted two fairly clean-blooded horses, and rode off through the arched gateway.

I asked the patrón if there was a gypsy gathering of any sort in the neighborhood. He said that there had been, a few nights before, a large camp at the rock crevice where the Virgen de Cabeza had first appeared to a young shepherd who was searching in the fastnesses for a lost ewe with her lamb, on a stormy night in the thirteenth century. There is no more hallowed spot in all Spain than the shrine of Our Lady of Cabeza. Later, on the road I saw some of the high-wheeled, white-hooded carts used for the loveliest of pilgrimages, the Romería del Rocío, which starts in Seville, winds through the streets across the Guadalquivir and so through Barrio Triana, out into the open country, tracing lanes through sweet grasses to camp at night under the silvery green tents of olive trees.

Perhaps of all the allurements Spain has to offer today, the Romería del Rocío is, from beginning to end, the most magical of all pastoral festivals. It is for the Andalusian country man and woman—the *Majo* and *Maja,* whom Goya so often painted—as well as gypsies from Triana. *Majas* wear gypsy dress, crisp full skirts of spotted cotton, and the cavaliers who ride cobs to escort the wagons affect short white or gray jackets over tight black breeches, tooled leather aprons fringed and tasseled as are chaps in the American Far West, and córdoban hats slanted at a dashing angle. As I passed by the carts women sitting high up on piled white mattresses smiled and waved. Some were polishing the copper cooking utensils kept hanging from the pole between the wheels, others were dressing the Triana dolls one can buy in the shops in Seville. Young girls were weaving garlands of wheat and fresh flowers to decorate the wagons for the night of dancing at an encampment by some stream.

I once stood on a river bank, late at night when I was visiting a friend at his *estancia* near Fernán Nuñez. The Romería encampment was on his land. In a slight declivity, ringed with olive trees, was a scene from *Midsummer Night's Dream*. The carts were drawn up in a circle with the nomad tabernacle, white curtains drawn, like an altar in the center. It was, I remember, a shiny night of stars, but no moon. The high, rounded covers of the carts seemed of moth-wing softness; in some a light in front of the Virgin glowed dimly. The air was still, not a sigh among the leaves. Bonfires were dying down to embers, and the wail of *saetas* seemed hushed in low cadences. At midnight the white curtains of the shrine were looped back, the candles lighted to glow on the figure of the Virgin in her golden robe and turn the trees to limpid green. Slowly, in a kind of ritualistic dance, men and women moved down to the stream dipping in their fingers as at a holy water font. Then the dance began to weave around the shrine. At intervals a piercing shriek split the silence, to die away as the *saeta* became a murmuring in the night. One by one the dancers sank to their knees around the woodland altar.

Into Ubeda I drove with a high heart, for this is invigorating country. The pure mountain air and the architectural excellence of Ubeda and its sister town Baeza only a few miles away, offer a traveler unique lift. This is still Andalusia, but in Jaén Province of the millions of olive trees, so close to proud Castile, her bosom forever borne up in a corselet of gold and silver etiquette, that from the terrace of Parador Don Ortego Cabiro the view is no longer the hot languors of Andalusia, but the mountain coolness of Castile.

The *parador* is a remodeled palace of the Cabiro family (sometimes called the Palace Davalos) of great antiquity, where many persons spend weeks at a time in summer or winter. In summer, they use this *parador* as a base, then drive to Seville, Córdoba, Granada, Ronda, even as far as Valdepeñas for the vintage festival. In winter, sportsmen shoot stag and wild boar in the adjacent mountains. I dined on game pâté and wonderfully prepared venison as promised when I had telephoned the manageress from Linares.

All the houses in Ubeda and Baeza are a gradation of one subtle color. The stone, quarried near Linares is a pale faun, a shade as delicate as bisque, lightly flecked in brown and plum-color like the shell of a plover's egg.

There are many fanciful buildings in Ubeda. It is impossible to describe in the detail they deserve all the variegated beauties of stucco, dovetailed stone, and marbles. Two houses in particular attract the eye immediately. The exquisite Plateresque School for Lacemakers is so redolent of theater that I have always wanted to reconstruct it in some appreciative city as a playhouse. The walls are embellished with plaques of the Muses, and a wide band of lace-like carved figures of nymphs and satyrs in the age-old Saturnalia, definitely of the theater, surrounds the door and windows.

The Palace of the Condes de Benevente is, by any standards, surely one of the loveliest Gothic tracery houses standing today, looking as swept and garnished as the day it was built. A Spanish interpretation of Florentine "banqueting house" style. Instead of the usual manner of hanging balconies in front of windows from which to watch tournaments, festivals, and religious ceremonies, there is a long pillared loggia across the top story, between two half circle columns, huge in girth, topped by palm tree capitals supporting a "ladies' bower" in delicate carved-stone filigree. The wall between the columns has tremendous import and is the delight of architects the world over. Big, square cabochons of stone form a diapered pattern (like the fleurs-de-lys stenciled on the walls of Florentine palaces) to be lightened, by the same delicate tracery around pointed Gothic windows, like that which caps the "ladies' bowers." If I were asked to describe Palacio de Benevente in one word, unhesitatingly I should say *style*.

In Spain, when some out-of-ordinary sight suddenly meets the eye in a city plaza or possibly fifty leagues from nowhere, never ask questions, or even wonder why. Just accept it, and in most cases enjoy it. To elucidate: I came into the Plaza de Santa Maria de Ubeda at mid-morning. A storm was brewing. As in a bull ring, the square was cut in half by livid sunlight and sharp black shadow. Thunder was reverberating among the distant mountain peaks. I felt a downpour was imminent. The doors of a priory school opened and out strode a religious procession at high speed. Prelates of the church, altar boys bearing a cross and swinging silver thuribles for incense led about fifty boys of assorted ages, every one in ecclesiastical scarlet. The boys wore red serge cassocks, the prelates walked high-chinned in moiré silk. For a moment this churchly pageantry struck clarion color in the sunlight. Suddenly the heavens opened, and the deluge fell. I ran under the arcades, but the procession proceeded (I afterwards saw them at Fuente de la Plaza Populo, chanting in Latin, bedraggled as red roosters left out in the rain) straight across the square. As quickly as the storm came, it passed. But oh, what a wetting those scarlet boys got.

The word for Jaén is drama, in capitals. A great sprawling town built on riffled hills, as if Ocean had been tortured into mounting waves, then on the instant transformed into stone. From the heights it is a strange spectacle, like a city kneeling, for most of the houses are low, no more than two or three stories. All shades of dusty yellow prevail, with ancient red tile roofs, the color blotted out by centuries of bronze and gray lichen. Sharply accented are a few roofs of new, fiery-red tiles. Rising in immensity out of all proportion, like some palace from an empire of Aztec gold, bulks the cathedral, a melange of pillars and pediments and soaring cupolas. The *placing* of this exaggerated church in the midst of indifference is as important as the grandiose façade by Pedro Valdelvira, who started to build in 1530. He died, an old man crowding a century, from marble dust clogging his lungs, for he worked with the marble carvers until his death. Had he lived two centuries longer, he would still not have seen this elaborate edifice to the greater glory of God completed. Workmen were busy as ants running up and down scaffolds at one side of the sacristy, when I spent an entire day examining the beautifully-articulated marble capitals, and made sketches of the strongly-built but fragile-appearing domed temples which crown the twin belfries. When I asked a verger if this work was reconstruction, perhaps from Civil War mutilation, when so many churches in Spain were desecrated, he said, "No, señor. We are still carrying out the Valdelvira plans." I nodded, thinking they must be very dog-eared by now. But no, I saw them on parchment, thumbmarked but not torn.

Enormous as the cathedral of Jaén appears, it is a deception. Backed by the undulating gray-violet Sierra Magina, the lower slopes dotted by thousands of olive trees, it gains in majesty, a great bulwark in stone and marble, isolated in the center of an old hill town where times vary from riches to dire poverty according to how good the olive crop was that year.

Cuenca should first be seen from the promenade in the lower town so one may get the improbable profile of this Moorish town set high on a gorge in a remote region of New Castile. The rock face rises three hundred meters sheer from verdant meadows and a serpentine river. The old Moorish houses are built cheek to jowl with wide balconies from which to view the sweeping panorama of river meadows and Sierra de Valdemeca. These airy pavilions jutting out into

MOUNTAIN
FARMERS.-
NAVARRE

space twenty feet or more from solid rock have an individuality seldom seen. I am reminded of an Oxford professor I met on the Puente de Trinidad arching the River Jucár, one of the eight bridges over two rivers dividing the town. The man was petulantly regarding the houses hanging half in space.

"Footlin' way to build. Eccentric lot of beggars. That's what." He turned to me yelling, "*Eccentric*, don't you agree?"

Aside from building their houses on air, the people of Cuenca support a cathedral of undisputed splendor, containing wrought-iron *rejas* accorded as fine as any in Spain. There is also a great rock-crystal candelabrum branching one hundred candles of spangle-decorated wax. Another monumental piece of eccentricity, if you like. There are one or two old palaces in Mudéjar style. One was occupied by the "warrior queen," as she styled herself, Doña Maria de las Nieves, wife of the Pretender Don Carlos. As late as 1874, during the Carlist Wars, Doña Maria ordered Cuenca sacked. She later commuted that order to "submission" so Cuenca would not be destroyed. Afterwards she spent some time in the house pointed out as Casa de las Pendones (the banners) because when in residence Doña Maria flew the flags of Anjou and Spain, including the device of each Spanish province. In the entrance hall of the house these weather-beaten banners can be seen stacked like spears in big Chinese jardinières.

Hotel Iberia is not the best hotel in the province but the food is good and the location excellent. The waiters, wearing gold-braided red Zouave jackets, copied from a painting of Doña Maria in Zouave uniform on a white horse, add dash to the white dining room. But in your room don't try to get service by ringing a bell. There is none. Just open the door and shout, as everyone else does.

The way to Zaragoza lies through extremes of terrain over the wide River Tagus, lying flat as Toledo steel, so shallow I could look over a bridge and see incalculable numbers of red and silver fish, more minute than whitebait, glinting like quicksilver. These fish are gathered in shallow baskets of rushes, then tossed into boiling olive oil and sold along the road, as crisp as *patatas fritas*. I stopped at a little town built like a Moorish casbah on the side of a hill near Villarquemado in the Sierra Albarracín. On a remote hill, far from any sign of habitation, rose a ruined abbey. The vast building is a gray-gold shell, roofless to the sierra winds, and from the foot of the hill the long cloisters and church of cathedral proportions look like a village of dormitories, a magnificent raddled monolith to destroying Time. To add just the right touch of the quick and the dead to this wild landscape, a boy in a white wool cape stood on a ledge tending a few goats. He was burned black as a Moor. He soon left off regarding me and gave attention to his job of tending goats, meanwhile flailing the air with his crook to ward off attack from a swooping eagle.

Through the Province of Guadalajara to Albarracín is a distraction in road travel, there is so much to see. Not that anything is so important, just beguiling. Such things as a farmhouse painted in stripes of red, green, and turquoise blue, like the rainbow Campanario Palace at Utebo, one of the mysteries of Spanish Mudéjar architecture. But my farmhouse had a shiny tin roof, as if crowned with mirrors. Near Tragacete I saw a farm roofed in golden straw, with four little turrets of straw at the corners, and a high wall of wattle and straw surrounding a plot of some green growth. This I learned later was opium poppy for medicinal use, and the turrets were lookouts for men to shoot at flocks of marauding birds.

Albarracín is an entertaining town with a Moorish wall that marches up a barren hill, becomes a square castellated fort on top, and marches right down on the other side. Women walk the walls proudly in dark red shawls, embroidered in black scrolls, and black skirts bordered in yellow flouncing. In the hilly streets of Albarracín these wide skirts give them the appearance of Hindu nautch dancers in the Rajputana temples. I like Teruel just across the border in Teruel Province of Aragon, for the spectacular way the red-roofed houses sweep upward to the high walled citadel. The towers are like minarets, green, purple, and blue in the sun. In the church of Santiago reposes a relic supposed to have miraculous powers to help the poor. It is a dun-colored cloak of heavy wool, almost an Arab caftan, coarsely woven, stained by wind and weather, ragged and threadbare. But this garment is surprisingly edged and lined with cloth of pure gold. According to legend, one cold, stormy night in the fifteenth century a wandering mendicant sought shelter in the town. Like the Holy Family in Jerusalem he was refused shelter at every door. Weary unto death and half frozen, the mendicant knocked at the last house by the wall, a miserable hut. The door was opened by an old man in the same state of rags as himself, who offered the stranger all he had, a pallet of straw. It was bitterly cold in the night and the old man moaned in his sleep. When he awoke at dawn the stranger had gone, never to be heard of again. Wrapped around the old man was the ragged cloak of the mendicant, but now it was lined with pure gold. Since that time many people, wanting help in a crisis, have touched the cloak, which is stretched flat in a reliquary. During the Civil War this relic was buried in a secret cave, but poor persons, "led by the mystery of its golden rays" it is said, went to the cave to pray.

Calatayud seems more of a Moorish dream from the realms of hashish than Granada, Córdoba, or other "Oriental" cities in Spain. One of the largest towns of Aragon, the approach is spiked by minarets in Mudéjar style as if the parasols of sultans had been raised against the black and gray striped hills, where the dark mouths of hundreds of caves lend a strange effect of patterned lace, or at night, when lighted, like huge glow worms. This is called Morera. Above these caves towers the shell of a Moorish castle, the ruined walls as delicate in line, as in its color of pink pearls.

For all this Moorish overlay, the history of Calatayud goes as far back as Phoenician days. A vast smithy for welding armor was erected at Bilbilis close by. I went out there to see the walled enclosure where Romans held horse fairs said to have corralled ten thousand horses at one time. There is little left to see except waste land and stone cubicles that were once horse pens. But to me these are evocative acres. I could see on the retina of my eye the whole picture of heavy-rumped mares and stallions, their tails switching, the beautiful muscles of necks rippling, and hear impatient pawing of hooves, as the sound of bargaining voices rose on the air.

The ancient mosque turned Christian, Colegiata de Santa Maria, still bears the little fretted Moorish porches, so like the houses in Tetuan and Fez. During Corpus Christi there is religious dancing in the Camino de la Soledad. The men wear Roman armor, as once it was made in Bilbilis, but the women in light colors are as Oriental in appearance as the visioned houris of Paradise promised to every true believer by Allah in the Koran.

After passing the lakeside village of Gallocanta and across the sluggish River Jilota, the first hint that one is coming to the chestnut forests of Zaragoza is the amazing greenness of the countryside, with long avenues of trees leading to farms and spacious manor houses. If the sun is shining there may be a glare of light spears radiating from the snow-capped peaks of distant Pyrenees. Zaragoza has the look of culture from the moment you drive under Puerta de la Aljafería and on past the Castillo de la Aljafería built by a Moorish caïd, but greatly remodeled as a royal residence for the Kings of Aragon. The University gives the city its tone. I have not seen so many bookshops, libraries, and stationery stores mixed with shops for Roman, Gothic, and Mudéjar antiquities anywhere in Spain. The first thing I did in Zaragoza was to buy typing paper of fine quality, a rarity in Europe. Zaragoza is actually a very large city, in many ways distinctly up-to-date, with numerous tree-lined squares and parks.

There are three reasons for climbing Monte Torrero, nearby: an unimaginably satisfying view of green woodlands, composed of great groves of walnut and chestnut trees, rivers, and far off the Pyrenees, with Sierra de la Peña a purple swath in middle distance; a telescope, far greater in range than the one at Ventorro Telescopio in Cádiz, although here is no mystery man from the Basque country to present you with a rosette for guessing the planets correctly; and a third compensation which no one could imagine. A whole menagerie of *Gigantones del Leon.* Unlike the immense puppets of Pamplona, Tarragona, and Burgos, which satirize human beings, these are giant-size animals dressed as potentates, mandarins, or Roman legionaries. The first rhinoceros ever to be exhibited in Europe traveled from Hamburg in 1748 (there is a medal of him struck in Nürnberg), across France, survived the passes of the Pyrenees, and was shown to the children of Zaragoza on Torrero Hill. That started the idea of animal puppets, which someone with wit and vision has carried with flourish to a circus finish, for which I am sure every child in Saragossa blessed his name. The king of beasts, from which the charade takes its name, is sixteen feet high and wears the red and gold armor and plumed casque of a fantastic Roman general, the lion's shaggy mane being outrageously crimped. The rhinoceros is an African chief or Oriental potentate, I could not tell which. The elephant is a fanciful Corsair. The monkeys, baboons, and so on of the simian group, are delectable Chinese mandarins in red, green, and yellow satin mandarin coats, and pigtails. These figures are kept in a pagoda-roofed house and brought out occasionally to entertain visitors on days of fiesta.

The Cathedral, La Seo, is more palace than church, with long corridors of gilt and mirrors, yet every prelate in Spain would like, when death sounds the trumpet, to lie in state under the baldaquin with its black spiral Salamonic columns, the curtains of gold and silver lace falling to drag for yards on the tessellated floor. This is a church where richness is upon richness piled, with the ardor only Spanish churches can show. There are acres of carved choir stalls. Instead of a *single* robing room for bishops and cardinals about to officiate before the high altar, there are whole apartments of flagrantly ornate white stucco rooms crammed with gilt and red velvet.

In the Cathedral of Nuestra Señora del Pilar, the sacristy where the jewels of the Madonna are kept is a marvel of brilliance. "La Pilaríca" is a black Virgin of great beauty of feature. She resides on top of a silver pillar with clouds and stars of spun glass behind her diademed head. On the occasion of important religious ceremony she is hung with a collection of real stones such as few queens, save perhaps Theodora of Byzantium, have ever worn, and carried through the streets. The Avenida de Ebro, along the river, is a beautiful promenade where in the evening young students from the university walk in groups, reciting the lessons for tomorrow in chanting voices like those of little boys reciting passages from the Koran, which one hears while passing schools in Fez and Marrakesh. This method of studying lessons may easily have originated in Zaragoza from Moorish source.

Museo de Tapices is housed in long, high chambers in La Seo. There is nothing comparable in Spain to these examples of the weavers' art of pictorial arras, with the possible exception of the "History of Tarquin" tapestries in Zamora, which I prefer. The Museo de Tapices collection is chosen from the finest tapestries of La Seo and El Pilar cathedrals. *Las Naves* is narrative needlework at its highest pitch, depicting the story of the expedition of Brutus (nephew of Aeneas) to Aquitaine. Ships, horses, all the soldiers fantastically equipped for war, and the sails of the galleons are imagined as great sea birds in flight. Only one of three panels is known to be in existence. Another, purported to be of this set, was found in Arras in 1700 covered with caked blood and cow dung in a byre, but damaged beyond any hope of restoration. It is known that these tapestries were woven in Arras. In one room in the museum, pure theater rears its head. The chatelaines in *Till Eulenspiegel*, seem to parade before one's eyes in a panel where a group of medieval ladies wear impossibly tall hennins fashioned to ape the horn of a unicorn. All the dames are walking in extreme sway-back *enceinte* fashion, thus satirizing the legend of the virgin and the unicorn.

To be so close to Navarre and not go on to Pamplona seemed a mistake. I planned to drive by way of Huesca, on to the inimitable

Las Cinco Villas in the hills and see the houses that Señor El Loco (the madman) built for non-existent children, then on to Pamplona, to Miranda de Ebro, and so on through Monasterio de Rodilla to Burgos.

The way from Zaragoza to Huesca lies through El Castellar valley, and beside the River Gallego for a good part of the way. This is "the ramparts of Navarre," country of most inspiring mountain scenery, the towering castle-like crags glinting with quartz deposits rising from pine forests. It is also a wonderful way to drive because the valley road has a stone bed and is wider than most in Spain.

Huesca, in the province which bears its name, lured me to its fastnesses to see the Gothic cathedral and twin palaces, half Moorish, half Gothic. The cathedral is built on the site of a mosque and the palaces were once pavilions and mirador colonnades resided in by twin caliphs. It seems curious to think that so close to the Pyrenees and stern Navarre was once a Moorish citadel. Even the walls that follow a partly ruinous line to the town of Jaca, were erected by Moorish overlords to provide a pleasance over which they might ride on horseback or be carried indolently in litters to take the air, view the mountains, and in Jaca buy Greek slaves.

In the cathedral is a *retablo* in alabaster by the most noted sculptor of his time, Damien Forment, a Valencian of the fifteenth century. He brought back from Italy ideas greatly foreign to the taste of Spanish clergy. Two of his first works were destroyed as sacrilegious. But after he had carved the *retablo* in El Pilar in Zaragoza he was reinstated as a genius above criticism. In the cathedral in Huesca the subject is the Passion, under a series of ascending canopies and traceries as delicate as spun lace, which form a frame for the triptych. I drove into Jaca to witness a ceremony in the cathedral, rare even in Spain. Young men and women in superb medieval costume of the district, all the jewel colors of red, green, yellow, and violet with a great deal of gold and silver galloon on skirts and jackets, dance the *jota* down the center aisle and in front of the altar. In the choir stalls stand men playing on Navarrese bagpipes and tambourines as big as drums. The fusing of solemnity, ritual, and abandon, with overall the eerie wail of bagpipes, sent me out into the night aching to paint what I had just seen on a vast canvas.

The oddly shaped region called Las Cinco Villas is a series of little hills topped with trees. There is also a scattering of shepherds' huts and a wall of dark cypress, doubtless once clipped in arches like that wonderfully somber colonnade of sable arches at the hunting lodge of Carlos III near Brihuega. Behind this now untended ragged barricade, is a grove of chestnut trees. And if you look closely, for no one is allowed inside the gates, you will see five miniature castles of white stone. Each is different in design but bears a family resemblance to the other. All bristle with turrets and crenelations. Most delicious of all, each is named after the imagined occupant and has its own entrance gate and driveway. A dilettante romantic bachelor in the early nineteenth century had a desire for sons and daughters with none of the bother of begetting them. So he had five dolls fashioned. Boys and girls. He built each a "villa," naming it after each doll child. So these little white castles set among hanging gardens and hibiscus fringed lakes are *Elysium, Atlantis, Propontis, Fons Juventae,* and *Ophir.*

The last few miles across the rolling meadowlands as one approaches Pamplona have an air of Normandy. There is also in Navarre the breath of Les Basses Pyrénées and of Biarritz; and Basque legends form a great share of Navarrese songs and poetry. Long lines of mountain poplars line the road, and the Pyrénées rise in graded peaks, like cut-out scenery against a backdrop of wind-blown clouds. A date for travelers in Spain to keep well in mind is the 7th of July. This is the Festival of San Firmin, as important and brilliant in color and excitement in Pamplona as the *Feria* in Seville. Runners of rush matting are attached to the walls of the houses as safeguard for both man and bull. Young bulls, destined later for corrida, are let loose and aspiring young toreros chase them through the narrow alleys. Rose-crowned young girls lean from second- and third-story windows to shout encouragement. All is pandemonium and slashing color on the move. This is the time that improbable crew of *Gigantones* are carried bobbing, nodding great pudding heads, and curtseying in mock formality to balcony parties, by men who usually carry a bottle of wine under the skirts of whatever plaster giant he may be locomoting. It is a spectacle lurid, bizarre beyond belief, and curiously frightening.

The traditional costumes of Estella, near Pamplona, are a triumph of cold elegance, with something of the glitter of Pyrénées snows against a darkling sky. The women wear sky-blue satin skirts heavily banded in black and silver, with long-sleeved bodices of dark red velvet and superbly-ornamented stomachers encrusted with filigree silver balls and hung with pearl chains. A peaked hat of the pale blue satin is a foundation for a cape-like shawl of black velvet, turned back in revers of blue silk heavily banded with silver. It is a dress for court functions, for the pavane, for the *présentation d'honneur* to be seen in the light of tapers held by flunkies. But against the rocky landscape it fits in just as well. High dog collars of rose quartz, pearls and silver are worn with dark red dresses by women in the markets of Olite.

The bull ring at Pamplona is one of the most handsomely appointed in Spain, with restaurants and great arcaded entrances for promenade. I could wish the hotels were as comfortable as the bull-ring restaurants. La Perla is a fairly good hotel and Hostel del Rey Noble excellent for food. But a great many persons who come here for the San Firmin show drive to San Sebastian, to stay the night at the Continental Palace or Hotel de Londres, two splendid hotels on the north coast.

The old part of Pamplona is by far the most interesting, like a setting for a great Spanish tragedy. Dark narrow streets, with men in long circular black cloaks lurking in shadows, seeming part of the darkness. In the old markets where a fervently ripe local cheese is sold, the stalls of Navarrese Gothic contribute vastly to the scene, for the market women wear a tent-like garment of saffron-dyed linen, and wide black hats. This is called the Quarter of the Rock; above it, crouching in the somnolence of old buildings far past their usefulness, is the castle erected by Philip II in 1571 to be the strongest citadel in Spain.

Along rivers raging in torrents, past the grandly spacious *estancias* of Navarre, I drove towards Miranda de Ebro. The houses are built of stone, or thin brick, in the old Roman manner of indenting or obtruding the brick to get a pattern of diagonal trellis lines or chequers on the walls. There are always two high, machicolated towers flanking the façade, or if the house is older in date and the family of great prominence in the province, four towers rise at each corner of the main block. When a great carved cartouche surmounts the big entrance arch, this makes a most imposing rural dwelling, in keeping with the phrase heard so constantly, "proud Navarre."

The old Monastery of Rodilla dreams away the years in the midst of a cloister which surrounds the big square refectory like a many-arched wall. I saw over a hundred young novitiates all in white robes, their waists loosely girdled with olive wood rosaries, walking in this cloister. In one hand each carried a loaf of bread to which he gave half attention. In the other hand a breviary to which he bent the other half. All was still, not even the sound of sandled feet in motion. The walls were black with masses of ancient ivy, the first vines I had seen thickly covering walls in Spain. I drove on my way. In a short time, out of a sunset haze ahead rose shafts of gray lace, more intricate yet powerful in design than any other Gothic carving I know. The Cathedral of Burgos.

Chapter 12

PROUD ARAGON AND CASTILE

COMING into Burgos, the road winds through a disused quarry. As early as the ninth century faun-gray stone was cut from these riven cliffs to build the walls, the tall harsh-faced houses fronting on streets as narrow and branching as a labyrinth, and, in a later century the greater part of the cathedral itself. I noticed that even today huge blocks of this stone are piled unsteadily in pyramids; some unwieldly looking pieces, bearing ancient markings and dates, lie scattered about half hidden by rank grasses. It may be these blocks of stone have been here since El Cid walked through the quarry selecting stone to build his twenty-towered castle of which only an arched gateway and great round tower, with its curious superstructure bulging above the castellated archers' walk, remain. (Puerta El Cid in Valencia is a copy of the gateway.) The closer I came to the most famous cathedral spires in Spain, the more I realized that for all their appearance of indomitable strength that has weathered centuries of bitter wars and schisms, the carving is so delicate that the spires remind me of a cluster of wild hyacinth bells, giant in size, trembling against the pearl-gray sky.

My mind ranged back through the weeks since I started at night from Port Vendres, splashed through a cloudburst in the Pyrénées, to spend lyric days skirting the Catalonian shore and the sensuous beauties of Valencia. Standing in the carven northern sternness of Burgos I liked to remember the Costa Brava. The serpentine waver of those cactus barricades above sandy beaches gleaming like gilt foil against the bluest of water. Days and nights of driving across well-nigh interminable *vegas* of baked red earth in Andalusia, where

196

at least I was heartened by occasional oases of olive trees, and on the air the tincture of citrus fruit and grape. How pleasant were the days following the path of Romería del Rocío through grassy meadows and river valleys and then grading upwards, higher and higher into the rocky fastnesses of Aragon and Navarre, where hoary old castles frown from every crag and the gray shells of long-deserted monastic houses rattle and crumble in the wind. And now Castile with its cold formality and stupendous treasures waving in the blazonry of dead kings. Without this variety I would not be in Spain.

I have been told the cathedral at Burgos is the greatest treasure house in Spain, "an ecclesiastical Prado." Because of its position on a windswept plateau, the church, undeniably impressive as it is, gains in architectural importance from the low, plain-faced houses around the base which seem to be acting as humble caryatids lifting to the skies the transepts, flying buttresses, pinnacled dome, and the twin spires.

In the thirteenth century Fernando III of Castile decreed that Maestro Enrique and Juan Perez should build upon the site where once had stood the cell of the hermit Fray Rocio (a saintly man and patron of travelers) a cathedral to magnify the devoutness of Castile. Fernando had just wrested Córdoba from Abd-ar-Rahman, bringing to his court a scorched green banner saying "I have burned the Omayyad yoke." But building was slow, and many years passed when work fell off to the point of ceasing altogether. Then some royal conqueror would renew operations at a feverish rate hoping to blaze abroad his name and his deeds. Gil de Siloë finished the western transepts and spires. Additions to the church were made during the fourteenth and fifteenth centuries by Juan de Colonia whose style was more restrained and delicate in ornament. The interior is like a stone forest where aisles of silver trees branch into a misty blue heaven. This illusion is caused by the smoke of innumerable candles burning in front of alcove chapels and the high altar. A ravishing effect of gold trellises is achieved by broad rays of sunlight that slant down from lunette windows under the roof to crisscross the pink marble floor of the nave.

The whole edifice is so extraordinarily rich in *retablos*, holy vessels, and altar garniture, that one understands why Burgos Cathedral is considered one of great triumvirate of cathedrals with Toledo and Seville. A short way out of town is Cartuja de Miraflores, harboring the wonderful Golden *Retablo* which springs to life in candle light

197

to show a pageant of full-rounded medieval life from the cradle to the grave, in a sumptuous pattern of deeply incised figures, all against a flowery meadow. Much grander in conception and more vigorous in treatment is the tomb of Juan II of Castile and Doña Isabella of Portugal. This catafalque raised on a stepped dais seems to me a remarkably compelling mélange of royal heraldry, even in the Cartuja, which is amazingly rich in ornament, arms, and banners. The effigies of this royal pair lie side by side on the catafalque shaped like an eight-pointed star. Gil de Siloë wrought in alabaster the jeweled crowns and magnificently-patterned damask robes, touching genius in his carving of cabochon rings on every finger of Isabella's hands with one finger keeping her place in a prayer book. I looked long at this carving of jewels and found it as exquisite in detail as the Han dynasty jade ornaments strung on yellow silk, often seen in the "reception room" of a Chinese emperor's tomb.

Tremendous pomp is added to this splendidly conceived composition by pairs of rampant lions supporting armorial shields to mark the eight corners of the dais. I have seen many carved effigies in all the splendor of royal trappings; for one, the unforgettable kneeling group of Charles V and his family in the Escorial, but somehow this pair of sleeping figures seems a tour de force in beautifully sensitive handling of the bone structure of long aristocratic faces, and lean bodies under rich fabrics. The eye is arrested by such telling detail as the slight rise of the queen's right knee as if gently restless in her sleep.

In the Museo El Cid hangs a round Moorish shield of damascened black bronze entwining the ciphers A and S. This perhaps designates a title of honor. The title of El Seid was bestowed on Rodrigo Diaz de Vivar by Abar the Moorish king of Zaragoza, when he offered allegiance—"my sword and my knights"—to this most fanatical and devious of all Moorish rulers in Spain. Vivar fell out with Alfonso VI after a stormy session in a tent on the field of battle outside Zaragoza. In a white heat of rage and exasperation he accused the king of weakness, a "blow-hot, blow-cold" manner of conducting his crusade of Christians against Moslems. Flinging himself out of Alfonso's presence, he called his few hundred adherents to his banner, shouting he would fight only with a brave man. This started the years of fantastic successes when power piled upon power for El Cid. One can see a collection of great parchment portfolios documenting with astonishing clarity the life history of Rodrigo Diaz de Vivar, who was born near Burgos. Although his name is wrapped in fable, I believe him to be no mythical hero, but a conquistador of courage and vision as vitally alive in the tenth century as are the tales of his adventures today. A good bit of his history is written in English and on sale, handsomely bound as an exciting chronicle.

It is told that El Cid all during his adventurous life was a practical joker. His vaulting imagination earned him a reputation with women of another Barbarossa, who delighted in upsetting the calm tenure of an entire village by amorous pranks. Among other sobriquets coined to enhance the name of El Cid was "sire of half the bastards in Spain." He warmed to the theatrical in all things. Notwithstanding his huge size, he once impersonated a rich widow who was to have married a pompous notary of Burgos. The woman was forcibly detained in her house while the Cid, muffled in veils, took her place. It was not until the notary was being carried, protesting loudly, to the town fountain to be unceremoniously ducked by his powerfully-built "bride," that the awakened townspeople knew of the nocturnal jest taking place. The story of the Cid and two money lenders, the brothers Raquel, is fairly well known. He chose two heavy wooden chests stoutly bound with iron, their intricate locks so rusted as to resist the great keys hanging at the Cid's girdle. These chests were moved to a house he owned close to the city gate. He told the money lenders the chests were filled with Moorish treasure for which he wanted them to advance him gold, for he must fly into exile. This the brothers did to a considerable sum in gold marks. El Cid tossed brother Vidas the keys and called for his horse to be brought around. He leaped into the saddle. Before the sound of galloping hooves had died away, the chests were opened to disclose bags of sand and some old, much-mended harness. Today in the cathedral crypt where the legendary conquistador is buried, stands one of the age-blackened chests filled with girths and bridles of moldering leather. I noticed big areas of furry mildew inside the chest. It being cool but dry in the crypt, I wondered about this. The guide shrugged his shoulders, so I manufactured a fragment of ghostly lore to add to his tale to visitors.

"Tell them," I said, "that this dampness is caused by unending floods of tears shed by the brothers Raquel when they discovered the hoax. Both fellows are probably still mourning somewhere around here."

The man looked over his shoulder a shade uneasily, but promptly wrote down what I had told him in his little book.

The Arco de Santa Maria, like the gates of many old cities throughout Spain, is a compelling "set piece" of theatrical stone work, let into the walls of Burgos. In this case the architect seems to have been carried away by inventiveness. A soaring proscenium surrounds the gateway, which started out to be a castle and ended up as a galleried pleasance whereon figures of knights in armor, cap-a-pie, and ladies in court robes balancing towering steeple headdresses, stand in niches as if to wave and curtsy welcome to all who pass beneath. A medley of crenelated turrets across the top of the gate gives the effect of a pointed crown. There is a winning, childlike "sand-castle" pomp about this massive frivolity that leavens the general austerity of Burgos. Everybody seems to want picture postcards of the gate, and I notice many painters find it a perfect subject for sketches. Museo Arqueologico has now been opened on one of the floors of the gate house, so the friendly knights and ladies are kept constantly busy entertaining.

The ancient Castillo elevated above the town has magnificently florid carved ceilings and doors set in alabaster portal arches hugely scaled in the bold Castilian manner. This stone pile is another one of the seemingly tottering shells of masonry, like the exquisite Cartuja near Jerez de la Frontera, which have breasted the centuries and will probably do so for many more. My room at the comfortable Hotel Condestable (Constable) was massive in scale; the doors and window shutters opening inward were carved in the flowing style of the finest Castilian manor houses.

Within a radius of forty miles of Burgos are two extraordinary religious houses as different in intent as one can imagine. These should not be missed. One is the Cistercian nunnery of Santa Maria de Real de Las Huelgas; the other the little-known, remote, and utterly lovely Romanesque monastery, Santo Domingo de Silos.

On my way out to Las Huelgas I passed three tall square towers, grim, rough-walled and more or less alike standing stark against the sky, one in a plowed field, the other two on mounds, in the midst of blowing grasses. Scarcely a window pierced the walls but each tower displayed opulent escutcheons above arched doors. Doors in Castile are wide and high as gateways. Built of chestnut wood, these are studded with bronze bosses as big as cannon balls. On a kind of balcony above the door of the tallest tower stand stone wild men, over life size, bearing clubs, naked save for the skin of a shaggy animal thrown over one shoulder.

These sculptured figures, blatant in frankness of masculinity, act as caryatids for a floriated coat of arms surmounted by the Crown of Castile and the Lion of Burgos. I have learned these deserted towers (used as cow byres now by local farmers) were once banqueting houses, when the court of Ferdinand and Isabella hunted stag and wild boar on this plateau which, until the sixteenth century, was a thickly-wooded royal hunting preserve. In the seventeenth century continuous seasons of drought and devastating forest fires greatly reduced the forest areas around Burgos.

The royal convent of Las Huelgas was once a place for retirement in summer for the Spanish kings. When Alfonso VIII turned the palace into a nunnery for ladies of royal blood who wished to withdraw from the world, he, perhaps unwittingly, established a vast royal tomb of blinding magnificence. Altar cloths, carpets, tapestries, and vestments are exceptionally rich, for most of these were brought from the palaces of some of the greatest grandees in Spain when a member of which ever family entered at Las Huelgas. A jeweled habit, intricately worked in Stations of the Cross, in gold and silver on blue velvet, was worn by the first abbess, born a princess palatine. Each novitiate brought a considerable personal wardrobe of brocade and tinsel-woven velvet, gowns which she continued to wear, even after her vows were taken under a dolman-cut habit of dark purple silk. These ladies walking in couples through the cloisters or kneeling at devotion on velvet cushions embroidered with the arms of their ancestral houses, must have resembled more a complement of maids-in-waiting on a Castilian queen than ordained nuns. Today the order is much depleted in numbers and the habit worn by the nuns is far more subdued.

Everywhere in the convent is the muted patina of pure gold. *Retablos,* altar furniture, embellishment for tombs, in effect this nunnery is a *palais d'or.* When Aztec and Mexican gold from the New World was flooding Spain, great religious houses such as Las Huelgas, used as royal asylums, were literally plated in gold. While the Escorial is the most outstanding evidence of this in Spain today, there are many monasteries as richly appointed, in proportion.

I saw at Las Huelgas the tombs of six kings and over a score of princes and princesses. Circular palls of crimson, dark claret, or tawny orange velvet, stiff with gold galloon, are thrown over the coffins. Long trumpets with heraldic tabards jut out in rows from the walls, creating a swaying forest of sumptuous leaves of silk and metal gauzes. This is veritably a hall of dead kings, like, in size and stillness only, that empty cave of stone where dead kings walk, the Castle of Dunluce on the Irish Sea. There is now a small museum at Las Huelgas where medieval jewels and priceless brocades from some of the tombs which have been recently opened may be closely examined. This is a completely dazzling sight, given point by coils and thick braids of golden hair, keeping the dominant golden note of Las Huelgas to the fore. Quite possibly this is Plantagenet hair, for Alfonso VIII and his Queen, Eleanor Plantagenet, daughter of Henry II of England, were buried here, as their kneeling effigies attest.

Unlike the tomb-nunnery of Las Huelgas, Santo Domingo de Silos strikes the note of rare simplicity and quietness. A harbor for restrained beauty in architecture where a few notable treasures are to be seen, and over all is repose. I felt only the memory of splendor in the gardens, or when walking in the singularly lovely double colonnade cloisters. Here one forgets time or place. When the organ is being played at evensong one's senses seem lifted by unearthly music. If there still exists such a place as retreat from the world, I should say Silos is it. One comes upon the monastery by precisely the right approach. The road from Las Huelgas leads through the little town of Covarrubias. As I passed, harvest was being gathered. In a far-off circle hyacinth blue mountains shimmered in the haze of perfect harvest weather. In the foreground the browns, golden yellow, and russet red of Castilian meadows and uplands lay, not dry *vega* but moist, productive earth. All around were piled, high, temple-pointed stooks of barley, wheat, and maize, in the curious way only Castilian farmers seem to know.

The monastery appears to be asleep in a hollow on the banks of the murmuring Arlanzón. Distributed in a pattern of different heights, the rose-gray tiles gleam against a background of leafy orchards and cool meadows. Gaunt walls and an ancient Roman arch remind one of the monastery's early greatness. The present Santo Domingo de Silos was built in one of the noblest ages of Spanish architecture. Neither money, labor nor the sure taste of simplicity in great scale and unpretentious surfaces was spared in its construction. The Colegiata encloses, as in the sublime shell of a nautilus, the sepulchres of Don Fernando Gonzales and his wife Doña Sancha, the founders. There is a museum displaying an unexpected group of paintings. The two finest are a fourteenth century triptych of the Epiphany and a marvelously luminous Zurbarán of St. Dominic bearing the famous staff, now encased in silver in the library.

The double cloisters are so unique in architecture that they have become a kind of mecca for architects traveling in Spain. So spacious is the continuous flow of line, so deeply incised each column, capped by lotus petals, that this lower cloister steals the thunder from the upper tier, which on close inspection many find more graceful in detail but not so startling in vigorous line. Next to the Zurbarán, the treasure at Silos which interested me most is a carved casket of ivory inlaid with green enamel in the ingratiating Arab script with quotations from the Koran. The casket bears an inscription in Arabic on the lid to the effect that it was made by Mohiamed-ben-Ziyar at Cuenca in the year of Hegira 417 (1039). A plaque in enamel of St. Dominic flanked by two angels bears close resemblance of feature to the Zurbarán. The Benedictine monks who now occupy the monastery are intensely proud of the most complete library in existence on the far-flung travels of medieval saints into "the unkown wilderness of men," their martyrdom, and canonization, in thousands of volumes. In fact, I was interested to find that travel in all its phases impelled these brothers, so unadventurous, so hidden from the world, to collect everything possible on the subject; and they discussed Spanish Morocco, from where I had but lately come, India and Italy, Austria and Ireland, with knowledge and ease, solely from reading of these countries. All through the monastery are traces of Mozarabic craftsmen who, more than any other early artists, helped to glorify Spain.

My road now lay through Palencia, an ancient Iberian town with arcaded streets, renowned for having cradled the oldest university in Spain. It was founded under royal seal in the year 1208 by Alfonso IX who invested the students and faculty with royal colors. Today the college "dons" wear crimson shoulder capes while the students wear capes of purple. The crossing and recrossing of these two factions, coming and going from classes in the plaza before the university, forms an arresting St. Catherine's Wheel of slashing color, in an otherwise drab town. There is a highly interesting collection of all the minerals mined in Spain in the museum here. I was immensely surprised at the wealth buried, waiting untouched for uncounted centuries, in the rocks of the great mountain ranges, and no other country seems to have so many sierras. Cobalt, copper, zinc, silver, quicksilver, many semi-precious stones, and marble in the Sierra de

Gredos and Navarre as well as the Spanish side of the Pyrenees. Coal, the phosphates, and sulphur are waiting here, in variation of quality and incalculable quantities, for so little of the mineral riches of Spain has been exploited.

I drove out of my way to lunch at Albergue La Baneza where last year I had enjoyed an Asturian specialty difficult to get anywhere save at a farmhouse table. It is called *pote*. The preparation varies in ingredients in various localities. I like the pure Asturian way of preparing it. At La Baneza I ate my fill of turnip greens cooked in beef stock with pork. Huge copper pots of Old Castile aromatic mustard, aged and carefully selected for vintage, is served with *pote*. I looked at a label on the mustard pot. The date was 1910. Nearly as rare, for a mustard, as Napoleon Brandy for a cognac.

During lunch I learned a bit of news which caused me to make one of my famous volte-face in plans, and drive like one demented all through the afternoon. Once a year the shepherds who tend goats and sheep in the mountains and grassy slopes around Najéra in the Sierra de la Demanda region hold high festival dedicated to the pagan god Pan. I stayed the night at Albergue de Aranda de Duero, one of the most agreeable of the Spanish Tourist *paradores* which, happily, increase each year in number. A romantic air drifts about this old castellated house, almost hidden in gardens as inviting to walk or dine in as any I know. The pagan rout was held not far away and was well worth my furious drive, miles out of my planned way, but I would not have missed it for worlds. Nearly three hundred shepherds ranging in age from fifteen years to, I should judge by the look of some, near a century, were attired in a picturesque diversity of costumes which are their everyday attire. One youth told me, pointing to a green leather jacket he had embroidered in red and black cord in his endless spare time, that this was an addition to his daily apparel to honor the god Pan. Some of these herdsmen come down the mountains but once a year, just for this festival. The gathering is held in a field where rises a small knoll. Here under the stars had been raised a crude altar of rocks decorated with grapevines and boughs of oak and chestnut. All night long (I left the celebration around three o'clock in the morning) the men danced in groups among themselves. I saw dances of Navarre, the classic Muro-Urriza. Dressed in white scalloped knee breeches with wide garters of bells, and white lamb's wool jackets, aflutter with embroidered ribbons, the men showed masterly precision and accent with castanets. This dance is very popular for weddings and religious ceremonies in Navarrese towns. Like the old Morris dance of yeoman in the English shires, Muro-Urriza is a classic dance with pagan undertones, stemming from the mists of antiquity. The cool night air throbbed with the wail of Aragon bagpipes creating slow-paced tempo for wild mountain dances aping the randy antics of goats to such perfection I felt it was a good thing no women were present. The Navarrese tambour is a deep-toned drum; when properly beaten, as it was here, the roll reverberates through the mountains like the crack of doom, I liked best the versatility with which the youngest boys performed on different kinds of Pan pipes made by themselves. I am told these boys lie for hours during long, lonely vigils of herd-tending, "conversing" with one another, though out of sight, by a language of their own, produced by notes on the pipes. Many of the youngest shepherds danced, carrying in their arms kids and lambs with gilded hooves and collars of oak leaves streaming with ribbons. As I looked at this pagan scene on a Spanish hillside in 1952, I felt the flavor of antiquity was never so strong upon the air.

By mid-morning, when I left Nájera to drive to Valladolid, I passed close by the foot of the hill. The altar where lately pagan revels ruled was deserted. But I noticed a good many revelers sleeping it off, strewn about on the sward which looked like a littered battlefield. It had been, I reflected, for many shepherds, a battle with Bacchus.

Perhaps more than any other city in Spain, Valladolid wraps itself in a great cloak of hauteur, regally embroidered with some of the most fantastic architectural novelties to be seen on the peninsula. Valladolid never lets anyone forget that it was once the capital of Spain. In the church of Santa Maria la Antigua, the oldest Romanesque church in Castile, founded about 1200, there hangs a curiously intriguing banner of yellow silk. Embroidered on this in red and black is a chronicle of histroic events which have taken place in this city since the building of the church. A few of the salient facts ring with names which have made history.

Valladolid is called the "City of Colleges." The University, now housed in a vast Baroque building, is far famed as a seat of learning to which students come from all over the world. Just to wander through the hundreds of rooms in this ornate pile is to see the Baroque and Rococo styles at their most entertaining and freely interpreted best. However ornate the façade is, beautifully alive and flowing in ornamentation, it is the painted ceilings in great rooms that set the sumptuous note. Painted in extreme *brio* by Italian artists and Spanish painters who studied in Italy, Juan Güas, architect and painter, stars as a bold dramatic draughtsman, while Juan de Juni shows a mastery of color brushed in with vivid chiaroscuro.

Christopher Columbus lived in Valladolid the last years of his life in utter dejection. His house is pointed out, a plain-faced dwelling of no distinction, shuttered now, as it was when he lived there almost completely recluse. Excitement must have run high when Ferdinand and Isabella los Catolicos were married in the cathedral when it was far from finished (it is still unfinished by half) under a maze of scaffoldings. A number of fatalities among the great personages assembled is recorded. A violent storm of wind and rain raged all during the wedding ceremony, causing stones from the groining in the nave to collapse, and plaster to shower down. There is a book in Archivo de Simancas which lists the yards of satin, silks, velvets, damasks, jeweled embroideries and "pure" gold galloon used in the decorations and robes for the clergy and court for this royal mating; the amount of yardage, to say nothing of the cost, staggers the imagination.

Cervantes' house is now a library. There is a charming enfilade of rooms along the front and sides of the house. Each room has two windows and handsomely carved doors. There is a "widow's walk" on the roof where Cervantes went to enjoy a view of a green and agriculturally rich countryside. A dramatic view doubtless inspired him to write. Remember that when Cervantes lived in Ronda he had a room with a sweeping view of the eagle-haunted sierras. The entire city is as redolent with the memory of extraordinary persons as it is of dream-sequence architecture by ebullient Juan Herrera and the unrestrained brothers Churriguerra. There are many palaces here showing the hand of these architects who must have enjoyed a very field day of unbridled expression in Valladolid.

El Cid thundered all over the place. He built gates and castles regardless, which he promptly ordered torn down when days of vexatious exile dogged his heels. Only a few castles were destroyed apparently, for on every hand one is shown something built by this tireless adventurer.

Alleged the most beautiful woman ever known in Spain, Doña Maria de Padilla, vain, extravagant mistress of Pedro the Cruel, King of Castile, rode through the streets in a litter borne on the backs of

CHARRO
COSTUMES
SALAMANCA

tigers from Africa, muzzled in gold. It is said Doña Maria affected a double train to her jeweled velvet gowns. These trains dragged for yards on either side of her litter, so that the crowds in the street would not press close to her, for to step so much as a toe on this dragging velvet magnificence was to suffer cruel punishment, perhaps total "disappearance" if she gave Don Pedro the name of anyone guilty of such effrontery.

The most splendid but infinitely poignant palace in the vicinity of Valladolid is Castle Tordesillas, built by Alfonso X, called El Sabio (the Wise), as a retreat for study of the planetary system. When his son, Pedro the Cruel, came into possession, all was changed from scholarly grandeur to a whore's realm. He had a room with walls of lacquered kingfisher feathers. Another used as bedroom for his mistress Doña Maria had walls curtained in a waterfall of crystal and pearls. Don Pedro finally gave this castle, with Moorish baths and fantastic turrets spraying fountains, to Doña Maria. Later, when it became a royal convent, Juana la Loca was imprisoned here for nearly half a century, first by her father, who vacillated from remorse to defiant shouting that he had imprisoned his daughter only to protect her from her malady and from unsympathetic eyes and tongues. Far more infamous was the scene following the death of Ferdinand. Juana's son, Charles V, promised her removal to a private, less strict incarceration and then reneged, because of the prophecy of a sooth-sayer that his mother would be the instrument of his assassination if freed from Tordesillas. I recall no story more moving than that of Juana la Loca maundering her life away racked in bodily pain by self-inflicted wounds. This daughter of the greatest and proudest queen Spain ever knew, Isabella the Catholic, spent her days and nights wandering the corridors of the castle showing to real or imaginary persons her hands and feet, pointing to the bleeding wounds of her fancied perpetual crucifixion.

Approaching Valladolid I passed a pink and yellow country villa set on the edge of a lagoon not far back from the road. Once, evidently, a pleasure retreat the house was now grimly shuttered. The fripperied elegance seemed moribund, partly because the lagoon across the excessively ornate façade, in highest Churriguerresque style, was bone-dry, reflecting nothing, and the long lane of peepul trees leading to the front steps and bordering the highway for over a mile, were disconcerting in the constant agitation this curious tree is subject to, even in dead calm atmosphere. Each tiny scimitar-shaped leaf shuddered as with a life of its own, showing first an almond-green side, then a turquoise-blue one. The whole landscape, as I drove through the lane of peepuls, seemed in a state of violent ague.

When I reached Conde Ansúrez Hotel in Valladolid, I sent in my bags and started to do a round of sightseeing. In this city I know my way around fairly well, for I have been here three or four times. But always after leaving, I either realize, or am told, that I did not see this, that, or whatever. Now, since my way to Zamora lay so close to Valladolid I decided to stop the night at the Conde Ansúrez and go out to Villadefrades on the River Sequillo, to see a museum lately opened in an old castle where eccentric ship models had been collected by succeeding generations of one family. With a friend in Salamanca I had been discussing the museum of Catalonian maritime history in Barcelona. He said, "If you want to see some really rare collectors' items in ship models, go to Castle Sobria in Villadefrades near Valladolid. I will be eager to hear what you have to write about some of them." More he would not say.

When I arrived in the loney little village, the shut-eyed houses all seemed to be sliding slowly, but surely, into the stagnant green pools of what answered for a river. But my disappointment at finding no castle to house a collection of anything was brightened when a beggar in all the panoply of vilely odorous rags, patch over one eye, sores on legs, the whole traditional mendicant trappings to woo pity, split his face in a craggy, cavernous smile and informed me that of course there was a castle and a museum. His hands quavering in mid air, palms upward in venal expectancy, of course, he directed me farther along the river.

"It is but a kilometer or so, señor, of little way, to Belver de los Montes. I used to own property there before the wars."

As I gave this human wreck a peseta or two for setting me on the right road, I added, "Property you say? What sort of property?"

The man polished my coins on his scabrous knee. With his one shifty eye he looked up at me. "That is a long story, señor. I am of the old aristocracy of Spanish beggars. If you ever traveled here in the old days, the days of the monarchy, you would have known our guild."

I nodded. "I have given members of your guild many's the coin in my time."

He spat copiously between his gnarled feet. "Yes, señor, so did every tourist. *We* were one of the sights of Spain."

"And of all Latin countries," I echoed.

"We owned houses, vineyards, oil presses," he grinned evilly, waving his hand to encompass all Spain, "and brothels. Is that what you call the houses of content for women, señor?"

I nodded. "There are other names, but that is a good one. Go on with your story. I am much entertained."

He then treated me to such a wise, searching, and apt highlight on the ever-present topic of the extreme poverty to be seen in Spain, that I was deeply moved by it, considering it completely coincides with my own summing up.

Always, he told me, three quarters of Spain's inhabitants have been poor. The church, powerful beyond all calculation, has amassed vast treasure by working on the pious credulity and the love of pageantry and ceremonial pomp so deeply embedded in the Spanish nature. The kings gave richly productive lands to a small group called, roughly, grandees, *hidalgos*, or landowners. To give alms to the afflicted gained the giver heavenly reward, so beggars waxed rich and as many men became professional beggars as went into the church.

"And of what moment, señor, is a lost leg, or a few patches and sores if one is rich?" he asked.

Irritating perhaps, but for centuries the reward was there in quantity for the reaping, gained by whines and the sad cry for "Alms in the name of God, alms. Alms, so the Holy Virgin will smile on you, alms." The beggar waxed dramatic. "A profession, yes, as good, as honorable any day as that of a painter of pictures—Goya," he shrugged and spat with fervor, "or a matador. Oh yes, it has been a rich, good life."

Then came the Civil War. He told me about the fall of the monarchy and the church tottering, the priests gasping out their life and vomiting up their guts when saturated in petroleum and burned alive in pits.

"Republicans, Falange, no good in any of them. Now, you see, señor, we are not rich beggars any more. Almost *everyone* is poor now. There is no aristocracy in being a beggar." He shook his head sadly and drew a royal crown in the dust with a flexible great toe. "Spain is no poorer these days than it ever was, only poverty shows in a more scattered way. There's too much talk of poverty anyway. Tourists see a lot of poverty but they talk about it too much. That is not the way for me to get my property back." He fingered the coins reflectively. "No, señor, you are kind, but I will die here." He pointed to the stone where he sat in front of the big, empty, gloomy looking church. "I will die a poor beggar, not the rich one I once was. Poor, like Spain is poor."

My confidant on matters pertaining to the "too-much-discussed-and-nothing-done-about-it" poverty in Spain had given me a particularly sketchy steer towards Belver de los Montes. "One kilometer, señor, of little way," he had said. It turned out to be fifteen kilometers at least, but I did not hold it against his odoriferous memory. In all the bizarre contrasts of terrain through which I had driven in these past weeks in Spanish provinces I had seen nothing quite like this countryside. Yellow and purple gorse ranged in breaking combers of color on both sides of a narrow cart track. Tall, black, sepulchral trees stood straight and close together, like the iron bars of a cathedral *retalbo*, against a cloudless primrose sky as flat as a china plate. The silence was oppressive; not a bird sang, nor did any game bird rise to whir above my head, and make my trigger finger itch for a gun. It was as if I had been compelled by nature to drive endlessly through a sea of flowering waves. Finally I passed a ruined castle on a craggy mound of rock, just to remind me that at least I was still in Spain. Then the inevitable black speck rose ahead of me in the road. This turned out to be a young boy with snapping black eyes and gay grin, sitting on the rump of a burro and singing a *saeta* at the top of his lungs. After my question he called out, "Yes, señor, ahead is Castle Sobrio. But why does the señor want to go there? It is a dead place."

I called back, "I am going to bring it back to life, like the prince kissing The Sleeping Beauty in the Silent Wood, or whatever the correct words are."

He yelled with laughter and I drove on through the ballet-setting countryside. A long, mossy wall appeared, then a humped bridge over what was for Spain a fairly rambunctious stream. There on an artificial-looking hill, as if it had just been formed by stones and mud turned out of a giant child's pail, was the village of Belver and the castle. For the village there is not much to dwell on. A scrawny church, looking oddly caved in, like the raddled cheeks of a woman who has been *there* and *back* too many times for her age. In the church a wheezy organ was being played. A cluster of shuttered houses—it was the hour when Belverese would be just kicking the covers off from siesta—and the gates to the castly standing invitingly flung wide. Cocks and hens of radiantly brilliant plumage were scratching in the driveway. It was all utterly quiet, pastoral, and in no way gave me a hint of the enchanted two hours in store for me.

I was received at the ornate portal by a charming young girl dressed in the full skirt of red and white striped cotton and black satin apron of the local peasantry. Yes, she said, the museum—"Museo la Barca" she called it—was to the right, would I follow her? At first my eyes, a shade dimmed by coming into semi-darkness from flat brilliant light, could make out nothing more than that the room was long, immensely high of ceiling, and lighted by porthole windows near the roof. The girl busied herself opening shutters painted in ships all firing cannon. Then I began to get the entire picture. Four windows ranged one wall. These were hung with blue, yellow, and green striped silk curtains. Hanging from cross pieces were ships out of some sea of dreams. More of these oddities were resting in cradles on shelves and a few large, important ones were shored up by gilded wood braces on long dark tables down the center of the room. A few of the most outstanding items, unique in shipbuilding, real or in miniature, are these. A ship carved to look like a lion floating, front paws outstretched, head (in which were captain's luxurious quarters) thrown proudly back, mane windblown in hyacinthine curls. A flagrantly Rococo lion-hull ship, it might have been carved in the heat of leaping imagination by Bernini himself. The hull of a wedding barge is entirely crusted with porcelain flowers. All kinds of flowers, and in the heart of each flower is a small round mirror about the size of a half dollar on which is painted a cherub's face with red, golden, or raven black curls. The sails of this fantasia in ships, to sail a halcyon sea, are of pink and silver shot silk. To bring in the rough, "blow-blow-blow-the-man-down" nautical note there is a coaster or trawler, high-prowed, low in the water, and broad of beam. This is carved ruggedly in cedar wood and the sails and rigging are saffron-dyed huckaback linen. Strange half-Moorish signs to ward off evil spirits are painted in crude colors on the sails.

A beautiful craft of superlative workmanship was all carved with a small pocket knife from bits and pieces of wood and bull's hide by a sailor of Napoleon's navy, who lived twenty years as a prisoner, forgotten by his captor, in a dungeon in the Castle of Oropesa. An old jailer, who had taken a fancy to the man, procured for him the sparse materials to carry on his work. Old uniforms or such cloth was used for sails. Pigtails, worn by sailors at that time, and hairs from his beard increasing in length and strength as the years of confinement advanced, were pulled out and employed as rigging. Rusty nails became anchors, copper nails were hammered into guns and the sailor's own gold earrings became hinges and initials for the door to the captain's quarters. The chief ornament is a gold signet ring bearing a crest, which still gleams as a scutcheon figurehead under the bowsprit; this is formed from the handle of a dust broom. A beautifully articulated ship, an utter beauty in suave lines and purity of balance, standing on a keel needing no cradle, it is named *La Belle Patrie*. I looked carefully at almost hidden detail through a magnifying glass provided by the custodian, who gave me data on the various models, after he arrived, a little dopey from too long siesta. The infinite patience, the skill required to fashion this ship was little short of incredible. I reflected that whatever this imprisoned French sailor's overwhelming difficulties and lack of proper material, he was always buoyed up by the hope, however faint, that some day he would again see the place after which he christened his ship of the line. I wonder if he ever did?

It was extremely late at night when I got back to my hotel in Valladolid, having hung over the ship models far longer than I had ever expected to do. But one of the most comforting things in Spain is the fact that no matter how late one arrives at one's destination, from a village inn to the grandeur of the Ritz Hotel in Madrid, with many strata *paradores* and *albergues* in between, there is always some one up and about to give welcome, and a meal will always be forthcoming. Not a hot meal, perhaps, but bread, cheese, a salad, eggs cooked in whatever way one likes best, and the amazingly good hams cured in oddly attractive ways, such as those that are cured in the mountain snows of Navarre, to become importantly vintage.

Wine of course is always ready, and usually a good strong black coffee freshly made. All this will be served by an attractive waitress or a handsome young waiter, not in the least surly at being kept long away from a well-earned bed. For nowadays in Spain hotel staffs are wisely chosen as much for their good looks and charming manner as for efficiency, which ranks high as well.

So, at half-past one in the morning I was served thin, succulently tender slices of veal tossed in sherry and sautéed in butter, with just the right whiff of garlic to spike an already rampant appetite. To give this after-midnight repast just the proper touch, the point one remembers, a platter of broiled mushrooms—"Fresh picked today in the Torozos Mountains, señor"—was brought to table. These were served with a flourish by my waiter Pablo who, I learned, was an embryo torero. I noticed he handled the platter with the grace and sureness that he hoped one day to display in handling the *muleta* and sword when delivering *buena suerte* in corrida. He was a lithe, extremely handsome youth, with the long, slender close-boned hands of an artist. I spoke to him about his hopes. Was he worried about a "proclaiming debut," the *novillero's* acceptance by a committee that is required for true matador status?

"No," he replied. "I had a vision."

"Not like Santa Teresa, I hope," I said.

Pablo laughed. "Oh no, señor. I mean in this vision I am in the ring wearing a pink satin suit with much gold embroidery and tassels. I am delivering a deep *suerte*. Much blood. I am acclaimed as in thunder. Oh yes, it will be true. Next year you will see of me."

I told him I would come to see him dispatch Miura bulls by the dozens, then asked him, apropos of my mention of her, had he ever heard the story of the grim-lipped, no-fooling-around-with-me Saint Theresa when she was unsuspectingly hurled into the river?

Pablo swung round on his heels with the consummate grace of a born matador. "No, señor, but I shall hope you will tell me."

Over searing-hot, Stygian black coffee I began my tale.

"Santa Teresa had been having one of her bitter moods. We all know she was a handful at times, a stoic of the first water, and a reed, like a rod of Toledo steel for bending but not snapping. One day she was striding along a path beside a rushing river."

"In Spain, a rushing river?" Pablo interrupted incredulously.

"Yes, this was probably in Navarre or Aragon. They do have rushing rivers there." I paused, then went on. "Probably she was muttering to herself. Suddenly, with no warning, there was a loud clap of thunder; by unseen force Teresa was most unceremoniously heaved into the river. She did not scream nor falter but went about the business of getting herself out of that predicament. She stood upon the bank, shook herself like a water spaniel after a swim, looked up to heaven and in even, but distinctly annoyed tones, said, 'God, I don't wonder you have as many enemies as you do, considering the way you treat people,' and strode on her way muttering."

I went up to my room as dawn was breaking, escorted by the peals of high laughter of Pablo Montez. Instead of *buenas noches* I had wished him *buenas suertes,* and more visions of the same.

Chapter 13

SALAMANCA AND THE MIURA BULL

For a short way out of Valladolid on my way to Zamora I drove through a world of silver veils. One could scarcely call it fog, for it was light as a sigh of content, what we in the south of Ireland call "the grace of the morning." It was an eerie way to explore the road into the Province of Zamora, for I could see little, but hear all manner of farmyard noises to right and left. Over all, the clang and crash of church bells, tolling, ever the obligato to Spanish life.

I had just passed under a half ruinous Roman arch when I noticed coming toward me, walking in dead center of the road, what looked to be a most monstrous breed of humans with four arms. Then, as the mist was lifting rapidly, I saw these creatures were ordinary men and women from the Torozos Mountains, wearing flowing cloaks of azure blue wool and wide-brimmed, steeple-crowned black hats. These mountaineers come down from the uplands to Valladolid daily, to sell the giant mushrooms gathered at dawn on the misty slopes. What had given them the effect of an extra set of arms were the huge carved-wooden yokes, as heavy, one would think, as the pole of a farm wagon, from which great clusters of pink and sepia fungi hung like tassels of goat skin and bright wool from a Berber caïd's saddle bags. Of course whenever I see in Spain a reminder of something Arab I know there is a reason for it, a hold-over from Moorish times. At street corners in the town all during the forenoon, vendors set up ovens. They will fry these giant fungi, as pungent, as fresh-tasting as dew, for you to eat right there or, put up in a hastily curled cornucopia of red or yellow paper, to take on picnic. I like to buy the

216

mushrooms right off the yokes and eat them raw, dipped in olive oil spiked with a squirt of lemon. I almost turned the car around to follow the mountaineers back to Valladolid, then I had a better idea. I hailed a woman trailing behind the rest and bought four big clusters of juicy looking mushrooms. I would have them put into an earthenware pot with a cover and tossed in olive oil and red wine over a hot fire for my dinner.

By the time I hove in sight of a small town called Toro, the mist had drifted away. Now the day was sparkling as crystal, with a cool breeze from off the "mushroom mountains" of Torozos, to lend added zest. I was so occupied in trying to recall details of "The History of Tarquin" tapestries, I almost passed without noticing what proved to be a thoroughly entertaining house. I decided the place had been built as a retreat from something or other, an architectural whimsey nonpareil.

By the tone of the whole establishment it probably was a hunting lodge. I looked around the silent park to see if a name of any sort was visible. Often these fantasies in architecture are given ironic names—for example, Casa del Labrador (Laborer's House) in the gardens of Aranjuez, which turns out to be a sumptuous palace of Charles IV where everything is done in the grand manner. There is an enfilade of glittering reception rooms almost overpowering in splendor. Twin staircases mount upward to disappear in a frenzy of white and gold floriations. From the exuberantly painted ceiling hang crystal chandeliers like frosted acanthus plants reversed in growth. The *casa* displays a collection of fragile porcelains from China, and Russian malachite urns, jewel or sweetmeat boxes, and tops for gilt consoles, considered the finest in the world.

Of course there are different interpretations of a "laborer." In a simple sense it is a man who works with his hands for his daily bread. Then this bright "Laborer's" pavilion for, say, Oberon and Titania seems a shade ostentatious. All over Europe one comes upon these fanciful houses, but I believe nowhere quite so extravagant nor so ironically named as in Spain and Portugal.

Having passed through Toro I was now regarding a house in no way so extravagant as Casa del Labrador but infinitely gay in spite of abiding solitude. The beautifully wrought-iron gate was locked and no one was in sight. However, through the bars I got a fair idea of the detail of an octagonal house built of pink and black marble squares, alternately veined. It is, of course, sham marble, but the pink

217

veins painted in extreme Italian *bravura* on black, and black veins on the pink, gave the walls distinct character. The top, or fourth floor is surrounded by a balustrade aping fern-sprouting rocks and fallen logs in pink and black stucco. Forming a frieze, an entire hunt is in full cry; the horses and mounted gentlemen and ladies, modeled life-size, dash round and round after an assortment of stags, wild boars, and slavering wolves. There is a sense of gay enchantment about the whole conception, as if a delightful merry-go-round party was in progress. I learned more about this lodge in Zamora. Philip II gave it to his mistress, the Duchess of Eboli, to spike her errant fancy, for she was a woman who, before the tragedy of her fatal imprisonment, gained whatever she wanted from Philip by becoming periodically afflicted with cooling ardor. I have always maintained that down the centuries royal mistresses in Spain or elsewhere had all the luck going. The method of obtaining their desires may have been devious, certainly extremely varied in attack, but so often the landscape is embellished with castles and pleasure pavilions built by lust-besotted kings and lesser noblemen, to satisfy these nostalgic priestesses of human frailty.

It was not long after leaving the gates of the merry-go-round lodge that I saw in the distance the long, graceful bridge spanning the River Duero (to become the Duoro when it crosses the frontier of Portugal). This bridge is a lightly articulated series of sixteen stone arches of great antiquity, providing a most inviting entrance to Zamora. I had kept watch of the changing sunlight and drifting cloud patterns on the dome of the cathedral from two or three kilometers away. In all Europe there is no more remarkable conceit in masonry. It appears to be an airy silken tent pavilion, perhaps for Tamerlane or Suleiman the Magnificent, floating in some cloudland battlefield.

Grouped in a circle around the central dome are a collection of round towers, the top of each one delicately pierced by a columned colonnade capped by a dome in form like a Saracen warrior helmet; these domes are replicas in miniature of the powerfully curved bulb of the central dome. This Oriental-looking edifice is complete in itself and seems in no way a part of the Romanesque cathedral, albeit adding a supremely handsome finial to the whole. I went out onto the roof through one of the eight carved doors. If, instead of springing from a mass of lichen-gilded tiles, this Saracenic pavilion was reflected in water surrounded by syringa and the jet-black of cypresses, it would attract as much attention and admiring comment as the myrtle courts and miradors in the Alhambra.

To my mind the rose-red and black "History of Tarquin" tapestries in the cathedral are alone worth a trip to Spain. I have never had nearly enough time to absorb the infinite details, the exhilarating sense of pageantry, the sweep of line and, overall, the extraordinary vibrance achieved by so limited a choice of colors: a range of rose-reds, tawny gold, white, and black skilfully juggled. Although the red and black predominate in the grand design, the gold and white are placed in juxtaposition to gleam like jewel colors and accent the tremendous impact of *black*.

Tanaquil, the wife of Tarquin, wearing a gown of black and gold in a design of lilies, and crowns borne on the ruffed-feather backs of eagles, rides a white palfrey among warriors in fantastic armor mounted on black chargers, the helmets aflourish with black plumes. Slim pages with flowing golden hair, wearing long black hose and doublets blow upon trumpets, pet doves, plait garlands, or nonchalantly shoot arrows from a bow into space.

Under a canopy of rose- and gold-tracery damask Tarquin sits enthroned. Eye-compelling in black robes, he is crowned beneath the eagle which, legend says, flew or hovered always above his head. A court of nobles, severe in black-furred gowns, surround him. Behind this throng, masons work feverishly to erect an amphitheatre which symbolizes the strong walls and aqueducts of Rome. All this epic composition is translated into early Gothic style in architecture and dress. The palaces of patricians cresting the Seven Hills of Rome form the far background as a frieze. Towers and turrets, drawbridges, barbicans, and hanging gardens flaunt the extreme delicacy of Gothic ornament. All this scene is given vivid movement by forests of spears with rose and black banners streaming out upon the Appian wind.

This triptych panel is from the looms of Tournai, a town which, with Arras, formed the two incomparable centers in France for weaving of tapestries during the Middle Ages. When I see these mannered, magnificently evocative narrative panels of mythological legends or historic facts woven on the great French looms, I think of the brusque answer given by Voltaire when a visitor to his study in Paris pointed to a great winged chair covered by a fragment of needlework depicting the rape of Lucrece. "That has a hint of lechery. Where did it come from?"

"From the womb of Tournai, of course, where all great needle-work is conceived."

The set of tapestries of the wars of Troy, of earlier weaving than the Tarquin Saga, are hung in another room in the cathedral. Again Attic Greece is expressed in Gothic terms. The series is incomplete. Originally there were eleven panels; only four are hanging here. "The Rape of Helen," a rampageous composition of confusion in all reds and yellows is the finest in drawing. The figure of Paris is shown as a simpering buffoon clothed in the top of fancy dress. The panel showing the expedition of the Trojans to the realm of Neptune is made glorious by masterly composition, centering a looming golden galleon, sails belling, rigging snapping and torn asunder by a raging wind to form a pattern, unforgettable in movement of whipping power. Were the gods to give me my choice of one of these panels it would unhesitatingly be "The Tent of Achilles," with thousands of upright lances forming a wall in the background. Dimly seen behind the spears, as through slanting rain, are the delicate, shaven-eye-brow faces of Gothic beauties. The ladies smile encouragement from the Walls of Troy to the knights in desperate conflict, littering the plain with armored corpses.

Zamora has other interesting points, but nothing to compete with the tapestries. A medieval fortress, Casa de Momos, now brooding alone on its hill, is a splendid example of Gothic Plateresque, less cluttered and far more elegant, because of the alternation of embellished spaces and plain areas to set each other off, than is most Plateresque ornament.

Only a little way out of Zamora on my way to Salamanca I again encountered charcoal burners on the road. A far larger contingent, this one, than the lone man with the rascally eyes and touch of genius in his fingers, from whom I had bought a set of forest denizens carved from wood, on a misty road through a Catalonian cork forest. This present trek included whole families, loaded down with camping gear. They were moving from one pitch in a walnut or chestnut woods to another grove where fresh faggots would be found. From the smallest child to old men and women, their hands and faces bore the blue-black patina of wood smoke. Indeed, some of the oldest faces seemed as though carved from obsidian, as black as any Moor with Nubian blood. I was instantly reminded of the Veiled Tuaregs (men who veil the lower face, though their women are not veiled) I had seen and painted in Timbuctu and the bleak wastes of the

Hoggar-Hadramaut Plateau, who still rule by savagery and fear a vast Indigo empire; they dip their garments in cold-water indigo dye and rub off the blue tint on their skin. The bluer the cheeks, the hands, arms, and legs, the greater the beauty thereof. But with these wandering Maragatos, a race of obscure origin who once lived in walled towns near Astorga, it is smoke from constant fires which causes their dull blue skins. Until fifty years ago these Maragatos were, almost to the last soul, itinerant muleteers. Both men and women are a breed huge and strong-sinewed, dressed alike in red wool smocks and black kilts. Winter and summer they wear great, hooded capes of animal skins. Just as the untouchables in India are traditionally street sweepers and guardians of railway crossings, so were Maragatos known all over Spain as indefatigable walkers of the roads, delivering all and sundry on the backs of their mules. A man in Jerez de la Frontera told me that he remembers his father running a sort of mule-express route from town to town with Maragatos to deliver his wine in small casks. Every road in Spain once knew these Maragato muleteers. Now they have lost their walled towns and taken to the brush and the forest cooking pot.

The weather in both Old and New Castile had been mainly cool. But the sun was distilling vibrations of heat as I crossed the plains stretching on all sides away into the old Kingdom of León and the olive-bronze flanks of Sierra de Guadarrama. The *vaqueros* who ride the plains of Andalusia and Salamanca have a song which they sing when riding into this exciting old city driving young bulls from the famous *ganadarías* to corrida or steers to be sent to markets. The import of the song is the love of women and bulls. In every verse it is the bull who triumphs in the *vaquero's* affections. A kind of Spanish Frankie-and-Johnny, "She left me in the lurch" lament. Each line ends with the word "bull." One stanza runs:

If you love women you love bulls,
Women are jealous if you talk too much of bulls.
I'm sleepy tonight so I think I'll sleep with bulls,
Women won't let you sleep, they think you're as strong as bulls.

A young *vaquero* at a well-known *ganadaría*, raising the famed Miura bulls for corrida in Madrid, told me he knew one hundred verses to the song. He added, "When I was free to take women any time, I used to make them fierce with jealousy when I sang to them the bull song. Now I have a *novia* (betrothed), and will marry soon. I am forbidden to sing the song in her hearing. But on the plains it is all right, only my horse and the wind hear me."

I drove through La Velles and saw the *vaqueros'* houses in a long row painted bright colors. At the end is a big arch advertising with pride that in this region are some of the most renowed *ganadarías* in Spain. Signs at crossroads bear the names of notable breeders of bulls for corrida instead of towns and villages. Seeming to crawl lazily across the gently undulating plain are whitewashed stone walls dividing fields, with here and there a few sepia-dark bulls placidly feeding. Low, red-tiled bull pens give the landscape a toy-village aspect. But I noticed far off on higher ground, knee-deep in a grassy meadow, a magnificent black bull, sculptured against the pale sky. *Salud, Toro Bravo*. He looked every inch the monarch of all he surveyed.

The definition of Salamanca is "great architecture." That is a point everyone concedes; whether they may know all the fine shadings of periods in dove-tailed and carven stone does not signify. Salamanca is one Spanish city where the buildings and palaces show off to best advantage because there is plenty of space to get perspective, which is far from the case in a greater part of the huddled cities of ancient lineage where magnificent monuments are half obscured by narrow alleys and crowding roofs.

To my mind Plaza Mayor in Salamanca is the handsomest, certainly the most impressive square in Spain. Designed by Andres Garcia de Quiñones, it stands alone with no competition, for there is no other plaza even remotely so spacious or so beautifully dressed. It is immense in scale, sweeping to the four corners of the compass in four majestic arcades. Here are Plateresque façades, early and late Renaissance, with carefully considered scale in soaring doorways and pedimented windows, in themselves forming most happy unity of design. Frontings designed by the brothers Churriguerras display airy balconies, garlanded and festooned window facings, and trellises of flowering branches to crosshatch the walls and cast light and shadow like jeweled traceries against that extraordinary velvet texture of rippled stucco which seems to have been a Churriguerra secret.

Some consider the University of Salamanca to be the most glorious example of Plateresque style in existence. It was first founded in 1208 in Palencia by Alfonso IX of León.

The University continued under the patronage of Alfonso X, called El Sabio (the Sage). So learned a man as this king was a constant source of wonder and admiration to his subjects. Fully versed in Spanish, Greek, Latin, and the legion facets of Moorish culture, he was conversant with all branches of the arts to a degree almost unimagined in his century. The library, enriched many times by a Royal inheritance, is as much a museum for rare volumes and folios as it is for constant historical research by the students. The Ayuntamiento, or town hall, a masterpiece of Quiñones, was built to house visitors for bull fights which were held, until 1860, in the Plaza in the manner of the annual Palio of Siena which is a horse race run around the piazza in the same way it has been done since the thirteenth century.

The Seminario Concilar not only dominates Plaza Mayor but continues around arcaded patios into another square. Arcaded streets and squares are a feature of many European cities. But the sweep and tremendous style of the continuous undulation of arches around the entire Plaza Mayor has no counterpart. The two cathedrals which are so much the heartbeat of all Spanish towns are Siamese twins in Salamanca. One shoulders the other with a door connecting. The Old Cathedral is a magnificent gesture in Romanesque built by royal decree in the twelfth century. At this time architects of religious houses leaned far toward the Byzantine style. This cathedral, possibly more than any other in Spain, is largely Byzantine in mood and detail, particularly in the lovely, quiet cloisters. The New Cathedral was begun in 1509 but took nearly three hundred years to build with much left undone as far as completion, even now. Many styles of architecture are embraced in the New Cathedral. Starting as a Spanish Gothic cruciform plan there is Plateresque and not very good Renaissance in evidence. However, no building is beneath notice in Salamanca; in fact if anything the city has an embarrassment of extraordinarily notable buildings, vastly different in character, but each one holding its own.

The Convent of Las Dueñas reminds me far more of a palace of worldly pleasures than a religious retreat, though the nuns are exquisitely gentle and saintly. The cloisters are supremely beautiful, reminding me of old summer palaces of the sultans of Turkey I once saw along the Bosporus. Saint Theresa is at Las Dueñas in spirit, with a vengeance, for it was in the cloisters here that she beheld many visions and was "frozen" into silence from her eternal haranguing, a kind of "still-pond-no-more-moving" attitude, two months duration, during which time only her eyes moved, flashing angry fire.

The Palace of Monterrey is in richly patterned stucco, the façade resembling a gigantic cut-pattern for damask or brocade, unearthly cloud textures, caused by the change of sunlight to shadow. The Irish Nobles College is a splendid gesture of high Renaissance where the roster of students has, since its inception in the sixteenth century, been predominately Irish. It is a museum as well as college of arts and sciences and shows to an extraordinary degree the close association between the Irish and Iberians since the tenth century. From early times the interchange of Irish and Spanish commodities has been unique in merchant history. Four Spanish barbs (heavy horses of Moorish-Spanish breeding) with a coach of olive wood upholstered in tooled córdoban leather formed part of the dowry of a daughter of the Costello or Consadino (Considine in Ireland) family, when she journeyed to Donegal or Galway (most of the Hispano-Irish marriages were in the West of Ireland counties). In return the Irish nobles and tribal chieftains sent their sons to the Nobles College in Salamanca along with linen, tweed, and various woolens, with gold- and silver-wrought jewelry. Now and again a merchant or noble would include in the cargo a violet-eyed daughter, fresh and healthy from the peaty bogs, to carry her smiles and wit into the austerity of some Spanish family. There has always been tremendous rapport between youth in the two countries. Passion and daring in the Iberian male have mated well with ardor, exuberant health, a leaping poetic sense, and an alluring wildness in the Gaelic woman.

Equally important in the exchange between Galway, Bilbao, Vigo and Waterford was the importation to Salamanca of Irish map makers. In the sixteenth century a group numbered sixty-four men formed a guild of their own. For anyone interested in beautifully drawn and illuminated maps of the world, as sometimes conceived in fantastic ignorance of reality down the centuries, there is a notable collection to be seen today at the University of Salamanca in a room dedicated to Fray Luis de León.

Casa de las Conchas has been photographed nearly as much as the Alhambra and compared to half the houses in the world. To me it is singularly individual. When I look at the strong shadows cast by the conch shells studding the walls in high relief, the diapering of the beautifully grooved and fluted shells seems to form a trellis, illusive but vital in design. Each time I am more sure that las Conchas is not only the handsomest house in the style of Spanish Renaissance (it was built to honor a visit of Ferdinand and Isabella the Catholic to

Salamanca) but the finest example of that combination of extreme beauty and arrogance in design so emphatically desired in Spain.

I felt I could not leave Salamanca without going out to pay my respects again to the uncorrupted body of Saint Theresa of Jesus lying just as rigid in death as she habitually held her self in life, in the Convent at Alba de Tormes, which she founded. Of all the saintly women in the roster of canonization, Theresa of Jesus is the one I would like to have known more than another. This Amazon who knew her own mind, and stood up to all and sundry persecution with a witty retort ever on her lips, must have been a rarely entertaining character. She always ran true to form, took every indignity in her sweeping stride, and was never mawkish. Added to this, she carried double chips on her shoulders. For her temper flayed the fools she met. Stupidity she could not tolerate. In short she was mad the whole time. Not mad as was Juana la Loca, whose piety led to dementia. But just plain *hopping* mad.

I walked through a garden where a few olive trees leaned perilously near to cracking from the wind. The Convent Alba de Tormes is unpretentious, almost meager, after the improbable magnificence of so many religious houses in Spain. I noticed on the air a smell of fresh-baked bread, always a heartening one, and in the cloister a nun was polishing a silver censer. A pilgrimage of women from La Alberca, chanking like nautch dancers in the panoply of silver chains and amulets, worn for occasions, had just crowded into the crypt where the body of the saint lies. I finally managed to slip past a woman, stiff as if armored for tourney, in her red, black, and silver dress, but I caught only a glimpse of the mummyfied saint. Cold and rigid these many centuries though she has been, I could see the face as a woman in front of me sank to her knees. Hardly discernible, I thought I caught the slight flicker of an eyebrow, and the twitch of a nostril, age-old gestures from an amused mind. It was as if Saint Theresa was trying to say to me, "So—you are telling that story about me being heaved into the river, all over the place. Well—mind you tell it well." I walked out of Alba de Tormes content.

I had been asked to dine at the *ganadería* of a retired matador who breeds bulls near Villa de Peralonso, a few miles from Salamanca. Señor Tomé greeted me at the door of his house with the news that he was expecting Manola Vázquez, but did not know when he would arrive. As I passed through the door I noticed the polished walnut planks were studded with black iron heads of Miura bulls. Portraits,

Señor Tomé told me, of famous ones he had dispatched. Underneath each head was a name plate complete with the place and date of the corrida. As soon as I entered the patio I smelled the tang of saffron. I hoped there would be a *paella* for the main course. There was an impressive ceremony of drinking a white *manzanilla*, pungent and faintly resinous, which had been brought that day from Señor Tomé's vineyards in the Asturias. Each of the guests was handed a small silver tray by a tiny, gnome-like creature, who had been valet to the great matador in the days when his double *verónicas* and agility with the sword had been the most famous in the bull ring. On each tray were a small lily-shaped glass, a Triana-ware flask of *manzanilla*, and small dishes of olives, anchovies, *langostinos*, slivers of *jamón serrano*, and hot French-fried onions. What might be called a Spanish smörgasbörd. By half past ten Vázquez arrived from Madrid enroute to Valladolid where he was due to appear in corrida. A shy, darkly handsome youth, his dark eyes holding a look of one dedicated to an idée fixe. In this case, not at all difficult to guess the *idea*. As he walked among the guests I felt he typified all the romantic young gods of the bull ring. The dinner was excellent and of great bounty. What I enjoyed most, after an epic *paella*, was a big tray of cheeses. There were three kinds I had not before tasted in all the times I have been in the country: Burgos Monte, a creamy, rather bland variety with a haunting, pleasant aftertaste, an Estramadura goats' milk cheese, heavily smoked by pine wood; from Asturias a hard, pungent Montañés and from La Mancha, a *Manchego* rather like Italian Parmesan. I stayed the night at Señor Tomé's, and of course we talked bulls, all the fine points from breeding to the last thrust of a sword. I went to bed at sunrise after, according to my lights, a satisfying and memorable night such as is seldom granted me in this age.

Next morning I drove to Ciudad Rodrigo to stay at Parador de Enrique. This is a fourteenth-century castle, remodeled with great care and extraordinarily sure taste, to the end that all comforts may tempt the modern-minded traveler, without sacrificing the ancient charm of the castle. A big, solid square tower rises from four flanking baileys all within a castellated wall. The rooms command a magnificent view of far-reaching plains and river valleys, as well as the romantic region known as The Four Sierras: Sierra de Gata, Sierra de Peña de Francia, Tras la Sierra Béjar and the towering, snow-capped Sierra de Gredos, rising 8,000 feet into cerulean skies. This

Gredos area is indeed legendary country, where blue trout leap in the mountain torrents, gray wolves and red foxes slink near hamlets by day and bark or howl at one another by night. The loveliest sight of the wildness is the ibex with his scimitar horns pausing for a second, arrested in motion, then darting away, a black and white arrow against the snows. Villages in the Gredos are hidden from view among the rocks and forests with no way of reaching them save on foot or donkey back. Oddly enough the industry, if one can call it that, of these lost villages is raising cocks and hens for market: pampered birds with beautiful, irridescent feathers, carefully tended to make a splendid show on market days, so different from the grimy, raddled fighting cocks at the sunset fiesta in Barrio Santiago. Coming down from a mountain hamlet one day I met men and women at a crossroads coming out of a valley, on their way to market at Tornavacas. The men walked in Indian file on one side of the narrow path, the women, muffled in red and black striped cloaks, which were the top layer of voluminous skirts hiked up as a hood, walked on the other side. Between them plodded a heavily laden string of burros, the high baskets of criss-crossed willow withes on their backs filled with a motley of roosters and hens, so brilliant of plumage, which fairly crackled in the hot sunlight, that at first I took the fowl to be some exotic breed of birds and this a circus crew traveling from one small village to another. But no—it was simply the Guadarrama and Estramadura barnyard fowl, strident in every shade of purple, red, orange, green, and black, flecked in bronze iridescence, all capped by the dagged combs of vermilion. I stood aside in wonder to let this parade pass by. Then it was I caught the illusive pattern. The brilliant birds acted as a foil to the embroidered skirts and bodices of the mountain women and the serape capes worn by the men.

Next day I went to a fiesta in La Alberca in the hills. Here I saw at close range, and in impressive numbers, the most amazing, barbarically beautiful, traditional costumes worn in Spain today. And there are an amazing lot of villages whose inhabitants still wear, almost daily, heirloom costumes of astonishing richness and ingenuity in conception as well as fashioning. The highroads of Spain are one long pageant of spectacular color, rich materials, and embroideries. Many of the heirloom costumes in Castile and Aragon defy the wear and tear of time, considering some of the dresses are three hundred years old and worn every few days to market or some religious celebration, generation after generation. In La Alberca, three women, each one a raven-haired Juno or an Amazon, more like—for there is an uncompromising, strongly-chiseled beauty in the faces of many of these mountaineer women—stood together on a flight of steps. One woman was elevated a little which gave her the prominence of a figure on a pedestal. Immediately to my mind leaped the memory of a pagan figure carved in carnelian and clotted with silver ornaments I had once seen in Corinth. Some pagan goddess, or was it a sacrificial idol once set up on the wave-lapped altars of Thrace? Here was the comparable figure stark before me. Stiff, wide skirts of black velvet worn over an underdress of red cloth. The black skirts are banded in diagonal design of red and gold. The long-sleeved bodice, cut to flare at the hips, is of red, green, or black silk heavily appliquéed in velvet in one of those contrasting colors. A square of heavy white lace is laid over the head with a point partly shading the eyes and falling to the bridge of the nose. This strikes a pure Arab note. The glory, the considered impact to one's senses, of this costume is the improbably rich, hieratic plastron of multiple chains of looped silver hanging to below the knees. Strung on these chanking links are crosses, pierced silver plaques as big as pomegranates, silver eight-pointed stars and amulets from Berber days, silver saints of various sizes, filigree balls for musk and amber, and latticed silver cubes. This whole incredible mass of ornaments is entirely of silver which sways and clatters when the wearer moves as if a platoon of armored cavalry was in full charge. And from behind this metal harness the women are darkly handsome in a wild, pagan way. From under the tab of lace their eyes regard you as an eagle does.

One day I caught one of these women from La Alberca off her guard. I was walking along a road looking for a spring I had been told was to be found, cool and clear, in a rock crevice. It was hot and dusty and I had found no spring water. At the entrance to a deeply-shaded mountain road stood a woman from La Alberca resplendent in all her velvet and silver hardware. On the grass beside her I noticed a large tub of water in which bobbed some of the big yellow melons of the region. I stopped to buy some and I made it fairly plain that I wanted to taste one first. The woman produced from among her chains a wicked-looking long blade knife. With a deft flick of her wrist she cut the melon in half in one swoop, then held it out for me to see. It looked cool, ripe, and juicy. I bought two melons and gave her a few pesetas. In attempting to make change

HELMET HATS
ESTRAMADURA- MONTEHERMOSO

Collection of Margaret Mower

the woman became panicky and got her hands, the pesetas, and the chains into an unholy tangle. Suddenly she threw her head back and roared with laughter—good, lusty roars fit to shake the amulets into a symphony of rattling sound. I finally went on my way with the melons, a few pesetas change, and the realization that this was the first time I had ever seen one of these flamboyantly-garbed women even smile, let alone guffaw.

I asked later in Béjar if the La Alberca women wore this extraordinary collection of necklaces, these heavy velvet and gold trappings every day. I was told not *every* day, but since the woman was attempting to sell melons on a road frequented by tourists she wore her barbaric finery to attract attention to her wares.

Béjar is a grand, pulsing-with-life kind of town in the heart of bullock-raising country. Broad, grassy meadows surround wide-spreading farms. In this locality a farmhouse is built in crescent form. The living quarters are in the wide center while in the tapering ends are granaries, wine or cider presses, and quarters for live stock. Béjar men wear baggy red breeches with leather aprons divided in the middle like a Wyoming cowboy's chaps, and carry lethal-looking bull whips with a lash six yards long. Terrible fights have been known to take place when men have been lashed to bleeding ribbons by these whips in the hands of some herdsman crazed by jealousy, a violent quarrel over land or live stock, or sometimes simply by wine. This is primitive land and men's passions are primitive to match it.

The comparatively small area comprising Palencia de Negrilla, Salamanca, La Alberca, Montehermoso, and Lagartera might be called the open-air museum of traditional costumes in Spain. Apart from the incredible richness of materials, true inventiveness of design, and the individuality achieved when assembling these trappings into a complete picture, most compelling is the immediate use and the dashing style with which they are worn. Visitors motoring through the countryside are continually astonished to see a betrothal party or perhaps a wedding procession wending through a country lane or along the broad highway, in brilliant array.

For the most part these almost heraldic garments are heirlooms for both men and women, carefully guarded, kept in perfect repair down the years. A bride of Montehermoso or Lagartera will proudly display to you the heavy materials of her three-times-great grandmother's wedding dress. These dresses are "everlasting" because of being "built" as carefully as a fishing smack, for both must breast heavy seas. "Yes, señor," a young bride from Lagartera said to me, "this dress has lasted many lifetimes, and will last many more." There is no place for the constantly changing whims of *haute couture* in the hinterlands of Spain.

At the Parador Oropesa, the castle where the Dukes of Frías once gave shooting parties of thirty or more guns to hunt the scythe-horned ibex in Sierra de Gredos, I watched a wedding ceremony take place. A young couple from Lagartera, a love enslaved Paolo and Francesca of the sierras. The costume of the young man was definitely of the theater. It combined sophisticated elegance with rustic charm. Dark-purple knee breeches were gartered in gold and olive green over plum-red stockings. A gold-embroidered white cotton shirt was partly hidden by a jacket of claret velvet ornately braided in green and gold, slung carelessly, hussar fashion, over one shoulder. The touch superb was a broad-brimmed black felt hat, rakish in line, the crown encircled with gold braid and the tail feathers of a cock pheasant. The bride had fresh auburn coloring greatly enhanced by a gown of red and brilliant green silk brocade, the skirt so thickly banded with gold lace and tiny sequined tassels it stood away from the figure like sheet metal and thrummed like a harp in the wind when the girl moved. Her apron of green velvet was similarly embroidered in red and gold. Under a slashed bodice of the brocade her vestee was sewn with seed pearls. When the wedding party left after a tremendous spread of food, venison, and wild game roasted on iron spits in an outdoor oven crowned the feast, it was in a hooded cart set high on red wheels very like those used in Romería del Rocío.

I saw a Charros fiesta in Palencia de Negrilla where immense hoops of roses, jasmine, and grape vines were used in a profusion of most bewildering movements. The women wearing costumes of black, pink, and wine-red velvet embroidered in gold flowers, spun the hoops to and fro as do small children in a park. Some dancers hurled the hoops high in the air, and, as they descended, leaped through them. It was a marvelous measure to behold for the long tabard streamers hanging down the women's backs gave the effect of flamboyantly-plumaged birds darting in and out of a flowery forest. The magnificent white lace head shawls of Charro costumes stem from a gift of one hundred meters of heavy Castilian lace sent to the women of Palencia de Negrilla by *Los Reyes Catolicos*, as Ferdinand and Isabella are usually described, after they had witnessed in the Ayuntamiento in Salamanca the dances of Charros. On the forehead of each woman wearing this traditional costume is affixed a gold crucifix resting on the royal arms of Old Castile, in embroidered velvet.

The much-remarked costumes worn by women in Montehermoso are completely feminine, not barbaric, as in La Alberca. Perhaps the most lavish in number of embroidered skirts, petticoats, and aprons, worn one over another, in all the provinces. It is, however, the high-crowned, beribboned poke bonnet which gives to the whole display a tremendous chic. The poke is dipped far forward over the eyes to allow a waterfall of yellow or pink silk shawl to trail to the heels in back. During the Peninsular Wars a regiment of British Infantry was encamped outside the walls of Montehermos. High-crowned Shakos ornamented with cockades and tasseled cords were worn by officers and privates. When the Duke of Wellington ordered the army to leave Spain, the Wellington Shako, was adopted by the dejected women in memory. The dress is usually of heavy ribbed black silk, the durable silk which the Spanish know so well how to make. A wide black velvet fichu is crossed over the breasts. Yellow, green, purple, and various shades of red petticoats hold the overskirt out like a bell. When the wearer chooses to sit in a chair these skirts must be flipped up over the chair back in the way a peacock spreads his tail.

The Sierra San Pedro region which embraces the curious course of the Tagus River gorge deserves to be better known and more widely visited. From Monroy and Alacántara through Arroyo del Puerco to Albuquerque and so into Badajóz, there is no terrain even remotely like it in the whole of Spain. The landscape has the "fever-bright, eyes-alight" quality of pictures from a folio of Albrecht Dürer. High mountains, thin and peaked, gashed with quartz deposits, flash iridescence to the sun. The day I passed through this enchanted valley even the clouds which wreathed the crests took on pastel colors lending an air of fragile impermanence to the whole, like the final transformation scene from hovel to palace of the Ogre King's daughter in a Christmas pantomime. Suddenly the Tagus gorge changes from pastiche to deep plum-brown and purple-red rocks, where a sound of rushing water is heard but no subterranean water is seen. Two tall, golden rock pillars appear plumed with stunted pines and here again we have the greatest gesture Spain has to offer. Pure theater. Whether in the crypt of a gilded, tapestry-hung cathedral, or the shadowed corridors of a river gorge, Spain is *theater*. I sketched this Tagus scene, in all its grim Spanish richness, with even the clouds massing above the rock pillars in red and gold opulence. For no detail in the landscape of Spain ever falters in doing its part to make the whole display of mood memorable and *Iberian*. [As I finished the last stroke I took a last look at the gorge, then back to my hastily brushed in picture. The dark reds and sepia-purples were held as in a proscenium by the towering golden rocks. I thought "What a setting for Ravel's *Pavanne to a Dead Infanta*."]

Albuquerque is a somber town where stand serried ranks of palaces of a defunct nobility; nearly all are shuttered, and I am told each one is full of "theatrical props" in disheveled furniture and the objets d'art and statues of members of the family. These mawkishly-sentimental sculptured portraits have a kind of embarrassing fascination. I shall never forget one instance which curdled my blood, not from horror, but writhing embarrassment. I was taken to visit a widow who lived in Sedano in Castile, to see a collection of Russian malachite given to her late husband in St. Petersburg, where he had been stationed. In the salon where the malachite boxes and other objects were laid, I noticed a figure of a little girl of about ten years old standing on a pink cushion in a niche which was heavily draped with golden-yellow silk curtains. The child was fondling a white Angora cat. As no one spoke to her, and she did not move, I wondered "What on earth is this?" I was soon shown. The mother, handkerchief brought into full play, turned on a bare electric light bulb and there in all its ghastly lifelikeness was a sculptured and painted counterpart of her dead daughter Pilar. It was, of course, a triumph of *trompe-l'oeil*. The hair was real (from the child's own head). The lace collar and cuffs on the lime green silk dress were real, but the dress was marble. The jet buttons on the marble patent-leather shoes were real, so was the ribbon and silver bell on the cat. Finally I became groggy trying to find out what was real and what sculptured marble. It seems that Pilar loved her cat, playing with him by the hour in this curtained niche during her lifetime. So what more fitting and companionable to a grieving widow than to have her child always in a happy mood right in the room? In so many places in Spain I have seen variations of this obsession for keeping the dead close by, in effigy. In chapels are the figures of whole families dressed in the height of fashion of whatever period they lived. Some of these, singly or in groups, are well known and may be seen all over the peninsula. Sometimes young women of grandee families are buried in transparent coffins, the dress and satin cushioning sprinkled with jewels and wax flowers.

I walked through the market place in Albuquerque to see the carved animals used as fountains (now dry) lining the paths. The market was built in the center of a park and still flourishes. The chief house is Palacio Domar with a most beautiful scutcheon over the door emblazoning a carved pelican feeding its offspring with an enormous frog. On pointed hills ringing the town are castles, mostly ruinous now, once belonging to the powerful Albuquerque family whose ramifications spread over Mexico and into Peru, in fact into every country where Spanish conquistadors penetrated.

Montijo is a curiously dormant town. Tight little houses like wedges of cheese of pale greenish white stand in narrow gardens with hedges primly cut, again in animal designs which seems to be a fetish in this vicinity. In the plaza I had the fleeting memory of recently reading in a biography that Eugénie Montijo, when a slim golden-haired countess, had driven a pair of white goats with gilded horns, harnessed to a red cart, through the streets of this slumberous village long before she entertained the idea of becoming Empress of France. She is also said to have lived in a house with a pink and blue tiled façade, but I could not find it. Oddly, I reflected, the few people I saw about the streets made no impression. This in itself was an unusual state of affairs in Spain. After I had crossed over the bridge spanning the feeble trickle of the River Alcazába I turned to look back. Always I shall think of the place as "pucker-mouthed Montijo." I have never seen such an air of primness. Frowning Montijo said to me, "Good-bye; come again if you like, but it doesn't matter a jot."

Mérida was just waking from siesta. A monumental quiet reigned. I felt as if the town with all its inhabitants had not been fully awake since the great days when, as Roman capital of Lusitania (Portugal), its riches and importance in the Roman scheme was immense. Humped bridges stand remote in fields where once waterways dug out of rock by Roman engineers cross hatched fields brought to noble fertility. There is a ruined temple to Ceres, or Demeter the Roman Earth Mother, near Mérida. Gauntly the shells of four aqueducts stand like the remnants of a herd of tired elephants, to shelter huts for herdsmen, even to protect their flocks at night in pens built under the arches. Mérida is almost as whitewashed as Cádiz. But it is a distinctly Spanish town. The shadow of the Moor in Spain has not lingered here. On foot I crossed the magnificent arcaded bridge which was built by the Emperor Trajan, over the Guadiana, to the utter rage of three storks building nests who had decided to walk down the middle of the road and resented my treading on their scattered sticks. Storks are everywhere in this particular stretch of country. Even in Andalusia where it is said, "for every chimney there is a stork to cover it," I did not see so many. In Spain I came to know that a fledgling stork is the clumsiest, most ridiculous bird in nature's aviary.

After leaving Mérida the scene changes again. This time to the cleanly drawn, sweeping economy of line in treeless hills, a kind of country which crops up so suddenly in nearly all parts of Spain. There is a most curious bridge over the River Alcazába, as decorative as it is bizarre, but completely pointless. Four stone pedestals rise to the height of ten or twelve feet. On the top of each one, in "stand-at-guard" stance, is a cast-iron figure of a British Grenadier in the uniform and busby of 1800, all painted pillar-box red, a relic of Wellington's sojourn. The effect of this extravaganza in a lonely landscape reminds me of the Cuatrel (fortress) de Bibataubin at Granada where figures of Prussian Guards in white tie-wigs and miter hats line the Rococo cornice of the red and white barracks.

I crossed the bridge hearing loud grunting and sharp squeals. A herd of slab-sided swine were fighting to rub their backs on the rough stone pedestals of the bridge. These unsavory looking beasts were, I judged, more of the same half-wild breed I had heard feed on vipers in the Sierra de los Víboras a few miles away toward Portugal, said to be infested by every sort of reptile from small golden hoop snake to dragon lizard. Hams from these viper-fed swine are considered a rare delicacy by gourmets. In the eighteenth century, London merchants who catered to the finicky appetites of the aristocracy were the chief importers. Each time I order *jamón serrano* in Spain I ask, hopefully, if it is from the viper gluttons. Always I get smiles and shrugs, just as always the ham is delicious. I have a feeling I will never know for sure, if my ham is viper-fed, or not.

As I so often do when coming into a town lying slightly below or above eye level, I stop and either sketch, or just take in the whole effect, for I find towns and cities have as much individuality in silhouette as in separate buildings or detail. Now it was Badajóz. It seems,

I thought, like a vast fortification. Notwithstanding that Badajóz had been pulled into battle formation by the engineering genius of a French general, Vauban, the walls stood up from Spanish earth, with the proud immensity of Spain.

Chapter 14

THE TAGUS AND TOLEDO

ALBEIT the day was rapidly darkening there was still a slash of primrose light in the sky which set off the ponderous gray fortress of Badajóz to perfection. I wondered where the renowned French military strategist Vauban had ever been able to quarry such Cyclopean stones to build his walls which are said to be sixty feet thick at the base, containing overall barracks for thousands of soldiers. I thought, too, of the pride the population of Badajóz take in their cold, proud city. And remember that pride is the keynote of the Spanish character. A Spaniard has an overweening personal pride. This is matched by pride of family, pride in his birthplace, his province, above all, in Spain. There are two proverbs often heard to point this up. One is "Pride is not spelled p-r-i-d-e. It is spelled B-a-d-a-j-ó-z." The other is an old wheeze, nonetheless very apt. "From Badajóz to Heaven, and in Heaven a loophole to look down at Badajóz." It is well known that whatever city, town or village a man hails from, when quoting this proverb he substitutes the name of his birthplace for Badajóz.

There is one magnificent gateway to enter the town, so floriated and boldly carved in almost Bernini *bravura* that the escutcheon over the arch, bristling with figures blowing trumpets, seemed to blare out of tune with the church bells, which were tolling for evening Mass. Badajóz is so close to the once restless frontier of Portugal that for centuries it has had little knowledge of peaceful pursuits. This explains why so many of the houses with the embattled look are fortified, or rise guardedly behind high spiked walls. There is a tremendous military grandeur about Badajóz which arrested my attention to the point that I sketched and photographed all one morning. I was taken through a bleak house near the citadel where Wellington lived. Going through the gaunt, disheveled rooms I realized fully why in after years he bristled at the mention of Badajóz. His usual description of it was, "Stone, stone. That old fort, where even my bed was made of stone."

From the Alcazába, perched precariously on a craggy hill, one looks toward green fields where long, low, white farmhouses drowse, covered in passion flower and trumpet vine, the whole landscape intersected by four wide rivers flowing into the cork forests of Alentejo Province in Portugal. In Badajóz are made a type of heavy pottery soup bowls (a thick hearty vegetable and meat *pote* is the staple dish of this region). The largest bowl ever made in the Valós potteries was for Francisco Goya, who boasted he could eat six bowls of *pote* at a sitting. The potters heard Goya was staying at Sanlúcar de Barrameda, living all but recluse, seeing only his "duquesita" of Alba. He was invited to come to Badajóz where at a banquet in his honor he was presented with a yellow and black bowl, as huge in circumference as a first-prize pumpkin. For the presentation the bowl was filled to the brim with twelve ordinary portions of game, ham, and sausage *pote*. It is said Goya finished the soup with gusto and later, in gratitude painted a picture of the scene. On the hem of the apron-size napkin tucked under his chin he painted his name, the place and date, adding a small, round spectacled face, with a cockscomb of obstreperous hair sprouting from the forehead. From the lips is issuing a very convincing belch. Later on Goya designed for the potteries exciting sketches of the bull ring, which are still used to decorate big white soup bowls.

Estramadura Province deals in space. Unlimited space. The dazzling white houses, like sentinels in the plain, solitary, or sometimes companioned by one tall hazel tree, stand out flat in the landscape as if painted on the sky. And the sky is the backdrop of the province. A lone horseman on a nag resounds in the landscape like a thunder clap, just by being a moving object in the solitude. I passed one such *vaquero* and wondered where was his herd of cows. A few minutes later I saw a black speck and puffs of dust moving across the plain far off to my right. It was the *vaquero* riding the range after one lone calf. Not until I was approaching Guadalupe did I see any more activity. Suddenly at least ten *vaqueros* and hundreds of cattle were looming out of nowhere.

The heart of Estramadura country is a province remote in time and space, as if forever wearing a black velvet mask to hide the beauty of villages hidden in mountain gorges or forests of cork. Estramadura is full of jealously-hidden secrets and surprises. Vast plains are surrounded by groves of evergreen oak trees, each savannah carefully planted in such a manner that it seems like a fairy ring of dark emerald. Always one's eyes are regaled by the rusted-blue of distant hills backed by dark jagged crowns of three sierras. The nearly inaccessible towns of Estramadura are exciting to come upon for one finds the inhabitants enjoying a spirited life full of pageantry and joy in the daily round, and most courteously ready to share it with any tourists with enough imagination to penetrate their fastnesses.

Topping a pointed hill, Béjar crowds around its white castle, Gothic with Morish overtones, houses as brightly painted as a stained-glass window; the swathes of color added to by hanging gardens and baskets of growing vines and ferns swung in festoons from the eaves. Suddenly the road dips down a long grade into the quiet tree-shaded streets of Baños de Montemayor. Here one finds some of the most comfortable, old-fashioned, but luxurious hotels in Spain. Baños de Montemayor has long been a fashionable spa where generations of *hidalgo* families have come to bathe in the electricity-impregnated waters. A long *alameda* lined with cafés, shops, and pavilions leading to the public baths, is like a page from an illustrated weekly of the period when Queen Mother Christina took ten-year-old Alfonso in a white satin suit and long black silk stockings to "take the waters" at the spa. The improbable slimness approaching the skeletal of the Infante Alfonso caused the townspeople to coin a phrase when discussing anyone with a skinny frame. "As thin as the royal giraffe."

To come upon the thirteenth-century Cathedral of Our Lady of Guadalupe is a startling experience. Chestnut trees on a hill hide the tremendous edifice until one is immediately at the base of towering walls. I have heard it called "the lost shrine of Guadalupe." Perhaps no cathedral-shrine anywhere is so remotely situated, so far off the beaten track. Miles upon miles of bare plain, dust, heat, and weariness. Suddenly there it rises, a mighty fortress, springing against the sky as if a part of Altamira Rock. All the stones used to rear this religious monolith to a Madonna only one meter high, came from the bowels of Altamira Rock. Yet there is no sign of this quarrying

239

on the face of the rock itself. A superhuman task comparable to the building of the Pyramids, one would think.

Of all deeply loved Virgins in Spain, none is held so precious in the hearts of persons of every walk of life as Our Lady of the Hidden Brook (the Arab words *guada* and *lupe*). I stayed the night in the monastery where the Franciscan friars show travelers rare kindness and a memorable hospitality. After a meal in a long room with a beamed and painted ceiling I was happy to see a monk carrying a charcoal brazier toward my room. As the sun set and night came down, it had turned cold with the sharp, crystal coldness of the mountains. Next morning I walked in the *camarin*, behind the altar, its brilliance faded long since Luca Giordano painted the walls in primary colors. There is a silent dignity about the two-story cloister, an inspiring sense of lift to the flow of arched line. This double tier is much more grand in scale, but I believe not so delicate in detail or elegance of slender serpentine columns as the cloister at Santo Domingo de Silos, which will always be a criterion in my mind by which to judge Romanesque or Mozarabic architecture. I had but lately seen Silos, and it came to memory now as I walked in the sacristy at Guadalupe where hang eight panels by Zurbarán, depicting the monks at daily tasks such as gardening, churning butter, baking loaves of bread, and the like. Silos has only one Zurbarán, the superb St. Dominic with his staff, far richer in conception and brush work than these at Guadalupe. Yet these are very fine. No one who ever lived can surpass Zurbarán as a draughtsman.

Then I walked slowly into the cathedral to stand in front of the shrine. It was early for tourists to be about. Save for ten or twelve pilgrims and a few countrywomen I was alone to absorb this tremendously strong fare. I am used to scale in the grand style. It has been said that in my painting and architectural drawings I deal in it. But the vastness of the nave is almost an enormity against scale. It is stupefying. In contrast, the figure of the Virgin, said to have been carved by St. Luke, scarcely thirty inches high, looks tiny. For seven centuries the Madonna was buried in a cave near where the cathedral now stands. With the expulsion of the Moors she was brought from the cave to be surrounded by the offerings of treasure which had accumulated in her name during all those years. It almost transcends the imagination to realize only a part of the drama of human emotions that have taken place before this shrine. The treasure house of the cathedral was actually started when Alfonso XI, in full armor, en-

tered the church and threw down bales of richest stuffs, gold vessels
and jewels looted from the Moors, as an offering to Our Lady of
Guadalupe for her protection and aid in his victory. Ferdinand and
Isabella the Catholic prostrated themselves before this simple figure
with downcast eyes. The queen lay on the stones overcome with
religious fervor. It was feared for a time her reason might be impaired. When the royal pair returned to Valladolid they sent to the
cathedral a wagon train of treasure of immense value and a ruby ring
with F and I intertwined in the setting. On a gold chain this hangs
about the neck of the Virgin. Numerous conquistadors draped the
Virgin with captured banners taken in battle from enemies of Spain.
Pizarro, the fabulous son of a swineherd of Trujillo, hung heavy
chains of gold from the New World about the slender neck of the
tiny figure. Cortez heaped about her ingots of the most precious
metal from the storehouses of Montezuma. Possibly as dramatic as
any moment recorded was when Cervantes entered the nave of
Guadalupe, ill and travel-stained. He knelt at the Virgin's feet to
offer her the rusted chains that had manacled his legs when he was
taken as a slave to Algeria. The vestments and treasure kept in a
crypt are comparable in richness, perhaps even in value, to those in
the cathedral at Toledo. Vitrines hold copes and chasubles, miters,
altar cloths, bales of velvets, and brocades for ceremonial baldaquins
as well as every conceivable jeweled ornament and device. Many of
these are presents from persons wishing to remain unknown. Legion
stories are told of grandees and noble ladies who have arrived at the
shrine incognito wrapped in heavy cloaks or veils. Some women
have even been carried down the nave in a hysterical frenzy of ex-
piation. To my mind the outstanding episode for pure drama is the
story of the woman—to this day no one knows for sure who she was,
though there has been much conjecture and even ribald gossip—who
arrived at the cathedral in 1820 attended by an entourage of silent
persons all in black. She herself was in black robes heavily jeweled.
A throne chair, brought from her traveling coach, was set in front
of the shrine, for it was given out that an infirmity made it impossible
for her to kneel. For three days she sat, bowed under heavy veils, and
prayed, refusing all food, retiring to a canopied litter at night. Finally
on the morning of the fourth day, as the organ was being played for
Mass, the woman stripped off her jewels and called for sackcloth.
Leaving her rich garments on the floor the penitent woman was
carried weeping from the shrine to her coach. The jewels scattered

at the feet of the Virgin were gathered into a sack by a duenna in the retinue of the mysterious woman. These were entrusted to a friar, the duenna asking that they be hidden until such time as the donor should no longer be alive, explaining that the jewels were of great worth and of such splendor they would surely be recognized. A few years later a letter was delivered to the padre saying that the jewels could now be displayed on the breast of Our Lady of Guadalupe. The courier who delivered the letter wore the livery of The Dukes of Alba.

Driving along the River Guadiana in Ciudad Real Province, I came, just at dusk, to a strangely compelling sight on the opposite river bank. At first loomed what looked like the gaudy insubstantial towers of a White City amusement park. It turned out to be Puebla de Don Rodrigo. A crumbling castle built by El Cid, to add to his formidable collection for protection of his stolen boundaries, merges into tiers of cave dwellings in so subtle a fashion I could not tell which was which. Sufficiently intriguing was the firefly flickering of hundreds of candles and blue Madonna lamps as inhabitants of roomy caves went about preparing the evening meal. There was plenty of activity and sound. Haunting *saetas* rose and fell in cadences. Children cried, dogs barked. Somewhere a man strummed a guitar and a pursued fowl protested stridently that it was not his turn to go into the pot. Until a few years ago superannuated members of the Rodrigo family still lived in one wing of the castle. I have never seen the puebla in the light of day. Except that the Guadiana flows lazily at the base of the ledge-piled cliffs, the place probably does not differ greatly in appearance from the other cave habitations scattered all over Spain. But I did notice one difference in the fast fading light. From the topmost tower of the castle hung wooden dovecotes suspended by chains like baskets of hanging ferns or geraniums from the eaves of a summer châlet. A great deal of pother in fluttering of wings was going on, as well as the arrival and take-off of winged messengers. I learned a great deal about this puebla later. The tall, round tower is a military post for training carrier pigeons which are still greatly in use during army maneuvers.

Near Tetuan in Spanish Morocco a similar tower was used during the days when the bandit chief Rasuli harassed the resident Spanish troops out of their minds. In some way the bandits high up in the Riff Mountains at Rasuli's fortress hideaway used to shoot down or snare the messenger pigeons. The bandits would eat some of the birds but a few of those snared were sent on their way to the Spanish outposts bearing obscene suggestions of where the Spanish should go, and what to do when they got there. One officer collected these suggestions which he in turn sent anonymously to officers or persons with whom he did not see eye to eye. I have seen a few of the collection and I must say that for picturesque lewdness and descriptive simile concerning the libido these Riffian quatrains hit the bull's eye every time.

Ciudad Real is a small town in the high, imperial style mightily concerned with self importance, taking the name Royal City seriously, somewhat like a Valladolid in miniature. The houses have ornate façades with armorial bearings above many entrance doors. The city was given royal charter by Los Reyes Catolicos, who often stayed here for the autumn vintage ceremonies at adjacent Valdepeñas. Until the fall of the monarchy (Alfonso XIII) these annual festivals to Bacchus were the most elaborate and well attended in the country. Wherever the court was in residence, no matter how short the sojourn, nobles ever watchful for royal favor, built houses as close as possible to the royal lodgings. Many of the most beautiful towns in Europe today owe their inception to the vagaries of some king who could not stay long in one place. We have the magnificent castle of the Mendoza family at Manzanares Real in the environs of Madrid. While not royal, this family was immensely powerful at court. Families of lesser nobles squandered entire fortunes to build elegant *petits palais* in Manzanares near the great Mendoza palace rising in greenery, a trellised bower of grape vines.

When I drove through the dark streets of Ciudad Real I wondered at the shuttered houses and utter silence riding the place like a funeral pall. Then I noticed a poster announcing a fiesta at Valdepeñas. I soon found out that everyone save the lame, the halt, and the blind had been in the hills for two days attending the first of a number of fiestas to celebrate the vintage.

Valdepeñas is noted for a light, eminently drinkable wine which has enjoyed notable popularity from the days when Roman emperors had huge hogsheads sent back to Rome to age in the cellars of their villas. Then the seal of approval from the Castilian and Aragones kings gave the wine further renown. In fact, I have found most travelers prefer Valdepeñas and (or) Marqúes de Riscal above most Spanish wines. I venture this is because both have fragrant bouquet and are agreeable on the palate, with no lasting ill effects.

YOUNG NOVIOS
TOLEDO

Collection of Mrs. John Adams Mayer

The town lies in the midst of lovely rolling vineyards in Ciudad Real Province. I left the deserted Royal City under a bright moon to drive to Valdepeñas hoping to catch some of the gaiety still at its height. I had driven about half way when I came upon a well-nigh indescribable gesture in architecture looming solitary, as do so many of these unexplainable edifices in Spain, in a lonely moon-drenched countryside. Confronting me was a long stone bridge across the River Jabalón erected, I felt, on the instant, by the touch of a wand in the hand of Fata Morgana. A fanciful illusion, evoked from froth and fribble to get me in fiesta mood for Valdepeñas. But no, the bridge itself stood firm on, I found later, Roman arches. The grandiose ornament of urns spouting suns, moons, and stars, in pure Aztec trumpeting of shrill yellow plaster which flanked the bridge approach, was half crumbled away. Like Puenta de Toledo by Pedro de Ribera in Madrid, the exaggerated convolutions were taken from crude drawings of barbaric palaces of Andean princes brought back to Spain by the conquistadors. In the starshine this raddled magnificence seemed to veer like flames with a light wind that had sprung up. Stucco fragments fell every once in a while with a splash into the water below.

The square at Valdepeñas was bright with orange lanterns and flares set up under arbors of grape vines. A hundred or more couples were dancing on the cobbles of the plaza. Light from the flares cast huge, wavering shadows of the dancers on the house fronts. Music from primitive instruments was loud and piercing, competing with the explosions of powder bombs masked in gay paper, without which no celebration in Spain is conceivable. Strongly colored carpets and banners hung from second- and third-story windows. Wine passed freely among the crowd, and everyone ate great, thick sandwiches made from slit-asunder loaves of bread with slices of cheese, ham, and sausages between, munching contendedly while whirling in the dance. This is ancient land, a province where legends are immediate and old usages prevail. The vine tenders and grape pressers live in the old Spanish way.

Costumes traditional to Valdepeñas are not remarkable, in fact extremely simple in contrast to the gold lace and embroidery of many other provinces. The older women wear black skirts and bodices with red banding and white cotton head shawls scalloped in red. Younger girls wear red and white full skirts patterned in red flowers and birds on white or the reverse. The stockings worn by men and women alike are knitted in brilliant stripes fit to shame the rainbow. It was the visitors from Ciudad Real who left no doubt in the mind that they hailed from a proud "royal-charter" city. The women wear red velvet aprons appliquéed and embroidered with scrolls and eagles in gold with a kind of *madroñes*, or chenille balls spangling a mantilla of red silk worn over high-dressed black hair. The men are as splendidly accoutered as the kings and jacks on playing cards, in yellow tabards, some belted, others rolling free, appliquéed in heraldic manner in red, black, and gold.

I left about dawn to drive through the sunrise to Manzanares of sad-eyed palaces. Except for the Mendoza vineyard buildings, the houses seem lonely and forgotten, left stranded on the threshold of a world whose way of life has long since departed. After Manzanares the land becomes more rolling, with sudden juts of rock. Like a breath of eternal spring the rock-rose blooms on banks beside the road casting a carpet of faint pink crocus petals far into the receding hills. I am reminded of Corinth by the giant acanthus plants (without which Greek sculptors could not have left the glorious floriated capitols in Corinthian style to delight posterity) which dress the *vega* in arresting floriations. The curved movement of the leaves, notched in silver, are vital as the movements of flamenco dancers. I cut some of the great leaves. One that I used as a specimen to sketch was curled back, so writhed upon the center I had to straighten it out. To my surprise the uncurled leaf measured seven feet.

Cervantes, minus his chains, seems now to walk across the plains arm-in-arm with Don Quixote and Sancho Panza. This is La Mancha, the country where every schoolboy, in imagination, has tilted at the patched sails, lazily turning on the walls of tall stone windmills dotting the landscape.

I stopped at a *taberna*, the walls washed with pale cerulean blue, standing solitary sentinel beside the road in the plains where even a windmill was a rarity. The meal was as frugal as one usually finds in remote districts. But the Valdepeñas wine was excellent, cooled to the right degree, in bottles sunk in a great cask of spring water, and the pungent flavor of La Mancha cheese allied with fresh butter and a dark barley-flour loaf sent me on my way rejoicing. As soon as I had put Taberna Tio Chorizo (a joke on someone, I suspected, for the name means Uncle Sausage) a few miles behind me, a phalanx of whitewashed, black-capped stone windmills sprang up from the plain with no warning, until I was surrounded by waving canvas sails. The sky was a particularly intense blue dome over the windmills of La Mancha today. Against the sky the white towers and gray or sepia linen arms to catch the wind intensified the color of the sky until the bright day seemed to darken with cobalt shadows. I stopped the car, got out, and tried to paint a white tower to catch the sense of slow, majestic rhythm of the ochre yellow sails against the cloudless sky. I found myself using brushfuls of strong, pure color straight from the tube, brushed in with an economy of line. Red earth, white tower, ochre sails, and deep cobalt-blue sky. There, I had it. With a last sweep of the brush—La Mancha.

I drove to Albacete for only one reason, to buy knives. The most important town commercially in the Province of Albacete is historically famous for light-weight, strongly tempered steel cutlery. A man told me once, "Albacete is as important to the international hotel trade for its cutlery as is Toledo for its wonderfully flexible, damascened blades."

The Street of Apprentices was first Roman, then Moorish. It is still a sort of informal school of the art of grinding and polishing steel knives, but is frowned on now by slick young factory workers as something left over from the Middle Ages, which indeed it is. It reminds me of some of the metal workers' shops in the souks of Fez or Meknès where young boys sit cross-legged humming sentimental love songs or chanting passages from the Koran while they hammer out beautiful as well as useful utensils.

Chinchilla de Monte Aragon is not the oldest village in Spain by a long shot, but by the color of the houses alone it might have been buried under desert sands for a hundred centuries. The Phoenicians held cavalry maneuvers here and the Romans built a stadium for games. Little of this remains except a few plinths of the sort erected to victorious athletes; the names have long since been obliterated by the winds of time. The color of the narrow alley-like streets is only the memory of color, dimmed to a blanched-pearl whiteness. Yet I noticed in the ancient arcades a fragment of Phoenician wall, and farther on a group of Romanesque columns once painted with rich reds and purple blue. But most of the town, including a Romanesque church, is pastel colored; in the shadows the tones deepen. As accent, a breath of life as it were, tubs of the curious blue geraniums, seen only in Spain, decorate the bare plaza, and the women effect the severest of black hooded capes.

In Santa Maria la Antigua Convent there is a madonna of gilded wood in black and gold robes hung with countless ivory rosaries and moonstone amulets. The carving of ivory (from Africa) and polishing of moonstones were ancient arts in Chinchilla, and examples of this work are highly prized by collectors. Now only a few antique caskets and religious ornaments are to be seen.

I drove to Toledo by way of Alcazar de San Juan, carefully hiding my boxes of modern cutlery, for it seemed somehow sacrilege to enter the ancient stronghold of the damascened-steel workers with shiny, spanking new knives I would use to pare off juicy slices of beef and venison or the undercooked breast of game birds. I would make it right with Toledo by choosing a brace of rapiers and a serpentine sword.

Nothing could be more felicitous than to drive into dreaming Orgaz with the thought of Toledo not far off hovering in my mind.

Like the overture to a great dramatic piece to which one has long looked forward, Orgaz strikes the first soft but reverberating chords nobly. It is a village of no size, but great age and beauty, because of its houses built of metallic stone. Heavy veins of iron crosshatching the rock, all this heavily rimed with bronze-green lichen. Castle Orgaz glows above a tremendous stand of darkling pine trees as a golden crucifix suspended on a green enamel cross. There is nothing more to the village than this, except a golden quietness on every hand. Then comes a stretch of silence in the dusty, silvery-rose *vega*.

As I came closer to Toledo the storied city seemed to be a mirage of castles and temples forever receding. The walls and turreted towers are the color of myrrh, amber, rose, amethyst, gold and dusty green. I wonder who crushed all the hoarded jewels of Byzantium and the laden East to crystals, then poured the glowing dust upon the plain to form Toledo. El Greco saw this illusive color too, for when painting the town from the bridge over the Tagus he mixed on his palette muted colors I have never seen elsewhere.

It is said that when Francisco de Villalpando, who designed the glorious gilt *rejas* of Capilla Mayor in the cathedral, walked through the streets he wore a robe on which was finely embroidered the whole city of Toledo in panorama, save across his shoulders where space was left to embroider the Capilla Mayor *rejas* in gold thread. I wonder if the radiant garment is today somewhere preserved, or only dust added to the mounds and towers of myrrh. This is what Toledo does to the mind. Images of long-dead magnificence crowd present manifestations before one's eyes in such a way it is hardly possible to tell where imagination and reality divide.

In the thirteenth-century cathedral there is much visual excitement of various periods. For sheer *brio* in movement, perhaps nothing of the Rococo period surpasses El Transparente, sculptured by Narcisco Tomé. This immense set piece extends from marble floor to ceiling, in a kind of symphony of exultation. If ever carved marble was articulate this is true of El Transparente. No artist was ever better served by light and shadow, Tomé having directed masons to pierce the upper walls with lunettes the better to display his Virgin ascending to Heaven, rapturously greeted by seraphims and billowing angels, all extending hands to assist Her to join the seated figure of Christ in Glory. Even on a gray day there seem to be floods of golden light from the cleverly hidden amber glass in the lunettes high in the walls of the nave.

Another great piece of religious theater is the "flight" of choir stalls carved in chestnut wood by Rodrigo Aleman, beautifully imaginative, because he used as motif, figures from curtains embroidered by Moorish women for the Borgia (Borja) family of Játiva. The subject is the conquest of Granada and in translation from worked silk on velvet to carved chestnut wood the vitality and incident of the original story has been miraculously preserved. The choir stalls are arranged as a series of steps. So great is the height of the cathedral, these seem to reach into the clouds of incense forever drifting across the ceilings of Spanish churches. There is a ceiling by Luca Giordano, a great colorist, which glows like the morning of creation in spectacular range of yellows and limpid greens. If for no other reason on earth the Cathedral of Toledo is triumphant for the vast collection of jeweled and embroidered vestments and altar garniture. While there is loot from the Moors and presents from foreign monarchs, the greater part of stuffs, embracing every facet of brocades, damasks, satins, and velvets, came solely from the looms of weavers to the medieval kings of Spain. The use of pure gold and silver thread in high embossment, or the clipped-fringe ends to catch points of light, is rich past belief, when combined with velvets in green, black, glowing reds, and orange, the entire range of blues and purple, the honey-yellow of Aragon and the pale rose known as bister, used for the farthingales for infantas. Many of the vestments dating from the sixteenth century are cut and fashioned from heraldic banners carried before far earlier kings and queens of Aragon, Navarre, and Castile, as well as robes used at their coronations. A few years ago I was in Toledo for a week, during which the anniversary of the Battle of Lepanto was celebrated on the first Sunday in October. The banner flown by Don Juan of Austria from the stern of his galleon is displayed as a battle tent in the nave of the cathedral. The sun streaming in on the crimson-, black-, yellow-, and gold-embroidered arms of Los Reyes Catolicos set the colors vibrating until they seemed as pulse-stirring as the music of a harp. Color against sound, to challenge in volume the notes of a paean to victory played by a hidden organist.

The El Greco painting, "Christ Stripped of His Garments" in the sacristy of the cathedral is darkly handsome and sufficiently tortured for the subject, but in no way touches in greatness his "Burial of Count Orgaz" in Santo Tomé. The church of Santo Tomé is hidden in a dark side street, the walls are seer and bleak, coming to life only at Corpus Christi when the outside walls of the churches, as well as many of the buildings and old palaces, are completely covered by arras and tapestries from the cathedral collection. Then the town sings with every color in the spectrum and my color-conscious eyes seemed to find shades I had never before dreamed of. Alone on a white wall, hangs El Greco's painting, with the limp figure of Orgaz in golden armor being lifted up to Heaven by magnificently-vestured St. Augustine and St. Esteban, while an impressive assemblage of *hidalgos* in stark black, their lean, sallow faces embedded in white ruffs, watch this divine elevation with mingled emotions. A small boy, said to be El Greco's youngest son, dressed as a page in black doublet and hose, occupies the front of the canvas. Never in all portraiture have I seen a boy so winning or so impertinent. Wearing the most supercilious expression, this black-garbed stripling engages your attention while he is pointing to Toledo rising above the Tagus which forms the background to the picture. I was told by a verger in attendance at the stall, where one can buy photographs of the entire painting or details of the figures, that almost everyone wants a copy of the full-length detail of this boy.

The house where El Greco lived is on a hill with a small tree-lined plaza in front. One passes through a series of patios and arcaded alleys to reach it. From upper rooms in the house is the view over the roofs of the city and across the ancient arched bridge over the Tagus to the somber color of the plains, so often seen against a tortured sky in his pictures.

In Toledo I haunt one particular shop where Toledo blades, either plain steel or damascened, are made. There is still a Court of Apprentices (directly across from the entrance patio of the El Greco museum) where young boys sit in the wide, windowed booths intently hammering metal blades, inserting gold and silver wires into steel in the rich and graceful Moorish art of damascene. Each boy well-schooled in the tale, will tell you about the origin of the process in Damascus where first the metal belts and breast plates worn by harem beauties were so decorated. Sultans and caliphs desired this contrasting tracery design, gold on silver for sword hilts and scabards. Later pictorial stories of victorious battles were set in bright wire into the body armor and greaves for knightly warriors and kings throughout the Christian world. Every apprentice is divided between wanting one day to be a famous matador and the next, a famous armorer. There is a museum connected with this shop where ancient Moorish shields, damascened stirrups and saddle pommels, even great lotus-flower fans once fashioned to be carried in ceremonial processions, can be seen.

I saw a bull fight in Toledo. An unusual thing happened during the corrida. Domingo Ortega decided to place his own *banderillas* in the shoulders of the bull. A slender arrow he looked, in almond-green and gold. He chose the most dangerous way to do this trick. Standing stock still before the bull's charge, only at the last split second did Ortega force the bull to alter his course by a sudden sway of the body to one side. The bull, unaware of this deceit, thundered past as Ortega swayed back to his original position to place the darts expertly, one on either side of the gleaming black shoulders. Not until Ortega turned to acknowledge the frenzied roars of the crowd did I notice that one horn of the bull had ripped off swatches of gold galloon from the green *traje de luces* (knee breeches) or that smears of the bull's blood striped the famous pink silk stockings which all toreros wear for luck.

After Ortega had delivered a swift *suerte* to his third bull there took place a little ceremony. He was carried on the shoulders of admirers, jostling each other in high excitement, to the box of the *alcalde*. Here, after delivering a severed ear of the dispatched bull to an official guest in the mayor's box, Ortega was presented with a flexible Toledo blade. Next morning I walked to the shop of the apprentices near Plaza Marqués de la Vega Inclán (named for the man who gave El Greco's house to the city for a museum) and bought a sword with an undulating or "reflection in water" blade, serpentine in line and so flexible I can bend it double. I had long had my eye on it. That evening I was showing my prize to a man at Parador Oropesa a few miles outside Toledo on the road to Madrid, where I was staying.

The man examined the thin blade carefully. "What will you do with it?" he asked.

I replied, "What I will *do* does not signify. What does one *do* with quicksilver, or moonlight on water, or sunlight on a field of ripe wheat? Just look. At least I can look at this blade whenever I choose. I have other plans for this slithy beauty as well."

There being no good hotel in Toledo, many people stay in Madrid, two hours' drive away. I took the old Roman road to Aranjuez. Many times I have walked in the gardens of this old town where time seems to stand at ease, forgotten and forgetting, for the ilex and pomegranate walks never change. The faded beauties of the summer palace of the Spanish kings beckon one to wander in nostalgic mood. The palace is well tended but more than a shade poignant with memories of long-past grandeur. In the throne room, rows of tattered silk banners move restlessly against the cornices. I always sense a whisper of gossip. Everything about Aranjuez whispers of yesterday. Either one is in a mood for reflection, or the gardens create it. I always feel the illusive presence of ghosts in these long green alleys where so few flowers bloom. At evening, nightingales sing their hearts out, as if calling back the lovers of the past. Aranjuez has known great happiness and greater tragedy. When Isabella la Catolica lived here during the first summers of her marriage, she wrote that they were the happiest days of her life. Later she fled from Valladolid to Aranjuez for solace, when her mad daughter Juana was imprisoned in the Mudéjar patios of the royal convent of Santa Clara at Tordesillas by her own father.

The Casa del Labrador, which I have already mentioned as being ironically named, was built in the most secluded part of the jungle gardens of Aranjuez by Charles IV (guides always refer to him as Charlie Four) for his son Ferdinand VII. Charlie Four was an inveterate builder of palaces—"to occupy my time," as he had carved over the doors of these establishments. Of all those I have seen I favor the pale green stucco and white marble Venetian-style Palacio de los Rejas in a narrow, crowded street in Cádiz.

Ferdinand VII from early childhood was a problem. He had to be constantly entertained or he had tantrums. It is told that when he was given a set of chessmen of exquisite Chinese jade, he promptly decapitated each one with a large silver spoon. For a time La Perla, a famous singer of the time, lived at Casa del Labrador. One night she was strangled with a yellow satin ribbon threading a matchless pearl, which she always wore. Her body was found floating in the lagoon by a gardener. The murderer was never brought to book. Madrileños will tell you the singing you hear in the gardens is not all from the liquid throats of nightingales. La Perla is restless and distraught that her murder is still unavenged. She prowls about the gardens matching her voice with the singers in the trees.

Garden restaurants situated along the shaded banks of the Tagus at Aranjuez are delightful and attract many smart Madrileños who motor the thirty odd miles from the capital for lunch or dinner. They consider it the nicest possible way to entertain visiting guests. Of all the "grotto" restaurants El Labrador is perhaps most charmingly appointed and the food is either French or Spanish cuisine. This is a great place for people who cannot sit down to food cooked in olive oil but must have everything cooked with butter. I went to a dinner party one night at El Labrador given for me by friends from Madrid. We sat down to dinner at half past eleven o'clock. The dinner was not elaborate. Everything was beautifully cooked. At one o'clock the sweet came in, it had been especially prepared in my honor. I was told by my hostess "Because you are an Irish horseman. Just wait until you see." Four candelabra of luster were brought in and placed at the corners of the table, the better to light this culinary *objet d'art*. All of us sat still, eagerly waiting. A waiter came in bearing a huge gold tray on which was a remarkably true representation in sculptured ice of a famous fountain in Madrid, the Goddess Cybele in her triumphal chariot drawn by lions. The candle light struck thousands of facets of green sparks from the ice goddess. All around the lions were piled mounds of apricot and pistachio ice cream. I looked at my hostess and saw that she was frowning and biting her lips. Something had gone decidedly askew. I caught her eye and gently shook my head, because the chef was standing in the entrance to the arbor where we were seated, beaming from ear to ear, in pride of a really monumental achievement. We all clapped our hands. I bowed towards the chef, then there was a moment of wondering quiet. It appears that the chef thought that anyone who liked horses would like wild animals just as much. He could not carve a horse in ice to his or, he thought, to my liking, so he used a stock set of molds into which water is poured and frozen. This is perennially used to regale foreign ambassadors, and came from the kitchens of the Royal Palace, so to his mind it was the supreme gesture.

The ice cream was delicious and we enjoyed the diplomatic handling of the incident by the chef. We all agreed, better a good representation of the Plaza de la Cibeles fountain, than a clumsy carving of an Irish horse.

Chapter 15

MADRID HAS EVERYTHING

IN the classic manner I was rapidly reviewing in my mind various things I had heard recently about Madrid, as well as remembering how this metropolis, spread star-shaped on its high plateau, had impinged on my imagination when I was first taken there at the age of twelve years. Of all my remembrances, what has remained clearest in my memory is the answer to a question I received from my Grandfather Reynolds, whose opinion on anything under the sun I considered unassailable. The evening before I was to leave Rathgannonstown in Ireland to journey with my mother to the Spanish capital, I asked, "Shall I like Madrid?"

My grandfather lifted a small magnifying glass which he habitually wore on a black moiré ribbon around his neck. Using it as a quizzing glass he looked sharply at me and delivered, straight thrust, "Why wouldn't you now? Madrid has everything."

I now catalogued just what I would revisit and in what order, for I have been many times to Madrid since the twelve-year-old visit, and find something new always rears its head among all my favorite haunts.

Yes—Madrid has it all. Superb pictures, rare manuscripts, and the finest collection of illuminated parchment maps in the world, an equally splendid collection of armor, showing in thrilling array the history of the Moorish art of damascene. There is a remarkable collection of the finest examples of the gold and silversmith's art. A whole museum given to jewelry from Roman, Visigothic, to Medieval times, and so on down the centuries. The tapestries, both Spanish needlework and French, from looms of Tournai, Arras, and Beau-

vais, are displayed in conjunction with sumptuous medieval brocades and velvets. The embroidered and jeweled ecclesiastical damask
vestments rival those in the Cathedral of Toledo. Architecturally,
Madrid is varied and richly endowed. There are numerous wide
avenues bordered with attractive shops, old streets, and quarters
where the palaces of Spanish grandees are well worth seeing, for
they are usually built in Mudéjar or restrained Plateresque style.
Madrid is famous for its many gardens. Some are natural wooded
spaces left more or less as they were first laid out when the cult was
for trees and shrubbery as nature intended them, more than the
eighteenth-century contrived delights of parterres and clipped hedges
as background for studied flower effects. But gardens in the style of
Le Nôtre are here as well, notable for his style of combining magnificent flowers, topiary work, and fountains.

Then, when all else is said there is the Prado Museum, and a short
way out in the hills the tour de force of Baroque style palace-monastery, El Escorial. No city anywhere can boast greater treasure than
these. I wager no one will die of boredom by this banquet of beauty
though it is possible to be overcome by intellectual flatulence.

Aside from all other attractions, Madrid is the cleanest city I have
ever been in. A passion for keeping the streets and gardens swept and
neat seems to vie with the Madrileños' passion for corrida. Matadors
are the very emblem of Madrid. Ever ready on the tongue springs
forth eulogy of its heroes, from idolized matadors to the least considered little old picador who may once have blazed his dexterity
with the pic across the history of tauromachy. Madrileños do not
forget. Any man who dedicated his life to outwitting El Toro for
public entertainment occupies an inviolate niche in the collective
heart of the city. Even more than in Barcelona, out-door gossip at
the street cafés is the "newspaper" of Madrid. Newsboys may hawk
their wares right under the noses of a group of Madrileños sitting
at a sidewalk table, to no avail. Avid for news, both internal and of
events exploding in the outside world, the men prefer to get it via the
route; "He told my brother and my brother told me." I asked a
friend in Madrid just why this is so. He replied, "Cold print is not
dramatic, however much the news itself may be. But to be told
startling events by a friend with gestures, over a glass of *manzanilla*,
ah, one can make a real drama out of that." He added that almost no
women in Spain read newspapers. Yet most Spanish women, particularly those I have met in Madrid, seem extremely well informed on

what goes on in the world. This again is gained by word of mouth from male members of the family during the nightly ritual dinner, a kind of family conclave which no Spaniard ever misses unless he is away from the city. The matriarchal system prevails among all classes in Spain. Always garbed in black, frequently carrying the family fortune in jewels on her person, the matriarch reigns supreme.

One is always aware when approaching Madrid, which occupies a plateau in the exact center of the country, that the Sierra de Guadarrama rises in sheer, striated beauty due north of the city, to form a magnet for fierce electrical storms during nine months of the year. Always the sight of this range is heartening, for dense forests of dark umbrella pines on the slopes paint a swathe of cool green against gold-gray granite. No matter how hot the summer may be in Madrid, the peaks of Guadarrama, when suddenly enveloped in writhing black thunderheads, split by forked lightning, seem to form a curtain of coolness which, whether the rain sweeps down on the streets of Madrid or not, will temper the air most pleasantly. This same coolness from distant mountains is true of Granada as well, where the eternally snow-clad peaks of Sierra Nevada Range stand sentinel, a backdrop to this ancient Moorish town. In Spain there are said to be thirty-two sierras of great or lesser degree. Over three-quarters of the country is covered by hills or mountains.

Twice in my life I have arrived in Madrid when the city was one great *feria*. Here I was again in the midst of a pulsing crowd of Madrileños strolling in the middle of the streets, sitting at cafés, all endeavoring in various ways to kill time agreeably until six o'clock. It is of course not unusual if one arrives in any Spanish city on Sunday to find a corrida scheduled for evening performance. Sunday is the day when the working man can attend the bull fight with his wife and very often his entire family including in-laws. On all counts Sunday is a gala day in Spain.

It was late in the afternoon as I wove through the traffic. Open carryalls drawn by white mules, festive in Andalusian harness of vermilion and green, ajangle with silver chains, drove at a smart pace along the wide street leading to Plaza de Toros, so that everyone could see the bull fighters in their gold and satin finery. Litri and Aparicio, two crack matadors, great friends since childhood, always work together. Both matadors are extremely brilliant performers in totally different style. Litri is cool and collected, always appearing blasé in the face of the most slashing lunges of a bull. His *suerte* is

257

lethal. Every move he makes is expert, but somehow, to me, uninspired. Aparicio is less austere. There is a glow about his person. He is far more the performer to the gallery. His swiftness and grace are proverbial in Spain. I contend he would have made one of the great male dancers of classic ballet of the century, had he not dedicated his life to corrida. After the last *suerte*, the parade round the bull ring with both Litri and Aparicio borne on the shoulders of admirers frantic with delight, I was taken out of the city to a small *hosteria* on the road to Guadalajara. A celebration for Litri and Aparicio was in order, given them by a famous grandee of Spain who is a breeder of notoriously fierce bulls and a leading devotee of the sport. The party numbered fourteen. The staff at Hosteria El Morillo was putting on a rather unique party, as it turned out, for it was the birthday of the *patrón* of the inn. The Spanish love for dressing up was brought into full play. A master of ceremonies was highly effective in the costume of a matador of 1800, pale-blue satin braided in black, copied from a Goya painting which hangs in the wine room of the *hosteria*. The waiters and musicians all wore the red, white, and black *charro* costumes worn in the Province of Salamanca. This was a broad compliment to the six Salamanca bulls dispatched that day by the two matador guests of honor. When I remarked that I had seen these *charro* costumes, or very like, in Chapultepec Province in Mexico, I was told that *charro* costumes had been copied almost identically after a ship load of families from Salamanca Province had gone out with the conquistador Pizarro to the New World.

Hosteria El Morillo takes its name from the sobriquet of a former owner, an immensely strong, burly man. The fellow was built like a bull with heavy, muscle-padded shoulders, a long-waisted barrel torso, and short slim legs. He further resembled El Toro by having a large swelling on the back of his neck, like the *morillo* or humped muscle so noticeable behind the skull of Miura bulls. Food was a long time in coming and the big stone flask of strong, colorless *aguardiente* was passed many times round the big table. I noticed both Litri and Aparicio drank only cider from Asturias. I took particular notice of the withdrawn face of Litri. What goes on in the mind behind the set mask of a bull fighter? I have often wondered. Tonight, tension and fatigue had given the pallid face a drawn, bleak look, a very Spanish look. There was pride and glitter and bravery in the eyes of Aparicio as he diverted his listeners with some anecdote of the late corrida. I shifted my eyes back to Litri, because one can read all Spain in the

VAZQUEZ   SEGOVIA JR

face of a matador. The "penetrating-the-tomorrows" look. What will tomorrow bring? Just as the past has been one of sorrow, of pain and often death, so must the marching tomorrows whisper of insecurity and dark forebodings. In this case the shadow cast by the lamp light on the wall behind Litri's head took the eerie shape of a pair of horns.

Food came at last to interrupt my thoughts, and high time, too, for I was getting in deep with morbid shadows and I was mortally hungry to boot. The specialty of the *hosteria* is beef, brought from the bull ring, the great abattoir of most Spanish towns. The dish of honor this evening was *estofado de rabo*, a monumental stew made from bulls' tails, in flavor very much like ox-tail soup, with a Spanish accent of garlic, tomatoes, and anchovies. As an entrée we had a delicacy much favored in all Spanish countries, even to Guatamala, and La Paz in the High Andes. This is slices of bulls' testicles fried in oil, served with a purée of mushrooms. I find it excellent, if somewhat strong in flavor. *Clarete de Valdepeñas* or *Marqués de Murrieta*, each a distinguished wine, is drunk with this epicurean dish, much favored in ages past at the banquets of Lucullus where the testicles were served with a sauce of lampreys. The beef to strengthen the blood, the fish to aid processes of the brain, or so the renowned gourmet claimed in his treatise on food. Perhaps as a result of this diet, the vitality of the Spanish male, even in regions where hunger stalks ominously, is marked.

In Madrid I always go first to the Prado to steep myself in medieval Spanish art as portrayed by the great Spanish masters. Then, the day before I leave the city I go again (how many times I go in between I am not saying) to take a last look at my particular favorites. Velazquez' "Las Meninas" hangs in resplendent isolation in a room to itself. For so great a human document this is right and fitting. It is a triumph of shimmering light. Cross lights from painted windows and doors in the room where the Infanta Margaret stands, allied with the imaginative lighting in the room in which the picture hangs, enhance the clarity of the composition to an unimaginable brilliance. The expression on the face of the Infanta, at once haughty yet quizzically smiling, remains always in the mind as perfection of technique in painting. Her companions, the dwarf and the gentle guardian mastiff, give such a vivid sense of life in the round that I always feel as if I am taking part in the court ceremony of having my portrait painted along with the princess. Perhaps the enigmatic smile on her face is the knowledge that the king and queen are looking into the room where she stands, for their surreptitious reflections are sketched in a mirror on the wall, for posterity to marvel at Velazquez for such daring.

Velazquez is in sterner mood in his mighty canvas "Las Lanzas" (Surrender of Breda). The superbly rich and stirring composition of a very court of generals in brocade and velvet under body armor, plumed hats sweeping the muddy battlefield, form a frieze of surrender when war was conducted in a courtly manner. In the background the *lanzas* form a delicately serrated but impenetrable black wall of lances against a rain-drenched sky. In the portrait of Doña Isabel de Bourbon, the depiction of strongly-limned assurance, the full possession of self, stands for all time as criterion of a portrait of a beautiful imperious woman. "El Bufón," leader of the *bufolitos Majos*, is a subtle mixture of bravado and poignant sadness. These tiny people, dwarfs said to have been found by the dozens in the stews of medieval Barcelona and in the mountain town of Miranda de Ebro, a town remarkable for breeding dwarfs, were trained to serve the king as mountebanks and jesters or as pages for Infantes and Infantas. During the reign of Philip I, *bufolitos* reached such prominence in the affections of the court they were given apartments with red and gold furniture covered in embroideries and damasks, scaled to fit their small persons. In the Palace of the Infantado at Guadalajara may still be seen one of these ornate apartments in doll size. There is a story of a dwarf who fell in love with a lady of the court. In pretending that he was as strong and desirable a male for her couch as another man, he tried on a suit of armor belonging to a man of normal size. On his way to show himself to the lady, the visor of the helmet fell over his face, blinding him. Stumbling, he took a wrong turning and fell to his death from a high balcony to the flagged patio below. The tiny gallant was buried with full honors by the family of the man in whose armor the *bufolito* had been killed.

The Prado offers a feast of Zurbarán, José Ribera, Murillo, as well as examples of the sharp-faceted talents of Francisco Goya y Lucientes. Here, as in no other place, one can study the work of this exceptionally gifted painter. Goya was born of Aragonese peasant stock to rise in rapid strides, once his talents were recognized. He became court painter to the House of Bourbon. He became the at first exultant, later remorseful, lover of the Duchess of Alba, acknowledged to be the most fascinating if not wholly beautiful in the accepted sense, prideful and exalted grandee of her time in Spain. Every phase of the steady rise of Goya as an artist is to be found in his paintings at the Prado; his cartoons, for tapestries (as well as the finished arras), etchings and a portfolio of searing pen and ink sketches, *Desastres de la Guerra* (Disasters of War). Such annotations on the margin of man's cruelty to man have never before nor since been so rabidly depicted. José Luzan Martinez, teacher and long time confident of Goya, said of his friend, "Francisco is a rapacious artist. He is a glutton for human emotions. His blood boils all the time for one wrong or another. His touch can be exquisite as gossamer when painting a gauze veil over a woman's breast, yet as quickly disembowel you with strokes of his scathing pen."

A poignant story lies behind the murals by Goya that one can see in the tiny circular chapel of San Antonio de la Florida facing a disused market place in the outskirts of Madrid. This chapel was built as a penance by a rich patroness of the parish in 1730. For some reason not divulged, the interior was never finished. Slapdash, whitewash-covered walls were bare of all ornament. One day Goya, attacked by vertigo, sought shelter from the hot sun in the chapel. At this time he was a cruelly upset man. His consuming love affair with the Duchess of Alba had reached a desperate crisis. He was aging and far from well. His nights were tortured by dreams wherein he saw the ravishing beauty of his "duquesita," as he fondly called her, tainted by excesses. There exists a set of his etchings, which scandalized Madrid society, to prove it. Goya, resting in the quiet chapel, was suddenly startled when a young girl, who had been kneeling at the shrine of Our Lady, burst into floods of tears, so uncontrollable as to cause her to fall into a half faint. Goya revived her and taking her gently by the elbow led her out into the air. He learned that a cruel, avaricious mother was forcing her into a marriage with a rich suitor old enough to be her father. This she loathed, for already she loved elsewhere. After the girl had gone on her way Goya stood brooding, regarding the blank walls around him. Suddenly he made up his mind. He would paint on the walls of San Antonia de la Florida a panorama of his disturbed nights, a phantasmagoria of human frailty. The faces of all the silly, the predatory, the greedy women he had known in his constantly amorous journey through life, which he felt was about to draw to a close. Within a week Goya started to paint. One gazes up at a circular mural painting, a seven-foot-high frieze, a few feet above the altar. On a balustraded terrace are grouped perhaps thirty figures of women. Women leering, women smiling, a range of smiles from simpering indecision to the lustful, come-hither smile. It is a parade of extraordinary virtuosity in painting skill, depicting this crew frowning in anger, greedy eyes glinting, through the roster of depravity to the fat, sensual, besotted libertine. The frieze is a triumph of decoration, for all the women are shown in crisp muslins, bright ribbons, and gauzes of the period when Goya lived, or in tawdry, bedraggled finery of an older time. The color is remarkable for its misty freshness, the like of spring flowers. Goya painted his troubled heart out on these walls. This decoration might be called "The Expression of Two Minds"—the abject lover and the bitter disapprover.

All important schools of painting are hung on the walls of the Prado. Four enfilades of high-ceilinged, beautifully-lighted rooms are built around a central gallery reached by two grand staircases. Ribalta (1555-1628), a Valencian painter, was perhaps the first man to carry dramatic *chiaroscuro* to a point where his highlights and shadows seem brittle as glass. Later Zurbarán became a master of this style by softening the intensity of his sharp contrasts yet losing none of the excitement. An Andalusian, one Alonso Cano, never quite made up his mind whether he was sculptor or painter. In 1632 he made a tremendously effective statue of San Martin to adorn the austere tomb of Archbishop Talavera in Toledo. This statue was destroyed during the Civil War but a half-size model remains intact. The Italian school is splendidly represented by Fra Angelico, Andrea del Sarto, and Tintoretto, Titian, and Tiepolo, the "trinity of T's" as Goya called them. The Flemish School is chosen perhaps more for decoration than inspired painting. Van der Weyden, the brothers Huyprecht and Jan van Eyck are somber; Rubens' pictures, in the last gasp of Baroque *bravura*, throb in color on the walls as a foil to the restrained beauty of the muted palette of Memling's magnificently moving "Adoration of the Shepherds."

The French School does not come off so well as the Dutch and German. However, when one takes all in all there is nothing on earth to compare with Prado, either in the amount or the quality of great and rare pictures and sculpture.

The amusement side of the roster in Madrid offers a long and varied page of entertainments. There are lots of delightful music halls where the shows are gay and witty. Lope de Véga is a variety house where the acts are sophisticated and smartly costumed, for the Spanish flare for style and color in dress extends itself to brilliance in costuming a theatrical piece. There are many lesser music halls for all tastes. All these have shows beginning at eleven o'clock. A few kilometers outside of Madrid is a notable cabaret called Villa Rosa. Dinner is served at eleven o'clock in a garden festooned with electric lights surrounding a good-sized stage. The proscenium is a trellis of different varieties of roses. On the stage Pedro de Córdoba, assuredly the leading male flamenco dancer in Spain, dances with his troup of gitanas, each one picked for being individually good in rendering saetas and flamenco.

One night I sat at a table in the softly lighted, rose-scented garden of Villa Rosa waiting for the show to start. Immense Lunar moths, half the size of doves, floated through the air to singe their pale, opalescent wings to cinders in the amorous flame of a candle in front of me. Only when the dancing was over and the curtains had swung dustily together on a storm of castanets and wildly clattering heels was I conscious of a smiling waiter hovering a shade nervously at my elbow. Then I remembered I had ordered broiled shrimps, marinated in white wine. The waiter raised his strongly marked black eyebrows. "I did not wish to disturb señor until the interval. I shall serve now?"

I replied, "On the instant. I am more than ready." Then, with a little touch of ceremony which the Spanish dearly love to impart to serving food, I was brought the shrimp en brochette, piled high on a platter surrounded by braised celery lightly dusted with saffron, the whole doused in brandy which the waiter set aflame with a flourish. Just as the flames died down and I had tasted the first forkful of shrimp, to find it a miracle of flavor, the lights concealed in the hearts of glass roses on either side of the proscenium went on again. We were off; this time the dance was a spirited jota.

It has been said that Madrid is an Arcadia for lovers and children because of the parks, spread in such plenty and magnitude of massed flowers and secluded groves throughout the city. One can literally get lost in some of the parks. One morning I walked through Parque del Retiro. If it had not been that I was able to follow the tanbark bridle paths to an exit gate I might be there still. I counted thirty fountains and nine equestrian statues in open spaces or hidden in leafy alleys. Retiro has a Promenade de las Infantas dedicated to nursemaids. Many of these young women are magnificently built Junos, of heroic hips and breasts. It is almost a tradition that these nursemaids to children of aristocratic Madrileños come from the villages of La Robla and Villapadierna in the Asturias, in the same tradition as in the Pincian Gardens in Rome, the pink-and-white-, or blue-and-white-skirted nursemaids having for centuries come from Frosinone near Monte Cassino.

I noticed whole groups of children obviously not of the class to be watched over by a nursemaid, laughing and playing games with the rather sallow-faced children in the charge of the Villapadierna women. Everyone, the nurses included, was laughing gaily. Then I remembered being told that these nurses are chosen for their notoriously happy dispositions as well as their flagrant good health. They wear provincial costumes, consisting of full skirts and tight-fitting bodices in carnation pink, lemon-yellow, or heliotrope cotton with black satin aprons banded in heavy lace identical to that which the women crochet while keeping a weather eye on skittish charges. The caps are wings of the lace, with floating streamers of embroidered ribbon. Even if the gardens had no flowers these nursemaids present a most flowery picture against the feathery mimosa trees, and the exclamatory blackness of burnished ilex and evergreens.

Of all the parks one may enjoy in the heart of Madrid or in close proximity, I like Retiro best because of its grottos and myriad fountains. The park encompasses over three hundred acres but seems limitless because of inventiveness in contriving artificial lakes and rides cut through the trees which again end in little theatres where the scenery consists of artfully-contrived screens of greenery pointed up by snow-white statues of the Muses or gods and goddesses truant from Olympus. In one semicircle there is a dramatic bit of bombast featuring over-life-size statues of all the kings of Spain. As in the verdant retreats of Aranjuez, or the sable silences of cypress aisles at Briheuga, or again in the syringa gardens of Granada's Generalife, nightingales are heard to sing at twilight in the density of Parque del Retiro.

The Fountain of Cybele is an arresting pile of stone. The tiara-crowned goddess sits enthroned in a triumphal car surrounded by trophies of Art, Learning, Science, and Astronomy. She seems oblivious to the lean-flanked, shaggy-maned lions, teeth bared savagely, that draw her chariot. Indeed her nonchalance is matched by little boys and girls who love climbing up to ride astride the lions' backs until the Guardía Civil, in black and gold three-cornered hats, walking always in pairs, chase them away.

The shopping streets of Madrid are notably fine. From Puerta del

Sol to Carrera de San Jeronimo a stroll will enable one to pass the most up-to-date shops for jewelry, the world-renowned Spanish gloves and shoes, and all kinds of leather work of superb quality and finish. Here too are to be found the traditional Spanish perfumes —Oil of Jasmine, Attar of Roses, Violeta de Granada, Pomegranate Blossom, and the illusive Heliotrope, "Perfume of Love," which Goya used to present to the Duchess of Alba in tiny crystal flacons from Fez which he would conceal in the thumbs of her gloves. When she started to put them on she would discover his attention and always wrote him a note of thanks sprinkled with a few drops of heliotrope essence, which in Spain means the lady is eager for a return visit from the recipient.

There are many shops where antiquities of Spain are beautifully arranged. Lace shawls and mantillas are companioned by tortoise-shell combs and ornaments. I am always fascinated by the shops which feature bonbons and marrons glacés. The marrons, sugared or in syrup, are arranged in a bewildering assortment of crystal jars and bottles so fanciful that they alone are worth the price of admission.

The Royal Palace can now be seen as a museum. On entering, the first thing to startle the eye is the tremendous double flight of marble staircases reminiscent of those in the Paris Opera House. From the sweeping corridor at the head of these flights of bisque marble steps opens an impressive array of reception rooms decorated and furnished either in the French style of Louis Quinze or Venetian Rococo. The throne room, called the most grandiose in Europe, and in which the most rigid protocol was observed up to the last minute of the monarchy, was decorated by Tiepolo. The ceiling is considered by many persons as the Italian painter's most representative achievement and in many ways it is a great piece of theater. It is certainly ebullient and singing in color, its figures defying every law of gravity to gather in attendance around the chariot of Apollo, while maneuvering to escape a kick from the rearing white horses drawing his golden chariot. This is spirited brushwork, amazingly vital composition, and a sumptuous placing of rich ruby-reds and peacock-greens against the pearly empyrean. But to my taste Tiepolo's greatest imagery is in the Palazzo Rezzonico in Venice.

The collection of Russian malachite in the Madrid palace museum is superlative, particularly in showing the variety of objects for decoration or for use that can be made from this exciting green mineral.

While the general tone of Madrid is that of an extremely elegant modern metropolis, it stems from an ancient city dating from the ninth century (some chroniclers give a flexible margin of eighty to one hundred years on the date) when the Moors built a casbah on the highest point of the plateau where now stands the Palacio Real, calling it Majrit. In the "old town" are to be seen markets and buildings varying in dates. Majrit was actually a wide spreading *souk* or market place, the hub for all surrounding villages like the Place Djemaa el Fna (square of death or destruction) in Marrakesh, the largest open bazaar in the world. Under the palace there are dungeons left from the Moorish casbah, tunneling six levels into the solid rock. In the old Torre de los Lujanes on the plateau, Charles V imprisoned his admired, but mortal enemy, Francis I of France, who was wounded, then captured, on the battlefield of Pavia. When Francis was freed from his prison, the walls were found to be covered by exquisitely drawn flowers scratched into the stone with a nail from his shoe. The undaunted king had colored the petals by mixing the red and yellow earth of his cell floor with soup and water. When Philip II passed through Madrid in 1560 he was attracted by the flower-diapered walls of the cell. He ordered that lacquer be brushed over the walls to preserve the design. Coming out of the dank prison he sniffed the champagne clarity of the air. He also reveled in the beauty of the pine-clad Guadarrama Mountains. He decreed that henceforth Madrid should be the royal court city. So it has remained, the capital of Spain, save for six years when the royal residence was moved to Valladolid.

The wide avenue called Castellana is flanked by gardens which stand sentinel to imposing stone mansions. Unhesitatingly I would say that no city I have ever visited takes such pride in its hotels to suit every standard of living as Madrid. Long acknowledged by discriminating travelers as the first hotel in Europe, the Ritz faces Paseo del Prado and has as its neighbor the Prado museum itself. Rooms at the Ritz are beautifully furnished and embrace every comfort. Both the indoor restaurant and the garden grill, where enchanting latticed dining pavilions are shaded by tall plane trees, are famous for French and Spanish cuisine. Distinguished by being termed the largest hotel on the Continent, the Palace is only one block away, closer to the Carrera de San Jeronimo where you will by this time have flattened your pocketbook and perhaps have to sleep in the park.

The Palace Hotel is noted for its gaiety, centering on a large lounge with a crescent-shaped American bar. The restaurant is famous for a bountiful buffet of cold foods arranged in something of a spectacle. My only criticism of the Palace is the continuous din. About as restful to lunch or dine here as in a boiler factory. But then its popularity proves that few persons share my view. There is a long, wide promenade leading from the Paseo entrance to the dining room which more or less bears out what once was said of the International Bridge across the Bosporus "that silver scimitar across the Golden Horn" in Constantinople of the sultans. It was a by-word that if one waited long enough at either entrance to the bridge, guarded by janissaries in gray, white, and crimson, standing beside immense plaster cornucopias filled with "the sweet waters of Asia and Roses of Sharon from its meadows," one would see pass by every nationality in the world. Times have changed now in essence, though the world still travels widely. The byword now is, if one sits long enough in the foyer of the Palace Hotel in Madrid, not only every nationality will pass through but all one's friends as well. Madrileños call this corridor, "the gilded beehive of a thousand Queen Bees." I add to this, the Queen Bees are all American.

Hotel Emperador on the beautiful Avenida de José Antonio is an excellent place to stop. Hotel Velazquez, Hotel Carlos V, and Hotel Florida are of first-class rating and all within easy distance of the parks and entertainment quarters. For restaurants as good as they are varied the list is impressive. I can give only a few that are for some particular reason different and distinctive. Las Cancelas is ripe Andalusian in atmosphere, decorated with all the fiery sweep of a gitana's switching train. *Novilleros* gather here. These are young bullfighters eager to show off how, once given opportunity in *corrida*, they will do this or that, a *verónica* or *suerte*, for each embryo matador has a carefully worked out theory or system of how to "dominate" the bravest bull. The great dish here is *pollo del pais*, a fricassé of strong chicken broth and dumplings. The wine served with it is Ribeira, an Andalusian wine, a slightly fizzy red variety combining the hot color, lingering musky taste, and lift of the spirit that one comes to expect from Andalusia. After a few glasses of this wine the young *novilleros* whom everyone invites to his table and treats, cannot tell a waiter from one of their number who impersonates a bull.

Botin is a very old establishment housed in an ancient crypt. Dim and romantic, the flickering light from candles casts huge shadows on the pale citrus-color walls. Delicious black bean soup with red cabbage and crackling, roast suckling pig are the great dishes at "old

Botin's." Horcher is unashamedly costly, in this case rightly so, for immense trouble is taken to please the guest, and one long remembers a meal at Horcher's that is as superior in every way as it is expensive. The *cave* is unexcelled in Europe, especially for all the Rhine and Moselle wine of distilled sunlight and delicate bouquet. Everyone who visits Madrid should go at least once to Horcher. Gastronomically, it is the epitome of elegant Madrid. The restaurant is in a once noble house. I always feel a dinner in any of the beautifully-proportioned rooms, which seem in some subtle way in close affinity with the superb cuisine, to be a codicil to the last will and testament of Lucullus who left to his gourmet cronies, "the memories of symposiums around my table, where food was poetry and Cyprian wines led us immoderately to dance."

The drive out of Madrid to Guadalajara is through curiously silent villages, clean swept. The pastel-colored houses fronting on the long dusty central street, which is the king's highway, seem to "palely loiter" as if marking time, with no women sitting in the doorways threading lace or making straw-embroidered belts for the men of their families. Most Spanish towns near large cities are beehives of activity and ripe with incident. But the people of this locality, save infants and ancients, work in the allotment gardens along the river raising fruits and vegetables for the legion restaurants and hotels of Madrid.

Guadalajara is chiefly notable for one of the saddest and most unearthly beautiful palaces left to us out of long past romance, a kind of melancholy abode transfixed on the spear of Time. The Palace of the Dukes of Infantado. Even the name is nostalgic of great, highly colored days when the glory that was Spain shone as a beacon of golden splendor to Europe and the New World across the Spanish Main. This tall miradored house was a veritable casket of richest treasure due largely to conquistadors who paved its courts with gold ingots of the Incas and sheathed walls and ceilings of oval and cube rooms with sheets of pure gold metal hammered into a design of birds and flowers. At Infantado Philip II married Elizabeth of Valois in the Salon de los Linajes (Hall of Genealogies) in a ceremony which for unbridled magnificence of trappings had never before been equaled. Carpets of cloth of gold, embroidered with the lilies of France in blue and silver and bordered with pearls, were spread on the flagstones of the courtyard. Because the weather was unseasonably warm, great fans of swans' wings, peacocks' tails, the black and white quills of ibex and tawny sierra eagles, their wings spread out for two yards, were carried by Arab boys from Tangier, who kept the fans constantly in motion to cool the air surrounding the royal dais. This magical scene has been preserved in embroideries worked in gold and jewels upon yellow satin. Now, the Palace of the Infantado is a cavern of mystery, desecrated and fallen upon evil days, dying upon its foundations, the once gilded rooms clogged with the debris of disuse. When Juan Güas designed it he studded the bister-yellow façade with faceted stone ornaments fashioned like the opening buds of giant lotus flowers. The entrance doorway is columned in porphyry wreathed in delicately-carved oak leaves, above which extends for two stories an entablature of ancestral arms supported by naked satyrs. The top story under the eaves is Moorish in feeling. This is a palace in itself, a kind of terraced village, like the immensely ornate cupolas, chimneys, and dormered pavilions which glorify the Mansard roof of Chateau de Chambord on the Loire in France; one of those added extravagances to an already splendid house which give it world renown. A long arcaded balcony terrace at Infantado has inset miradors, semicircular in shape. A dado crosses the whole façade carved in festoons of fruits featuring the artichoke, a detail in early architecture often confused with the later introduced pineapple finials, symbolical of hospitality. After Francis I of France was captured on the Pavian battlefield, his wounds were dressed and he was brought by litter on a tortuous journey to the Infantado Palace to recuperate, until Charles V made up his mind just how his prisoner should be treated. Charles entrusted the French king to the Duke of Infantado, head of the powerful Mendoza family, to watch over until he should have recovered from his wounds. The duke and Francis became great friends. To amuse as well as honor his guest, the duke arranged a tournament. Held in the plaza in front of the palace, Francis looked down from the miradors which are framed in stalactites of golden stone. It is said that the French king was so handsome in velvet and satin, slashed and dagged as are fritillaries in the spring, a plumed cap set aslant his auburn curls, that the ladies of the palace fought like tigresses to wait upon him, to ease his bandages and to comb out his russet pointed beard. It was probably thoughts of this dalliance in the miradors of the palace which sustained Francis later and tempted him to etch spring flowers on the moldy walls of Torre de los Lujanes. While the shell of Infantado and the great double colonnaded courtyard remain largely as they were originally, vandals have de-

stroyed or removed much of the interior beauty, such as carved porphyry, lapis lazuli, and obsidian mantles and chimney pieces, which
are described in documents as being glorious beyond description.
These have been removed, but whether piece-meal or intact, and to
where, no one knows.

The Hall of the Hunters (*Cazadores*) is still a room of majestic
proportions. Parts of the ceiling are of thin sheets of hammered gold,
applied as light as thistle silk, and fragmentary painting of scenes of
the chase remains on the walls.

The Hall of Genealogies (*Linajes*) is decorated with scutcheons
of the one hundred most famous pedigrees in Spain, featuring, of
course, the Mendoza coat of arms on the ceiling. All through the
palace are rooms of the most exciting invention in decoration. Ranged
on four sides of the courtyard are double tiers of arches, the columns
supporting grotesque lions with the heads of griffons, their locks arranged in Byzantine curls. The Infantado has been used as an orphanage run by nuns, but I believe is to be completely restored, as
was the Alhambra, by the government.

The morning I started for Ávila it teemed with the kind of downpour that seems to come from the sky down and the ground up.
When I was a few miles from the town the rain stopped as if by
magic. Before me was the most stupendous walled city in Spain, and,
to my mind, in the world. All the high lights and shadows I could
handle, I realized as I sat sketching one of the heraldically-emblazoned
gateways, played upon the walls. Ávila offers one a feast of miles of
castellations, barbicans, and eighty great and lesser towers. The
machicolated walls are breached by fourteen impressive gateways.
The color of the stone is a paler faun than most of the golden cities
of Spain, yet in the shadows there is a deep raisin-rose color, dark
amaranth as the lees of wine. All around lay fields, the sere yellow of
coarse sheep grass, or the red *vega* earth which surrounds the walls.
All this towered medieval splendor is posed against a pearl-gray sky
slashed with bands of matrix blue, more green than is the usual sky in
Spain. El Greco with his uncanny skill and feeling for painting life
into cold stone work would have reveled, would have wielded a sure
brush if he had sat on the rocks beside the road and painted Ávila
on this erratic, now gray, now bright, day. What strikes the beholder
most deeply, perhaps, is the remarkable state of preservation of the
walls of Ávila. Some restoration has been done to repair the damage
of wars, time, and the rasping winds that even as I sketched swept

across the plains, but it has not impaired the grandeur of the fortifications. According to old chronicles, two master builders, Casandro and Florin de Pituenga, who set the first stones to "ring around a fortress" in 1080, gave the plan of how to build the existing walls and towers to Alvar García who, after the work had been abandoned for a time, again took up the task in 1090 and worked unceasingly for nine years, until he completed what we see so vitally alive today. It is supposed that about two thousand workmen were employed most of the time, and quite probable that conquered Moors were pressed into a kind of slave labor to rush the walls to completion. The comparatively short time it took to build such monumental and extensive masonry makes it one of the great engineering feats of history.

Because of its position on a plateau of rocky soil 3600 feet above sea level, Ávila is called "the city that lives nearest Heaven," withdrawn, noble, wrapped in quietude. The very abruptness with which the walls rise from the plain typifies Old Castile, a hard yet delicate world faceted like a diamond, difficult to discover, revealing the brilliance of its heart to the spiritual and material eye only after polishing by tours of discovery. Ávila has to me the true Castilian dignity more than any other city in the province. And of all Spanish cities, it seems closest to the Middle Ages. Even the inhabitants in streets and market places, with their long-jawed, ascetic visages, closely resemble the carved medieval saints in the west front of the Cathedral.

It is a very old city; down the centuries there were the usual Roman, Visigothic, and Moorish upheavals when Ávila cannot be said to have had a clear identity. Then in 1105 the townspeople took military enterprise into their own hands. Under the red and green banner of Sancho Sánchez Zurraquín, flaunting a black *capra hispanica*, the scythe-horned mountain goat, emblem of the people of the Gredos, they defeated the Arabs in Zaragoza. This was the thin end of the wedge heralding comparative freedom for the population of Ávila. There were more skirmishes and two major battles before there appeared from the fastness of Sierra de Gredos the legendary figure of Nalvillos (second parhaps in adventurous performance to El Cid), an indomitable fighter whose adherents proclaimed him king. An important figure in the life of Ávila as it rose to take its place in the Spanish sun was Alfonso de Madrigal, known as El Tostada, who wrote many books. He was made Bishop of Ávila in 1449. De Madrigal was so miniature in stature that it is said that when he was granted an audience with Pope Eugenius IV, the Holy Father thought the bishop was on his knees and told him sharply to get up.

The expulsion of the Arabs which coincided with the exodus of the nobles toward the court was a heavy blow to Ávila. The population, once numbered five thousand, was reduced in a few weeks to less than two thousand.

Surely in the whole history of Ávila the most remarkable figure to emerge was Santa Teresa de Jesús. The city now revolves around her memory as it has done since her extraordinary life of martyrdom and death. To the Ávilese she is their buckler and their shield. While most of the stories concerning Teresa de Cepeda's persecution and her stoic acceptance of it can be believed, there are many stories of divine visitations and instant protection to the pursued or oppressed that even the people of Ávila say one cannot trust. One story concerns a beautiful virgin, Santa Barbara of San Segundo, who, to preserve her virtue from being constantly assailed by men of bad nature, asked God to destroy her beauty. In answer to her prayer a beard covered her face and a coat of fur sprouted on her body and limbs. A similar miracle is said to have taken place at Lull when La Bella Mallorquina was changed from a simple maiden into a she-goat with long face and shaggy hide. Perhaps we can impute most of these stories to the crackling imagination of Fray Isidro, a conceited archpriest who once officiated at San Segundo's tomb. He was a scandalmonger rampant, who was finally driven by disgusted townfolk from Ávila. However, he left behind him a legacy of weird and dubious tales.

There is a strange quality of fanatic morbidity in the decoration of the façade of the cathedral of Ávila, both interior and exterior, which is as diverting as it is compelling. The edifice is a wonderful and infinitely curious barbaric fortified temple whose period of decoration, as well as the age of its raddled stone walls, would be difficult to place. I have never seen a religious house remotely like it. I venture that the towers and circular chapel are tenth century. The two main towers and the naves are undoubtedly of twelfth-century construction, while cloisters, vaults and two offertory chapels are sixteenth-century French Ogival with English Norman overtones. The cathedral could easily be taken for a fortress, with its fortified east tower, its three great circular battlements, covered galleries, and drill square paved with Cyclopean stones worn in ridges by centuries of mailed boots.

Actually it did serve as a fortress as well as a cathedral during four centuries. Not until the sixteenth century did it lose its double military-ecclesiastical character, when the Bishop of Ávila abolished the military barracks in order to put a stop to the frequent territorial disputes arising from the question of whether it was a fortress for warlike pursuits or a house of God for holy worship.

The grandest single detail to be seen is the sweeping line and massed figures so vitally carved in stone which sums up the Porch of the Apostles. The porch, of fourteenth-century work, consists of a proscenium of five pointed tympan-vaulted arches. In niches stand the magnificently garbed apostles playing on musical instruments. It is impossible to catalogue all the extraordinary detail of figures such as Famine, emaciated and bloated at once, slavering Greed, hysterical Passion, simpering Virtue. A beautiful, placid figure of a woman by Pedro de Vineigra called Life, holds hands with a cadaverous monstrosity called Death by Vasco de la Zarza. Chained lions carved from black-veined gray stone line the raised dais which surrounds the Porch of the Apostles and flanking side terraces which in turn lead into the Plaza de Cathedral. It is said that wonderfully rich garments of red, green, blue, yellow, and black velvet heavily banded in gold galloon were once used to robe the figures of the Twelve Apostles on feast days. One day a verger in his cups sold the entire wardrobe to a rag man who promptly disposed of the loot, to whom he would never say, and built a house on the proceeds, in nearby El Espinar. It is a good thing for Ávila that the tremendous crimson velvet curtains which hang in the dimly lighted Corridor of Tombs in the west Portal are so immense in scale and weight that the drunken verger could not rip them down to sell to old "rags and bones" along with the ceremonial robes of the Apostles. The heavy, dragging folds of dark velvet edged with a two foot band of heavy gold galloon are the definition of sumptuousness, lending a grand-opera touch to an otherwise dim gallery. Everywhere are signs and relics of Santa Teresa but I think the most entertaining and immediate are her "playthings" as this little cache of objects is naively labeled. A yellowed collarbone (whether hers or another's is not stated). A stone desk she used with a hole for ink and a little "furnace" to heat wax. The log, pleached as white as ivory, which she used for a pillow. A heavy thong of hard, uncompromising black bull's hide, nicked with many notches, numbering her irking visitations. *Los Morales de San Gregorio*, a treatise written by her. A letter to her great friend Sor Maria Briceno with whom she studied at the age of seventeen.

274

(The letter is woefully ink blotted.) A stone jug from which she drank (her obsession for surrounding herself with stone objects carries even to eating and drinking utensils). The flute and rattle with which she amused herself, the rosary which was clutched tightly in her hands when she died, and, last but not least, the rudely put together ladder she used to gather plums and from which the Devil made her fall. An extremely personal collection, doubly interesting because of its authenticity.

As I stood looking at this collection of heterogeneous objects which had been so closely associated with Santa Teresa in her daily round, I felt somehow these brought back the spirit of the courageous woman who sought and achieved against insurmountable odds as near perfection of soul on earth as is possible. But she did it with spirit and her head held proudly, not bent in maudlin meekness. I have always admired this saint above all others, perhaps more the woman than the saint. Once I was asked to give a lecture on Baroque architecture in Spain, at Trinity College in Dublin. I mounted the rostrum. Soon I was well away on my subject. Then I started to describe the Baroque temple, a shrine to memory, which has been built on the site of the house in Ávila where Teresa Cepeda was born. The shrine is not ornately elaborate but is impressive in its simplicity. Before I was aware of my words I was giving a full length lecture on Santa Teresa and the coolness, the persistence with which she combatted papal envoys, cutting miles of red tape, skeined about her spare figure by ecclesiastical witlessness, in her dedicated effort to purify the Church of Spain from within. She lost the long battle because she was one woman against the Pope in Rome. She won many small but important skirmishes to lasting effect. When my lecture was finished I wondered whether I might not be reproved by the Dean, who had asked me to give a lecture on Spanish Architecture. He was a prince of understanding, saying, "Well, Shamas, there is architecture and *architecture*. You presented an entirely new side light on Santa Teresa and her *architecture* of life. The boys enjoyed it as I certainly did myself."

Across the plaza from the Cathedral is the magnificent Casa de Valderrabaños with soaring arched windows, fifteenth-century sculptured doorway and flamboyantly carved heraldries, which was given by the city to Gonzala Davila, an impoverished grandee, after his heroic conduct during the conquest of Gibraltar. The steps are guarded by huge stone watchdogs with human faces. One wonders why these beasts are so oddly mutilated. It seems the behinds of the watchdogs were so eloquent that they became the target for all sorts of jokes and pictorial obscenities. So Don Gonzala had the offending ribald members lopped off.

I think Palacio de Bracamonte is one of the most charming small palaces in all Spain. This is a two-story pavilion of white stone with sharp black *rejas* in three tall windows supporting fluidly carved coats of arms. The scutcheon is in itself an arresting piece of sculpture, featuring a harp contrived from the horns of rams that is indigenous to one Gredos region where shepherds spend the greater part of their lives high in the mountains playing out their hearts to an audience of stubble-cropping herds, low-swooping eagles, and the high-piled cumulus clouds. Over the windows are bas-reliefs of pastoral flutes and crude bagpipes. The door is of polished bull's hide. Centuries of rubbing with olive oil have given the leather the clarity of a bronze mirror. Twin gazebos rise at the corners of the façade from a roof of curiously violet-brown tiles which are dyed by the residue of wine vats at vintage time. I once saw this operation take place. Huge buckets of wine dregs, so heavy it took two men to lift them, are raised by ropes to a man on the ridge pole. He empties the lees of wine over the tiles. I shall never forget the cascade of rich red dregs which ran along the runnels of the tiles like a Niagara of blood.

Once inside the awesome walls of Ávila, perhaps what most interests visitors is the Medieval Bazaar, unique in Spain, and one of the few ancient craftsmanship bazaars to remain in its original state in all Europe. In the narrow streets, so quiet, so intent on industry, people of all ages fashion hand-made wares of simple dignity, beautiful in design and quality. Surpassingly fine, soft wool blankets and authentic pottery and hammered brass ware. I was particularly struck by the exquisite lace, some marked by vital design, some as fine in stitch as Irish Rose Point. In all their craft can be seen traces of a lost band of Crusaders who were cast up on the coast of Málaga, to wander aimlessly through Spain to the Pyrenees. They paid their way by shedding spoils of war brought back from the Holy Land. From the Crusader's Shield, with its red Maltese cross, come many of the designs I saw on metal trays and boxes. The persons living within precincts of the quarter do not marry outside their guild any more than a *gitano* would ever marry a Gazi or non-gypsy. The Ávilese of the bazaar think it best to keep the traditions of working and living unaltered in the hurly-burly of shoddy modern machine-made wares.

I went out to villages lying in the vicinity of Ávila to see the local costumes which are worn at all time, save when the peasants work in the fields or among the elaborate system of dykes and irrigation ditches set up in 900 by the Moors and still grandly functioning. Piedrahita El Barco de Ávila Hoyos, even as far afield as Salvatierra —a town of odd aspect, being curiously jagged looking with its once proud walls so undermined by spring freshets in subterranean springs that the stones have caved in and houses have been built in the breach. But I was eager to see the widely discussed costume of the women of Salvatierra. The traditional dress is a dark red wool habit, much the same in cut as the long skirt, tightly buttoned bodice, and veil-encircled hat worn by a lady of fashion when riding in the Bois de Boulogne during the reign of Empress Eugénie de Montijo. The whole appearance is medieval in tone, for the *gorra*, a tall helmet-shaped hat of curled straw, is so high it resembles the hennin (or *henning*) from Flanders which was so widely worn by women of rank in the middle ages. The *gorra* is lavishly adorned with pompons of wool and silk intermingled with cunningly-designed ornaments of straw, not unlike the figures one hangs on a Christmas tree. What gives this helmet its cachet is a sharply pulled-down visor to shield the wearer's eyes. Hanging over the bridge of the nose is a heart-shaped ornament of metal on a background of velvet. The color varies according to the wearer's condition. A spinster wears bright green, a married woman red; while a widow affects memorial black. The women of Salvatierra are very rightly proud of these handsome headdresses, and they make them to sell in the Medieval Bazaar in Ávila, or in shops in their own village. In the most unexpected places, whether in Ávila at Museo Provincial de Bellas Artes, or along the road to adjacent villages, I saw clumsily-carved stone animals used either as finials to roofs, on gate posts, even heaped hodgepodge in courtyards, or lying neglected in tall grasses along the road. The Celtiberians who inhabited these parts during earliest times left these caricatured images of Iberian bulls, pigs, goats, and lizards, big as crocodiles, and a long-barreled animal with a zany head rather resembling a hyena or jackal. The Ávilese say these monstrosities are deer with antlers broken off, or dogs. I believe they are an animal that is now extinct.

Because there is a great amount of wild game in the Sierra de

Gredos with many hunters constantly passing through Ávila, the ancient art of taxidermy is of a high order here. There is a very entertaining street of shops with big windows presenting a series of pictures of naturally poised deer, mountain goats, foxes, wolves, and wild boars staring glassily in the manner of the mounted beasts in a natural history museum. Mounted trophies of the hunt decorate the walls of almost all country houses in Spain.

Sierra de Gredos is a world in itself. Wild flowers bloom amid snows; murmuring mountain streams never run dry. Wild animals of not too frightening tendencies dash across the slopes or pause as if waiting for camera or gun shots. Most memorable of all is the crystal clarity of the air. The Parador de Gredos I consider one of the most beautifully-situated and comfortable hotels in Spain. In Ávila there is Hotel Continental and a most agreeable Hotel del Tostado in the plaza of that name. Close by is the handsome Casa de Velada, with a machicolated tower of architectural importance, the whole façade enriched by impressive heraldic shields supported by lions' heads. During the four days I was in Ávila, and the surrounding villages I stayed out at Parador de Gredos, largely so I could eat myself into a coma on brook trout, fresh from mountain streams, as well as the tender veal of the locality. Sliced paper-thin, then sautéed in white wine and olive oil, this is a dish to complement ravenous mountain appetite.

From Ávila I took the road to Segovia by way of Madrigal de las Altas Torres of the hauntingly lovely name. If ever a town is a "song of the high towers" it is this drowsing demi-paradise. An indisputable air of ancient lineage hovers around the ruins of the once high towers, a few more or less intact, proudly silhouetted against the sky. A circular wall of yellow stone is so overgrown with red trumpet vines it seems more a hedge of greenery hung with orange lanterns than stone wall. The houses of the town are clustered around a large park run to weeds and ragged cypress trees. In this atmosphere of desuetude, given a latent kind of life by swarms of buzzing honey bees and dragonflies darting across a stagnant pool, stands the once noble Mudéjar house where Isabella la Catolica was born. Later it became a nunnery which at one time held the center of the stage for a scandal that rocked the steps of the throne. The natural daughter of Don Juan of Austria, an inmate of the nunnery at the time, was wooed in secret by a mysterious adventurer who styled himself King Sebastian of Portugal, but who was in reality a pastry cook of Madrigal. When the rash love trysts of Doñ Barbara and her "kingly" lover were discovered, he was forthwith hanged upside down from a spike set into the gate post of the convent, while the wretched girl was sent to a remote convent in Medina de Rioseco, in the mushroom ridden wilds of the Torozos Mountains to endure years of solitary confinement.

Near the nunnery of Madrigal there is a vast, echoing barracks of a friary, now sheltering only a fraction of its usual roster of monks. A most frightened appearing, timid-eyed young monk showed me around. Like a fortress in tawny brick, lichened as with green and silver lace, I thought the place seemed more an assemblage court for bats and raucous night birds already stirring in the rafters than a retreat for timorous monks. Still a kind of life and beauty was infused by the groined arches over which darted shadows of swaying branches. At sunset, when I was offered a glass of diluted wine in the lovely orange light of the cloisters, I looked through an arched window giving on to the refectory, long and high as a cathedral nave. There I beheld a sight, astonishing in many ways. On a background of dusty black velvet hangs a superbly carved Christ on the Cross. The life-size figure is in ivory, the cross hewn of olive wood from the Mount of Olives. Rivers of blood, composed of strings of garnets, vein the face, breast, and legs of the figure.

At a small, completely excellent *hosteria* in Arévalo in the Province of Segovia I had an appetizing meal. The chief dish of this Castilian province is suckling pig. It is customary for the girl who serves it to bring the roast pig to the table on a metal platter, but she cuts the pig with an earthenware plate to show you how perfectly it has been cooked and how tender the flesh. This rite of cutting roast meat, of any variety, with a plate is a source of pride among good cooks of the region.

Regaled with good food and wine, I started out to my car. Suddenly the saga of the discovery of America, and the storied conquistadors were brought into focus at Hosteria Arévalo. I looked casually at the names written in the visitors' book, lying open on a long table in the red-tiled hall. Condesa Alicia de Illúcan was dashed across the page in flowing script. I know her to be Alicia Moctezuma, a direct descendant of the last Aztec emperor of Mexico. I recalled, too, there is a Christopher Columbus in the Spanish navy. He is Duke de Veragua and Admiral of Castile. The night had come on definitely chilly. There was a tall aristocratic-looking Spaniard standing in the entrance hall smoking a cigarette. He was wrapped in a black wool

Béjar *capa*, one of the few romantic garments left to wear by a man in modern clothes. When laid out flat a *capa* forms a full circle. It is cut full, so that the wearer can throw one edge, sometimes velvet lined (I have seen some lined in fur) over the left shoulder. An extremely warm, pleasant-to-wear and dashing garment.

Next morning I crossed the *vega* in a drizzle. The sun was striving to win through, so the first glimpse I had of Segovia was sunlight filtering through a pink mist, caused by the rose-red earth of the plain from which the moisture took its color. I cannot imagine a more perfect way to see the multiple turrets and cunningly grouped towers of the Castle of Coca than in this unearthly light. There are in the world many fantasies in stone. I am persuaded this castle leads all the rest. There is a fable told and retold in the Vale of Kashmir, of a Rajput emperor who commanded a genie to conjure from the floating islands of pink water lilies on the Dal Lake, a palace where he might install an houri, more beautiful than all the adjectives usually called in to describe these paramours. Commanded, it was done. The palace climbed cloudward, a conglomeration of pink walls, terraces and minarets. What lent the last touch of magic to this absurdity was that it could be ordered to float on a carpet of clouds to any spot desired. One night the emperor discovered that while he had been away in a distant part of his kingdom the houri had taken to her bed a stalwart young fisherman from a lake village. Search high, search low, no trace of the magic pink castle could be found. Even the genie, bellowing his lungs out until the reverberations of his shouting caused whole mountains of snow in the Himalayas to avalanche, had no effect. So the heart-broken emperor, enraged at this turn of events, induced the genie back into a stone bottle of distilled honey, always a trap for unwary genies with a sweet tooth, and the centuries passed. I am persuaded the Castle of Coca is the magic *pavilion d'amour* from Rajputana settled in the wastes of a Spanish *vega*. Certainly it more nearly resembles the contrived balconies, cupolas, miradors, and traceries in pink stone of these pleasure houses of Ind, than a Spanish fortress.

As the sun broke through the clouds and every buttress of the castle was sharply revealed I had the same feeling I have had before that the foundations of the castle, gripping the arid earth from which no vegetation springs, are like the talons of enormous eagles clutching destructively at a crumbling ledge of rock. I have seen Coca in the rigid grip of winter winds, when it was so cold one's breath froze in lances of ice; in the brilliance of a hot, red October sunset when it seemed consumed in flames, and in the purple, black, and green lividness of an approaching storm, deceitfully masquerading in summer trappings by keeping the sun bright as a decoy. Through every vagary of nature, Coca remains rosy and serene, *in* Spain but not *of* it. Actually Coca was built by a man steeped to the nostrils in vainglory, one Alonso de Fonseca, Archbishop of Seville. Fonseca, dressed in a purple and white toga, his head wreathed in a victor's wreath of triumphal bay leaves, used to drive a chariot of hammered silver, harnessing four black horses abreast, around the walls of the castle, while his guests numbering hundreds waved languidly to him from the clustered turrets. Coca is now the property of the Duke of Alba, who gets little time to stop in his score of castles, but the very fact that they belong to him assures that the monuments will be well preserved.

Presently out of the mists loomed the gray-green arches of the aqueduct which, for many centuries, has stood uncontested as one of the world's wonders of engineering construction. It is said that Emperor Trajan dreamed that a famine of water was to come within his span of life, when all Spain would shrivel into a desert. As life for anyone is precarious, he called his engineers in conclave and in a few weeks work was begun on the aqueduct we see still functioning today. The date carved into enduring stone is A.D. 98-117. To the local peasantry this is "The Devil's Bridge," so-called from an ancient legend attributing its construction to the magic of "El Diablo." The double tier of stone arches with a promenade for pedestrians and "chariots" along the top is a marvel of ingenuity. The gigantic blocks of stone are cunningly fitted together without mortar. Standing at one end of the structure I am always unbelieving of what my trained eyes see. The receding perspective from close up to where the great stone serpent drags its tail across the rusty plains to disappear into the shadowed crevasses of the Guadarrama Mountains nearly passes credulity. Yes, in Segovia I can drink clear cold water from the springs of Sierra de la Fuenfria, only a few miles from Madrid, which has always been the source of the water supply. The Rivers Eresma and Clamores may shrink to trickles in the long summer droughts peculiar to this region, but the aqueduct still supplies cool water in plenty to Segovia through the same system of stone syphons that was introduced when this giant aerial waterway was first built. These syphons were rehabilitated in the thirteenth century. Except for a general in-

spection every few years, the system of stone flues needs little attention. What a heartening, imagination-stirring sight to evoke out of
antiquity—the Emperor Trajan with his cronies, escorted by Roman
Legions driving along the "Emperor's Way" (to give it the early
style of reference) which crests the length of the aqueduct. At evening Trajan would take the air and view the mountains rising behind

the city in the plain. Today one can walk along the same way to
breathe the mountain air and revel in the same panorama.

It is wonderful to see Segovia from this height, lying wrapped like
a woman in many shades of pink draperies, on a sort of couch formed
by a declivity in the plain. The city has many beautiful old buildings
to admire. Romanesque architecture predominates, though the Moors
held out against the Christians long after the fall of Toledo not far
away. Whether the Moors ever raised any outstanding buildings in
Segovia or not, there is little of their lovely art here now. The Alcazar has suffered many fires, enlargments, and not too wisely handled

282

restorations since Alfonso VI built it as a citadel in the late eleventh century. Its chief beauty is to personify the castles in Spain we all dream of in the night watches, on top of its terraced green hill. When Isabella of Castile was crowned in the great square of Segovia, she caused the tall pointed turrets to be encased in silver, to catch and throw out as a beacon the moon's rays, and to be hung with silver bells so that the evening breeze would bear the message of their music to herald her coronation, far out across the *vega*.

A moonlight night is the time to see the Alcazar of Segovia for the first time, if it can be managed, for then, as if carved in translucent white jade, in sheer beauty of rising walls and towers, Alcazar is a sight to catch one's breath.

Chapter 16

EL ESCORIAL–THE PANOPLY OF
MEDIEVAL SPAIN

L YING athwart a valley thirty odd miles from Madrid is a man-
made tableland, shored up by tremendous breastworks of
intersected ramps and buttresses of stone blocks, comparable in rough-hewn majesty to those Cyclopean stones used in the
Roman walls which may still be seen in fantastic ruin at Tarragona.
This skillfully contrived plateau is laid out in gardens from the midst
of which rise the walls of the palace-monastery of San Lorenzo del
Escorial. Built of dovetailed stone, cleanly dressed as is monument
marble, pale mauve-gray in tone, the far-flung structure bulks arrogantly four-square to the elements, giving no quarter down the
centuries to tempests, either those sent whirling down the valley by
God unleashing the four winds, or the more treacherous tempests
whipped up by papal politics and devious court intrigue. Grimly
serene, El Escorial is silhouetted against pine-dark mountains, its
walls accented in length by a preponderance of windows. Numerous
times, from different vantage points, I have studied the well-con-
sidered mass of the monastery, with its four airy pavilions giving lift
and lightness as soaring finials to the four corners. I have ever come
to the conclusion that it is these north, south, east, and west pavilions,
which lift the Escorial from monotony, for, if considered in detail,
the long unadorned walls are in truth just what Washington Irving
said of them—"a tiresome, architectural monotony." It is the pinnacle
hoisting on each pavilion, ending in a needle-sharp spire piercing the
heavens, that gives to the monastery the effect of a Gargantuan ship
about to set sail on a return voyage down the valley.

Philip II, always morose, restless, and an inveterate letter writer, penned to his court architect, Juan Herrera, a letter of complaint, that had all the bluntness and force of a papal bull. This letter stands for all time as a model of verbosity. Page after page of heavy parchment is covered with Philip's infantile calligraphy stressing his dissatisfaction with the plans by Juan Bautista de Toledo to whom he had first entrusted the building, and who was his architect from 1563 until his death four years later. After pages of complaints, Philip makes known in no uncertain terms his wishes for Herrera to design "a palace to incorporate a private chapel above a tomb, wherein we will ensepulcher all the Spanish kings." Further on Philip waxes devout—"a house to exemplify my devotion to the greater glory of God that will extol the virtue of simplicity, nobility without arrogance, avoiding all that is tainted with worldly pleasure or the grandiose. Above all, elevating majesty without ostentation."

After more pages of this sort of rhetorical verbiage Philip, having considerably warmed to his subject, cools slightly, adding a last admonition. "On the whole, severity must be the keynote, for we will tolerate no cavil against extravagance." While everything in this world is comparative, after reading this letter it is still a trifle hard to reconcile El Escorial, as it stands so proudly today, with the kind of monastery-tomb-palace the fanatically religious Philip II conceived. If there stands a more extravagant temple to unbridled magnificence anywhere under the canopy today, I do not know where it is.

I like to stand on the wide terrace of Hotel Felipe II overhanging a ravine, with the village of Escorial below, sun-drowsing during the day but twinkling with lights at night, and look down on the monastery. If it is a sunset in the Spanish grand manner the windows within my line of vision (there are over three thousand windows in El Escorial) will burn bright orange, a mammoth set piece of conflagration, which flames in awesome steadiness for a time; then as quickly as the sun sinks, the windows are again blind and drear. I saw Escorial once in moonlight bathed in silver serenity; the illusion of a luminous galleon drifting in remoteness was startling. Again in a raging electrical storm, the walls and pinnacles were now green, now yellow, now livid white, sinking back into blackness to become a lumbering hulk.

A man whom I met told me he wanted to photograph the edifice for some magazine. I said to him, "Just to level a camera at El Escorial and snap your shutter doesn't signify. It is so vast and stark you want to stay in the village, preferably at the Felipe II, and wait for the elements to pull one of those sudden changes from calm to demented. Then, and then only, will you get spellbinding pictures of the monastery as it deserves. If ever a building needs mood in portrayal to convey its uniqueness it is this one." I showed the man some stunning photographs taken by a Bavarian youth, which have been bought by the Spanish Government for inclusion in a book on Madrid, and he agreed with what I said.

In the center of the building over the great circular altar rises a dome built to one-quarter scale in the image of Michelangelo's masterpiece, the dome of Saint Peter's in Rome. From a pine-shaded grotto on a ledge of a high escarpment Philip II was wont to spend hours a day sitting in his "Chair for Meditation," reading his breviary, muttering litanies, momentarily lifting his eyes to watch the building, the dream of his life, slowly coming true over a period of twenty-two years. It is said that the king, wrapped in a cloak of wool, or fur in winter, or stripped to black satin small clothes in the scorching heat of summer, ignored all rigors of the seasons to occupy daily his natural stone chair.

At first Juan Bautista de Toledo, whose stubbornness exasperated the king, was called every evening to the chair to report on the day's progress. Later, Juan Herrera, far more talented and closely connected with every phase of the building as we now see it, sought the grotto. For it was always Philip who made last decisions. Indeed, so closely was Philip II concerned with the erection of his dream, from the first excavations until the royal standards were flown from the four spires, that chroniclers say he took all credit for El Escorial, save, I expect, for actually dovetailing of the stone and marble blocks.

I shall never forget standing one day in early April on the ledge in front of the grotto. Behind me were the dark rustling pines. In front was the monastery in the middle distance, while Madrid hung suspended in the sky on the far, smoky horizon. Between me and El Escorial was a grove of flowering almond and peach trees, plum trees too I remember, for there was feathery white among the strong pink of almond blossoms. Through a lattice tracery of sepia branches plumed in delicate petals the strong, impregnable lines of the vast stone walls seemed to gain a gentleness they never knew. So—when persons say to me, as they do, "El Escorial? Yes, colossal, but so cold and forbidding," I answer, "Perhaps, in mid-winter with Guadarrama winds writhing the bare branches and torturing the towers. But not in spring, when the almond blooms."

The interior of El Escorial is grand in scale, fully equal in stunning impact to the exterior, though more directly magnificent in gold and rare woods and marble as befits a treasure repository of such magnitude. The oval sepulcher, reached by a winding marble staircase, is directly under the high altar. Although this crypt is shrouded in diffused light, the dimness in no way obscures the acres of gold leaf covering the sarcophagi of Spanish kings from Charles I (better known as Charles V, Holy Roman Emperor) to Alfonso XII. Save Philip IV, interred at La Granja, and Ferdinand and Isabella, los Reyes Catolicos, who are ensepulchered with Infanta Juana in Capilla Real at La Cartuja, and exile Alfonso XIII buried in Rome, all sleep here. I always stand for a long time looking at the recumbent effigy of Don Juan of Austria, held in the nostalgic spell cast by the beauty of the serene features of this improbably handsome and romantic young warrior. The day I walked round the crypt a beadle in a dark red gown and white ruff, carrying his staff of office and a gold candelabrum branching at least a dozen candles, was showing some V.I.P. the sarcophagi. In the light of tapers the plating of "conquistadors' gold" seemed to glow balefully against black marble molding on the tiered shelves and groups of obsidian columns. The concave ceiling is coffered and set with huge bosses, petaled like roses, covered in burnished gold leaf. A rarely beautiful example of Baroque design.

The long enfilade of rooms called "Goya Salons" is furnished in a Spanish version of the Directoire style. A great deal of black and gold lacquer furniture stands about, to point up the set of thirty-four panels hanging on the walls of the rooms, wherein Goya showed the simple pleasures of a country fiesta, picnics beside a river chattering over stones in a bosky dell, a race of bumpkins on stilts, and court ladies and beaux playing at milk maid and harvesters. This apartment has a light, gay air, a pleasant oasis in the overpowering richness of the majority of the palace rooms. The hidden apartment of Philip II, which is almost on the threshold of the altar, with a grilled window in his bedroom from which, during his long, exhausting last illness, he could see and hear mass, engages the interest of all visitors because of the human element, the extreme personal touch. Here is the king's writing table with a pair of gold-fringed gloves for a book mark, as if his lean, sallow hands had just pulled fingers from the soft suede. Slippers he wore when at ease are under the narrow ascetic bed and there is the quill pen, the plume nibbled to a matted fringe, with which Philip II of Spain signed his last official document, elevating Cardinal Sepulveda to an archbishopric.

I have stood for hours in the corridor leading to the Patio de los Reyes where the library of over fifty thousand books is housed among Santo Domingo mahogany carved panels, gazing at the immense panel painted on silk showing thousands of foot soldiers and a knightly company on the march. The exquisitely-painted detail is bewildering in fineness. Half the panel shows a medieval king setting his camp, to rest, feed and find diversion before a long march next day or perhaps a battle. Mercenaries doff armor to bathe naked in a nearby river to the enchantment of buxom village girls. Sappers build fires. Cooks prepare the evening camp fare. Horses are rubbed down while knights are valeted by pages and squires. Pennons blaze with heraldic devices, and a moon rises over distant mountains as musicians tune up for entertainment.

The other half of this narrative mural is concerned with daybreak and the flurry of breaking camp. Hundreds of knights, armed cap-a-pie, set out on the march. The little silk castle-belvedere of the king with its panache of herons' plumes is struck. Baggage wagons are stacked with gear, and the king in golden armor leads off on a curveting destrier. In all this panoply the painting of thousands of lances bearing bright pennons fluttering in the dawn wind holds a strange fascination for me. I want to be one of the cavalcade.

The library at El Escorial is a compelling room on all counts. Here are many relics both historical and religious, of which two or three are outstanding. One is the Sword of Dedication which Philip II used to bestow the name of Saint Lawrence (San Lorenzo) on the monastery. The saint was a deacon of Pope Sixtus II who stoically bore martyrdom, and the dedication was a memorial for the victory of St. Quentin in 1557 which occurred on his feast day. Then there is a remarkable treatise on the powers of healing attributed to precious stones, with annotations by Alfonso the Wise; and in a glass case by itself, the autobiography of Santa Teresa in her own writing. Her hand must have rushed across the pages, stabbing the parchment, for it is a vital, expostulating, but most untidy scrawl.

At El Escorial during the lifetime of Philip II, and down the centuries, hundreds of persons dressed in rich or tawdry finery lived as pensioners who took chancy place at court, but who never spoke to the king. The court at El Escorial when the Bourbons were in

PAGEANTRY
AND PANOPLY
from
CATHEDRAL
EASTER.
JR

flower is said to have numbered three thousand souls, with all but a few lesser functionaries housed within the palace walls. It is reported, quite naturally, that a bevy of distractingly pretty young women, and probably many not so young or so pretty, occupied an ambiguous position among the hangers-on. There is one large room, hidden away from most eyes—though anyone can see it who is sufficiently adventurous, or perhaps prying—where nostalgia rules the musty shadows, to recreate in the mind the days when the unending corridors opened onto a veritable rabbit warren of these pensioners' rooms. This room contains at least thirty sedan chairs. Some are glassed-in of painted leather, once luxuriously cushioned in red or yellow silk and damask. Others are simple wooden affairs, with cloth curtains or cracked leather fittings. These sedans were once used to transport the ladies to and fro from their own cubby holes to the rooms of whichever gallants had need of their company. The yawning caverns of corridors were so cold and gusty with Guadarrama winds that it was thought unwise for these lightly-clad ladies to venture through them on foot. Today these chairs stand in a long row against the walls of the otherwise empty room. Across the seats of some are folded robes of once lovely colored padded silk, a few deeply banded with fur. All have been prey to rats, mildew, and the unregenerate moth.

After leaving El Escorial, I drove to the hill town of Sepulveda. The appellation "honey-colored" or "golden," so often used to describe a town in Spain, was never more apt than here. In the afternoon sun of a lazy summer day it seemed a golden cock pheasant sitting warily atop a red earth hill, preening with its beak long tail feathers which are the narow, labyrinthian streets. Sepulveda is an ancient fortress town. Once the walls and stone-paved alleys resounded year in, year out, with the sound of steel ringing upon shield and buckler, for it appears that everyone who owned a sword wanted to wrest the rich, advantageously-placed town from anyone fortunate enough to have won it. Now quiet reigns. The chief pursuits are lace making, fine cabinet work, and perfecting a large, melon-bellied guitar of particularly musical tone which has long been a favorite of amorous *cabelleros*, with which to serenade Carmen, Lolita, Pilár, or perhaps Concépcíon, blushing behind the family *rejas*.

Spaniards love bravery in a man, whether he is matador or soldier, especially when the grand gesture is employed. So, in the town of Sepulveda I heard a story that is a legend of the cafés. The intrepid

Sir James Douglas, one of the foremost leaders under Bruce in the War of Scottish Independence, was chosen by the king, on his death-bed, to take his heart in a casket to Jerusalem and lay it in the Holy Sepulcher of Christ. On his way through Spain Douglas stopped at Sepulveda to recover from an infected wound. The brave Scotsman was of jovial as well as musical nature. He learned to play the fine guitars made by the instrument makers of the town. Recovered, he went off to help the king of Castile in his war against the Moors. Douglas took with him not only the precious casket containing the heart of the king, but a guitar which he said he would play to the Castilian king on the night of victory over the infidel. But things did not turn out that way. In the press of action, finding himself hemmed in, Douglas tore the casket containing the heart from his neck and flung it into the infidel ranks shouting, "Forward, brave heart, as thou wert ever wont, and Douglas will follow thee." After the tide of battle had turned, Douglas' men found him lying dead beside the casket.

San Raphael is a summer spa for pleasure. Hidden in a dense wood of pine, chestnut, and cork trees, many travelers pass it by unheeding, yet it has a popular season from July to September, patronized largely by Spanish *hidalgo* families who go there year after year. One may spend a delightful weekend here, motoring out from Madrid, pic-nicking in the grottos; some are coffee kiosks with music, others are secluded and quite private. The long stretches of gardens have stiff parterres and gushing fountains, which the natives of the village will tell you are like "a little Versailles. Just as beautiful—though not so large, of course." Not far away on the road to La Granja I stopped at an old Carthusian monastery now turned into a parador. This retreat is called El Paular, and I find it one of the happiest stories Spain has to tell. Ilex and Rose of Sharon, lavender-leaved peepul trees and chestnut, shade the old cloisters, where thousands of bright-plumaged birds and flashing butterflies darted over my head as I ate lunch out of doors. Everywhere are the flash and whirr of wings, for El Paular is an aviary and a bird sanctuary at once.

Medinaceli is a dead city, embalmed with that incense-laden atmosphere so indicative of the sumptuous, half-royal, half-ecclesias-tical progresses of Old Spain. A vast, gaunt cathedral, with gold emblazoned balconies, *retablos*, and sarcophagi—fifteen in a row— of the ducal family of Medinaceli, blazes with banners and accouter-ments of battle and worldly riches. The whole show is far more reminiscent of a museum than a place for worship. It is all stifling, heady fare, made bearable, or certainly memorable, by the sensational view from the terrace of Medinaceli Palace. The earth of Aragon spreads wide, straight out of the annals of Spanish history. Bleak fields are tilled in stripes, parched red and ochre, as if the land were carpeted with the flag of Spain. Far off flashes the metallic blue Jalón, a river famed and feared for incalculable depth and iciness from deep flowing springs. It is said that if an apple or a melon is weighted on a line and let down into the black waters of the Jalón, it is pulled up frozen, solid as a ball of ice. Always in Spain the far horizon is rimmed or jagged by mountains. From Medinaceli it is the dark purple ramparts of Sierra de Moncayo, saw-toothed and forbidding, where there are still a few outlaw brigands on the run from the Civil War, holed up and desperate, who create horrific depredations on villages lying in the valley below.

At last, after many false starts and detours for one reason or another, I drew into León. As is so often the case in Spain, it is the cathedral which dominates the landscape for miles, but this time with a noticeable difference. The Cathedral of Santa Maria de Regla is not a monument to sheer ornamentation. This time the church is a monument to imagination expressed more subtly in terms of shimmering crystal and stone. One is struck by the singular purity of line. Twin towers crowned by spires flank a Gothic window, the largest I have ever seen of stained glass. The whole beautifully-composed front achieves a completely harmonious façade. While there is much to admire in the admirable exterior restraint, undeniably one of the finest Gothic gestures in Spain, it is the interior which makes the Cathedral of León an exclamatory piece of architecture. Rendering a series of immense mural painting in sparkling color that is largely luminous light is an achievement unique in the annals of tinted glass. At Léon it has come off magnificently. Standing in the nave I gazed up into the crystal distances of ogival windows set above the clerestory and the two choir lofts. The color range is far greater in richness than any stained glass I know. I am reminded of the improbable colors of that flower from "Never-Never-Land," the *Ixia viridiflora*, of violent, intense green and electric blue, shot with jagged lightnings of strident pink, crimson and smouldering purple, which grows almost beyond the reach of man in the icy altitudes of the Chilean Andes. Just as it is daylight that makes these great windows at León glorious, so it is shattering mountain light that makes the acres of

Ixia viridiflora seem unbelievable. Possibly it is this radiance that causes one to experience the peculiar emotion aroused by the sight of these windows. I came out of the church into the sunset scene still bathed in a kind of "Gloria in excelis" and feeling that I rivaled the sun.

The cathedral has a fascinating history. Originally the town of León was built as a sprawling garrison or depot to shelter Roman Legion VII Gemina. Traces of a foundation for brick barracks of gigantic proportions can be seen today. Later a palace of Ordoño II, King of León, adjoined Roman baths of particularly scandalous reputation, which had been built and maintained as recreation for the soldiery. When public opinion soured on the flagrant indecencies which took place at the baths the edict went forth that they were condemned and must be leveled forthwith. But politics was brought into play and the edict was not carried out. A year passed. Finally incensed, the people rioted and in a wild demonstration the populace pulled down both baths and Ordoño's palace. Alfonso I of Spain, after conquering the Berber chief Muruza built a fortress in León. But evil days fell upon the city in the sandy, wind-swept wastes. León was deserted and so lay moribund for a hundred years, prey to wolves, and beggars who camped in a kind of thieves' den in the ruins of the cavalry barracks.

When Don Ramiro at last came to León to establish a Christian population he found the city half buried under mammoth drifts of sand. This picture of barren León of antiquity is in sharp contrast to the orchards and meadows which make the countryside delicious today. In the twelfth century Bishop Manrique de Lara built the cathedral on the site of Ordoño's palace and the infamous Roman baths. Like many another Spanish cathedral, down the centuries it has undergone additions and enlargements, suiting the style to changing influences in architecture. That the edifice has retained the cool ardor of pure Gothic simplicity as a setting for the jewel-like windows is no small miracle.

As contrast, in the Plaza San Isidro stands the church of the same name. The curiously polyglot architecture, a mélange of conflicting ideas, seems to writhe in eternal torment, one style trying to throttle its neighbor in the overall design. Mainly Gothic, the church underneath is crude Romanesque, overlaid by Renaissance detail and massive cornices; columns and a winged pediment are exuberantly Baroque. What gives cachet to this uncertain effusion in stone is a colossal equestrian statue of a truncated warrior which crowns the pediment.

There is a long dun-gray building of no outward distinction called "The Pantheon of the Kings." Inside, it is another story. Here the shadowy darkness, scented with age-old sandlewood and musk, is impressive in the richly faded grandeur with which Spain knows so well how to enshrine the days of her greatness. High, narrow chapels, barred in gold like gilded cages, preserve the remains of noble persons. As I walked along the middle aisle, the only movement in the musty air, was the flutter of candle flame fanned in the draught from the open door through which I had entered. I had the feeling that some ceremony had but lately taken place here. I nearly tripped over immense fat tassels of crimson silk threaded with tarnished gold, hanging from four black velvet cushions. There was a sound of high-pitched, adolescent giggling as two altar boys in red cassocks and wide black belts ran down the aisle lugging a canvas bag between them. Paying scant attention to me the boys gathered up the cushions and stuffed them into the sack making a great *do* of tucking in yards of the fat red silk tassels. When the sack was full to bulging and hoisted on the back of the bigger of the two acolytes, I noticed a name stenciled in black upon the bag. Guzmán, a name that has rung variously as a clarion or as a dirge of bells down Spanish history. Perhaps most discreditably when Don Juan Pérez y Guzmán, the vainglorious, luxury-loving Governor of Panama, wrote his report of the burning of his city by Henry (later Sir Henry) Morgan. This letter to the King of Spain was intercepted by Morgan's men en route to the coast and is now in the archives of the British Admiralty. As a monument to falsifying actual facts, this parchment remains unique in the roster of the written word.

As are all their other palaces in Spain, that of the Guzmán family in León is a superb gesture, in this instance a perfect example of Spanish Renaissance. The great upper gallery is as splendid as I have ever seen. In a series of niches immense urns of jasper, holding black and silver lilies, gleam in the changing light when viewed from the street, the petals of metal as flexible as the natural flower.

I found a lovely park to wander in for a while, with an equally lovely name. Parque Paperlaguinda de las Mimosas follows the river bank until it reaches the statue of the noble patron of León, Guzmán el Bueno (the Good) who built the palace and presented the Paperlaguinda gardens to the city. Despite a face that looks like a benevolent bull-frog, with eyes popping like cannon balls, Guzmán the good is presented as an impressive figure bearing in his hand a scroll annotating the names of all his generous presentations, not only to León but to all Spain.

In the environs of León, sufficiently far off not to be classed as suburbs, are a number of interesting towns, all rewarding to visit. Sahagun is gray and translucent under the curiously transparent sky of Galicia. The houses have a paper-thin quality, like a village built of playing cards, though this effect is merely a trick of the light, for all medieval towns in Spain are built mightily of stone. The town bears the northern, shut-faced air. However, I was considerably heartened to buy some of my favorite sausages to take along with me for lunch at Ponferrada. *Chorizo* is a form of salami made with pork and red peppers of a rich and piquant flavor. Like the lure of oysters or olives to the young palate, once one tastes *chorizo* the chances are that the taster will become an addict. My first taste was at a picnic on the beach at Santander when I was thirteen years old. I spit out the first mouthful because the *pimienta* nipped my tongue. But I well remember the after-taste was so pleasant I tried again. Since then I resort to bribery to get *chorizo*, or theft if necessary. Once in a little mountain town in Castile I filched a long sausage when a shopkeeper was tardy in answering my call *"por favor."* I left him what I thought would be more than enough money to cover it, and departed. An hour later a breathless urchin, his eyes and nose streaming with the effort of running at a high altitude, caught up with me. I was eating my lunch by the roadside, enjoying the valley scene where a thunderous waterfall fed a stream that I was sure harbored delectable trout. The boy bore two more *chorizos*.

"Señor, I saw you leave. Señor Pedro says you must not give him charity. Your pesetas cover these two *chorizos*." With a sweeping bow, worthy of Guzman the Good, the boy sped like a mountain goat back over the road he had come, his café au lait bottom showing half out of ragged breeches. An instance of Spanish pride which disdains charity, well laced with the impeccable honesty one meets in all localities in Spain. Well, perhaps with the isolated exception of certain quarters of Barcelona.

Ponferrada is an old town on the river Sil. The rime of age is everywhere apparent, but in age lies its beauty. Ageless beauty has stamped the town walls and the Castle of Ponferrada. While the castle by the bridge is one of the most famous in Spain, the banks of the Sil bristle with castles of great or lesser importance, for this was once a kind of Maginot Line against the Moors, so the walls of towns on one side of this river were designed to be impregnable. There is a softness as of old velvet about the walls of Ponferrada Castle. Perhaps this is due to the porous clay stone from which they are built. The ribbed and pitted texture of the sepia stone is intensely interesting to paint. Flickering now red, now gold, in the long shadows of sunset, the castle was the illusion of some lost Gothic tapestry-town sharply etched against the pale violet reaches of conical peaks which define Montañas de León, sentinel ramparts between the Province of León and the Atlantic. I ate the last of my *chorizos* and drank hard cider of the region, sitting on a stone plinth while I sketched the castle walls where once had risen "the fifty towers" (there are but twelve now), according to the historical essays of Alvar Pérez de Quiñones in the Museo de San Marcos at León. Quiñones goes on to say that once "half an hundred towers threatened the sky to make glorious the battlements of Ponferrada." The walls stretch out on either side of the main barbican in a snaky chain of arches and cells, a kind of caravanserai (in the Moorish sense of cubicles for travelers to stop in over night). This halt was famed throughout Spain for pilgrims on the way to Santiago de Compostela.

The road to Pontevedra is winding, up hill, down dale, differing from most of these switchback roads in that the climb and sudden descent is not over mountain passes, but vine-clad hills, gulleys, and dark gorges made musical and coolly fragrant by tumbling waterfalls which the Province of Galicia seems to collect.

Sierra de Picos, where battalions of pines march up and down red stone ridges, is now a reforestation preserve. A magnificent flash of color against the pale aquamarine sky and dark green flanks of the mountains proved to be the Spanish flag. Two red horizontal bars with a yellow stripe between on which is displayed the Imperial Eagle of Spain in exclamatory black. The bare yellow flanks of Sierra del Laurel are so gashed with gorges it shunts the River Cabrera in zig-zag pattern across the plum-colored barrenness of the *vega* called El Bierzo, flat and uneventful as a deserted ballroom floor. I stopped for the night at Puebla de Trives in a small *hosteria* undoubtedly primitive but redolent of the atmosphere of old Galicia where hospitality to travelers has ever been austere but generously given. Outside steps scaled the ancient blue-washed walls of Los Quercus Suber, named for the cork oaks which are planted in a grove to ring the inn with shade. I found this delightful old house a rabbit warren of patios and twisting stairways, with no two rooms on the same level. Mine was a huge square room at the top of the house with two windows above the tree tops, fronted by an iron balcony from which I had an unobstructed view of the River Miño, called in the province "the Madonna's pearls," for its habit of widening out at intervals to the size of a small lake, giving the effect of pearls on a string. An over-life-size figure of the Virgin of Monforte de León, carved from indigo-blue stone, stands high on a ledge in a rocky shrine overlooking the largest lake, quietly contemplating her pearls.

Pontevedra has the windswept, clean-drawn look of so many fishing villages on the coast of Maine. The houses of Galician fishermen are sturdy stone cubes with flat shale shingles and many of them are topped by a squat tower to entice storks to build a nest both to breed their young and assure good fortune. In Galicia, as off the Western coast of Ireland, the Atlantic kelp is strongly impregnated with iodine where the long combers roll in steadily upon the rocky shore. Consequently the nets and trawlers' weirs of bamboo, shaped like giant butterfly wings, are hung up to dry against whitewashed walls and the piers of the old Roman breakwater. The white surfaces are dyed the yellow-green of absinthe by the iodine. This causes the walls to gain a patina of yellow crosshatching which stands out like golden tracery in the rays of a setting sun. There is one small, white house in Pontevedra that is a shrine, but a shrine with a difference. It is the house of a poetess who came to spend her summers and to write with understanding and poignant beauty, as no one else has done, of her native Galicia; of its simplicity and the courage of its people and its stirring legends. Rosalía de Castro, as are the majority of poets, was of retiring disposition. Still she kept open house to anyone who called to wish her well. For she was greatly loved and her poems are learned by heart and recited by peasants and fishermen who cannot read the printed page. This method of learning by heart to recite history, poetry, and the legends of a province is a Moorish custom kept alive and immediate in Galicia, Castile, Aragon, and Navarre, indeed in all the Northern provinces. During long winter evenings, shut away in snow-bound, windy mountain fastnesses the people gather in one another's houses for a kind of symposium in the Roman sense, to dance, to sing, and to keep vitally alive the old way of life.

On the road to Santiago I again met pilgrims, some of them walking the long way, others, luxuriously lolling in auto-buses, much as

I had seen a few weeks ago on the road to the shrine of St. Francis at Xavier. Just before I drove into Silleda I met wild-eyed young goatherds gazing anxiously towards the town, vexation riding their grimy faces, because they could not dare desert their flocks to join in the crowds running in the direction of the big Roman gates in the walls of Silleda.

When I swung into the dusty plaza I was stopped by a heterogeneous crowd. At first glance it looked as if a platoon of cavalry had taken the place over. What I saw was a newly-arrived pack train of mules and burros loaded with bales of spongy outer bark of the cork tree. The slabs of cork were piled high in rope saddlebags, loosely woven like fish nets. Cork in this raw state is dingy, a muddy, yellowish pink, but there was plenty of color, rampant color, in the bridles and breechings of the animals. In Spain I have seen all manner of ingenious contrivances to harness donkeys, bullocks, and horses. Here I had a banquet of ingenuity. For the most part the trappings were red or yellow wool and twisted cord tassels, the elaborate kind made in Ronda or Granada and worth many hundreds of pesetas. Close to me was a tiny burro standing knee deep in golden straw which he was reducing to a few scattered wisps in great gulping mouthfuls. His head was submerged behind a red and green bridle far too big for him. Then I noticed a heavy band of fringes like a hackamore bit across his tiny muzzle. The man who owned him said this was used to prevent a young donkey from suckling on the road, thereby holding up the caravan.

"Good God," I said, "you don't expect a donkey not yet weaned to carry pack loads, do you?"

The man smiled. "Oh, Alfero is much older than he seems. He is *bufolito* (a dwarf) and he just refuses to be weaned. The sight of a teat when he is hungry, and he stops everything until he is fed."

This pack train had come all the way from Calzada de Calatrava near Ciudad Real, a good eight hundred miles away by mountain trails and circuitous detours. The muleteers were Basque from Vergara near San Sebastian. They make this trip twice a year to bring this fine grade of cork, used exclusively for fishing-rod handles and sport appliances. It fetches higher prices in northern provinces where it is scarcer than in Valencia or Andalusia. I liked the way the men and boys, numbering in all about sixty-five, treated their pack animals. Spanish muleteers have for long made pets of their donkeys. The willing little beast is a friend as well as co-worker, the story of

Sancho Panza amusingly illustrates. When a thief stole his ass in the Sierra Morena, Sancho was inconsolable, crying aloud, "Oh, my children's pet! Solace of my cares! My brother, half supporter of my person!"

Chapter 17

LA CORUÑA AND THE BISCAY COAST

THE attractions along the road from Pontevedra to Santiago de Compostela are varied, indeed so compelling that many travelers take three or four days to do sixty kilometers, making frequent stops over night and detours by day to visit the vineyard villages set on slopes running down to the sea. There are simple but totally pleasant inns and fishermen's *tabernas* at Ulla and at Padrón, which seems a village carved from lapis lazuli or viridian, owing to the custom of spraying the grape vines, many of which form arbors for the houses, with Paris of silphium.

Rijano is a village naive as a country maiden, where stone urns are set at the corners of the up-slanting plaza, to be filled with the choicest bunches of grapes so that visitors may inspect or taste the splendid yield of fruit from Rijano vineyards. All along this vine-bordered coast the roads are excellent and the scenery unmatched in Spain for that unbeatable combination, seascape allied with rolling uplands and lofty mountains.

I drove into Santiago de Compostela by way of Touro. The first glimpse I had of the most holy of all pilgrimages, after Rome and Jerusalem, was a green hill surrounded by a greener forest. A procession of tawny marble figures seemed to wend their way on the tree tops down to the indigo waters of the River Tamore, where it widens into a bay to empty into the Atlantic Ocean. The effect of this marble coterie of exalted personages, hand-in-hand, as it were, with saints and winged angels of the fiery sword, is startling. To me, sitting far below the tree-hidden cathedral, it was as if these heroic figures, restless with forever balancing on the cornices of El Obradoiro, were walking the tree tops to welcome me. Soon I turned into a long ride cut through the trees. As a far-off finial, splendid beyond words, rose the grouped towers and dome of the shrine.

Santiago, apart from the cathedral and monastery, is a city of unlimited architectural riches reminding me in many ways of Rome, or is it Venice? Perhaps when I look more closely at the splendors of Baroque palaces it is Prague I am recalling. The more I range the streets of the city I realize it is a combination of all three cities, with overtones wholly Spanish. I walked at night along the streets, in and out of plazas. A moon close to full bathed lace-like frets and cornices molded in vital high relief that would delight the eyes of Palladio. Volutes and counterfoils ornament the clustered pinnacles and the spires of El Obradoiro. The essence of this scene was that of some exotic temple half smothered by the tenacles of jungle vines in the steamy forests of Cambodia. Santiago, so diversified in architectural ornament, is the most bewildering city in Spain to place in any given epoch, or indeed in any given land, yet the atmosphere over all is of Spain.

Standing off a way to get a perspective of El Obradoiro, it is again the translucent light of Galicia that triumphs over architecture. For without it the spires, rising in two massive but delicately slender plinths, would not appear so airy, nor give off such radiant color. The stone is not remarkable in texture or ornament, but gains in the color of Orient pearl by being silhouetted against an irridescent sky. The center façade engages Corinthian columns flanking the entrance door. Purely ornamental, the columns appear to support a magnificently flowing proscenium or "tiara" pediment. From the scrolled apex, seeming about to take flight, is poised a vigorously sculptured heroic figure of St. James. The cathedral has four façades, each one individual in itself, but artfully designed to fuse perfectly with the whole. It is only when examining the detail of ornament that one is conscious of the differences. The design throughout is pure Baroque at its highest gleam. If in itself El Obradoiro were not one of the most perfect gestures in Baroque architecture in the world, it gains immensely in splendor by complement in the buildings facing it in the plaza.

There is the important Gothic-Renaissance Hospital Real (Royal Hospital). San Jeronimo College with Neo-classic façade, patios, and chapels. The Rajóy Palace, veritably an alfresco portrait gallery of busts and plaques in Plateresque style. According to an old legend,

SANTIAGO de COMPOSTELA.
GALICIA

St. James the Apostle (Santiago) was decapitated in Palestine by order of Herod Agrippa. His disciples then took his body by sea to Iria Flavia (the Roman name of Santiago), where it was buried in a "marble ark," in the Liberum Donun mount. Some say the tomb was discovered early in the ninth century by a swineherd whose herd was rooting for truffles. A town grew in ever spreading circles around the holy spot until the inhabitants numbered ten thousand.

When the news of the discovery spread to the rest of the Christian world pilgrims began to arrive in the town of Compostela. Since the eleventh century, when King Alfonso VI gave the province of Galicia to his sister Doña Urraca as dowry on her marriage to Raymond of Burgundy, Compostela has been an important center for monasteries, pilgrims' hostels, and churches. Now the cathedral rises as a Baroque jewel in a setting of the finest Romanesque to be found in the Province of Galicia, a province mainly Romanesque in architectural monuments.

Fountains featuring horses as ornament occupy a special pigeon hole in my cells of memory. At Viterbo is the winged bronze Pegasus in the spray-filled grotto at Villa Lante. The Swim Bath in a square in Salzburg was built by an indulgent cardinal to indulge a horse's love for cavorting in water. Dramatic in vitality is the tremendous Castor and Pollux fountain in elevated Piazza Quirinale in Rome, where the stallions crouching on their haunches seem about to leap into the space below, carrying the Heavenly Twins with them. Now I add another equine group in marble. In Santiago de Compostela, the fountain of the horses (de los Caballos), is a fountain of great scale in the classic Baroque tradition of sweeping line. The Gates of Quintana in the Plaza Literarios are again in the lofty Baroque principle of Roman Vitruvius. Here at eleven o'clock every morning a perambulating symposium takes place. Students from the somewhat over-precious Rococo seminary (formerly the Monastery of San Martin Pinario) walk about discussing all phases of literature, particularly that which has been fostered in Spain since earliest Celtiberian and Iberian times, some of which was found incised on the walls of caves. I once saw a celebration of the traditional feast held annually in July to commemorate the discovery of the Apostle. The high point of this feast is the swinging of a huge repousée silver censer, seven feet in height, called *Botafumeiro*. Like the "fiery furnace," belching scented smoke through filigree, *Botafumeiro* is swung in perilous arcs across the church from transept to nave by groups of ecstatic altar boys in red and purple habits. In the rapt silence of the multitude gazing upward, the screech of silver chains propelling this greatest pendulum ever seen is nerve wracking, albeit the spectacle is glorious.

Meanwhile a procession of acolytes and the choir, headed by the archbishop in splendid cope and mitre, jeweled crozier in red-gloved hand, walks slowly around the temple, seemingly oblivious of this smoking censer thundering through the air only a few yards above their heads.

Laracha stands garlanded with vines on a hill where vineyards stretch to the town gates like streamers of green ribbon. The accent to this laughing green countryside is latticed vines. In some of the smaller villages I drove through, such as Mesia and Cambre, vines are trained to form a canopy right across the street. All this gay note is a foretaste of what one finds in La Coruña. It is a delicious town with a singularly personal kind of magic, posed athwart a promontory jutting out into the Atlantic Ocean between two bays. In many ways, La Coruña is unique in Spain. Flaunting the high-colored, tinselly air of an Easter bazaar, it is at once vitally alive and dreamy, a "city of lusters" for all the houses facing the sea, varying from six to eight stories, have before every window a glassed-in balcony. The glass is either palest pink, amber, or violet to catch and distill every sliver of sunlight all year round.

La Coruña is most happy in its climate. Ironically, the port enjoys sun and soft breezes all the year round just as if it were set down in the semi-tropical embraces of Costa Brava. No one has ever been able to fathom this freak of nature, considering La Coruña's latitude and longitude. Only twenty miles away the rigorous Galician winters howl with gales and send crystal-laden storms down the valley, isolating inhabitants for days at a time, while this equable port of call for liners of every nation is a sun pocket. Equally happily, La Coruña is never hot in summer. Atlantic breezes temper the atmosphere. In mid July it was so cool I wore a top coat most evenings. The streets are lined with palm trees and everywhere are flower gardens. Under the arcades on which mainly the houses are built hang great wire baskets of variegated petunias, frilled, striped, or deep, rich solid colors. The hotel and restaurant situation in La Coruña is perhaps the best managed in Spain, with a long heritage of pleased clients. There are many old hotels of great reputation and two or three new ones. Hotel Finisterre is a palace of infinite delights. The rooms are wide windowed to the sea. The food is notably good with a menu as large as a daily newssheet. Anything, or everything, on the list is yours for the asking. Sanchez is the major domo at Hotel Finesterre. He is "most old," but indomitable. He rules his staff with a mental and verbal rod of iron, with the mind and grand airs of the Dowager Empress of China whose portraits, I told him, he not a little resembled, to his instant delight. Like Santander and San Sebastian, La Coruña has, for a century, been a gathering place, during the season, for international celebrities of all classes and talents.

Gaby Deslys loved Hotel Finesterre, as did Clemenceau and Lily Langtry. French cocottes, the most expensive *belles poules*, took apartments along the sea, living luxuriously in the crystal, jewel-casket atmosphere. For all the populace to see, La Belle Otero danced in the plaza by moonlight to please a grandee lover, who wished to refute without resorting to rapiers the imputation made in the Casino (now closed) that Otero "could not dance for viper-pigs" (an insult of stature in Spain).

Hotel Bahia is comfortable and charmingly Victorian. The café and restaurant at Hotel Atlantico are always crowded and gay in modern Spanish taste. The sport program at La Coruña, all year round, is formidable. The city has over one hundred thousand inhabitants, and almost everyone seems to be sport minded in one way or another. One young man told me, "In La Coruña we think only of yacht races, bull fights (all the crack matadors long to fight corrida in the beautiful Plaza de Toros by the sea), pigeon shoots, food, and dancing." I waited, knowing a certain something would be forthcoming considering the man is Spanish. He took a pull at his glass of wine. "Oh—yes, football, fiestas, celebrations for the saints, tennis and pretty girls." He smiled wryly. "And pursuing girls in this town *is* a sport. It tires me out."

At the café restaurants along the sea-front promenade all the famous Spanish sea-food dishes appear on the menu. I tasted for the first time the extraordinary *centolla* (*Cancer pagurus*), a crab with a tremendous spread of claws shaped like horns, as fearsome and tenacious as the talons of a Ronda eagle. The flesh is firm and pink. No other crustacean I know of tastes so definitely of the sea. The shell of this crab is as large as a fish platter and, like the claws, is coral pink and beautifully marked by great marbled streaks of black. The Iberian fisherfolk of Galicia (along this coast the people insist that they are the oldest race in the peninsula, therefore Iberians), cleverly strip

305

the huge, perfect specimens of meat without harming the shell, leaving the claws suspended intact, the top shell hinged as a cover. After drying thoroughly in the sun, these coral shells are lined with black silk to sell as work boxes.

By this time my readers know my predilection for lighthouses. Visually I collect them. On the topmost crag of the promontory stands the most ancient and certainly the most exciting Phoenician "drum lighthouse" in existence. It is called the Tower of Hercules, which incidentally figures in the coat of arms of the city. According to tradition, it stands on the site of a tower built by the Celtic chieftain Breogan before he set out for Ireland. This stone tower, immense in circumference, may have first been built by Phoenician mariners, certainly, it was restored by Roman engineers, for the method of laying the stone is undeniably Roman. There is one stone near the base which bears a nearly obliterated name and date. This would place the restoration as during the epoch of Emperor Trajan, that inveterate builder of colossi. There is a stone ramp where once was a lofty gateway for the passage of country carts laden with wood. A constant flow of logs was needed to feed the fires that served as a beacon for mariners, and was never let die out. I went up to the top of this stone monster, feeling the stone along the way. It was rough, warm, and friendly to my touch. From this height I could view the tremendous panorama of the sea, which the Phoenicians called the Mists of Limbo, two ranges of mountains and the mouths of the estuaries of The Bay of El Ferrol, now called Ferrol de Candillo, and several towns: Betanzos, Sada, with its whirlpool of waters forever in turmoil, and Puentedeume where twenty captive desperados, escaping from their guards, were drowned during the eighteenth century. The bodies were later found embalmed to the hardness of stone by some chemical properties in the waters. There, on the spot where the receding tide revealed the corpses, the petrified images still stand, set up like ten pins in an alley for bowls.

I saw on a small island the tissue-thin shell of the ruins of once magnificent castle Andrade, which proves once more that however insubstantial these great stone castles may look in their ruinous state, the walls stand impervious to time and the elements.

Andrade is buffeted by Atlantic gales from all sides, but medieval building was for the ages. The Monastery of Sobrado de los Mónjes is of great architectural beauty. It was founded in the tenth century and one can trace many periods of construction until it became a predominately Baroque church in the seventeenth century. I like to wander in the fifteenth-century kitchens where a whole ox could be roasted in the cavernous fireplaces and great, rusted spit chains now drag on the stone floors. The monks were a liberal-minded order, keeping great state. Nearby is an artificial lake in which to stock fish, first dredged by the monks of Sobrado.

At Betanzos close by there is a fourteenth-century church to Santa Maria del Azogue, who has strings of acorns and pungent black truffles looped around her neck instead of jewels. This Virgin has an enchanting face. The lips curve up slightly at the corners in an enigmatical smile which prompts me to think her a humorist. She is the patron of shepherds who from time to time come down from their lonely fastnesses and brave the company of men to hang the earthy necklaces there, a propitiatory offering of simple faith from surely the most innocent class of men still left in the world. One must go to Greece or remote parts of Italy, but more generally Spain, to realize that the antique profession of herdsman, lonely of human companionship beyond reason, relying on Pan pipes for entertainment, is still flourishing.

The interior of the Church of San Francisco is given over to shadows. In the darkest part is embedded a sumptuous mausoleum, nearly hidden under tarnished gold and mildewed velvet palls. This is the final sanctuary of the celebrated knight Fernán Pérez de Andrade, whose castle on the island trembles in the estuary winds. His body was desecrated, then moved by relatives from place to place to hide it from his enemies who swore by San Martin to burn it. At last it was brought home. His effigy shows him to have been formed like a gorilla, almost a monster in torso, with short, bowed legs. But his serene face is as beautiful as a Knight of the Grail. Not the least interesting point about this great Galician warrior is his title: O Bóo.

Oviedo is a dramatically placed town rearing against the sky which was massing with black storm clouds as I arrived under the blue slate gateway. The most noticeable thing as one drives through the countryside nearing Oviedo are the storks which build messy twig nests on top of the loosely laid thatch, which is not of straw but bundles of gorse twigs. The whole effect is wildly disheveled. Storks nest on the chimneys in the town too, but seem to be more orderly here. There is a continual flapping of stork wings and the irritating sound of storks sharpening their long bills one against the other. The grim cathedral is bare inside, but for a gigantic crucifix made from the spars of a ship. There is a small monastery in the cellar of which is a *Baños Agua Nilacrosa* whose waters are said to have cured countless generations of victims with gallstone, including no less a personage than Lord Horatio Nelson.

Driving along from Oviedo, through slanting rain I noticed the farms of this locality, so prone to sudden deluge, had granaries elevated on stone pillars, a custom left over from Visigothic days Within a radius of thirty miles of Oviedo are to be seen the largest number and certainly the finest of Visigothic churches and granaries. The one effort these "destroyers" made at cultivation was to sow and harvest crops of maize and barley used in brewing a potent kind of mead.

The old Roman walls of Lugo are its chief interest, built of an oddly colored mottled-brown and slate-blue stone. The streets are dark and narrow and cramped, in the way of walled towns.

I stopped at an inn which had once been a friary. The bedrooms were once cells for the friars who may have my bed back at any time to continue its disciplinary role in the monastic life. I have never slept on a harder surface, even on beds of baked mud without blankets in Timbuctu. I had a meal here which started out with broiled mushrooms and I should have stopped there. But I ordered *jamón*. I shall always remember Lugo for the ham of strong flavor which had been cured in sour wine. Next day I was not only stiff as a ramrod from the hard bed, but I had a sandpaper-raw throat from eating the ham.

The oddest manner of building fences I have seen the world over is in this part of Galicia. Great paving stones of blue granite are up-ended to form a breastwork to mark off a farmer's fields. Near Vigo I ran through a valley banked on either side by steep hills. The houses are of stone with roofs composed of wide strips of bark laid lengthwise like shingles. Both house and shingles are stained black with a tar solution. The houses, scattered haphazard on the green hills, have the curious look of a flock of black goats complacently feeding on the slopes. I saw capes of red cloth and black Phrygian caps worn by the men around Vigo. Over baggy black breeches and thong-wrapped goatskin leggings the voluminous red capes worn with one end thrown over the left shoulder are reminiscent of those worn by farmers harvesting wheat fields on the shores of the Straits of Corinth.

Vigo is a noisy port given to entertaining a transient tourist element, always in the fever of embarking or debarking. Of all cities in Spain, Vigo reminds me most of New York in its exasperating tempo of living. The accent here is on ships and shipping and there is not much reason for stopping in any one of the surprisingly good hotels, save to make daily excursions to villages like Redondela and Porriño, both gay fishing villages. In Porriño are circular houses painted pillar-box red and white. The fish dishes at *tabernas* in any of these little sea coast villages are of a freshness, delicately seasoned in any way you wish. Everything is cooked after you have chosen your fish or crustacean. Galician *langosta* is one of the most agreeable memories you will take out of Spain.

The Basque port of Gijón is noisy too, but somehow the proverbial Basque reticence seems to temper the atmosphere. During the day ship sirens and whistles blow, there is clamor and flurry in the streets, but at night, when most Spanish cities come to life, Gijón, except for the waterfront brothels and bars, becomes a morgue. The countryside behind the city is lovely with pastoral abundance. White farms stand in orchards of the big, spicy Asturian apple. Large cider presses are housed under blue slate conical roofs. Tipsy bees hum around the vats. There is a sharp tang in the cool air. The highway through the lordly Province of Asturias leads close to Covadonga. And just here, when the road reaches a plateau, appears in the valley a sight to stir the most hardened emotions. As if carved in white jade, the Baroque Monastery of Covadonga lies embedded in a forest of dark pines, surrounded by even darker green mountains. Around this religious house there hovers a pure unearthly beauty of repose that one must see to appreciate. It is only from this vantage point that one can fully savor this white wonder in its rich green setting. Once the gates are entered, there is no way to get a perspective, for the trees encroach so close to the walls. The day I saw it, two white herons were sailing majestically around and around the spires. I looked closely into the sky for an attacking eagle. But none was in sight. Perhaps the unregenerate eagle of Spanish sierras respects the air of sanctity wreathing the monastery. In the hearts of pious Spaniards, Our Lady of Covadonga is nearly as revered as the more ancient Madonna of Guadalupe. The treasures of jewels and vestments of the former church cannot compare with those at Guadalupe, but Covadonga harbors the bequeathed crowns of many kings and queens of Spain. The history of the Virgin reigning in this shrine is that she was presented in commemoration of the first battle against the Moors fought by Don Pelayo in the early part of the eighth century. Our Lady of Covadonga was crowned with a diadem of jewels taken from the captured infidel commander. On certain holy days, and to commemorate annually Don Pelayo's entrance into the long drawn out Holy War against the infidel, the Virgin raised on a palanquin is taken on a procession through the countryside. This is a procession I should like to see. I have photographs of it showing a small army of young men dressed in the ancient military costume of Don Pelayo's time, all carrying magnificently emblazoned banners. A group of children represent the chorus of angels who are alleged to have sung in the clouds above the battlefield to hearten the Christian soldiers.

On all sides, the Asturian mountain ranges fill the eye. However, it takes Picos de Europa to top them all. This mass of rock has no parallel in Europe for its formation in ascending strata of variegated rock and quartz. Dark plum- and sepia-pitted rock stripe the base. The whole incredible mass soars 8800 feet into the empyrean cloudless cerulean ether to be literally *crested* by spikes of rose, violet, and amber-green quartz. Valleys, carpeted with lupins and marsh iris, sweep away to the sea on one side, and to Peña Prieta and Sierra del Berzo, famous for musical waterfalls, on the other. In the meadows are rushing brooks full of fish to attract the ardent angler. No one ever fails to stop by the roadside to feast his eyes on this picture of fantastic mountain, farmland, valley, and wild flower garden, on one hand, with the sea coast on the other.

Santander is justifiably proud of its reputation as a fashionable watering place. But there is more to it than that. For one thing there is the old quarter of the town that never heard of fashion, with the most entertaining shops. Dummies, fully dressed in finery to attract a sailor ashore with his pay still intact, are skied up on stilts in front of the shops, modeling clothes for himself and the gaudy doxie who will entertain the fellow for a few nights and then strip him clean. Papier mâché dummies, these caricatures are, with the garish appearance of circus clowns, used to display everything from synthetic Basque costumes for tourist trade, to baskets of fruit or flowers borne on the head, or lace mantillas draped over high tortoise shell combs. There are *tabernas* in the little fishing villages that string out along the coast like the brilliant tail to a kite. In patios dappled with sun and shadow from fish nets slung across the roofs to dry, or on a terrace fronting the sea, one can eat succulent *frutos de mar* (fruits of the sea). There is one tiny *taberna* where the terrace is enhanced by carved wood figureheads, collected from barkentines and old coasters, some of them wrecked while sailing the treacherous Bay of Biscay. One Venus with a waterfall chignon and a bustle attracted me strangely. Her bodice plunged to a desperate decolletage. Her opulent breasts were caught in a gilded fish net. At night I had only to push a button and the nipples lighted up, one red to stop, the other green to go.

The hotels at Santander rank with those of Madrid and Seville. Hotel Real stands secluded in a magnificent garden. The Rex and Gran are equally fine. I can give them no greater praise than to say, they are run in the manner of Hotel Alfonso XIII in Seville.

I like to walk out on the Magdalina Peninsula where the sailing boats in regatta cut around the point, the masts leaning far over at a perilous angle. From morning until night there are regattas at Santander. On the peninsula stands an ornate royal palace, silent now, but its rooms once echoed to the shouts of children at play, and music at night, when the royal family of Spain came here for the summer. This was favorite of all her palaces with Queen Victoria Eugénie (Princess Ena of Battenberg) to stay with her children. I noticed this time that, deserted or not, the bead curtains at the upper windows, are still there. I had seen them before, and once in a jumble shop in Madrid saw some very much like them. These are a fantasy in crystal bead fringe, hung with tiny glass bells in the manner of Chinese temples. The curtains not only discourage flies but tinkle pleasantly in the ocean breeze.

To the casual visitor, the first impression of Bilbao is of a stern front and no humor for gaiety. This is not entirely so. Behind inscrutable black eyes, and the stiff, dark-blue Basque blouses, the people of this commercial city are wonderfully hospitable. Bilbao is not on the sea as many persons suppose. It lies on the River Nervión, ten miles inland. The wide river mouth is the harbor for Bilbao. The streets of the old town, which I greatly prefer to the clanging new city, are narrow, riven with high black iron shutters, and somber with much dark-blue paint on house fronts in the way of Basque towns across the Pyrénées.

Paseo del Arenál and the Gran Via are handsome streets bordered with trees. From seven o'clock in the evening until midnight all vehicular traffic is detoured through side streets so that the populace may walk as slowly as they will, unhindered by hooting sirens or traffic regulations. The slightly disconcerting Spanish custom of a group of strollers engaged in conversation, oblivious to surroundings, who suddenly stop dead in their tracks to gesticulate and harangue, needs this kind of unchallenged jaywalking, or casualties would be overwhelming. The brightly lit cafés on Gran Via burn brilliant Roman Fire in front of the terrace at night which gives a spacious sense of fiesta to the scene. Greatly in the mood of Picos de Europa, the road leading to Mondragón presents some of the most stirring mountain scenery in Spain. The evergreen bordered road constantly presents vistas of Carretera de Orduña, a serrated range, like appliqués cut from colored jades. The tremendous white mountains, veined with quartz crystals, shimmer in sun and haze to form on orchestration of light. Light in flashing movement can be as musical as the sound of wind instruments or the crashing notes of brass.

Zumarraga, as dashing as its name, concedes nothing to the Basque. The town lies on the outskirts of San Sebastian, the capital of Guipúzcoa Province where the people are arrogantly Navarrese. Plum-colored, slate, and tawny stone houses brighten the landscape. Many of them are *petite palais* with colonnaded top floors and grandiose armorial bearings hung at a precarious angle over the pillared gates leading to patios which are like private armories, with suits of armor and fan-shaped array of swords, pikes, and lances on the stone walls. There still is enacted a nostalgic ceremony in Zumarraga which takes place in the spring of the year. Ladies of the town, dressed as Amazons in armored cuirasses, greaves, pleated kirtles and helmets with great blades atop from which wave red, yellow, or black horsehair plumes, ride magnificently caparisoned horses through the streets and out into open country in a race to the shrine of Santa Maria del Rocío. This is to commemorate the midnight ride of a woman of Zumarraga who, in the days of Roman occupation, rode breakneck to save the lives of outlying farmers, by warning them to take refuge within the walled town against a scourge of wolves from the Pyrénées. During a winter of iron cold, hundreds of wolves hunting in packs killed livestock and humans on farms of the surrounding countryside. This wild ride of Roman Amazons is a thrilling spectacle to watch. The women train for months beforehand, until each is *one* with her mount, a very centauress, armored, and helmeted in streaming plumes.

Down a hill I drove into San Sebastian. The note of extreme fashion, the element of chic, is stressed here, even more than in Santander. It is San Sebastian that wears the crown. I drove to my hotel along the Avenida de Calvo Sotelo. Next morning I did a lot of shopping in the Avenida de España which rivals the Corso in Rome, the rue de la Paix in Paris, or Fifth Avenue in New York, for smart and beautifully-appointed shops where everything to ensnare one's acquisitive instinct is on view. I stopped to admire the contents of one window in Avenida de España, for the ingenuity and taste of its display. Bags of gold gauze studded with sapphire, ruby or emerald stars, lace paper in silver or bronze, and bead-embroidered net, contained *marrons glacés*. The chestnuts come from groves at Durango de Bilbao, through which I had but lately driven in the luminous morning and seen heavy clusters of spiny green chestnut burrs hanging like Christmas ornaments on the wide-branched trees. The gathering, grading, and preparing for market of these chestnuts is an important industry in the north of Spain, and like all else is attended by strangely compelling rites and ceremonies peculiar to whatever province or locality. In Spain it is the frequently met pageantry of processions carrying the Virgin or patron saint or some Holy Relic in a gilded, plumed, and flower-festooned tabernacle along the roads to some grove or orchard to bless the sowing or the harvests thereof that makes a journey through the countryside exciting and memorable.

San Sebastian is racing minded, largely due to the late king's father, Alfonso XII, who built the handsome Hipódromo Lasarte, abetted by his prime minister Canovas del Castillo, an ardent horse lover. Some of the finest racing stables in Europe have for over a half a century sent their best blood to race here in August and September.

In the sunny reaches of Parque Alderdi-Eder, unfurled fan-shaped leaves of magnificent old chestnut trees sweep down over the heads of the evening throng of smartly turned out habitués, drinking Bilbao chocolate, or, more recently fashionable, *el cock-tail*.

Alcoves of greenery are placed like sylvan opera boxes in a semicircle at the edge of the cleared space for tables. From one of these alcoves I sat one evening watching the *mise-enscène*. Across my mind passed the recollection of a large painting I had once seen in an old house in the back country of Virginia, not far from Charlottesville. One day I had been taken by a friend to see the gardens and, if it were possible, the interior of the Jeffersonian-Palladian house. I saw the gardens, neglected but romantic, nostalgic of another time when a great romance budded, flowered and withered away in the dark secrecy of the box alleys. I asked for the chatelaine. We were told she was indisposed and saw no one now. We might, however, see the lower rooms of the house, if we would be quiet. When my eyes became accustomed to the shadowy rooms, I saw a vast canvas hanging on the landing of an exceedingly grand staircase. I walked closer. Here was a galaxy of beauty if I ever saw it, portrayed by a facile brush. In a garden perhaps twenty men and women sat at wicker tables under the low sweeping branches of chestnut trees. The ladies were painted in the high bravura of Boldini, with great rose or plum-laden picture hats set rakishly atop pompadours of gleaming gold, auburn, or raven-wing black. Some of the ladies sipped tea or chocolate from fragile cups, as others opened ruffled parasols to ward off the sun dappling through the chestnut leaves. I remembered an exquisite brunette gently prodding with the ferule of her parasol an impudent Pekinese just starting to lie down for a nap on the Nile-green softness of her swirling organdy train. This whole painted assemblage of rank and fashion was as delicious an annotation on the page of feminine beauty and luxurious dalliance during *La Belle Epoque* as I had ever seen. I looked closely at the words printed in black on a gold name plate on the frame. "Parque Alderi-Eder. San Sebastian—1895."

As I sat quietly observant in my alcove, ladies and their escorts strolled slowly past, looked for, and found, a table under dappled shade, settled themselves and ordered refreshment. The painting on the shadowy staircase in an all but forgotten Virginia country house was, I thought, spread before me, save that the dresses of the women were not so gracefully fragile as those in the painting from the brush of painter-sculptor Prince Paul Troubetzkoy.

Like Santander, the hotels here are world famous. It is hard to choose between the superbly situated Continental Palace, Hotel Maria Cristina, or the Londres. All these hotels have private beaches, but there are any number of delightful public beaches on the far sweeping curve of La Concha which is indeed a shell of silvery sand as fine as powder. Up and down the coast there is a collection of fishing villages offering attractions in the way of bathing, restaurants and the fascinating accumulations of nautical equipment and largesse from the sea. In a curio shop at La Mota I bought a pair of golden galloon epaulettes mounted on red felt, with the initials and date, "D.D.R. Serapis 1799," worked on the felt in yellow silk. The curio dealer told me the epaulettes had been washed ashore in his father's day in a bull's-hide seachest with compartments lined with lead. This accounted for the perfect state of the gold galloon. I asked the man what else, if anything, the chest contained.

"Boots," he answered. "Five pairs of boots—gold-tasseled, dress-uniform boots. Never had been worn, señor. I wore a pair as a young boy."

I remarked that it was peculiar no one had ever bought this handsome pair of epaulettes in all the years they had been on display.

The man shrugged his shoulders. "Not as peculiar as what people will or will *not* buy," he answered.

I detected a hint of sarcasm in his voice. I paid my pesetas and went out into veils of mist just starting to roll in from the sea. I had not told him why I had bought a fragment of the mysterious D.D.R.'s naval regalia. I took these, with other loot back to Ireland. After having a saddle maker in Athlone fit each epaulette with a stout hook I am using them for boot pulls. I find them useful in the hand and decorative hanging on the wall of my dressing room, as a reminder of what nostalgic memorabilia one can pick up in out of the way shops in Spain.

At the foot of gaunt, dragon-scaled old Monte Urgull, is Taberna La Mota where one may dine and watch fireworks. On Saturday nights during the summer season (June to September) rockets describe a parabola of sparks over one's head to reflect in the sea, while set pieces showing great ingenuity of invention are set off by the military from the ramparts of the old Fortress of La Mota, crouching on the shoulders of Monte Urgull.

There are museums and the usual complement of churches in San Sebastian. San Télmo is an ancient abbey church. When it was restored José Maria Sert painted vast murals in the nave, employing his favored rich monotones of umber, sepia, dregs-of-wine, and silver, in the composition.

Pasajes a few miles from San Sebastian at the top curve of La Concha still has the air of an old whaling village. The dour Basque whalers had only two religious ceremonies a year. In the spring when they set out, Madonna de la Barca was carried out into the sea up to her shoulders. Salt water was laved upon her face. When the whalers returned to the village in the late autumn, the whaling ships loaded and reeking with whale oil from North Atlantic waters, the Madonna was again brought out to bestow on the weary mariners a briny benediction. In the spring and autumn the rites of blessing the sea are still carried on, though only rarely do the whalers go out into northern waters.

In 1776, Marquis de La Fayette sailed from Pasajes for America with half the hold of his ship loaded with bay-leaf scented candles and kegs of apricot brandy from Durango de Bilbao sent him as a present by the Duke of Medinaceli. With this ducal *bon voyage* gift was an accompanying note. "To light your table with fragrance while you drink the sunlight distilled from Spanish fruit orchards." It is related, alas, that halfway across the Atlantic storms arose, nearly swamping the heavily laden ship. More than half of this desirable cargo, some of which would undoubtedly have been presented by the marquis to General Washington, had to be jettisoned to lighten the ship.

At Taberna Camara, famous in the litany of gourmets, lobster is boiled in a huge "gypsy cauldron" as you watch, served with melted butter and slices of lemon. The lobster is small and sweet fleshed and as fresh as the sea itself.

There is an old square called San Vicente in San Sebastian which probably brings the popular idea of the Spain of *Carmen* more nearly into focus than any other I can remember. All the houses facing the square have spacious balconies and rickety outside stairways of crazily-tangled iron work. Some of the houses still retain big black numerals painted on the walls behind the balconies indicating where seats were placed when the square was used (until 1910) for bull fights. A fiesta with an accent on dancing in which the dance measures ape all the traditional movements of corrida is still held in the square during *Corpus Christi*.

I left San Sebastian on a stormy day. Great layers of rain clouds cut off the top of the Pyrenees as deftly as if by the clean sweep of a Saracen's sword. I would soon cross the long bridge at Irún, and then the last of Spain. I loathed to leave, so I dallied along, stopping at intervals, making excuses to myself that I must sketch this house or that fountain. I already had three big portfolios of sketches, far more than I could ever use, in this book, were it to be as big as an Atlas. I even drove out of my way to lunch at Fuenterrabia on the coast. At a *taberna*, hanging right out in the sea spray, I ordered my last slices of *chorizo*. As I ate the spicy sausage slowly, I ruminated on these last months in Spain. My one hope is that I can make persons who read this book see in some measure the Spain that to me is truly *fabulous.* The Oxford Dictionary defines the word fabulous as "famed in fable—incredible." To me there is so much to be seen in Spain, the nearly incredible, that even when regarding it, I can scarcely believe my eyes. The treasures in the museums and churches cannot adequately be described. They must be seen first hand. One must absorb the blazing richness of medieval stuffs and the magnificence of the jewels in vitrines or glowing on the breasts of some revered Virgin, as Our Lady of Guadalupe or Nuestra Señora de los Reyes in Seville. The cathedrals, ancient monastic houses, abbeys, convents, palace-tombs, such as Las Huelgas, where lie ensepulchered the dead kings of Castile, Aragon, and Navarre, these are the *museums* of Spain. Far more so than a few collected pictures and statues gathered together in some ill-lighted room. The towns and villages take their tone from the province, each Province is an oracle and the people of the countryside gather in the towns for traditional diversions to listen, as did members of pagan communities. Were I asked to state in one word what I feel most outstanding in Spain I should say *variety*. Variety on all counts is the very definition of the Iberian Peninsula.

So—I left my table on the spray-drenched terrace at Fuenterrabia overloking the Bay of Biscay, with a kaleidoscope of bright particles flickering before my eyes. There was no order to these prisms of color, just a mélange made up of age-riven castles radiant in the sunrise, the heat of noonday, smoldering in the glorious Spanish sunsets, or gleaming palely in the moonlight. I listened. There was sound with my mirage of memory. Was that the wind or was it music from the mountains, played on shepherds' pipes? No, too soft. Perhaps it came from a far off gypsy *barrio*. A *saeta* from out antiquity, when bull herders roamed the marshes of Andalusia. At random I opened one of my sketch books. There, in swift strokes, I had caught dancers abandoned to some Eastern rhythm. I shut the book, for my mind leaped far ahead to arid red pueblas shouldering cool, pine-clad heights. I seemed to see the dark branches reach out to encircle rich cities alive with pageantry, or dead as carved alabaster. I brought my mind back, as from a far place, to see staring at me two small children, their hands outstretched for whatever I would give. I had seen eyes like these before in a dim cathedral, immobile and staring like a basilisk at faceted ecclesiastical jewels, with no thought save that of wonder. The thought of jewels conjured up before my eyes a big woman, tall, broad-hipped, built as Carthaginians were, clanking in barbaric silver chains as she walked along a dusty road. As if to

317

frame all this I saw the tempered light on cities of golden stone, laced
with the cadences of music and the somber beauty of primitive art
to captivate the imagination. I shut my eyes to jumble in my mind
the flecks of crystal as in a whirlpool. Quickly I opened them. Out
of all Spain what would I see? It was the Lady of Elche, that pagan
enigma in scarred stone—Virgin, sacred prostitute? We shall never
know. Know only that not anywhere is there such graven beauty in
sculpture.

Three peasant women from Tolosa passed me on the road. They
wore the black, gold-embroidered full skirt and tight-fitting red
bodice, a-swing with gold chains of the region. Each carried a sheaf
of wheat in one arm and balanced a brown pottery jar of oil atop her
swathed yellow turban. As I watched them disappear down the road
I thought, in a few more years the peasants in their sublime innocence
of adhering to ancient customs and traditional dress may feel the pull
of this modern world which stretches out nagging tenacles, even in

the remote hill towns of Spain. They desire, more than most people can realize to be left alone to their own desires and to continue the daily round to which they have been used for centuries. I hope the peasant simplicity and tenaciousness of their legends and way of life prevails, so as not to dissolve the dream.

At sunset I drove across the bridge at Irún into France. I heard myself whispering, "Spain—Fabulous Spain, the wonders of which will never cease."